No Place to Hide:
The South and Human Rights

No Place to Hide:
The South
and Human Rights

VOLUME I

by
Ralph McGill
edited with an introduction by
Calvin M. Logue

**MERCER
UNIVERSITY PRESS**

ISBN 0-86544-108-6 (Volume 1)
ISBN 0-86554-109-4 (Volume 2)

All books published by Mercer University Press
are produced on acid-free paper that exceeds
the minimum standards set by the
National Historical Publications and Records Commission.

Library of Congress Cataloging in Publication Data
McGill, Ralph, 1898–1969.
No place to hide

Includes bibliographical references and index.
1. Afro-Americans—Civil rights—Southern States—
Collected works.   2. Southern States—Race relations—
Collected works.   3. Civil rights—Southern States—
Collected works.   I. Logue, Cal M. (Calvin McLeod),
                          1935–   II. Title.
E185.61.M477   1984   305.8'96073'075   84-1044
            ISBN 0-86554-108-6 (v. 1 : alk. paper)
            ISBN 0-86554-109-4 (v. 2 : alk. paper)

Contents

Ralph McGill's Moderate Campaign for Racial Reform*

Calvin M. Logue

When Harvard University conferred an honorary degree on Ralph McGill, the citation read: "In a troubled time his steady voice of reason champions a new South."[1] Indeed, the South from 1946 to 1969 was a place of great social upheaval. During that period the South changed publicly from a radically segregated to a substantially integrated society. As editor and publisher of the *Atlanta Constitution* until his death in 1969, McGill spoke and wrote for the rights of blacks at a time when most whites remained silent or hostile to change in the social status of blacks. McGill's support for equal citizenship for black Southerners is analyzed in the following six divisions: the potential audience, McGill's resolve, his underlying rhetorical strategy, his 1946-1954 discourses, his 1954-1969 discourses, and a conclusion.

---

*Prepared for *Public Discourse in the Contemporary South*, a manuscript now under consideration by Louisiana State University Press; published by permission of Louisiana State University Press and Mercer University Press.

[1]*New York Times*, 16 June 1961.

Potential Audience:
Separate, Hostile, and Silent

In the South there was little talk prior to the 1960s of providing full citizenship for blacks. Clearly no market existed among whites in the region for a candid dialogue on racial discrimination. However, some whites were concerned. The Southern Regional Council, of which McGill was a charter member, was founded in 1944 to assist blacks, but not as "an organization of mass appeal." Virginius Dabney of the *Richmond Times-Dispatch* called for equal and separate facilities. While praising the South's culture and values, sociologist Howard Odum worked for gradual improvement of the more obvious racial inequities. Like most moderates, Dabney and Odum avoided the issue of segregation and stressed education, jobs, and voting. Lillian Smith and Aubrey Williams, on the other hand, denounced the "gradualists" and demanded that the cruel system of segregation be replaced by equal citizenship for blacks.[2]

Persons who criticized conditions imposed upon blacks risked immediate ostracism, loss of a job, verbal abuse, and physical harm. "Public opinion itself became a sort of mob which terrorized or silenced any who might oppose it," recalled McGill. Outspoken ministers, newsmen, and others were "subjected to abuse, often vile, and to threats." Mobsters resorted to the "rifle, shotgun fire, and dynamite."[3] As early as 1941, Lillian Smith told of an anonymous letter she received threatening her life after she had given a talk on racism to the students at Blue Ridge. Virginia Durr experienced the sacrifices demanded for talking publicly in the 1950s: "I am seeing down here this deathlike conformity building up, when to speak out, to take action of any kind, to protest, to write a letter, to hold a meeting, brings down on your head both social and economic ruin and there is no recourse in the law."[4]

---

[2]Morton Sosna, *Southern Liberals and the Race Issue: In Search of the Silent South* (New York: Columbia University Press, 1977) 55-56, 119, 121, 167-68, 226, 169.

[3]Ralph McGill, *The South and the Southerner* (Boston: Little, Brown Publisher, 1964) 251-52; "Cooper Union Lincoln Day Address," in *Ralph McGill: Editor and Publisher*, ed. Calvin McLeod Logue, 2 vols. (Durham: Moore Publishing Company, 1969) 2:161, out of print.

[4]Quoted in Sosna, *Southern Liberals*, 184, 171.

These intimidating acts plus the long-accepted tradition of racial segregation prevented most persons from talking about wrongs done to blacks. Noting the silence of moderates, McGill asked, "Where have the 'best people,' the 'good people' been?" They "were not there. There was a vacuum," he said. "There was no public dialogue." Too many people "stood back." Even when the bombings came, he said, there was no "outcry . . . for the record" from religious and civic leaders. "Save for a few rare voices," leaders at the state and local level provided no leadership for people who wanted "to obey and live by law." "The ideology of moderation was mostly myth." So-called moderate businessmen, clerics, editors, educators, and other citizens "remained aloof while affairs drifted into crisis." Moderates "gave consent to immoderation." There was a critical need for leaders to "inform—not inflame or deceive." The effect of inaction and intimidation was a "troubled and indecisive" public and "a vast mythology of confusion and distortion."[5]

Within this situation of social upheaval and change, Ralph McGill testified publicly that blacks had not been treated fairly and that the wrongs should be corrected. Persons who disagreed poured garbage on his lawn, made abusive telephone calls, sent threatening letters, demonstrated outside his office, and shot holes in his mailbox and window. Some persons directed that he be beaten, and the Ku Klux Klan named McGill "southern-enemy-number-one." In Columbus, Georgia, in 1959, McGill was denied use of both a superior court room and school facilities because as one commissioner claimed, his speech was an attempt to "ram . . . opinion down the throats of the people."[6] In 1963, "thirteen thousand copies of the official newspaper of the Episcopal Diocese of Atlanta" were "sold for scrap because" McGill "charged the local Episcopal leadership with 'hypocrisy.'"[7]

A Reformer's Resolve

What made McGill different? Why did he take a dangerous and unpopular stand? Why was he more teacher than crusader? McGill was

---

[5]"De Paul University Address," in *Ralph McGill*, 2:366-67; "South in Transition," in *Ralph McGill*, 2:359; *Atlanta Constitution*, 16 October 1958, and 11 December 1953; "Harvard University Law School Speech," in *Ralph McGill*, 1:226.

[6]*New York Times*, 1 April 1959.

[7]See "A Conversation With Ralph McGill," in volume 2.

motivated by what he called a "public philosophy," a belief that social progress depends upon individuals acting from moral strength. This ideal springs from a "spiritual self-confidence" based upon "ideals and integrity." "Emotional concern for human life is perhaps the most significant mark of . . . civilized individuals," he concluded. To improve the human condition, however, one had to go public with personal philosophy. To McGill, withheld principle was impotent. "Moral right" only made "might" if invested. Persons had to "stand out against what is wrong." "Laws are not enough unless they be just. . . . We cannot . . . clothe wrong in the garments of law or emotion and say, 'It is mine. You will please let it alone.' Moral right is slow and patient. . . . But, you cannot escape it."[8]

McGill's philosophy of "professed principles" reflected a strong system of values molded by a "standard of the spirit." Public spokesmen should "be believers in the great sense" and serve "the social, moral, and spiritual improvement" of all persons regardless of race, creed, color, or station in life. Meaningful social service depended upon "great convictions" and the fusing of "moral considerations with social inventiveness." McGill defined this "pursuit of excellent values" metaphorically as a "compass course for . . . life." Careful study of his speaking and writing reveals many of those virtues that he esteemed. These values confirm McGill's emphasis upon a *public* philosophy—upon a "common" principle—that evolves from the marketplace as well as from the pulpit. First there were the stock virtues of honor, integrity, intellectual honesty, common decency, human dignity, and common justice. McGill followed with values requisite to public involvement, confirming his preference for professed principle. He created his own terms for the basic freedoms: *civil liberties, opportunity,* and *promise*. Virtues that functioned as guides for involvers were: enthusiasm, "plain" unselfishness, realism, insight, self-comprehension, self-sacrifice, chivalry, ambition, wisdom, kindness, gentleness, stubbornness, unity, good will, and plain speaking.[9]

---

[8]"Oberlin College Commencement Address," in *Ralph McGill*, 2:295-99; "Institute for Education Speech," in *Ralph McGill*, 2:170-71; *Atlanta Constitution*, 27 February 1949.

[9]*Atlanta Constitution*, 25 December 1947; "Southern Journalism Speech," in *Ralph McGill*, 2:33; *Atlanta Constitution*, 14 September 1947.

Building upon these high principles, McGill developed several be-
liefs from which he argued for civil rights for blacks. Specifically, in his
speeches and writings he employed six premises from which he refracted
public arguments: individuals and governments should pursue policies
that are feasible; laws should be obeyed; free individuals have a moral
responsibility to oppose wrong; education is requisite to individual and
community progress; all persons should be granted the rights and privileges of full citizenship; Southern states should ensure the rights and
privileges of their own citizens.[10]

Certainly McGill had the makings of an activist. An optimist by
nature, he "liked the world," enjoyed his work, and felt that "life seems
pretty good . . . most of the time." The man was sensitive and kind-
hearted, even an easy "touch" for drunks who came to his office. A "notorious sentimentalist," he perceived himself as "cursed with a certain
sense of responsibility. The troubles of others trouble me." Also, he liked a public fight. Although "losing" went "awfully hard," McGill had
no "disposition to leave problems at the office," and he had to "walk for
an hour to get rid of the tension and excitement of debate." Yet, he enjoyed his role as public spokesman. Partisan by nature, McGill found
politics to be "a fascination that is almost narcotic." He relished "the
give and take," the "maneuverings, the organizing, the methods of
bringing in the sheaves." He could not "imagine a man who doesn't like
to discuss controversial subjects, but who avoids them out of fear of
being 'bothered.' " "If I crack up I will be the most surprised of all,"
he mused. "I like throwing punches and rolling with them. I do not
bruise easily." "Mostly I go along with the policy of getting in there and
firing both barrels—after you have something to fire."[11]

McGill was a peculiar social reformer, a reluctant crusader. He primarily pleased himself, thereby angering and frustrating racists, segregationists, and liberals. Racists called him a "nigger lover," and
liberals sometimes dismissed him as a "former liberal" and "practical
politician." While relatively fearless, he was reluctant to join special in-

---

[10]Cal M. Logue, "Ralph McGill: Convictions of a Southern Editor," *Journalism
Quarterly* 45 (Winter 1968): 647-52.

[11]*Atlanta Constitution*, 27 February 1946, 29 June 1946, 12 December 1946, 13
June 1948, 28 January 1949, 19 July 1946, 27 February 1946.

terests. He experienced "periodic attacks of melancholia" and "remorse of conscience," as he phrased it. Because he was "a worrier and a dreader and a fretter" and often "too serious about things," he continuously puzzled over problems, solutions, realities, and ideals. Seldom satisfied, even with his own assessment, he was forever looking ahead. "I cannot be a good crusader," he explained, "because I have been cursed, all my life, with the ability to see both sides of things. This is fatal to a crusader." "Extremists," he believed, "in either direction, almost inevitably provide dangerous and damaging leadership." McGill was also unique in that he worked up "a sort of affection for the tougher adversaries," such as Eugene Talmadge and Roy Harris. Further, although he wept easily "over sad songs and stories," he disliked expressing emotions publicly, another requirement of the crusader. [12]

McGill was fiercely independent, a characteristic that directly influenced the method and substance of his communication. Believing in Thoreau and Emerson, he attempted to "survive outside" his environment, no easy task for a daily columnist and persistent speaker. In subjecting himself to examination, McGill concluded: "I have always tried to develop a nonconforming mind, believing such a mind necessary to one whose job it is to comment on events and policies. I am by nature a nonconformist. . . . If man ever becomes tamed, and if he loses the one paramount freedom from which all others stem—the freedom of his mental processes—then all else is lost." Because of this independence, he refused to join any organization representing any cause, other than the Democratic party (a political arena) and the Masons, a group committed to brotherhood and biblical principles. He believed that if he did belong to a special interest group he "would not feel like sitting down and banging out a piece . . . about how [he] . . . disagreed with it." McGill observed that he did "not have to make a living being a professional liberal, but . . . [could] center on trying to be liberal." Being independent did not mean he was lacking in ideals: "I am not. . . . I expect always to be found in the middle of the road, just a little left of center, highly idealistic about life, but knowing that progress in government comes by politics and that they are practical problems." "I like a

---

[12]Ibid., 4 November 1947, 10 August 1955, 18 February 1947, 2 January 1950, 22 August 1948.

fight. . . . I expect to have more. . . . But . . . I like to call my shots. And aim where I think a shot is needed."[13]

A Rhetorical Strategy
of Public Instruction

In supporting blacks, McGill followed an underlying rhetorical strategy of public instruction. These mass lessons were consistent with his faith in professed principles, and suitable to Southerners hostile to social change. He engaged audiences in a search for understanding those admittedly difficult and, to some, threatening issues and events. Ranging from calm reflection to blunt ridicule, his lessons reflected a peculiar mix of intellectual honesty, realism, gentleness, and stubborn independence. Untamed by racist hoodlums or racial liberals, he carved a middle way precariously balanced between the realities of the hostile situation and the idealism of common justice. McGill's lesson plan was composed of three tenets: helpful participation in public discussion requires a disciplined and enlightened mind; progress in society depends upon individuals who will speak out; persuasion depends upon one's being realistic. Not only did McGill follow this prescription, he also attempted to persuade others to adopt this formula for meaningful involvement.

McGill developed and advocated disciplined thought and speech. To participate in public discussions effectively and constructively, one needed a tough, inquiring mind that would "doubt and question and test everything it encountered." An important part of preparing for open dialogue was knowing how to "read, understand, and express." To answer the troublesome question "Why?" demanded an intellectually stubborn individual. "There is no open sesame, no formula, no golden key," McGill advised, "let's don't be simplistic and/or seeking for simplistic answers." Communicators need to be aware of glib and "dogmatic formulae and answers." He advised avoiding persons "who can cut out a faith for you, and fit it to you as a tailor fits you a suit. . . . Faith . . . grows on a man, and it is always well-worn and never new from the fitters."[14]

---

[13]Ibid., 4 November 1946, 1 September 1942, and 29 February 1948.

[14]"Reynolds Lecture," in *Ralph McGill*, 2:472; *Atlanta Constitution*, 25 December 1947.

McGill practiced this posture of testing and searching in his speaking and writing. Claiming no certain answers, he began most of his speeches with this text: "Lord give me this day my daily idea and forgive me the one I had yesterday." "I cannot come to you with dogma," he told a University of Arkansas audience. "Whenever I go anywhere to make a talk, as one whose trade it is to use words, I try always to be humble before them." "Always be a seeker," he advised, "and never stop and say, 'This is all.' " Before audiences McGill performed "something like a teacher," stimulating inquiry, reading, study, and discussion. He encouraged groups to "meet, discuss and learn." He made appearances on platforms to "admit our problems," to create "better understanding," and to be "helpful." McGill educated listeners "to . . . orderly processes of education and law" going "behind the racial news" for a "balanced picture" that "makes people understand." Often his discussion included a lengthy analysis of the political and economic roots of a problem, explaining, as he said, that "these things are true, and this is why they are true and this is what we must do to correct them." McGill's instruction could be gentle or harsh. "Make up your mind not to vote for a prejudice," he coaxed during one campaign. Another time he ridiculed those participating in the Ku Klux Klan meeting on Stone Mountain as "brave boys" and "suckers" for lighting gasoline in the "form of Christ's cross."[15]

Thus, McGill's first rhetorical strategy suggested that constructive public instruction depended upon rigorous evaluation and investigation. Second, for society to progress, individuals had to speak out. This aspect of McGill's lesson plan was a direct response to the actions of fair-minded persons who avoided the issue of race and left decisions to extremists. He believed that private principle had to be expressed publicly to be politically potent. Also, means and ends had to be derived from public understanding. Public policy, he believed, comes from the "clamor of the marketplace"—-the more talk about a subject the better. Rhetorical inventiveness builds social progress. Democracy, he insisted, should not be a "careful, restrained, regimented, controlled existence." Social development "depended upon a bold and adventuresome spirit."[16]

---

[15]"National Education Association Speech," in *Ralph McGill*, 1:246; *Atlanta Constitution*, 14 July 1946 and 8 May 1946.

[16]*Atlanta Constitution*, 1 March 1950 and 20 November 1951.

McGill observed that more Americans needed to address problems in their towns, states, and country. The essence of government was respecting "honest differences" and "understanding the other man's problems." Ideal decisions then could be made by a majority of moral minorities. "A free people must be free to discuss and debate—because they have been informed." Debate and education, key aspects of McGill's strategy of instruction, were reciprocal rhetorically. Workable solutions should derive from people who debate, talk, write, and discuss. Besides being an unalienable right, to McGill enlightened communication was a means of public education. Communal participation was a form of societal counseling. "Our system not merely permits debate," he declared, "ours prolongs it, for years, if necessary. Our process is educational." "The Jeffersonian idea is mine, that the democratic way is slow, cumbersome, awkard and inefficient—but . . . after long travail, the voice of the people makes itself heard and felt." Applying this premise to civil rights legislation, McGill advocated "a fair and equitable law which will have public acceptance. It will come only because of the delay and discussion" and after "bitter, angry weeks and years of discussion and debate. When it does come it will mean something."[17]

The third tenet of McGill's rhetorical strategy was patently pragmatic; communicators must approach audiences with realistic expectations. "Man by nature is somewhat primitive," he believed, so speakers should not expect too much when addressing them. Audiences often were poorly informed and easily "lead . . . off on false trails" by means of old prejudices. Further, he believed citizens seldom act swiftly on issues so "man progresses by inches." "Mass thought is enlarged and improving—slowly." Communicators should teach rather than force an issue. Effective teaching necessitates realistic teachers. As "politics is the science of the possible" so was public communication an instrument of social reality. While radical crusaders could write, speak, and argue well from a distance, McGill stated, their actions were "pretty as a star and equally unobtainable." No ideal could work "unless it comprehend[ed] . . . human limitations." People should "be taught patiently and from the grass roots" when there could be "a benign and calm meeting of minds." Speakers could not "make all people just like" them-

---

[17]Ibid., 2 January 1959, 23 March 1949, 1 March 1950, and 22 August 1948.

selves. Rather, persons had to help "keep each other free and . . . work together." And, as the human "race improves through education and experience, we are all moved forward. But we do this step by step. Never by leaps."[18]

McGill coaxed and prodded his audiences more than he berated them, unless some specific event, such as the bombing of a school or church, demanded a different strategy. One cannot "get too far ahead of the audience you're trying to reach" he explained, otherwise "you find yourself" communicating "to just a small group." By deliberately adapting to dissent in the audience and countering it, McGill believed he was able to maintain a wider public. Speaking on the Chicago Round-Table program, he explained how he adapted his personal convictions. He had remarked on the forum that "while all of us know what the objectives are and are unreservedly for them, we know we must crawl before we walk, and we should know that while it is noble to die on the barricades, it is better for all concerned to get what one can in the name of progress." While always "pulling for the long view," he argued that he was "alive as of now and the tools with which" he "must work are the tools of today." McGill admitted that "there is schizophrenia" in "running with the hare and dropping back, now and then, to see how the hounds are making out" and there is "great frustration of spirit, but there also is Americanism and good politics as well." McGill further advised:

> You learn when you walk with men that an ideal is . . . worthless, and without power to do good, unless it understands human limitations. . . . So we must deal with the brick and the mortar we have. . . . We must work with the tools which will lift people and change their thinking. In this we can use ideals which understand human limitations. That's where I like to work. . . . It involves no surrender of personal principle. It accepts the inevitable fact that progress moves like an inchworm. It is accelerated only when human limitations are relaxed or removed.[19]

---

[18]"University of Arkansas Address," in *Ralph McGill*, 1:134-35; *Atlanta Constitution*, 21 October 1957 and 26 September 1948.

[19]"Logue's Interview with McGill," 29 December 1965, in *Ralph McGill*, 2:23; *Atlanta Constitution*, 14 February 1950, 2 October 1957, and 26 September 1948.

Discourses Supporting Separate and Equal Rights
for Blacks: 1946-1954

McGill's efforts for blacks can be divided into two periods: 1946 to 1954, when he advocated equal and separate rights and opportunities; and 1954 to 1969, when he increasingly supported full citizenship for blacks within a racially desegregated society.

During the first period, prior to the Supreme Court's school desegregation decision in 1954, a few liberals criticized McGill's stance of gradualism, but most white Southerners found his statements far too radical and threatening. McGill stayed his course, believing that support for equal-if-separate rights was honorable and realistic. Certainly during this period few white Southerners dared speak for blacks. Even by 1947, McGill was correct in believing that he had "been a voice crying in the wilderness for a long time." In writing and in forums McGill "held up and cried aloud" the "record of shame," proclaiming "the great need for improvement."[20] The explanation of McGill's public discourse in behalf of blacks from 1946 to 1954 will consider his emphasis upon a "separate but equal" arrangement between blacks and whites, and second, his support for specific civil rights.

Separate But Equal

Prior to 1954, McGill judged that enforcement of the Supreme Court's former decision requiring equal and separate rights was the most effective means of helping blacks. Unlike many Southerners who attempted to hold blacks in a state of degradation, McGill advocated this strategy to comply with the law and to accommodate white fears of a racially integrated society. Note how McGill prefaced his plea for social progress by paying homage to segregation as a means of maintaining his credibility with whites: "Believing now, as always, in separation of the races as the best and only workable system, it is possible to make a few comments." Often McGill extended this loyalty oath to the South by appealing to his audiences' sense of fairness and their need for economic security: "Thousands of good Christian men and women . . . believe there may be separation of races and still not have to mix with other

---

[20]*Atlanta Constitution*, 27 September 1947 and 9 October 1946.

workers; equal opportunity for education, without mixing in school.
. . . The South faces its greatest opportunity in history. Industry and
progress are coming. They will pass up a state which is filled with racial
tensions, violence and hate."[21]

The situation required McGill to invest much of his discourse re-
futing threats made by politicians, such as Eugene Talmadge, that any
change in the status of blacks inevitably meant social integration and intermarriage. Because so many whites feared racial mixing, McGill confronted their apprehensions directly: "There will be no 'nigger
policemen' [as politicians phrased it] arresting white people," McGill
explained. "There will be no mixing of races in the schools. There will
be no social equality measures. Now or later." "Negroes themselves do
not want" the "mixing of races." They desire "decent schools, good pay
and a fair chance at an education."

Although bowing respectfully to the tradition of segregation,
McGill developed his strategy of instruction by teaching what he called
a "primer of Southern thinking." When counseling in race relations and
citizen responsibility, McGill reminded whites that the repeated promise to blacks of equal rights and opportunities had been a lie: "We, as a
region and a people, have been dishonest in our segregation policy. . . .
We wrote our laws to say that while the races were to be separated we
would provide 'separate but equal' educational, travel, recreational and
other facilities. This we have not done." "We have said to let us alone
and we would do the job," McGill added. "We have not done that job.
Shall we have the moral courage to do it or not?"[22]

Over the years, in a continuous stream of morality maxims, the
journalist explained the "necessary actions" required to remedy the evil:
"honest facing up to facts"; "not a lot of cowardly retreating into dishonest refuges of phony values and prejudices"; "the issue is entirely a
moral one—and not political"; not a question of "protection of white supremacy"; answers lie with a "spirit of tolerance and courage"; "the only
supremacy which will endure is the supremacy based on justice, knowledge, and human justice."

---

[21]Ibid., 12 June 1946.

[22]Ibid., 22 January 1948 and 3 August 1948.

McGill told what it was like trying to follow a line of argument between the ultimate ideal and present realities. After speaking at an "interracial forum" at Spelman College, a practice totally unacceptable to most whites during the 1940s and later, he revealed that he felt

> like a sacrificial lamb. . . . The critics on one side damn you as supporting the Claghorn type of congressman. The Ku Klux type mind hollers that you talk to audiences with Negroes in them. Your mail reflects both criticisms. . . . While believing without reservation in human and civil rights, I cannot bring myself to be intellectually dishonest enough to oversimplify it as awaiting only the panacea of another law added to many others. . . . Here in the South there are old customs, traditions and walls of thought built by warfare, religion, economics and the forces of history. . . . We cannot remove them by a law. . . . The answer is within us, and it can be answered only from within the Southern pattern. . . . I want the South to do what is right. . . . This, I know satisfied no one [attending the forum]—not even me. But, not being beholden or in politics, I can say it.[23]

Support for Civil Rights

Although from 1946 to 1954 he compromised with what became in the 1960s an immoral "separate and equal" sham, during that period McGill declared that black Southerners had been "standing at the end of the line" in matters of law, education, employment, voting, housing and social services.

Law. In the 1940s, McGill demanded for blacks a fair trial and common and full justice without regard to . . . color. Exhibiting distinctive courage during this dangerous time, and preempting the call by many in the 1960s, he challenged the Southern tradition of a politically powerful sheriff structure by insisting that blacks be made "safe from police brutality" and given "equal justice in our courts." Although often conciliatory and inquiring, at times he was moved to attack the "lynching murders," "mob violence," and "corrupt country governments," asking that responsible persons "reestablish law enforcement which today is too often a mockery."[24]

While unequivocal in his stance for blacks' rights, McGill perplexed liberals by his independence in initially opposing a federal anti-

---

[23]*Atlanta Constitution*, 1 March 1948.

[24]Ibid., 14 July 1951 and 10 March 1946.

lynching bill. Two motivations probably influenced this decision: a desire to maintain communicative contact with Southern masses; and a conviction that local enforcement could work best. "A long time ago Mark Etheridge and I met in debate on the federal antilynching law," McGill wrote in 1947. "I took the negative. And lost. I still take the negative." Although he had "long opposed such legislation," he warned that no one "can stand and argue against it with much force when we recall the four lynch-murders in Walton County" Georgia. Typical of his pattern of reversal on other issues, as the years passed and conditions did not improve significantly in the region, McGill eventually urged the passage of a federal antilynching law. In 1949 he repeated that support, but with the qualification that the law not include "police power or coercion. That . . . should be left to the states."[25]

Education. Stating his passionate faith in education, McGill supported the public school as the foundation of America, arguing too that no system of private education could fulfill mass needs. Primarily he stressed the needs of blacks. "Let us admit our failure to provide equal educational opportunity," he advised. "We . . . have repeatedly insisted we want to be fair to the Negro. Let us admit that the record shows we have not." Blacks were not receiving a "square rattle" in schooling. Occasionally McGill linked educational inequities with segregated schools: "The school system is a segregated one and the Negro pupils and teachers have suffered by discrimination." A favorite tactic of McGill when speaking for civil rights was to warn whites how social and economic progress for all depended upon progress made by blacks: "The South will pay a heavy price for its discriminations." The region was entering an era that required "more formal education." A second recurring strategy was to challenge Southern states themselves to give blacks their "due in education," rather than forcing the federal government to require it.[26]

Employment. McGill pleaded for an end to discrimination in employment. When detailing how blacks had been denied their civil rights, he often defined the wrong and its motivation, and invited change: "Let us admit that . . . we redistrict Negro employment to the least rewarding fields of work. This denial is based entirely on prejudice." The results

[25]Ibid., 28 March 1947 and 7 January 1947; *New York Times*, 27 June 1949.

[26]*Atlanta Constitution*, 22 October 1950, 27 September 1947, and 20 March 1946.

of these evil practices were substandard income levels and poverty; the remedy was to "give to the Negro a right to work" based solely on "his skills and ability." Keenly aware that people are motivated by "what's in it for me," McGill emphasized to whites that employing blacks was in their own self-interest. Southerners could not "go on much longer carrying on" their backs "the economic burden of a people who generally do not have an opportunity to pay their way." Unless the black "can be made into a community asset, a citizen able to trade at the stores and earn his own way, we won't solve the problem," he contended. "We keep our economy poor by depressing him."[27]

Again, McGill insisted upon a Southern solution to unequal employment opportunities for blacks, opposing for some time the Federal Fair Employment Practices Commission (FEPC). As was the case with the antilynching law, this Southerner was adapting to his audiences' dislike for Northern intervention. Also, he did not believe a federal law would help. The proposed FEPC "is not a sound bill," he argued in 1947, because "it is largely political" and would "create as many abuses as it corrects." Unlike most Southerners, however, McGill did not stop there. He exploited the threat of the FEPC as a means of persuading the South to correct its own inequities: "The honest Southerner will have to admit that failure to allow the skilled Negro to work, even in segregated areas, gives proponents of the" FEPC "a whip hand." "The answer" he insisted, should originate in the South. "Federal legislation which transfers the same mentality and the same jury from the county courthouse to the Federal building is no answer at all." In 1950, McGill conceded that the South was not providing equal employment opportunities for blacks, and predicted from the FEPC "a fair and equitable law which will have public acceptance."[28]

Voting. McGill supported judicial directives, as when in the 1940s, the Supreme Court determined that blacks could vote in the Georgia primary elections. Anxious to reassure whites that he personally was not advocating political dominance for blacks, McGill deferred: "I do not at all mean to discuss here the pros and cons of Negro voting." Then he

---

[27]Ibid., 19 February 1948; *New York Times*, 5 January 1947; *Atlanta Constitution*, 23 July 1947.

[28]*Atlanta Constitution*, 22 June 1947, 7 June 1949, and 1 March 1950.

proceeded to do just that. He placed limitations on voting: "I have . . . an opinion which I would like again to express. The privilege of the ballot ought not to be given to the unqualified. Particularly do I think it should be withheld from those not literate enough to know the issues. I would oppose most vigorously permitting uneducated or otherwise unqualified Negroes to vote." To convince whites to allow blacks to vote, McGill reassured whites that they would continue to govern, and would not have to make it "easy for a Negro to vote." "Literacy tests and other qualifications" would protect the "enormous white majority" and prevent what irresponsible campaigners had claimed would be "nigger rule." After warranting whites' political dominance, McGill inched audiences forward to compliance with the Court: "At the same time it would be political folly, once the court decision is final, to bar those who are qualified." "Shall we be fooled by fear that one Negro voter can outvote 10 white voters in a primary in which state law requires the unit vote?"[29]

As the situation in the South and the nation changed, McGill expanded his demands. By 1949 he was advocating the elimination of the poll tax. In 1950 he predicted boldly: "Negro voting has leaped from about 200,000 ten years ago to almost 1,000,000, and will, within four years attain a total of at least 2,000,000. There are about 5,000,000 Negroes of voting age in the South, and they are on their way to the ballot box where they can, by their ballot, obtain a sounder basis of citizenship."[30]

Housing and Social Services. McGill supported the civil rights of blacks as required morally, economically, and judicially in the areas of law, education, employment, and voting. In doing so, he varied his rhetorical strategies from sarcastic indictments of abusive practices to expressed sympathy with specific means of limiting political participation by blacks. He extended his discussion of civil rights to include the desire of blacks for housing by resorting to sarcasm on occasion: "There is a great shortage of housing. I suppose it is very bad of Negroes that they don't dig holes in hillsides and live in them. But, for some reason, they like to have a roof, even if it is leaking and the house is poor." In his

---

[29]Ibid., 31 March 1946 and 3 April 1946.

[30]Ibid., 7 June 1949; "Daytona Beach Speech," in *Ralph McGill*, 2:46.

campaign for blacks, he also supported "a fair share of our municipal funds" for "playgrounds and the usual civic facilities such as paved streets, public health, sewers, and so on." In 1948 McGill wrote a pamphlet, "The Housing Challenge," for the Atlanta Housing Authority.[31]

Precursor of Desegregation

During the late 1940s and early 1950s McGill urgently tried to prepare Southerners for the social changes he knew to be inevitable. For years few saw the signs or took his regional prophecy seriously. As early as 20 March 1949, McGill forecast: "The Supreme Court . . . reported itself ready to rule on segregation. . . . That scares me because if they rule against segregation we have no machinery to carry it out." Without planning there would be "chaos and disorder." So as not to stampede his audiences, McGill claimed that he was not "trying . . . to argue pro or con . . . but to create some understanding of what we are up against." While personally hopeful that the Court decision would be delayed, he advised "citizens and leaders . . . to understand the Court is going to rule." McGill worried that "none of the Southern papers" discussed the potential decision. There could be "violent talk or worse," he accurately warned. "But the law would remain."[32]

By the early 1950s, McGill challenged segregation itself, shifting away from his previous emphasis upon equal and segregated rights. He argued that public education had become too expensive for states to afford two systems, even if the Court required it. Because education was so costly, "ways will be found to reduce the rigidity of school segregation." On 20 February 1950, McGill maintained that no honest person could defend compulsory segregation as a democratic institution. In 1953, he declared that "segregation by law no longer fits today's world. . . . The problem of the future is how to live with the change." Even so, he indicated, "at least five Southern states are preparing, if segregation is abolished, to make educational Saharas of their states by destroying their public school system."[33]

---

[31]*Atlanta Constitution*, 10 November 1946; "Ohio Northern University Address," in *Ralph McGill*, 2:435; essay on "Housing," in volume 1.

[32]*Atlanta Constitution*, 20 March 1949 and 30 November 1949.

[33]Ibid., 20 February 1950 and 1 December 1953.

Discourses Supporting Desegregated Public Schools:
1954-1969

After 1954, McGill escalated his efforts for reasonable racial changes. This section will reveal his recurring rhetorical strategy of public instruction by examining the social setting, followed by McGill's instruction on how to hold a public forum, his defense of the Supreme Court, his appeals in behalf of public schools, his opposition to violence, his exposing of myths, and his historical explanations for the causes of social changes.

The Social Setting

Concluding that black and white schools were unequal, the Supreme Court on 17 May 1954 ruled segregated education in the South unconstitutional. In 1956, the Court extended its ban on racial segregation to tax-supported colleges and universities. Other judicial and legislative decisions affected public transportation, swimming pools, courthouse cafeterias, seating on trolleys and buses, and private places of business. In 1960, a civil rights bill enabled "referees" to monitor "voting privileges denied" to blacks by local registrars. A bill was passed in 1964 regulating employment opportunities, school desegregation, voting rights, jury trials, and public accommodations. To enforce these federal laws, President Dwight Eisenhower sent troops to Arkansas, and President John Kennedy federalized troops in Mississippi and Alabama. Ten years after the historic decision, the Supreme Court declared that "the time for more 'deliberate speed' has run out," and ordered Prince Edward County, Virginia, to "reopen its public schools on a desegregated basis." In 1965, the Atlanta School Board was ordered to "speed up desegregation to two grades a year, beginning with kindergarten and first grade" that fall and "completing the entire system by September, 1968."

White opposition to desegregated schools was swift. Governor Herman Talmadge of Georgia said he did not recognize the ruling as a legal decision, labeling the act merely "judicial brainwashing." On 11 June 1954, governors or their representatives from twelve Southern states agreed to "seek legal means of circumventing" the Supreme Court's order. In 1956, a series of bills was introduced in the State Senate of Georgia to strengthen segregation. That same year, Virginia voters, by a margin of more than two to one, supported a plan to pay state money for tuition grants in private nonsectarian schools. Also, Virginia proposed a Pupil Placement Act, the "cornerstone of the massive resistance" to school desegregation, but the Court ruled it unconstitutional the following year. In 1958, the Court nullified Little Rock's attempt to lease "four high schools for private, segregated operation." The state legislature of Mississippi authorized its governor to close the public schools if needed. In 1960, the Court refused to stop integration of New Orleans schools." Until 1962, Florida law required total segregation of public schools.

Coercive efforts used to prevent racial integration included demonstrations, parades, catcalls, and murder. A "rowdy, angry mob . . . ran newspapermen out of town" in Clay, Kentucky, where "two Negro children tried to enroll." "Mob pressure" stopped three blacks from registering in Texarkana (Texas) Junior College. "Some 570 white children walked out" of the Weaverton Elementary School in Kentucky protesting the "enrollment of five Negroes." "Three explosions rocked" an integrated Clinton high school in Tennessee. "A dynamite bomb blasted a Negro elementary school" in Atlanta. In Athens, Georgia, "rocks were thrown through dormitory windows" when Charlayne Hunter attempted to enroll at the University of Georgia. "Night-riding arsonists" burned two black churches "connected with the desegregation drive in Southeast Georgia." Dynamite killed four black children in a Birmingham church.

The situation that Lillian Smith and Ralph McGill found intimidating in the 1940s became even more hostile after the Supreme Court supported desegregated public schools, restaurants, and other accommodations. To discuss civil rights and desegregation was dangerous. After 1954, the South faced a situation of revolutionary change. McGill perceived it as a "period complex, emotional, and difficult"; "an age of wonder, and of anxiety"; a "time of great change and ferment"; "a problem . . . immense and complex."

Even amidst the demonstrations and deaths, McGill offered calm instruction: "The world now is in one of those periods when the processes of history are speeded up," when "change or transition has been cranked up." "We cannot escape the economic and social effects of the massive changes now in progress. . . . It is folly not to think about them rationally." As was true in the days of the "Yanceys" and the "Rhetts," he advised, the "voice of reason and of moderation and compromise" is being "drowned out." Prejudice prevented "any sane and orderly discussion." There were only "irrational and bitter" words and "a mood of distrust." McGill felt as if he worked from within a "straightjacket." Tension was so great that Harry Ashmore questioned whether Emory University in Atlanta would be able to manage "an adult program concerning the 'Crisis in the Schools,' a forum in which McGill did participate.[34]

The Court's 1954 ruling accelerated the process of desegregation and forced citizens to make a critical decision. This was a "regional stage show," McGill assessed, about which persons would have "an opportunity to decide" between leaders who "are on trial" and others who "speak from pulpit, podium or press. . . . Somebody is wrong. That at least is obvious. . . . The debate is joined." The "choices narrow," McGill observed, between obeying the law and maintaining public schools, or disobeying and closing the schools.[35]

For many persons these were "bitter" alternatives. In a situation absorbed with hate and danger, McGill offered clear and judicious counsel. "We must make a decision," he told a Birmingham audience at a time when that city was under siege. "We can either join to assist court decision . . . or we can defy and encourage the violent to lawlessness." Emphasizing the urgency of the situation, McGill called for understanding: "Things are never going to be as they were before. . . . The South should not lie to itself. It is a critical time. We are . . . at a great pivot of history." He advised against heeding "only the angry, dogmatic voices of inflexible men" who were "prisoners of their own excesses." McGill urged citizens to use their influence to educate "people . . . to be constantly alert in their support and defense of our schools. . . . Today the political power pattern plans to close them in four or five states.[36]

---

[34]"Alfred M. Landon Lecture," in *Ralph McGill*, 2:432; "De Paul University Address," in *Ralph McGill*, 2:363; *Atlanta Constitution*, 22 October 1948; "St. Paul's Church Speech," in *Ralph McGill*, 2:100; "Ministers Week Speech," in *Ralph McGill*, 1:173.

[35]"Fayette County (KY) Bar Association Speech," in *Ralph McGill*, 2:228.

[36]"Birmingham Rotary Club Speech," in *Ralph McGill*, 1:217; "Augusta Rotary Club Speech," in *Ralph McGill*, 2:125.

How to Hold a Public Forum

After 1954, McGill continued speaking for blacks, pointing out how "shameful" and "un-American" it was to deny persons the right to vote and participate in civic decisions. Changing his thinking somewhat, he believed that only a combination "federal" and "local program" could provide new jobs for blacks. He repeated his conviction that making blacks "participating, taxpaying citizens by virtue of better jobs" would take them off the "white taxpayer's back." He declared that desegregation was "so very much a moral" issue "that it shames us all; it has become a matter of police and courts." McGill repeated that the South should right its wrongs. Addressing "the racial problem" as the "most grave and critical internal crisis the nation faces," McGill insisted that "we do not need new legislation. This is something we must find the will to do by ourselves." Each time Congress passed a new civil rights bill, McGill treated it as "a motivating force for action at the local levels." The bills were "nothing more than a beginning—a legal pivot toward equality in education, politics, housing and jobs."[37]

From 1954 until McGill's death in 1969, the primary struggle in the South was over public education. As he campaigned to save the public schools, McGill would question his audience rhetorically, "What can I do?" "Well, I think each man and woman must examine his own heart and conscience." He was not without hope and he urged people to continue their efforts for order, discussion, obedience to the Court, and public schools. Until the "peddlers of hate, distortion and falsehood" were answered, he insisted, they would be "more successful than we."

After 1954, many fairminded and law-abiding citizens finally realized that McGill's statements about desegregation were true and turned to him for help. Rather than turn away smugly, McGill seized the new audience as a means of supporting desegregation reasonably. He urged any person or group with access to a public forum to discuss the issues responsibly. "Three cooperating elements are required . . . the newspapers and other information media, the clergy, and business."

---

[37]*Atlanta Constitution*, 18 February 1961; "Civil Liberties Union Speech," in *Ralph McGill*, 2:319; "Massachusetts Institute of Technology Speech," in *Ralph McGill*, 1:244.

Interestingly, throughout this long and difficult period, McGill assumed that political leaders would inflame existing fears and prejudices. He did admit some understanding of their predicament, believing that to hold an office politicians often merely mirror the people's attitudes. Ministers, however, do have a pulpit, McGill suggested, contrasting their opportunity to speak candidly with the impotent position of politicians. While some clergymen had told their congregations that the "Bible condemned the court and government," others had "been forced out of their pulpits for declaring that Christianity is not a private club."

McGill knew from his own efforts that speaking would not be easy, no matter what the forum. "Editors too have a pulpit," he stated, criticizing "spineless newspapers" that were "unwilling to pay the cost which might ensue from engaging in controversy and debate." Business and labor leaders also must participate. Too many business persons had remained aloof from the fray, and "organized labor has not done what it should," all leaving a "vacuum" to be "filled by the extremists who defy the processes of law." "We can't abandon our schools," McGill insisted. Responsible citizens should "create a climate which will demand that schools be kept open and chart a way out of a chaos and deterioration." But public schools would be "preserved" only if people "speak out." "We must proceed . . . with unrelenting determination" and "stand up when we can."[38]

During McGill's speeches members of the audience asked how they could help when the situation was so explosive with hate. While McGill usually resisted simple formulas, at this time when the public schools were so imperiled, he sensed that precise, straightforward answers were appropriate. Drawing upon his own firsthand experience as a speaker, and following his personal format for offering public instruction, McGill explained step by step how interested individuals could return home and work to preserve law and order and the public schools. In an intimately familiar dialogue with his listeners, as preserved on tape recordings of his speeches and answers to questions from the audience, he recommended organization at the community level because there was little chance that any state political leaders could act responsibly even if

---

[38]"Birmingham Rotary Club Speech," in *Ralph McGill*, 1:217; "Ministers Week Speech," in *Ralph McGill*, 1:168.

they desired. But choose the community wisely, he suggested. "In some towns you can discuss" race and schools, and in "some you can't." More specifically, in his home state he felt that public discussions could be sponsored in Atlanta, Macon, and Columbus, while a person would "never get a discussion" in Echols, Baker and Clinch, and similarly hostile counties. McGill's sources told him there would be communication concerning the school crisis in "nearly all cities of any size except Augusta." Later he addressed the Rotary Club in Augusta, although there had been "considerable objection" to his speaking, "and it started some discussion" in the Augusta *Chronicle*.[39]

McGill recommended that persons arrange public meetings "with intelligence and with planning," reflecting again his belief that planners have to be realistic. In some places, he pointed out, "you may have to meet quietly. . . . You may have to be almost secretive about it." If possible, "bring in some of your political leadership," but do so "carefully and quietly" after evaluating the "community." Persons participating in a meeting should "stand quietly," "calmly," and "forthrightly." Speakers should be selected who are well informed and can "explain the depth of our dilemma" and the "agony of our situation"—as he had been doing since 1946! During the question and answer period after a speech at Emory University, McGill outlined a format he believed would work. Note that the procedure he prescribed followed exactly the form of instruction he had employed for many years in his personal campaign for improved race relations:

> Anytime a Christian church or leader or community can carry out by discussion, information programs, all to the good. I think that if you can get them out of the process of debate you will do better. Unhappily, a lot of people don't want to hear the truth. . . . But if you could have somebody who could project the real dilemma or have just a discussion, have both sides but let it be talked, the important thing is that it will be discussed. I think we have been in a position where we have been almost afraid to discuss this until the last few months. It was a subject that was taboo. . . . Now people are beginning to talk about it and a debate is beginning and I think that will be healthy.[40]

---

[39]"Augusta Rotary Club Speech," in *Ralph McGill*, 2:120-29.

[40]"Ministers Week Speech," in *Ralph McGill*, 1:178.

While instructing others on how to hold public discussions in their communities, McGill continued to address the problems himself. In his post-1954 lesson plan to save the public schools, he defended the Supreme Court, emphasized the critical need for schools, opposed violence, exposed false myths, and explained historical roots of change.

Defense of the Supreme Court

For those who opposed the actions of the Supreme Court, or failed to understand the Court's meaning, McGill attempted to explain: "My policy . . . has been to tell the people the truth about the court decision; namely, that it was a constitutional power of the court to interpret the Constitution." McGill taught that the Court "has not violated the Constitution because it can't." While citizens could "dissent" and "voice" against the decision, they should not delude themselves. "The ruling was final" and had to "be accepted, acceptable or not." McGill defended the Court as a "great umbrella" that "protects us from . . . domestic tyranny," a "shield and buckler," "the essential of life and government." Without obedience to the law there would be "anarchy." The lesson in all this was simple: no longer in public schools in the South could there be "educational segregation on the basis of race."[41]

Although often patient in interpreting the meaning of the Court for citizens, McGill was riled by what he perceived as the conscious deception of many leaders who rejected the desegregation judgment. He exposed the "extremist doctrines," "petty and unworthy values," and the "angry, dogmatic voices of inflexible men." He held them directly responsible for a "generation of children. . . . The bitter-enders and irrational persons who closed the schools were the worst enemies of the South." Remembering more chivalrous claims of honored Civil War veterans, McGill insisted that this time "I do not see how it would be possible for any one of these to emerge as the hero of a lost cause." McGill accused George Wallace and Ross Barnett of "practiced deceit"

---

[41]"Augusta Rotary Club Speech," in *Ralph McGill*, 2:129; "Editors View the South Speech," in *Ralph McGill*, 1:155; "Elijah Parish Lovejoy Address," in *Ralph McGill*, 2:183.

in claiming that the federal government was trying to control schools. "This is, of course, poppycock . . . to encourage defiance."[42]

Need for Public Schools

To win support for education, McGill emphasized the critical importance of public schools. Ironically, a chief argument used by McGill was the fact that even prior to consideration of desegregation, Southern schools had been inadequate. The National Education Association and others were quoted to show that the region provided "the poorest quality of education for children." Children in the seventh grade were "reading at about the fifth grade level." The curricula in many towns were inadequate to prepare students for advanced training in universities. Faculty salaries were lower, so the South was in danger of losing its best teachers. To destroy the limited progress that had been made, McGill argued, was "almost too fantastic to be believed."

Countering officials who called for segregated private schools, he maintained that no system of private education could serve the "great and growing population of children." Employing a recurring strategy, he predicted serious economic losses for the white establishment if the public schools were closed. Towns and cities that sacrificed schools were "inviting long-term economic loss. Industries will hesitate to build," he argued. "Engineers and technicians are the type who demand good schools." He then cited a study made of "three or four businesses" that "felt that there had been a very serious impact because of the school situation." Even more significant were the South's sons and daughters: "What really makes for frustration . . . is that it is children . . . who are to be the real victims of those who plan to close the schools. . . . The damage done them will be irreparable. . . . The schools may be closed in the Deep South. I cannot believe the people will permit them to remain shut."[43]

---

[42]"Crisis in Schools Speech," in *Ralph McGill*, 1:193; *Atlanta Constitution*, 30 May 1968.

[43]*Atlanta Constitution*, 22 September 1955; "Philadelphia Award Speech," in *Ralph McGill*, 2:485; *Boston Globe*, 24 January 1959; "Crisis in Schools Speech," in *Ralph McGill*, 1:205; "Sidney Hillman Foundation Speech," in *Ralph McGill*, 2:133.

Opposition to Violence

McGill was appalled by the violence in the region. Once during a wrenching discussion of the situation, even he concluded that it would be preferable to "see Georgia close its schools than to go into a period of violence and mob actions." He never submitted to the angry voices, shots, and bombs, however, insisting that no mob be allowed to make the South wear a "criminal's mask." The "red-necks and the violent haters" cannot become the "voice and face of the region." He deplored the "guns, dynamitings, beatings, and drownings." In his speeches and writings, McGill exposed the "harassment," "savage brutalities," "perversion of justice," "ruthless brutality," "filthy abuse," and "murder." "It is not possible to preach lawlessness and restrict it," he warned. Comparing University of Mississippi students to the "Nazi black shirts of the 1930s," McGill condemned their attempt to prevent desegregation of the university as a "grotesque . . . show." "Not all the perfumes of Araby will wash clean the political hands of Mississippi's Governor Ross Barnett." Persons who threatened the schools and the security of the region, proclaimed McGill, were "politically chained to the rock of prejudice, they are pecked and shrilled at by the vultures of fanaticism." Officials "in charge of the South must halt the destruction of churches and property and punish the guilty." "When the wolves of hate are loosed on one people, then no one is safe." "The wages of violence, like those of sin, is a sort of death. Something dies in a city or a community when there is an explosion of hatred." The "criminals," he continued, were "trampling out the vintage where the grapes of wrath are stored." "I mean no irreverence when I say that while public education may be crucified on a cross of willful destruction . . . it will rise again out of the wreckage."[44]

Exposing Myths

In speaking for schools, McGill broadened his strategy of public instruction to include a historical analysis of what made Southerners so

---

[44]"Rochester City Club Speech," in *Ralph McGill*, 2:347; "Massachusetts Historical Society Speech," in *Ralph McGill*, 2:402; "Massachusetts Institute of Technology Speech," in *Ralph McGill*, 1:242; *Atlanta Constitution*, 2 October 1962; "Birmingham Rotary Club Speech," in *Ralph McGill*, 1:218; *Atlanta Constitution*, 31 August 1962 and 18 January 1957.

hostile to the thought of racial desegregation. He explained the regional perception that seemingly prevented a reasonable consideration of limited racial integration. "The romanticized myth," he exhorted, "is a curse to those who live there. The myth still obscures the reality." These myths imprisoned Southerners in the past: "This business of changing images is important. Much of the South long was obsessed with an imagery that fits the old South—of song and myth. There still are some Southerners who are more devoted to this never-never land than they are to church or school. These Southerners presently are" engaged in the sordid business of a "retelling of old myths, a reopening of old wounds, and a reparading of old prejudices." To support open public schools, McGill exposed several "threadbare myths" he felt prevented many whites from accepting social change.[45]

The first "general image" McGill challenged was the concept of the South being "all of a piece." Referring to specific differences in attitudes, positions, and acts, he noted that "Southerners are learning that their states are not 'solid' Souths."

McGill identified a second myth to be the claim of the "unconstitutionality of the Constitution," a "passion" that had "prevented logical discussion." McGill refuted political leaders who insisted that the Constitution "is not law—that a constitutional decision does not have the effect of law."

Third was the "mythology . . . built around the word *sovereignty*," an "almost religious fervor, a sort of holy war for states' rights." "One of the confusing elements in attempts to have a national dialogue" on school desegregation, he explained, "has been the insistence, by extremist leadership, on state sovereignty." For example, McGill called Virginia's use of the "interposition theory" in opposing the Supreme Court's 1954 decision "a magnificent irrelevancy." For too long Southerners had "been prisoners of the deadly oratory of those who spoke of their 'sovereign states.' "

McGill analyzed how radical segregationist candidates combined Lost Cause arguments with the states' rights myth. Orators "deliber-

---

[45]"Civil Liberties Union Speech," in *Ralph McGill*, 2:319; "Alfred M. Landon Lecture," in *Ralph McGill*, 2:427; "Massachusetts Historical Society Speech," in *Ralph McGill*, 2:399.

ately, shrewdly choose the words they know will arouse the church burn-
ers. . . . They arouse the crowds with lies and false witnessing." They
are "fond of such phrases as 'We won't stop fighting until we drop to
our knees.' 'The Confederate guns speak to us from the past.' 'Our heads
are bloody but unbowed.' . . . 'We will never surrender.' 'We will show
the Supreme Court it can't tell us what to do.' "

McGill also challenged the persistent states' rights appeal by turning the argument to show the South's hypocrisy: "In the often grotesque
exaggerations which occur in the Deep South debate over the life or
death of the school system, the phrase most often used by those who lack
facts or logic is the ambiguous one of 'States' Rights'. . . . The states
utterly failed to carry out the separate but equal decision. State failure
to meet this responsibility, plus the march of history . . . produced a
constitutional" decision by the federal government.[46]

A fourth group of myths McGill challenged were those about blacks.
Some whites believed that blacks constituted "about half the population
of the South," when they formed only "about one-fourth and it de-
creases." But for whites who lived "where there are a great many Negroes," McGill attempted to redefine the negative image identified with
that race. He spoke of the "stereotype Negro—the one we don't like—
the one whose image we have as being dirty, ignorant, uncouth, inferior." Demagogues in the South claimed that "the Negro was not really
a human being." Through this distorted and selective mythmaking,
even "moderate, good people . . . inherited through the years, by a sort
of sad process of osmosis, prejudices which they do not always recognize
they possess." Some of the cruel images persisted because many whites
had never "known a cultured, educated Negro." The traditional separation of the races also prevented "white people" from knowing "what
the Negro community wants, thinks, or feels." Because of basic prejudices and lack of meaningful interaction between the races, whites often
concluded that the "sharecropper or tenant was happy in his shack . . .
that he was glad to be without the simplest amenities of life; that he was

---

[46]"United Negro College Fund Speech," in *Ralph McGill*, 2:237; "Cooper Union
Lincoln Day Address," in *Ralph McGill*, 2:162-64; *Atlanta Constitution*, 9 May 1952,
18 October 1965, 11 September 1962, and 16 December 1958.

delighted for his children not to have a chance at even an average education."[47]

Finally, whites feared that racial integration would mean intermarriage. During a speech at Emory University, McGill attempted to correct this assumption by discussing the belief among whites that desegregation "would mean mongrelization or amalgamation," and a voice from the audience said: "It always has." Startled by the overt response, McGill tried to explain that although there had been desegregation in Northern schools "the number of intermarriages . . . are down." "It seems to me," he amplified, "that the greatest falsehood has been imposed on us . . . namely that integration would mean amalgamation. I just think a little bit too much of the white race and the colored race to believe that only a law prevents them from rushing to the marriage courts (audience laughter). That's ridiculous in my opinion. And yet it's the overpowering one sentiment in this that it would mean mongrelization or amalgamation."[48]

From these myths about the unified South, nature of government, and motivation of blacks, Southerners, concluded McGill, created the "doctrines of white supremacy, of Negro inferiority, and a system of segregation whose moral, political, social and economic injustices, follies, and evils are just now being comprehended." Extending his explanation to the present, McGill taught that "ignorance, prejudice and shabbiness of mind and values are careless leaks in the dykes of the civilization in which man is a free individual. These forces must always be recognized for what they are and their presence and purpose publicly proclaimed and opposed." The old image of blacks is changing, he stated, "we somehow must rid ourselves of the stereotype Negro." The remedy is "really relatively simple. . . . It is to grant the Negro the rights . . . of full citizenship" and "to look at" a black individual and "see another human being."[49]

---

[47]"Carney Hospital Centennial Speech," in *Ralph McGill*, 2:312; "Ministers Week Speech," in *Ralph McGill*, 1:166; "American Association of School Administrators Speech," in *Ralph McGill*, 2:458; "Rosenwald Centennial Speech," in *Ralph McGill*, 2:288.

[48]"Editors View the South Speech," in *Ralph McGill*, 1:159-60.

[49]"Alfred M. Landon Lecture," in *Ralph McGill*, 2:429, "Augusta Rotary Club Speech," in *Ralph McGill*, 2:129-30; McGill, *South and Southerner,* 232.

Historical Causes of Social Change

Part of McGill's strategy was to teach why the South was unique. A recurring theme in his talks was "what made us 'Southern.' " His thesis was a "South in Transition." "To know what the job is" one must learn "what the picture is." "Out of experience comes the beginning of wisdom," he advised. Too few persons understand the " 'why' of the happenings." People should realize the "great forces with which we must contend." Borrowing words from Holy Scriptures for Bible Belt audiences, McGill said: "Each of us . . . is a part of the past" that has "touched us all, stopping at every door, passing over none." Southerners should comprehend how the changes affect them and why they paralyze.[50]

In his speeches and writings, McGill gave brief histories of the causes of changes confronting the South. His purpose was not only to make citizens aware of their own perceptions, but also to make them aware of the sources of their views. He explained the South's extreme sectional loyalty and her dislike for criticism. He analyzed the various forces that led to the "pattern called segregation." Specifically, he told of "the fogs of prejudice and distortion left from the Civil War and reconstruction"; how cotton, rice, tobacco, and the climate required to produce those commodities "demanded a slave labor" and thereby "set us apart"; how values were fixed by a plantation culture. McGill reminded audiences that desegregation was not "brand new" but had roots in the past and had "been coming a long time." So that listeners could see what had led to their present predicament, he isolated specific causes of social changes in the South: the Civil War and an "end of a social and economic system based on slavery"; the reality of a "melancholy, ruthless, sad, cruel, period" of reconstruction; the "seating of Rutherford B. Hayes, with Southern Redeemer support, in the winter of 1876-1877, that turned the South politically and economically away from the agrarian West to the industrial East"; "the enactment of statutory segregation, the various 'black codes,' the cult of white supremacy"; wrecking of the "cotton South" in "1919-1920" that "paralyzed the cotton economy";

---

[50]"*Hartford Courant* Anniversary Speech," in *Ralph McGill*, 2:332; "Crisis in Schools," in *Ralph McGill*, 1:192; "Ministers Week Speech," in *Ralph McGill*, 1:168.

"psychological impact of the Second World War to liberate the mind and soul of all men"; elimination of the "white primary" by the Supreme Court; and the potential for "two-party" politics in the South.

In assessing reasons for the inevitability of racial desegregation in the South, McGill stressed the importance of migration of people from town to city, from farm to factory. "Agrarian regionalism is moving off the stage—and urban regionalism is in the center of it." He predicted that the symbol of the "New South" would be "a test-tube rather than a cotton field." Since 1945, he said, the distinctive aspect of society had been its mobility. Quoting United States census data, he told how "from 1910 to 1930, almost ten percent of the population of the South migrated. In the decade from 1920 to 1930, it was almost 15 percent; in the last decade, ending in 1950, 18.9 percent." To dramatize the potency of migration, McGill provided poetic description.

> I can remember how the sharecroppers and tenant cabins emptied, some of them burned, leaving the chimneys there like silent sentinels representing something gone never to return. I saw . . . their wooden windows sagging, the doors sagging . . . the roof broken in, the old hearth places where people had dreamed and thought and perhaps sorrowed, and turned over, animals moving in through the buildings—1920s.[51]

McGill defined specific effects of Southern migration, all leading to the present harvest of inadequate education, jobs, housing and civil rights denials, as well as the conflict between the races. The first impact was economical. "Poor whites" and "colored" alike "moved to town" searching for "industrial jobs," but being poorly educated and unskilled many remained semi-unemployed. Although the "depression years slowed the exodus," World War II "plants required plain labor, semi-skilled labor." People "were picked up by the great engines of war . . . and put down, and there they are." The "industrial revolution of the 1950s was moving rural poverty in to be a part of the urban poverty."[52]

Second, migration influenced issues of race, a situation closely tied to economics. Blacks finally were exiting the plantation environment. "Only about one out of every ten Negroes is now a farm-hand," McGill

---

[51]"National Education Association Speech," in *Ralph McGill*, 1:248; "South in Transition Speech," in *Ralph McGill*, 2:350.

[52]"National Education Association Speech," in *Ralph McGill*, 1:250.

stated. "The rest are in the cities." The migration of blacks and whites redistributed the population into "new patterns" and "new characteristics." The influence of urbanization in the South was dramatic because "nowhere else . . . was the regional culture so completely associated with a rural, paternalistic way of life." Migration and historical events changed the South's racial patterns, explained McGill, not "Communists" or "alien influences." A third impact of migration was the continuation of "old agrarian points of view in the new urban areas." Many of the values, the prejudices, and the attitudes of the plantation culture, stated McGill, were transplanted to town. For example, persons employed in the "new little cotton mill, in the new timber plant, at a processing plant of some sort . . . were just about what the sharecropper and the tenant had been back on the cotton farm. And this is true today."[53]

The South, then, was ripe for change and conflict. As long as blacks were kept subservient to whites, there was little friction. But when the "white primaries" and segregation of schools, transportation, and public accommodations were ruled unconstitutional, and those pent-up forces described by McGill unleashed, a flood of fears prompted many whites to resist. He advised that change, while difficult, was morally right and regionally profitable.

Conclusion

While scathing in his criticism of irresponsible leaders and violence, McGill cushioned his criticism of the people. Even after 1954, he continued "seeking" with his audiences, believing still that "no generality" or "fixed opinion" would "fit any phase" of the race problem. He did not know all the answers and would not "speak with great dogmatic finality." He showed compassion for citizens who strongly supported segregation but were unwilling "to tear down the government with violence and anarchy." He refused to accuse or blame. Surprising to many who had heard him support civil rights and desegregation, McGill insisted that he had no program or policy of integration. "I don't know anybody that's demanding integration—a person would be a fool to de-

---

[53]"Crisis in Schools Speech," in *Ralph McGill*, 1:190, "Jewish Education Alliance Veterans Day Speech," in *Ralph McGill*, 2:77.

mand integration now in the Deep South," he concluded in 1957. He persisted in accommodating the fears of whites, stating that "going to school is not a social gathering," an argument he had employed in the 1940s to win equal rights for blacks. Still convinced that progress would come slowly, he spoke for gradual improvement: "Time works changes." He wanted legal suits delayed until a few border states had time to try desegregated schools as "precept and example" for the Deep South. Certainly "persons who preferred things . . . as they were" would choose the "beginning of integration rather than . . . lose the public school system."[54]

Increasingly, in the 1960s, McGill became more direct and candid in his call for resolution of the school problem. "Segregation is dead," he pronounced, "what remains" is the "effort to delay interment." The year before he died, McGill stated, "I am weary of the old hanging on of the dual school systems and the excuses and the evasion." "Must we forever keep on? Must a nation which has put a man in space still argue about where, and whether, a colored child shall go to school?" he asked a Birmingham audience.[55]

In his last newspaper column he saw printed, he called the "segregated system of education . . . viciously unjust . . . a disease that weakened all education." The day he died in 1969, he talked informally to students at Booker T. Washington High School in Atlanta of the "nonsense of supremacy" and "separation."

Unencumbered in the late 1960s by accommodating rhetorical strategies, McGill asked that somehow people "speed up the process of acceptance of what must be done morally . . . and what ought to have been done long ago without all the pressures." He exhorted the "good people, who have for so long listened to lies and political bombasts," to "accept the truth." A person's "rights cannot be compromised." "Law is not enough," he maintained, "the heart also must listen."

---

[54]"Editors View the South Speech," in *Ralph McGill*, 1:159; "Ministers Week Speech," in *Ralph McGill*, 1:163; "Augusta Rotary Club Speech," in *Ralph McGill*, 2:129.

[55]"United Negro College Fund Speech," in *Ralph McGill*, 2:239; "American Association of School Administrators Speech," in *Ralph McGill*, 2:462; "Birmingham Rotary Club Speech," in *Ralph McGill*, 1:219.

He supported the "Southern sit-ins" as a mechanism that brought to the "fore a moral issue heretofore obscured by politics and lawyers." Demonstrators involved in acts of civil disobedience would win, he advised, because "they have moral force on their side" and because they walk under the Constitution. The demonstrations changed the plantation image and mythology long held by whites of blacks.

Even in the final days of his life, however, McGill sought new methods and new understanding. After the street demonstrations and sit-ins, he asked: "Has this policy . . . played its limit? Has it attained what it can? And now is there need for another policy?" The day he died, a young black student asked his opinion of the "black separatist movement." When he answered, McGill must have thought back over the many years when he had struggled to remedy the old "separate and equal" system: "I don't think this will work. . . . You can't separate yourself from the world . . . from your fellowman."[56]

Ralph McGill was a crusader with common sense and, as the *New York Times* judged, a sense of humor.[57] The problems of people who were exploited bothered him. McGill addressed those concerns directly in his writings and speeches, but with compassion for all involved and with limited expectations. Convinced that social progress moves slowly, he generally assumed the role of social critic and public teacher by instructing readers and listeners in basic lessons of Southern history, social change, civil rights, and responsible citizenship. In searching with audiences for causes of conditions, he often was inspiringly poetic and, at times, "hodgepodgingly"—as he said—rambling. He angered racists and irresponsible political leaders, and disappointed impatient liberals. But always he acted with courage and considerable charisma in exhorting Southern audiences to look beyond the racism of their region. Persons who shared his dream of equality for all found encouragement and strength in his oral and written instruction.

During the difficult period from 1946 to 1969, McGill offered Southerners an alternative to inaction, hate, violence, and racial discrimination. For his pronouncements, he often was abused verbally and

---

[56]*Atlanta Constitution*, 3 February 1959; "National Education Speech," in *Ralph McGill*, 1:252; "Booker T. Washington Speech," in *Ralph McGill*, 2:505-506.

[57]*New York Times*, 5 February 1969.

threatened physically. Nevertheless he refused to bow to extremists on
any side, although "there was a time" at the *Atlanta Constitution*, he said,
in the 1940s and 1950s, when "some of the management . . . was opposed to" his "writing what" he "wanted to write."[58] McGill learned
that the only certain reward for a free and independent spokesman was
the "inner satisfaction of being able to face one's self." Thus, he took a
middle way, "just left of center," and spoke the truth as he perceived it
by insisting that civilized persons have a duty to oppose wrong. In doing
so, McGill personally helped blacks in their efforts to achieve equal
citizenship.

The essays, interviews, book reviews, and statements by McGill
that follow include carefully conceived and edited analyses of issues, opportunities, and problems in the South and nation, as well as brief and
impromptu responses to significant social needs. The works derive from
more than forty years of study and firsthand observations of people and
conditions in the United States. When McGill reviewed the book,
F.D.R. His Personal Letters (the review is published below), he concluded that "The entries are arranged chronologically, and as they march
through the years the reader is pulled along with them. It is almost as if
one were given a seat inside FDR's mind." A similar experience is enjoyed when reading McGill's works. While the first piece, "The Southeast," was written in 1958 and serves as an introduction to the South, the
others are arranged chronologically from 1938 to 1969. Also from the
collection one learns not only about issues, policies, and people confronting the South and nation, but of McGill's own development and perception of events, their causes, and possible actions to be taken. In some
of the pieces McGill simply praises Georgia and the South. In others he
offers penetrating assessments of racial discrimination in housing, the
courts, and schools, and of what must be done to correct the situation.
Taken together, the essays, reviews, interviews, and statements provide
McGill's understanding, criticism, and advice concerning citizens confronting social conflict and change. In an interview on radio in 1963 in
Boston about the rights of blacks (published below), McGill advised
that "You can't turn your back on this. There's no place to hide. There's

---

[58]"Logue's Interview with McGill," in *Ralph McGill*, 2:22.

no place to run." Following his own advice for social progress, for many years McGill publicly wrote and spoke for equal rights for all citizens. Many of those statements are reprinted below.

Acknowledgments

The editor expresses appreciation to the following persons for assistance and support: Ms. Elise Allen, Ms. Robin Gormley, the staff of Mercer University Press, Dr. W. J. Payne, Ms. Diane Hunter, Mr. Harold Buell, Mr. Grant Lamos, Mr. Jim Minter, the University of Georgia Library faculty and staff, Ms. Grace Lundy Tackett, Mrs. Ralph McGill, and Ms. Mary Jo Logue. The *Atlanta Constitution* and Associated Press were generous in providing photographs for the two volumes.

The World
of Ralph McGill
in Pictures

*Eleanor and Franklin Roosevelt relax on the sundeck of their vacation house in Warm Springs, Georgia, during FDR's first term. Roosevelt had been coming to Warm Springs since the 1920s for treatment of his poliomyelitis, and he made it a national center of therapy for victims of paralysis. It was here on this deck, overlooking a secluded forest of pines, mountain hardwoods, and native flowers, that Roosevelt designed many of the New Deal programs to combat the Great Depression that had afflicted and the South and the nation. (*Atlanta Constitution *photo)*

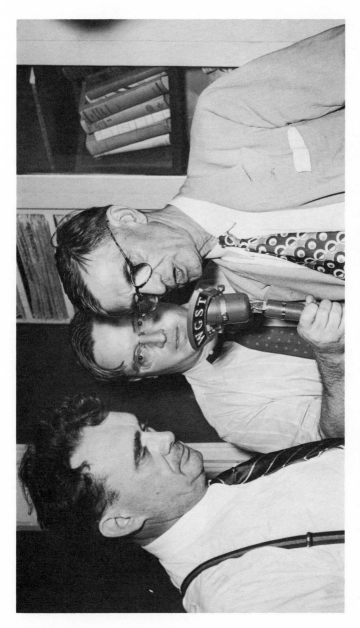

A dejected and exhausted Ralph McGill (left) listens as Eugene Talmadge declares himself the Democratic nominee for governor of Georgia, broadcasting from the offices of the Constitution in the early morning hours of 18 July 1946. Radio announcer John Fulton (center) holds the microphone. McGill and the Constitution had vigorously opposed Talmadge and his tactics of racial hatred during a hard-fought primary campaign. (Associated Press photo)

Ralph McGill (third from right) poses with President Harry S Truman (center) and a delegation of Southern journalists in the Oval Office of the White House. McGill wrote often about Truman, who supported civil rights legislation and other programs important to the South. (Associated Press photo)

A child reads her lesson in a segregated, one-room school in Appling County, Georgia, in January 1950. The cutline for this picture in the Constitution read, cryptically, "Stove Is Old, But Chimney Is Safe. Walls Are Ceiled. There Are No Desks, Only Benches." (Atlanta Constitution photo)

"Mama Sarah" Murphy reads a story with some of the 48 orphaned children she taught and cared for on a farm near Rockmart, Georgia. (Wide World photo, used with permission of the Atlanta Journal and Constitution.*)*

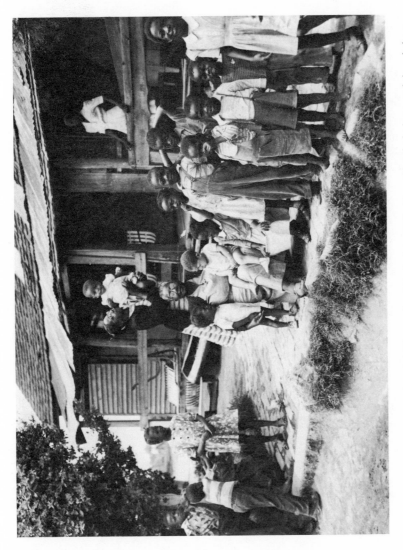

Sarah L. Murphy poses with orphaned children on her farm in June 1950. Since 1934 she had operated the only home and school for poor, black orphans in Georgia. (Wide World photo, used with permission of the Atlanta Journal and Constitution.)

Hostile whites are kept away from the entrance of Central High School in Little Rock, Arkansas, after President Dwight D. Eisenhower called in federal troops to police the first major crisis in Southern school desegregation. (Associated Press photo)

Dr. William Holmes Borders, pastor of Wheat Street Baptist Church in Atlanta, addresses an audience of 1,200 blacks after he and other black clergymen had successfully taken seats in the white section of a segregated city bus on 9 January 1957. Dr. Borders promised that the campaign to desegregate Atlanta's transit system would "go forward at whatever the cost." (Associated Press photo)

After seating themselves a second time in the "white" seats of Atlanta city buses, Dr. William Holmes Borders (right) and four other black clergymen find themselves in jail on 10 January 1957. (Associated Press photo)

President Dwight D. Eisenhower poses with a delegation of black leaders after a meeting at the White House to discuss civil rights issues on 23 June 1958. Appearing in the picture are (from left) Dr. Martin Luther King, Jr.; E. Frederic Morrow, a presidential assistant; President Eisenhower; A. Philip Randolph, president of the International Brotherhood of Sleeping Car Porters; Attorney General William Rogers, and Roy Wilkins, executive secretary of the National Association for the Advancement of Colored People. The black leaders had told the president that a recent court decision suspending school integration in Little Rock, Arkansas, had "shocked and outraged Negro citizens and millions of their fellow Americans." (Associated Press photo)

Ralph McGill (right) joins Palmer Hoyt of the Denver Post *and Turner Catledge of* The New York Times *in a televised interview with Dave Garroway (left) broadcast 24 April 1959 on the NBC "Today" program. McGill's appearances in such forums provided an opportunity for him to set events in the South and the Southern struggle for human rights in perspective for the rest of the nation. (Atlanta Constitution photo by Maurey Garber)*

Members of a black delegation take their seats for a public hearing on the issue of closing or desegregating Georgia's public schools on 24 March 1960. More than 1,200 spectators packed the auditorium of Henry Grady High School in Atlanta to hear 114 witnesses address a commission chaired by Atlanta attorney John Adams Sibley. At this hearing 85 persons representing a variety of community organizations favored keeping the public schools open, although they disagreed about how to approach desegregation. Only 28 witnesses advocated closing the public schools in the Atlanta hearing, but in other parts of the state many witnesses preferred closing to any form of desegregation. (Atlanta Constitution photo)

*A solitary white demonstrator representing the Atlanta chapter of the Congress of Racial Equality turns heads on a downtown street as she protests segregation in the city's business establishments on 3 May 1960. (*Atlanta Constitution *photo by Wiley Perry)*

A member of the Ku Klux Klan thumbs his nose at a photographer as he and other Klansmen picket the offices of the Atlanta Journal *and* Constitution *on 11 December 1960 in protest of the papers' editorial support of human rights. (*Atlanta Journal *photo by Charles Pugh)*

Seven thousand bales of cotton, saved from the flood waters of the Chattahoochee River, fill a street in the cotton district of Columbus, Georgia. Such a scene symbolizes the domination of the South's economy by cotton, a theme to which McGill returned again and again in his essays and editorials. (Atlanta Journal photo by Kirk Wooster)

The Southeast

One begins with geography.

The "South," which is the more usable name for the Southeast, sweeps south and west from Virginia, to Mississippi, Arkansas, and Texas. Through it, from a beginning in New Jersey and Pennsylvania, curves the great red- and brown-soiled crescent of the Piedmont Plateau. The great, many-folded Appalachians reach south and west, creating a vast, seemingly endless wilderness of peaks, ranges, and ridges in the Carolinas and East Tennessee, and thrusting buttresses into South Carolina and Georgia. Northward beyond the mountains are highlands with bluegrass and limestone streams. To the south are prairie lands rich and lush, wire-grass regions, and pinewoods. And farther on, the bayous, the tidal swamps, and the delta lands.

The region's settlers came first to the coastal plain and put names upon it—the "Tidewater" in Virginia, the "Low Country" in South Carolina. Two-thirds of Florida is coastal plain, which runs about three hundred miles inland into North Carolina, thrusts deeply into the Gulf states, and extends into East Texas.

Reprinted from Hardwick Moseley, ed., *The Romance of North America* (Boston: Houghton Mifflin Co., 1958) 177-221, by permission of Mrs. Ralph McGill and Houghton Mifflin Company.

The Appalachians were the great barrier to movement by the new settlers. Philadelphia was the first great port of entry. And from it men and their families pushed on, seeking a way through the Appalachians. They found the great valley in Virginia and followed it into Georgia and North and South Carolina. The probing, restless men discovered Cumberland Gap and pushed into the dark and bloody ground that became Kentucky.

Geography began to do things to people.

A land so divided by mountains and rivers did not make for unity or cohesion. Cabins and clearings slowly dotted the Piedmont. Grist mills were built on its streams and along the fall line. They were as separated from the great coastal-plain plantations, where rice, tobacco, and indigo had brought wealth, slavery, luxury, and a cultural tie with Europe, as if they dwelt in another world. And, in a sense, they did.

The coastal aristocrats were, for the most part, self-made, though the myth says otherwise. There were few cavaliers. They were mostly vigorous, middle-class stock, for whom the wealth produced by tobacco and rice made it possible to establish themselves in the English way. Their manor houses were named after the great halls in the mother country and furnished with English goods. Some few lived like feudal barons. But the aristocrats, barons, and the white-pillared manor houses were in the minority. Ownership of slaves was the usual identifying badge of the gentry. By 1860 there were only 383,637 slaveholders in a white population of more than 8,000,000. Of these, only 48,566 owned 20 or more. By 1860 the great body of Southerners were of the middle class whether measured by economic or by social yardsticks.[1]

From the beginning the planters, being more or less concentrated along the coastal plains, and possessing transportation and communication to and with Europe and its capitals, became essentially what the nobility is in England. They were able to put the stamp of the country gentleman so firmly on the South that even the rise of the cities, with

---

[1]See Kenneth M. Stamp, *Peculiar Institution: Slavery in the Ante-Bellum South* (New York: Vintage Books, 1956); John W. Blassingame, *Slave Community: Plantation Life in the Antebellum South*, rev. and enl. (New York: Oxford University Press, 1979); Eugene D. Genovese, *Roll, Jordan Roll: The World the Slaves Made* (New York: Vintage Books, 1972).

their commerce and trade, did not change it. The planter pattern held until the end.

The weather, like geography and the planters, put its stamp on the customs and the people of the region. Long growing seasons, heat, and high humidity were its features. In Virginia this season of growth was six months. In the deeper South it was nine. There was plenty of rain, but it didn't always come when needed. Summer droughts were common and winter freezes sometimes reached to the Gulf. Crops grew lush, but the soil washed away easily in the often torrential rains and the fields "wore out" within a few years where slave cultivation was careless.

The heat put its stamp on architecture. Ceilings were high. There were wide porches and balconies.

And, finally, there was the Negro with his influence to add to geography, the planters, and the weather. His exact contribution cannot be dissected out of the whole. Where culture and refinement were accepted, his labor provided the necessary leisure and opportunity. If in some places, he fostered a kindly paternalism, he provided, too, an example of loyalty and good manners which were a part of the plantation tradition. Psychologists think that, perhaps, by giving some men and women freedom from drudgery, the Negro made possible close family relationships. Fostered by security within the family came an attitude of self-assurance which somehow became a distinguishing attribute of the planter sons and daughters.

There was a trace of the Negro's inflections which found its way into the Southern tongue, and some of his laughter and superstitions found their way into the Southern personality. Exactly what the Negro gave to the sectional character and quality of the South is an inseparable part of both. Suffice it to say, he was a major factor.

There is one thing that may be defined. The presence of more than 4,000,000 dark-skinned enslaved persons in a population of not quite 12,500,000 created a race problem and made the section acutely race conscious, with a nagging current of accusing guilt in that sectional consciousness.

For many years, however, there was none of this—not even a hint—but only the surging nationalism of the new and burgeoning young Republic.

As 1820 began it could be said with truth there was no sectional America. There was, to be sure, the "West," and the "East." But the "West" was the frontier, the restless, never-fixed line of settlement.

In 1820 it was a straggling line of great unevenness. It had one end at Lake Erie. It made a sort of wedge-shaped line across Ohio and southern Indiana and Illinois on into Missouri. From there it cut back to middle Tennessee and Alabama. It was drawn not too deeply back from the coastline of South Carolina and Georgia.

Wherever this line of frontier settlement ran was the "West."

There was, in 1820, neither Southeast nor a South, though there were proud Southerners. They had shared and suffered in the war for independence, the struggles of the confederation, the War of 1812, and had helped to bring the Republic and its Constitution into being. There was pride in the fact that Southerners had made so positive a contribution, but in the main it was a national pride and not in the narrow regional sense. Indeed, the Southerners were, in general, satisfied with the government. They were, in 1820 as they had been since the founding of the Republic, playing a major role in the direction of national affairs. There was but one political party, the Republican (later known as the Democratic). Southerners came close to dominating it. In 1820 James Monroe of Virginia was president. Of four presidents before him, three had been Virginians. Three of his six cabinet members were Southerners, as was the powerfully influential Speaker of the House.

The Congress of 1820, contrasted with those of the twentieth century, seems too good to be true. There was no party rivalry. There was no Southern states' rights faction, no slave-state bloc, no farm lobby, no liberal or conservative factionalisms, no pro- or antilabor sentiment, and no regional nationalisms. The South was at peace with itself, with the nation, and with the Republican party. Yet there were fundamental regional differences which climate, crops, and events all too soon were to bring into focus.

In the region south of the Ohio River were ten of the twenty states making up the Republic. Five were on the Atlantic coast: Maryland, Virginia, North Carolina, South Carolina, and Georgia. Their population thinned out a few miles back from the sea. These were the colonial states. There had been in them a strain of loyalty to the king and the mother country which had made their entry into the Revolution a slower and more cautious one than that of Massachusetts.

Five were the younger states, hacked out of the inland frontier by the more restless and discontented ones from the colonial "East." These were Kentucky, Tennessee, Louisiana, Mississippi, and Alabama. The last two had but recently come to statehood. They had been admitted in 1817 and 1819, respectively, with the Indian war whoop still in their ears. Long years of harassments, pressures, and treaties had been slowly eroding away the lands of the Creek confederation, but not until 1832 would the Indian population be removed westward.

Some 14,000 persons had pushed into the territory of Arkansas. Florida was still a subject of bargaining with Spain. Mexico, of which Texas was a colony, was nearing victory in her war of independence with Spain.

While the Southeastern area, or the "South," had exactly half the states, there was a slow falling behind in population. The census of 1820 showed it a half million behind. There was a feature of the region which contributed to making it unique, or "different." Of the South's 4,298,199 persons, 1,496,189 were slaves with no right of citizenship. In addition, there were 116,915 "free persons of color" in the ten states. These, while free, were not citizens. The white population was 2,685,095, about half that of the North.

There were other population contrasts. The region had received little influx from foreign countries since colonial days. There was a smoothed-out homogeneity. In the whole South there were only a few more than 12,000 unnaturalized persons. The cities of the North had more than 40,000. The opening up of Mississippi and Alabama Indian lands was to have a further containing effect on the population. It did not push westward.

In 1820 one of every four Southerners was a Virginian. As the tobacco lands of that state, farmed since earliest colonial days, began to wear out, there was an exodus to the new cotton lands in Mississippi and Alabama. There was a like movement from other older states, especially South Carolina. The only Southern states which, in 1820, could boast of any substantial growth in the preceding decade were Mississippi, Alabama, Louisiana, Tennessee, and Georgia.

The slave population also varied. Wherever the plantation economy was best suited, the percentage of Negroes was high. But slavery was the one common trait, and as time would tell, the most meaningful. In each Southern state, save Kentucky and Tennessee, Negroes made up a third or more of the population. It ranged from 52.7 percent in South Carolina down to 19.6 in Tennessee. In Kentucky, Tennessee, Virginia, and North Carolina, the mountain regions not only contained few slaves, there was a feeling of resentment against slaveholders. This was not because of any antislavery sentiment but was rather due to class. The small freeholder yeoman of the Appalachian valleys and coves resented the ease and luxury of the great plantations. And, perhaps more, he regarded slavery as an unfair, even un-American competition.

By 1820 the South, contented and satisfied with national affairs, was thoroughly committed to an agrarian economy. And though none knew it then, this agrarianism was a road which inevitably forked off from national unity into regional nationalism.

Ninety percent of all Southerners were engaged in agriculture, as compared with 77 percent in the rest of the nation. But it was not "farming" as the North knew it. It was an intense concentration on huge money crops, and the market was the world. There were, of course, enough acres devoted to food to maintain the plantations, large and small. But it was very much a secondary operation. Cotton, tobacco, rice, and sugar were the preoccupation of the planters. Each crop had its kingdom, but King Cotton's was the largest and most powerful.

Tobacco had its domain in two wide areas in the upper South. Because it is a crop which requires great and continuing personal care, it was not well suited to large plantations and large numbers of workers. It came, finally, to be the crop of small farmers with a few slaves or none. For many it was a family affair.

Here and there hemp was a rival of tobacco, but it occupied only a small domain, never an empire.

Rice ruled a region of marsh and swampland inland along the Atlantic from the lower North Carolina coast down past Georgia where the fresh-water tidal rivers ebbed and flowed. South Carolina led, with about three-fourths of the total crop. Georgia was next.

As late as 1935 old Liverpool Hazzard, who had been a slave on one of Pierce Butler's island plantations off the Georgia coast, would talk to visitors about the rice fields, the harsh, heavy work, the mosquitoes, and the fevers. There was one memory which he savored. The rice birds came in great flocks, and old Liverpool would smack his toothless gums as he recalled them spitted over hot coals. The rice planters, of whom there were never more than 600-odd, were the real aristocrats, looking with a certain condescension on the vulgar mob which came clearing land to grow cotton or sweated down the tobacco rows. Some increased their wealth with Sea Island cotton, also a semi-exclusive crop, suited only to the islands and coastal strips. There, the percentage of slaves was high.

Sugar ruled in the lower reaches of the Mississippi River, with Louisiana as its major territory. Here was work which great gangs of slave labor could do well.

Cotton was something else. Anyone could grow cotton. By 1820 the value of the crop was greater than all the others put together. In 1819 and 1820 the crop was around 350,000 bales. Three-fourths of it was sold abroad at sixteen cents per pound.

Each decade, from then until the war began in 1861, the cotton crop just about doubled. There seemed no end to the demand for cotton. New, improved gins and better seeds and varieties at home were matched by the invention of new spinning machines in England.

Growing it did not require great capital or slaves for a beginning. But men who began small thought and dreamed big. The bales of cotton were stepping stones to the far-stretching acres, to hundreds of "hands," to the white-pillared mansions, to juleps stirred with a silver spoon.

Most of the wealth flowed overseas. The more prosperous Southern planters imported their literature, wines, furniture, rugs, and silver from England and France.

Government in the Southern states was centered in the counties. The counties sent men to the legislature. The legislature elected the United States senators and exercised, directly and indirectly, almost complete control over all affairs of the state. The right to vote was restricted largely to freeholders. Government represented, in the main, the opinion of the slaveholding planting class. This influence was great in national affairs, and so in 1820 there was no nationalistic "South."

But there was a growing resentment against the money power. Chief creditor of the land hungry who had poured into the new lands to buy cotton was the federal government which had sold public lands, and the banks. The constrictions of currency and credit which began in 1818 had extended into 1819 and 1820. By this latter year, discontent had united the frontier West and the South in economic opposition to the East and the Bank of the United States and federal policies and legislation dealing with tariff, land sales, and bankruptcy. The East began to agitate containment of slavery in the South and to argue more loudly than ever before that enslavement of human beings was a moral wrong.[2]

The charge came to dominate the debate over the admission of Missouri to statehood. From that time on, slavery was a dark Nemesis on American development. It began to color all attitudes and slowly to crowd aside most other considerations. Symbols replaced realities. All chance of defining the role of planter and industrialist, of farmer and worker in American life, was lost sight of in the fierce controversy over the extension of slavery and the deeper meaning of political control that was at the heart of it.

The three-fifths provision of the Constitution allowed a state to add to its free population three-fifths of its slave total for the purpose of determining the number of congressional representatives to which it was entitled. The faster-growing East, with a developing urbanism with its craftsmen and builders, was becoming more and more restive over the political strength of the planters in national affairs. They saw in each new slave state a strengthening of the planter influence.

Had slavery been merely a social and moral issue, it could have been met and resolved as such. But suddenly, out of nowhere it seemed, it burst on the young nation as the emotional factor of a sectional issue, linked to sectional rivalry and national expansion.

Before the expansion controversy began, there had been little difference between North and South in the vigor of expressed antislavery sentiment. Nor could the great surge of Northern moral indignation over slavery be regarded as the harvest of long years of Northern compassion for the slave.

To this day it is not entirely clear how what could have been a normal sort of sectional rivalry turned into a bitter, at times irrational, struggle between the North and South. Slavery became the symbol of the many differences between them. Soon, too, it became the symbol by which partisans were to prove "right" and "wrong," to define "progress" and "backwardness," "evil" and "good."

---

[2]See F. N. Boney, *Slave Life in Georgia: A Narrative of the Life, Sufferings, and Escape of John Brown, A Fugitive Slave* (Savannah GA: Beehive Press, 1972); Sue Karin and Joseph Logsdon, eds. *Twelve Years a Slave, by Solomon Northup* (Baton Rouge: Louisiana State University Press, 1968).

From 1820 there were forty-one brief years before the "irrepressible conflict" began. They were swift, sweaty years of sound and fury, of astonishing growth and vitality.

Regional nationalism, or sectionalism, which was thrust seemingly full-born into being in 1820 by the debate over the slavery sections of the new state of Missouri's constitution, was one of three dominant characteristics of American life in the period from 1820 to 1860. All were related. All moved swiftly.

Growth was rapid. The line of frontier settlement was never still. People came. People moved westward.

Population doubled in nearly every decade. By 1860 there were substantial settlements on the Pacific, in Minnesota, Kansas, Arkansas, and Texas which had ceased to be a republic to become a state. In that period the people broke a hundred million acres to the plow. Wheat and corn grew on the prairies. They had built cities and fought a war, adding by the latter land enough for a small empire in the Southwest.

The four great sections emerged and took on form and substance during these four decades: the Southeast or "South," the Southwest, Northeast, and Northwest. Each had differences within itself, but regional cultures began to grow and be shaped by their economics and their history.

Of these four, no other was so distinct and so set apart as the old South. Its great staple crops, dependent on a world market, its system of plantations worked by slave labor, had produced a unique social ideology, a way of life. The presence of slaves had held to a minimum the development of an artisan and craftsman class. As its weather, too, was distinct, so was its thinking.

The South thought of itself as different. There was a certain agreement in this. The three other sections also thought of it as different. From 1820 on it became more and more self-conscious. Myths began to grow about it. To the outsiders the South seemed to possess complete unity. Actually, in the colonial years and the early days of the Republic, its leaders had acted in cooperative accord. But as the nation expanded and prospered, the South developed internal conflicts. In weather, population, and political influence, the South began to be outdistanced. All this served to emphasize sectionalism, to create a slow-growing psychology of always being on the defensive. It spread from politics to religion, and in time caused the withdrawal of the Southern Methodist and Baptist churches into regional conferences and associations of their own. In the field of economics, this defensive push to withdraw was even stronger.[3]

Only the belief that John C. Calhoun would soon be president restrained South Carolina from complete defiance of the protective tariff of 1827-1828. Calhoun himself, seeking to avoid this revolution, came forward in 1832 with his plan of nullification or interposition. A sovereign state, he argued, could declare an act of Congress null and void and appeal to its fellow sovereigns to endorse or reflect that action. The South Carolina legislature adopted this action. President Andrew Jackson was brusque. The Union, he said, must be preserved. South Carolina failed to receive support expected from her sister states. There was a tariff compromise. But bitterness remained. And there was increased talk of state "sovereignty" and "states' rights."

The Mexican War, which began in 1846, soon became the issue of sectionalism. The abolitionists, joined by economic interests damaged by the war, cried that it was an unjust war of conquest and imperialism brought on by the slave interests. It was, they said, merely a war to extend slavery. The legislature of Massachusetts went so far as officially to describe it as such a war and declared that honest men could not support it.

Sectional hostility distorted and colored every issue. All differences came to be oversimplified by describing the South as a land of slavery and the North as one of freedom.

The Great Compromise of 1850, defining slave territory and free, attained after two years of bitter debate, dissension, and threats of secession, revealed the lack of unity in the South. But the agreement settled nothing. The absolutists, for this word fits them even better than extremists, had not changed their attitudes nor abandoned their objectives. In the North the abolitionists scorned the compromise and also extended their efforts to nullify the fugitive slave laws. In the South, Robert

---

[3]See T. Harry Williams, *Romance and Realism in Southern Politics* (Athens: University of Georgia Press, 1961); David M. Potter, *South and the Sectional Conflict* (Baton Rouge: Louisiana State University Press, 1968); Avery O. Craven, *Growth of Southern Nationalism: 1848-1861* (Baton Rouge: Louisiana State University Press, 1953).

Barnwell Rhett, William Lowndes Yancey, South Carolinians; and Edmund Ruffian of Virginia, were the fire-breathing absolutists who, during the 1850s, shouted down the moderates and prepared mass opinion for secession. They had many helpers, but more than any others, they pumped adrenalin into the political veins of the South.

The Southern states, driven by these men and inflamed by the abolitionist extremists, began to drive for economic self-sufficiency. It was a program too late to succeed. Failure and frustration induced a withdrawal both intellectual and spiritual. There were boycotts of Northern summer resorts, a rewriting of textbooks, the founding of Southern magazines, a glorification of all that made them and the region different. It increased in heat and volume as Northern abolitionists painted an increasingly harsh picture of a brutal and licentious slave power. Each made of the other a stereotype.

Thus was the ground prepared. There were many who sowed the seeds. Many of these seeds produced perennials which have continued to push themselves out of the soil to be reaped over and over again, long years after the deadly harvest of civil war.

Despite all this, the presidential vote of 1860 proved, without doubt, the majority of the people were still conservative. Lincoln polled 1,866,452 votes. Stephen H. Douglas, nominee of the Northern Democrats, 1,376,957; John Breckenridge, of the Southern Democratic wing, 849,781; and John Bell, candidate of the Southern states' rights conservatives, 588,879.

In ten Southern states Lincoln did not receive a single vote—or so said the grimly gleeful men who counted the ballots and announced the results.

But even the Southern people were of a conservative mind. Breckenridge carried the South but surprisingly did not win a majority of the popular vote. He had more votes in the North than Lincoln in the South, but they were few.

A minority President had been elected.

The parties, like values, minds, and emotions, had become sectional.

There were the moderates, in the press and in person, who pointed out that though Lincoln was legally elected, he could not hurt the South. There was, they said, no need for the secession. The South would still control the Congress and its important committees.

There were some who suggested that Maryland, Virginia, Kentucky, Missouri, Arkansas, Tennessee, and North Carolina create a border confederation by which the sane people of the South could escape the extremists of both regions. But the radicals of absolutism went their irrepressible way. Most of the moderates capitulated in bitterness of spirit, many of them with praise for the Union on their lips.

By 17 December 1860, Rhett and his associates had called a convention to order in South Carolina. Three days later a state ordinance of secession was voted. Within six weeks Mississippi, Florida, Alabama, Georgia, Louisiana, and Texas had duplicated that action. The Deep South, the Cotton Kingdom, began to look toward a confederacy. In Georgia, North Carolina, and Texas there was substantial, stubborn conservative opposition which fought a delaying action.[4]

There was a great surge of enthusiasm, but also a foreboding. There would be no war, men said reassuringly. A common saying was that a lady's thimble would hold all the blood that would be spilled. Sometimes this was varied by asserting that a handkerchief would wipe up all the blood that would be let. Many argued that reconstruction of the Union would be easier with the South out than in.

On 4 February the Montgomery convention met to form a new nation. In the elections on the ninth the fire-eaters were excluded from office. Jefferson Davis and Alexander Stephens were selected, respectively, as president and vice-president. Both were conservatives. Stephens was, for many, a bitter pill to swallow. He had fought against secession with all his skill, was a friend of Lincoln's and—many believed—was a Unionist at heart.[5]

When spring and April came, impetuous South Carolina fired on Fort Sumter. Lincoln called for volunteers. In the emotional upsurge that followed, the conservatives who had controlled in Virginia, North

---

[4]See J. Jeffrey Auer, ed., *Antislavery and Disunion, 1858-1861: Studies in the Rhetoric of Compromise and Conflict* (New York: Harper & Row, Publishers, 1963); Waldo W. Braden, ed., *Oratory in the Old South: 1828-1860* (Baton Rouge: Louisiana State University Press, 1970).

[5]See McGill's article on Stephens in *Southern Encounters: Southerners of Note in Ralph McGill's South*, ed. Calvin M. Logue (Macon GA: Mercer University Press, 1983).

Carolina, Arkansas, and Tennessee were swept aside. "Nobody," says an old letter of that time, "is allowed to retain and assert his reason."

An understanding of some aspects of the South of today and tomorrow may be had from that yesterday.

The Cotton Kingdom had come with a rush.

Sumter and the call for troops brought in Virginia, but the western counties which had voted Union began a new state movement. In 1863, under Federal protection, these were admitted to the Union as a state—West Virginia.

Arkansas, which before had voted not to secede, came reluctantly to secession. North Carolina and Tennessee followed, with a large minority dissenting.

Kentucky had in her political and emotional blood stream the tradition of Henry Clay. She hopefully determined on a policy of neutrality. Her strategic position made this impossible. The Confederates moved first. But Federal troops hurried across the Ohio and seized half the state. In December 1861 unoccupied Kentucky voted to secede. But the strategic area was in Federal hands, and they never relaxed the grip.

Nowhere in the Confederacy, for all the tumultuous support of secession, was there universal acceptance of it. The western parts of Virginia and North Carolina and the eastern areas of Tennessee and Kentucky were primarily Union. Had there been an easy military route into east Tennessee as into West Virginia, that region, too, would have been admitted as a loyal state.

Here and there about the South were islands of unionism, including two counties in Mississippi. One of these, Jones, was known as the Republic of Jones.

Where no or few slaves were, Union sentiment was strongest. And in the Appalachians the old legends of the Revolutionary War and pride in the mountain men at Kings Mountain held men to the Flag.

Certain Unionists, like the aristocratic intellectual James Louis Petigru of Charleston, South Carolina, were tolerated throughout the war.

The war itself was a curious one, bloody, glorious, and cruel. Any of the adjectives will fit at least a part of it. All through its four desperate years there were times when certain amenities were observed. Pickets often traded and fraternized. When General George Pickett's baby was born, Grant's troops lighted bonfires and sent congratulations. When

Lincoln visited Richmond, captured after so many delays, he visited George Pickett's house. "Just say an old friend called," he said.

Confederates cheered Meagher's Irish Brigade when it made its heroic charge up the steep slopes of Marye's Heights in the battle of Fredericksburg. The Federal army had great and undisguised admiration for Stonewall Jackson and for Beauty Stuart's great artilleryman, John Pelham. General William T. Sherman, for all his decisiveness, thought enough of the amenities to engage in a long, written debate with the mayor of Atlanta trying to make that unhappy man see the necessity of burning the central part of his city.

The war began with atrocity stories, but the actual atrocities were few. There were looting and vandalism. Much of this was done by irregulars or guerrillas, who sometimes plundered their own people. But crimes against women and civilians were so few as to provide exceptions. There was, on occasion, vast and sometimes wanton destruction of property, but never were there crimes against the people such as the world saw in 1914-1918 and on a larger scale in 1940-1945. To this day there is a controversy whether Columbia, South Carolina was burned deliberately. But as historians have noted, it is unusual that there should be a controversy at all.

Abraham Lincoln, who had planned to bring the Southern states back into the Union with honor, never referred to the Confederates as rebels. General Robert E. Lee had no harsh phrases for the men on the other side. To him, they were always "those people." The soldiers called each other "Johnny Reb" and "Billy Yank." There were some who felt hate and exercised it. The newspapers thundered for blood and the scalps of generals. They invented the scurrilous phrases, the rhetoric of abuse. The politicians also slandered, boasted, vilified. They, too, though failing more than any connected with the war, demanded success of the generals, many of whom were incompetents placed in commands by the influence of politicians.

It was an American war, a fact which made it unique. Even the German and Irish brigades in the Federal armies were fighting with new-country ideas in their heads. No old-country emotions stirred them. The flag they followed was theirs. In the South, soldiers thought of themselves first as being from individual states. As the idea of a national loyalty had not won a place above that of state allegiance, so the Confederacy never replaced the identity of self with state.

Even the commanding generals of the South thought of their regiments as state organizations, never as merely soldiers sworn to a new nation. Much of the morale of the troops on both sides came from this pride in state. To fail in a charge or to retreat was to disgrace the state.

There was not much talk of states' rights among Southern troops. This political obsession with states' rights later was to do as much to defeat the South as the opposing regiments. All through the war the governors and the legislatures were bickering and were increasingly difficult for the central government to handle. It was a matter for cajoling, and Jefferson Davis, an austere man, was not good at it. There was never enough unity.

Because it was the last war of the individual, the unmachined man, and since it was an all-American war with a great proportion of men in arms and otherwise directly committed with it, it has remained a personal sort of thing. The officers on each side had friends on the other. It was a war of brother against brother, especially in the states of Kentucky and Tennessee. But while the editors, orators, politicians, and many civilians carried on a war of bitterness and abuse, the troops fought bitterly but held each other in real esteem.

It was at once a war of the rank amateur and the best of professionals. There was never enough discipline. Nor was there ever adequate planning for medical and hospital services, for morale or welfare of the families of soldiers or sailors. The troops might fight and perform like mobs, or with a skill and perfection never attained in previous wars. Some of the battles and campaigns were ludicrous, preposterous caricatures of war—though nonetheless bloody. Others were so perfectly contrived from the viewpoint of tactics and strategy that through the years many of the general staffs of Europe have studied and imitated them.

It was a war, too, which called for all the arts of war, and for the invention of new ones.

For the first time in history the railroad was a major factor of war. The first Battle of Manassas was turned by troops hurried there by rail. Thereafter the railroads were a prime consideration of each opponent.

The telegraph, which largely followed the rails, also made its world debut as a factor of combat.

The Civil War provided, too, the first large-scale sea blockade which in part was countered by large-scale blockade running. Submarines played a small but significant role. There was amphibious war on beaches and the banks of rivers. The South made a great sweep into Pennsylvania. Pragmatic "Crump" Sherman marched from Atlanta to the sea, wholly lost for weeks to the top command and to Washington.

Though war had been talked and blustered for almost ten years, neither side was prepared for it. The South, of necessity, came close to marshaling all its resources. The North never did. From the administrative viewpoint the war was, North and South, a shambles. There was vast waste of human beings and materials. There was almost incredible inefficiency. Both governments suffered from the insistence of the states on playing state and local politics to the detriment of the respective national governments. In the North, Lincoln was better able to command support than was Jefferson Davis who was increasingly plagued, and destroyed, by states' rights.

Despite the failure of organization and bureaucracy, both armies proved enormously resourceful. The feats of engineers, both the Blue and the Gray, sometimes test the credulity of readers of history. They spanned rivers, great and small, with bridges. They built dams, dug canals, kept the railroads running—or prevented them.

In resourcefulness the South again led, for the old reason that necessity is the mother of invention. The Southern currency became valueless in trade soon after the war began. The region was agricultural, with few factories and no backlog of skills in its people. Slavery had stood in the way of the growth of a class of artisans such as urban and industrial centers require. Yet, despite all this, so well did the Southern people fill the many voids that not a single Confederate army or navy defeat could be excused for lack of arms, ammunition, or equipment.

Both sides were, with few exceptions, led by men of great and devout religious conviction. Both armies were swept by revivals. Each prayed to the same God, and quite humanly believed this same God looked upon them with favor.

The great lack of bitterness between the armies cannot too often be noted. The meetings to agree upon terms of capitulation between Generals Robert E. Lee and U. S. Grant, and a few days later between Generals Joseph Johnston and William T. Sherman, were emotional because of their lack of it. Both were significant for their compassion, understanding, and a recognition of the great American bond between them. There was a touch of humor in the Johnston-Sherman meeting, as there

was not in the momentous one between Grant and Lee. Somehow a bottle
of bourbon appeared on the table in the farmhouse meeting in North
Carolina. After they had talked terms over drinks, Joe Johnston proposed another. Sherman declined, saying that if he took another he
might be doing the surrendering.

The supreme tragedy of Lincoln's assassination loosed the hatreds
nurtured and aggravated by political and extremist ambitions for power
and revenge.

But, even so, the American character, which had placed its stamp on
the years of war, reasserted itself. There was no blood shed after the war.
The plans and attempts to convict the leaders of the seceding states fell
of their own weight.

The four years of war in the South were a time of elation and despair,
heroism and defection, self-sacrifice on a scale which has inspired all
generations since. It was a period, too, of greed and great callousness.
Defeat did not merely bring to a conclusion a society, a slave economy,
an era. It had a profound effect on the United States and its future.
(Since 1865 one of the South's preoccupations has been with the anatomy
of that defeat.) As there had been hope of avoiding war with secession,
peace movements continued throughout the war. Roughly two-thirds of
the Southerners owned no slaves at all and civilian bitterness grew out
of that fact as the fortunes of war declined.

It is possible to dissect from this resentment some of the political
"have not" attitudes which were to become so demagogic a part of cot-
ton-South politics after the war. A class feeling developed early in the
first year of combat. It was, an increasing voice said, a rich man's war
and a poor man's fight. Because of the South's desperate need for production, ownership of twenty or more slaves was made grounds for ex-
emption from military service. This ruling was abused. While
economically necessary, it was politically injurious. In the last years of
the war the discontented were saying, as letters to newspapers revealed,
that "if a man is poor—no matter how virtuous or intelligent he may
be—his poverty as effectually excludes him from the presence of the aristocracy as if he were afflicted with the leprosy or the smallpox." There
were proposals that once the war was won all soldiers who owned no land
be given fifty acres and a slave as a bonus. These are but samples of many
complaints, all on the same theme.

Peace movements, large and small, continued all through the war years. In 1863, Governor Zebulon B. Vance of North Carolina became so concerned over the strength of one in his state that he demanded of President Davis, in a letter of 30 December of that year, that the Confederacy make an effort to obtain an armistice.[6]

Davis was never in any sympathy with these movements. He regarded the separation as final. Even after Johnston's surrender, to which he reluctantly agreed, he nursed the hopeless dream of somehow escaping to return with a following to fight on to victory. Time after time he refused pleas and plans proposed by Southerners as ways to end the war. Davis wanted peace, but with independence. He tried, through agents secret and public, to create a peace demand on Lincoln from the old Northwestern states of Ohio, Illinois and Indiana whose southerly areas largely had been populated by Southerners. He failed, but he did create there the secret society—Knights of the Golden Circle—which promoted the Copperhead movement. The greatest Northern supporter of these Southern overtures was Clement L. Vallandigham, Ohio Democratic leader. For months the Union tolerated him in open defiance of the government. He was, finally, deported southward in the summer of 1863. There he was treated courteously but cooly. He at last sailed from a Southern port to exile in Canada.

In June of 1863, Vice-President Alexander Stephens, brooding on the cool veranda of his home near Washington, Georgia, wrote President Davis for permission to go to Washington ostensibly to seek ways and means to alleviate the sufferings of personnel, but really, once there, to discuss the possibility of peace. Stephens had few, if any, illusions about the permanency of the Confederacy. He informed Davis he wanted to negotiate on the basis of the sovereignty of each state and its right to "determine its own destiny."[7]

Davis, almost certainly with cynical restraint, withheld from Stephens the news that General Lee even then was making ready to invade

---

[6]Letter from Zebulon B. Vance of North Carolina to Jefferson Davis, 30 December 1863, in *Jefferson Davis, Constitutionalist: His Letters, Papers and Speeches*, ed. Dunbar Rowland (Jackson: Mississippi Department of Archives and History, 1923) 6:141-42.

[7]Letter from Alexander H. Stephens to Jefferson Davis, 12 June 1863, in Rowland, *Jefferson Davis*, 5:513-15.

the North. He believed, correctly, that Stephens would not have begun his journey had he known. But the frail and crippled little man did start by boat down the James. He reached Newport along with news of the Confederate failure at Gettysburg and of Lee's retreat back into Virginia. Federal officers turned him back.

Joining with Governor Joseph E. Brown of Georgia, Stephens created a peace movement in their state which coincided with that led in North Carolina by William Holden and Congressman William W. Boyce in South Carolina. State sovereignty was their slogan, and they attacked Davis for having destroyed it.[8] There was some sentiment for a second secession, this time from the Confederacy. In Richmond, President Davis remained as aloof as possible. He was wholly uncompromising on independence for the Confederacy and knew that any peace plan based on state sovereignty would be immediately fatal to the deteriorating government he headed. He had seen what a disaster states' rights, as exercised by a sovereign state, could bring to a central government. Vice-President Stephens, his dislike of Davis increasing, boldly charged that the Confederate leader wanted Lincoln elected, rather than the Northern Democratic nominee, George McClellan, who was pledged to peace and a restoration of the federal Union.

But Atlanta fell to Sherman, and Lincoln was easily reelected. Sherman marched through the soft autumn days to Savannah and in the South the talk grew strong that it was a rich man's war, that the politicians had made it, not the people.

Stephens tried once more. Francis P. Blair, a political figure since the years of Andrew Jackson, obtained permission in December 1864 from Lincoln to write Jefferson Davis about negotiations looking toward peace.[9] Stephens headed the delegation which in February 1865 met with Lincoln and William H. Seward, secretary of state, on a ship at Hampton Roads off Fortress Monroe. The Confederates went there bound by Davis not to discuss any agreement which did not include independence.

---

[8]See Joseph E. Parks, *Joseph E. Brown of Georgia* (Baton Rouge: Louisiana State University Press, 1977) 271-315.

[9]Letter from Francis P. Blair to Jefferson Davis, 30 December 1864, Rowland, *Jefferson Davis*, 6:432-33.

No minutes were kept. There were many versions. One is that Lincoln did say to Stephens that if he, Stephens would write "Union," he, Lincoln, would sign anything else. The writer has talked with two old men, close to the postwar Stephens, who said Stephens told them so. Lincoln almost certainly promised to push for congressional reimbursement of slave owners in exchange for emancipation agreement. He also pledged an honorable return to the Union and therefore asked for an end to the war, not merely an armistice. He was reasonable, even liberal, in everything save that one word *Union*.

History turns often on small pivots. Had Davis accepted peace at Hampton Roads, Lincoln would hardly have had his Booth. And without Booth there would have been no radical reconstruction by Thaddeus Stevens, Charles Sumner, and Henry W. Davis.

But Jefferson Davis was adamant. If half the men absent from Lee's army would return, he said, then Grant could be defeated. He sent out speakers. Ben Hill spoke four times in his all-but-disaffected state of Georgia. "We have all we need to win but fighting spirit," he cried, closing with a brilliant whiplash denunciation of Governor Joe Brown, "the subtle serpent which coils within our garden."[10]

There was a last surge of patriotic effort. But Georgia and South Carolina were effectively out of the war. Only in Virginia, where Lee was, and in North Carolina was there organized strength. Even this was melting away through desertion and illness.

Appomattox came almost with a rush.

Why was the Confederacy defeated? Why had the all-consuming enthusiasm of 1861 been greatly eroded as early as 1863?

At the outset the failure to ship every possible bale of cotton to Europe left the South without financial resources. Judah P. Benjamin had urged it. A majority in government insisted it be held so that cotton-hungry Britain would be forced to intervene to rescue King Cotton. When a prisoner in Fortress Monroe, Jefferson Davis mourned this fatal mistake. He estimated that before the Federal blockade became ef-

---

[10]See Haywood J. Pearce, Jr., *Benjamin H. Hill: Secession and Reconstruction* (New York: Negro Universities Press, 1928) 22, 86, 107-12, 152-55, 214-15; Benjamin H. Hill, Jr., *Senator Benjamin H. Hill of Georgia: His Life, Speeches, and Writings* (Atlanta: T. H. P. Bloodworth, 1893) 273-293.

fective three million bales could have been shipped to create a war reserve of a billion dollars in gold—enough for twice as many years of war as were fought. There were many other factors. But basic in them was the lack of unity and a general will to carry on. Arguments go around and around. "The seeds of destruction, states rights," were planted at the birth of the Confederacy, wrote able historian, E. Merton Coulter. These seeds "were destined to sprout and flourish," tended by the politicians most dedicated to state sovereignty.[11] Mrs. James Chestnut of South Carolina, whose famous diary is one of the great source books of the war, wrote, "The Confederacy has been done to death by the politicians."[12] Secretary of the Navy Stephen R. Mallory said in bitterness he regretted he had spent four years of his life in working for a people unfit for independence.[13] The Augusta *Constitutionalist* summed it up more accurately. "If this revolution has produced some of the meanest and most groveling of mankind, it has held an even balance by the example of some of the most exalted and aspiring souls."

There was nothing evil or immoral in the concept of one or more states seceding. To be sure, states' rights had rendered impotent the old confederation of states and brought the Republic and its central government into being. And it was the ambitions of the politicians which caused the concept of states' rights to be stretched into secession and, then, into false weakening of the internal structure of the Confederacy.

The armies of the Confederacy fought with a bravery and a devotion which has become legendary. Their ideals, courage,and dedication were equaled by many of those at home. As there was nothing immoral or evil in belief in the right of secession, the same could be said of the determination of men and women to fight for a way of life in which they believed. It was this ideal which caused the two-thirds of nonslaveholders

[11]E. Merton Coulter, *The Confederate States of America 1861-1865*, vol. 3, *A History of the South*, ed. Wendell Holmes Stephenson and E. Merton Coulter (Baton Rouge: Louisiana State University Press, 1950) 567.

[12]For related themes see C. Vann Woodward, ed., *Mary Chestnut's Civil War* (New Haven: Yale University Press, 1981) 517, 597, 620, 635, 799, 810, 820-21.

[13]See Joseph Thomas Durkin, *Stephen R. Mallory: Confederate Navy Chief* (Chapel Hill: University of North Carolina Press, 1954).

to stand with the third which did. The nation's great development and place in the world have ratified Lincoln's concept of Union.[14]

General Robert E. Lee published a message to the South a few months after Appomattox:

> The war being at an end, the Southern states having laid down their arms, and the question at issue between them having been decided, I believe it to be the duty of everyone to unite in the restoration of peace and harmony. . . . I have too exalted an opinion of the American people to believe they will consent to injustice, and it is only necessary, in my opinion, that truth should be known for the rights of everyone to be secured. I know of no surer way of eliciting the truth than by burying contention with the war.

But contention was not buried—as Lincoln might have been able to do.

The South was prostrate.

Two hundred sixty thousand Confederates had died in battle, of wounds, and of disease. If to those be added the crippled and maimed, the South had lost roughly one-fourth of her white population of productive age. Most of the war had been fought in the South. The destruction of railroads, bridges, cities, towns, livestock, and general property was great. Desolation and ruin set upon her.

There was left the land, the warm weather, the long growing seasons, the rains, and the Negro. The agricultural South began to rebuild on this foundation. There were heartbreaks; toil, harsh and unrelenting; suffering and self-denial.

To this was added a period called Reconstruction. In essence it was the antithesis of all the words, wishes, and plans of Lincoln.

Andrew Johnson replaced Lincoln. He was honest. He was devoted to his country and to the Constitution. But he lacked Lincoln's strength and flexibility. He was geographically and politically vulnerable. He had been a constitutional Democrat, drafted by the National Union Convention of 1864 to appeal to the War Democrats of the North. He was a Southerner, disliked by Southern leaders and distrusted by many in the North. Had Lincoln merely died of a heart attack in the box of the Ford Theater, the chances of his successor carrying out the peaceful policies

---

[14]See Emory M. Thomas, *The Confederate Nation, 1861-1865* (New York: Harper & Row, Publishers, 1979).

of Reconstruction, with federal assistance, would likely have been possible. But Lincoln had been assassinated and the plot had contemplated the murder of other leaders of government. There developed an almost pathological state of public opinion.

The extremists, the absolutists, moved in. "By the gods," shouted Senator Ben Wade, Lincoln's chief radical foe, on the day Johnson was sworn in, "there will be no trouble now in running the government."

But there was. Johnson clung stubbornly to the Constitution. But a radical Congress was elected in 1866. And that Congress, on 2 March 1867, angered by a presidential veto of the Reconstruction Act, passed it over that veto.

Military governors took over a South divided into five military districts. There was to be no civil government until the states were "remade and readmitted." All who had participated in the Confederate army or government were disenfranchised. New state constitutions, granting the franchise to all other males, of whatever race, color, or previous condition of servitude, were required, as was ratification of the then pending Fourteenth Amendment. Military governors were charged with carrying out all steps of the reconstruction. Political resistance was not possible. It went underground, emerging as the disguised and secret Ku Klux Klan.[15]

So great was the resolution of the radical Congress to allow nothing to bar its way that in February 1868 the House adopted a resolution of impeachment against President Johnson. The entire procedure is one of the most grievous blots on our history. Seven senators, withstanding abuse and unprecedented pressure from fellow members, the cabinet, and their home constituents, voted against impeachment and, by the margin of one vote, prevented it.

The Negro, unlettered, uninformed, landless, was, as Herbert Agar says in *The Price of Union*,

abandoned by the best men, North and South, and corrupted by the worst. . . . It was wicked to force the Negro to rule the disfranchised white man when

---

[15]See William C. Harris, *Presidential Reconstruction in Mississippi* (Baton Rouge: Louisiana State University Press, 1967); James Wilford Garner, *Reconstruction in Mississippi* (Baton Rouge: Louisiana State University Press, 1968); Alan Conway, *Reconstruction of Georgia* (Minneapolis: University of Minnesota Press, 1966).

everyone knew the position would be reversed as soon as the Northerners grew
sick of governing with the sword. . . . There is a limit beyond which only mad
moralists and the truly corrupt will go. It was the fate of the Negro . . . to be
sacrificed to an alliance between the two. . . . But he gave them his vote—since
they asked for it. . . . [16]

Here, not in the great war, developed the most grievous wounds, the
deepest prejudices, the evil which has extended into the public and political life of our time. Antagonism of the races was carefully, energetically, ruthlessly cultivated to push through all radical candidates and
measures. Out of this sprang the monstrous corruption, the incredible
extravagance, the violence, the chicanery, the mountains of debt erected
by that regime. It emotionally forced most of the white people into a single party. It meant that for generations to come political demagogues
would be able to poison the political wells with stories of the reconstruction and thereby create a solidly Democratic South. From this period,
too, came the power of the state and local extremists to exploit the race
issue when it was not even remotely involved, and to do so with great
and extravagant viciousness when it was. The effects of Reconstruction
were of long-range influence in shaping the whole political and economic life of the South.

The West, too, felt reverberations of it. National government was in
the hands of commerce, finance, and industry. In *The American Epoch*,
historian Arthur Lenk writes that:

> The reconstruction of national politics that began in 1861 had fully accom-
> plished its objectives by 1877. The business classes had executed a bloodless
> revolution. They had . . . wrested control of the political institutions from the
> agrarian and changed the character, but not the forms, of representative gov-
> ernment in the United States. [17]

Legislation had been passed during the war and in the Reconstruction years, having to do with tariffs, banking, railroads, labor, and pub-

---

[16]Herbert Agar, *The Price of Union* (Boston: Houghton Mifflin Co., 1960) 466-
67. An *s* should be added to "position," "their fellow Americans" should go between
"governing" and "with the sword," and "those" should be substituted for "the" before
"two."

[17]Arthur S. Lenk, *American Epoch: A History of the United States Since the 1890's*
(New York: A. A. Knopf, 1963) 5.

lic lands. At the end of the war the average rate on dutiable goods was 47 percent. In 1860 it has been 18.8 percent.

The National Banking Act of 1863 is a necessary piece of information for understanding why the bankrupt, postwar South clung so desperately to the one-crop economy of cotton and why it was for so many weary years a region of inertia and poverty.

The Banking Act of 1863 was not written with the needs of farmers in mind. Minimum capital of fifty thousand dollars was fixed for banks in towns with less than 6,000 population and one hundred thousand dollars for larger communities. Thirty years after, there was one bank for every 16,000 Americans but only one to every 58,130 residents of the South. In 1865 a ten percent tax was voted on bank-note circulation. Currency almost disappeared in the South. Only the merest fraction of huge federal sums spent on internal improvements was spent in the poorest states.

Here, in the field of tariffs and the restriction of capital, was the South hurt most.

Folkways, mores, traditions, customs and prejudices—all these grow slowly like coral, requiring a special climate and condition of the sea out of which they meagerly emerge, or remain just below the surface to wreck the unwary or unknowing. Reconstruction—and the long-range effect of it—was such a climate.

Reconstruction ended in 1877 after the election of 1876, which election was almost certainly taken from the victorious Samuel J. Tilden, Democrat, and awarded to Rutherford B. Hayes, Republican. And Democrats in high places assisted in the machinations. One of those popularly believed to have played a part in the great "compromise" was Henry Watterson, the brilliant editor of the Louisville (Kentucky) *Courier-Journal*. In speaking of the Reconstruction days a short time after 1877, "Marse Henry" said: "There was a time when amid the storm clouds on the Southern horizon there loomed another Poland, there lowered another Ireland, preparing to repeat upon the soil of the New World the mistakes of the old. . . . The hand of the South was in the lion's mouth, and my one hope, my only politics, was to placate the lion."[18] The price paid for Southern assistance was an end to Reconstruc-

---

[18]See Henry Watterson, *"Marse Henry": An Autobiography* (New York: George H. Doran Co., 1919).

tion and restoration of government to the Southern states. The South was given political autonomy. It could do as it pleased in matters of race policy, so long as it was done obliquely and with the appearance of legality. But what it really meant was that the North had politically abandoned the Negro. The *Nation* said as much. "The Negro," wrote that magazine, "will disappear from the field of national politics. Henceforth the nation, as a nation, will have nothing to do with him." Other Northern papers reached similar conclusions.

C. Vann Woodward, one of the foremost authorities on the great compromise of 1877, wrote in *Reunion of Reaction:*[19]

> If the compromise of 1877 revealed deep cleavages within the old party of Jackson, it also revealed the party of Radical Reconstruction in alliance with ex-Rebels and ex-Slaveholders. It revealed the party of carpetbaggery repudiating the carpetbaggers, the party of emancipation and freedom's rights abandoning the Negro to his former master—the South became, in effect and by choice, a satellite of the dominant economic region. So long as the Conservative (Southern) "Redeemers" held control they scotched any tendency of the South to combine forces with internal enemies of the new economy—laborites, Western agrarians, reformers. The South became a bulwark instead of a menace to the new economic order.

It meant, too, that the old mutual-interest combination of West and South was ended. Political control had been given over to non-farming interests, the banking and industrial entrepreneurs—all dependent on the North for capital and political easements.

"Redeemer Democrats" began to talk of "the New South," the first of many such prophecies. But, though there was a rush of building, issuing of bonds, and much plunder, the region turned slowly back toward cotton. It became a crop of discontent. The tariffs were against the farmers. Credit was hard to come by and rates were high. Cartels rigged the

---

[19]C. Vann Woodward, *Reunion and Reaction: The Compromise of 1877 and the End of Reconstruction* (Boston: Little, Brown and Company, 1951). Beginning with "If the compromise" and ending with "former master," McGill deleted "profound changes in the party of Thad Stevens and Charles Sumner. It revealed" following "it also revealed," and substituted "freedom's" for "freedmen's" before "rights" (p. 211). McGill took the passage that begins "the South became" and ends "the new economic order" from page 246 and added "and by choice" after "in effect," "economic" after "dominant," "(Southern)," after "Conservative," "Under the regime of the Redeemers" before "the South came," and "economic" after "menace to the new."

prices of farm implements and jute bagging. Rail rates crippled them by having wide differentials between raw materials and fabricated goods. It was a long hard road back. It was 1878 before the region's cotton crops equaled that of 1859.

There was the further strain in the bitter postwar years, of a population drain. Thousands left to take up homesteads in the West, chiefly Texas. In 1875 some thirty-five thousand white persons left Georgia. For a time there was a great campaign on to bring Europeans and Chinese to become field laborers.

There was, surprisingly, little Negro migration. Negroes were hungry for land of their own and where they could they began to buy. But opportunity was small. It was this yearning to have a place of their own that gave sharecropping such an appeal. A cropper was on his own. He had his own garden, chickens, and pigs. Sometimes he had a cow. He had half the crop as his. Out of it came charges at high rates and often cruelly padded, for the seeds, tools, food, and clothing advanced him.[20] Those lucky enough to meet with honest treatment soon came to own their own mules, wagons, plows, and tools, and could keep two-thirds of the crop. Some became owners and renters. For others the sharecropping system was little better than peonage. The breakup of the old plantations brought values down. Many of the prewar whites of the non-planter class bought land and began to grow cotton with croppers financing themselves with loans against the crop. The poorer ones became tenants, croppers. This acquisition of small farms was to have a profound effect on the economy of the South. Shortly after the turn of the century the region included two-thirds of the nation's farms.

They were all poor—the planter, the ex-slave, the croppers, and the new landowners. Credit was provided not by banks, which were few, but by factors and supply merchants. Cotton was the only crop which made such a system possible. And cotton was the only commodity on which a man could take a chance. It was not a perishable, though crops sometimes failed. The factors and supply merchants marked up their goods and charged interest rates which frequently were forty percent, sometimes higher. Debt and cotton came to be synonymous. Out of the dis-

---

[20]See Jay R. Mandle, *Roots of Black Poverty: The Southern Plantation Economy After the Civil War* (Durham: Duke University Press, 1978).

content of the cotton growers and workers and their just grievances grew
the explosive force of the Populist movement.[21]

In those days bitter and frustrated men, with the compassion
squeezed out of them by debt and disappointment, would sometimes
erupt with violence between themselves or in a swift, cruel nightmare
of bloodlust, not always racial, from some virus of hate and fear descended from the Reconstruction excesses.

In the "redemption days" legal devices for limiting Negro suffrage
were intricate registration and election laws. A law might limit the time
in a voting booth to two and one-half minutes—not enough for an illiterate Negro or white man. Petty larceny conviction as a disfranchising
factor was another favorite. Stuffing ballot boxes was a favorite form of
rather uniform corruption.

Not everyone was happy with these cynical procedures. Judge J. J.
Christian, a Mississippian, in arguing a bill of disfranchisement, had
the candor to say, addressing the chairman of a constitutional convention:
"Sir, it is no secret that there has not been a full vote and a fair count in
Mississippi since 1875—we have carried elections by fraud and violence
until the whole machinery is about to rot down." In getting rid of the
Negro in government, as left by the Reconstruction, the white government had been corrupted by the methods used. Rationalization brought
about a variety of means of disfranchisement.[22]

The heirs of the prejudices and fears of Reconstruction struggled,
too, with their consciences over public education. It was all but abandoned as the states struggled to refund or disavow debts left by carpetbag
governments. The rebuilding was slow and, in general, pathetic in its
inadequacy. This, too, was a breeder of discontent.

Surely, and not so slowly, a political crevasse appeared between the
gentry of the Black Belt farm lands and the uplands. By 1880 the Green-

---

[21]See Robert C. McMath, *Populist Vanguard: A History of the Southern Farmers' Alliance* (Chapel Hill: University of North Carolina Press, 1975); Lawrence Goodwyn,
Democratic Promise: The Populist Movement in America (New York: Oxford University
Press, 1976); Gerald H. Gaither, *Blacks and the Populist Revolt: Ballots and Bigotry in
the "New South"* (University: University of Alabama Press, 1975).

[22]See Emory M. Thomas, *The American War and Peace, 1860-1877* (Englewood
Cliffs NJ: Prentice Hall, 1973); Howard A. White, *Freedmen's Bureau in Louisiana*
(Baton Rouge: Louisiana State University Press, 1970).

back-Labor party, known also as the People's Anti-Bourbon party, was organizing and speaking out against the conservative "Redemption" Democrats for their favoritism to railroads, banks, insurance companies, and other corporate interests.

All over the South, from the debt-ridden small farms and the struggling small businessman, there was increasing criticism of the brutally inhumane convict lease system, the lack of public schools, and "Bourbon boss rule." A Republican paper in Knoxville, Tennessee, wrote: "We call on businessmen of all parties to take warning. Communism, Socialism, Agrarianism, nihilism, and diabolism are on the increase in America."

In 1880 the estimated true valuation of property in the United States was $47,642,000,000. The South's share of this was a mere $5,725,000,000. This meant a per capita wealth of $376 in the South as against an average of $1,086 outside. The national average was $870. The range inside the South was from $286 in Mississippi to $533 in Kentucky. The poorest state outside the South was Kansas, with per capita wealth of $577 as against $1,567 in Massachusetts and $1,653 in California.

Poverty was another legacy of war and Reconstruction. Yet, in a sense, this period, 1879-1880, was the darkness before the first real dawn for the South since Appomattox. A depression of magnitude enough to have pinched both American and British centers of capital came to an end in 1879.

Economic exploitation rapidly replaced political. Suddenly released capital rushed into the vacuum. The Southern empires of timber, coal, and iron were powerful magnets. Special trains brought speculators from the North. Sales of hundreds of thousands of acres of timber and mineral lands went to syndicates and individuals. Florida, in 1881, sold 4,000,000 acres of state land at twenty-five cents an acre to a group headed by Hamilton Disston of Philadelphia. In Louisiana alone forty-one groups of Northerners bought 1,370,332 acres from private owners. All over the South vast stands of pine, cypress, and hardwoods fell to ax and saw. The rivers were crowded with rafts. Railroads pushed out their lines, the legislatures often acting corruptly to aid them. In Texas twelve railroad companies were granted a total of 32,400,000 acres, which was more than the area of Indiana. English, Scottish, and American companies bought cheaply and heavily. Greatest of the foreign syndicates was the North American Land and Timber Company, Ltd. Organized in London in 1882, it bought more than 1,500,000 acres along the Louisiana coast at from twelve and one-half cents to seventy-five cents per acre. This venture, largely because of the energy and vision of the man hired to develop the land, was successful and beneficial to the region. He was a Midwesterner, S. A. Knapp of Iowa. He sold timber, but he also planted rice in upland prairies and used wheat threshers to harvest it. In five years Louisiana was a great producer of rice—and still is.

It was a time, too, of consolidations. Syndicates of Southerners, Easterners, and Englishmen began to buy and combine coal mines, railroads, trolley lines, infant electric and gas companies—all financed, and almost all directed, out of New York.

It was a time, too, of crusading fervor and of expositions to show the new machines and progress. Atlanta led with her International Cotton Exposition in 1881. Louisville and New Orleans staged larger ones, but Atlanta, and then Nashville, Tennessee, returned in triumph. The latter outdid the Chicago Exposition's emphasis on things cultural with a replica of the Parthenon.

As the New South burgeoned and gloried in the swift increase in cotton mills, new machines, and smokestacks in the sky, the Blue and the Gray held reunions. They were great successes. The soldiers had never disliked one another anyhow.

Voices of Southern editors began to be heard nationally. Henry W. Grady of the *Atlanta Constitution*, Henry Watterson of the *Louisville Courier-Journal*, and Francis W. Davison of the Charleston *News and Courier* were perhaps the most quoted. They preached the gospel of the New South—the industrial South. And their enthusiasm and gift for practical politics helped the new industrialists to govern.

"We are in favor," wrote the editor of the Vicksburg *Herald* in 1881, "of the South from the Potomac to the Rio Grande being thoroughly and permanently yankeeized."

And Henry Watterson could say, "If proselytism be the supreme joy of mankind New England must be pre-eminently happy, for the ambition of the South is to out-yankee the yankee."

But though industry was more varied and more widely distributed, this New South was still agricultural. The injustices of the economic system, geared for commerce and not for farmers, grew harsher. None of the glitter and precious little of the profits of the New South were reaching the farmers.[23]

There was a barrenness, too, in the arts and literature.

But there was an industrial revolution, and it was working changes in the Southern outlook, institutions and, particularly, in its concept of leadership. In England two generations passed between the establishment of factories and the Reform Act of 1832. In that period power passed from the hands of the landowners to manufacturers, merchants, and distributors. In the South this was achieved with much less industrialization and in a relatively brief period of time.

Nowhere had the farmer been redeemed.

In 1880 the size of the average farm was published as 156 acres. It had been 347 acres in 1860. This was deceptive. Each sharecropper assignment was a "farm." The plantation system was still holding on. But ownership was often absentee. In 1881, for example, the National Cotton Planters Association estimated that not one-third of the cotton plantations in the Mississippi Valley were "owned by those who held them at the end of the war." It was a plantation system, but not the old prewar plantation system. There was even less care of soil than in the inefficient days of slavery. The lien system imposed by the commission merchants was destructive. Interest rates ran as high as seventy percent. Rare, indeed, was the farmer who was a free agent. Prices dropped as rates increased. From an average of 11.1 cents per pound between the years of 1874 and 1877, cotton slid down to an average of 5.8 cents between 1894 and 1897. Charges for warehousing and commissions for dealers were deducted from this low price. As the value of the farmer's crop declined, his debt, in terms of bales and bushels, deducted as payment, went steadily up.

There was discontent in the corn belt. All farmers everywhere, fighting debt, droughts, and floods with no federal relief for the latter, grew more and more angry as they saw the federal generosity to railroads. They became more bitter as they read the offers, published in the North, of their state legislatures, offering subsidies, liberal franchises, and tax exemptions to manufacturers and railroads.

---

[23]See Joel Chandler Harris, *Life of Henry W. Grady, Including His Writings and Speeches* (New York: Cassell Publishing Co., 1890).

The Southern Farmers Alliance began in Texas and died of political dissension. Reorganized in 1886, it swept the South, and a major part of its strength was that it organized the Negro as well. More than 1,500,000 were associated in the Colored Alliance. Organizers preached that the alliance was "rate conscious," and neither race nor class conscious. In 1890 the Alliance scored "an agrarian triumph" in most of the Southern state elections.

It was in this period of political revolution that Southerners began to emerge who, seeking to build personal political organizations for their own ends, knew how to exploit the thunder and the gale. The name of Ben Tillman began to be heard outside his native South Carolina. Thomas E. Watson of Georgia and James S. Hogg of Texas also came to be well known as political magnets for the discontented.

Western Populism moved southward and most of the Alliance members and many old-line Democrats joined. It was a time of great emotions and violence. Nomination of Grover Cleveland angered Populists and Alliance men alike. They saw him as too compliant to the money and monopolistic interests. Ben Tillman shouted to an angry audience he would like "to stick a pitchfork in his (Cleveland's) guts" and thereby earned himself a picturesque nickname which was to be of great political value—"Pitchfork Ben."

In 1895, 195 Southern newspapers, mostly weekly, identified themselves as Populist. Populism was native-stock radicalism, and the stalwarts of "Redemption" were never able to make "Communist" or "Anarchist" stick. The Negro was an integral part of the movement. He was separate, yet included. He was represented on the party executive committees in some states. In Georgia Tom Watson told the poor-white farmers and the landless croppers, "They (the Conservative 'Redemption' Democrats) seek to divide and make you hate one another so they can exploit and use you. You are kept apart politically that you may be separately fleeced of your earnings."[24]

The Populists also denounced lynch law and the hideously cruel convict lease system. Negroes came to look upon a Populist leader with a

---

[24]See C. Vann Woodward, *Tom Watson: Agrarian Rebel* (New York: Oxford University Press, 1963).

sort of reverence and would often try to get close enough merely to touch his coat.

In the election of 1892 so violent were emotions that barn burnings, attacks on speakers, and gun battles were almost commonplace. In Texas's San Augustine County the Populist sheriff and five men were killed. In Georgia fifteen Negroes and several white men were slain. In 1894 economic depression added its complications of strikes, riots, and misery. The Populist Party that year reached its peak. In 1896 its leaders "fused" with the Democrats in the convention which nominated William Jennings Bryan. The rank and file were against it. "Fusion has destroyed Populism," said Watson. He was right. The "Redemptioners" or "New South Democrats" were more firmly in control.

The panic of 1893-1894 had placed the South's large, sprawling railroad system almost entirely in the hands of the Northeast, and the J. P. Morgan Company was dominant in control. Purchase of the Tennessee Coal and Iron Company at Birmingham was included in the Morgan venture into "redeeming" the South.

Textile developments were accelerated by New England mill owners. In 1896 they found that labor was forty percent lower in the South than in New England, and the working day twenty-four percent longer. Until 1906 the lowest legal work week in any Southern state was sixty-six hours and a seventy-five-hour week was not uncommon.

Coal mines, tobacco, timber—all came to be largely or entirely directed by trusts.

There were also the freight-rate differentials. Southern carriers charged higher rates per mile than did the Northern lines. Their rates and classifications were officially recognized by railroad associations. After 1887 the Interstate Commerce Commission recognized a "Southern territory." (As late as 1938 shippers of classified goods still had to pay rates which were thirty-nine percent higher in the designated Southern territory than shippers in the "official territory" paid for the same services.)

Commodity rates for raw materials, cotton, timber, coal, and so forth, were lower than those for finished goods. Steel shipped from the Alabama plant had a rate called "Pittsburgh Plus." This was the price of steel at Pittsburgh plus the freight charge from Pittsburgh to the place of delivery. Later this became the "Birmingham differential." A purchaser of Alabama steel had to pay the Pittsburgh price plus a differential of three dollars per ton, plus freight from Birmingham.

It basically was a colonial economy—with all its liabilities and its erosion of the soil, resources, and the human spirit. There also was wide disparity in the distribution of wealth. There were, of course, benefits. Some of the wealth remained. The wages were lower than paid for the same work in the North, but there were payrolls. The rail rates discriminated, but there was transportation. The living standard was raised. It can be, and is, argued that there was no other way—that the widespread devastation of war, the utter lack of capital, and the desperate needs, required a crash program by the great concentration of organized capital and experience in the East.

Basic still were the old problems—the overworked soil, called upon to sustain more people, the cut-over timber lands, the worked-out mines, the lack of opportunity for the educated.

And fundamental, too, was the problem of race. Disfranchisement laws, the poll tax, literary tests, the white primary law, the property qualifications, and various other measures had eliminated the Negro from the party ballot boxes. They also barred thousands of white men in each state. But extremists proceeded from the attack on the Negro as a voter to an attack on him as a Negro. There was an upsurge of racial violence. From 1890 to 1911 Southern states busied themselves extending and elaborating their laws requiring segregation. A credo began to be formed and stated. It was built on the premise that only the Southerner understood the Negro; that political equality meant social equality, and therefore, would not be allowed; that the South must be let alone to settle the question. The walls of both caste and segregation went higher and higher.

In 1895 Clark Howell, Sr., publisher of the *Atlanta Constitution*, pushed through, over great opposition, an invitation to Booker T. Washington of the new Tuskegee Institute for Negroes at Tuskegee, Alabama, to speak at the Atlanta Cotton States and International Exposition.

The speech became a sensation.[25]

---

[25]See Wayland Maxfield Parrish and Marie Hochmuth, *American Speeches* (New York: Longmans, Green and Co., 1954) 450-60.

The eloquent Washington declared his love for the South and his faith that reforms had to come from within. He said the Negro was more interested in vocational education and job opportunity than in political rights. It was, in fact, a renunciation of active political participation by the Negro. He was especially effective in reminding the South of the fidelity and love of the Negro during the Civil War. He identified his people with the industrial hopes of the South. As he had, in effect, agreed the Negro should not seek the ballot, he seemed, also, to suggest the Negro should not be unionized. He spoke of the Negro worker who "without strikes or labor wars," had helped build the South's industries and who would continue as a great labor force. Later he told Alabama industrialists that in the South alone, by reason of the presence of the Negro, was capital freed from the tyranny and despotism that "prevents you from employing whom you please."

To his own people he preached conservatism, patience, and the rewards of material progress. The friendship of the conservative whites and wealthy Northern capitalists offered more hope for the future, he argued, than agitation and protest.

The speech came to be known as "The Atlanta Compromise." Booker T. Washington became the most effective advocate of the doctrines and attitudes of the dominant Southern forces. No white orator could match him. His position had a profound effect on subsequent disfranchisement programs. Nor is it to be overlooked that a year later the United States Supreme Court, in *Plessy v. Ferguson*, handed down its "Separate but Equal" segregation decision enabling states which so legislated to segregate schools, transportation, and all public facilities. Negro labor history also reflects "The Atlanta Compromise." The young unions had not created racial discrimination, but it was widespread. When the greatest living Negro seemingly acquiesced, it was easier to accept and perpetuate it.

To this day, Booker T. Washington remains something of a mystery. In the East he identified himself with Northern capitalists who were, or were likely to be, interested in Southern properties, many of them large employers of Negro labor.

He, who had publicly renounced political equality for the Negro in the South, was more than once a guest aboard the yacht of H. H. Rogers of Standard Oil. He submitted many of his speeches to William H. Baldwin, Jr., vice-president of the Southern Railroad, which company employed thousands of Negroes. He was a welcome guest of Collis P. Huntington, railroad officer and builder of Newport News. Andrew Carnegie invited him to Skibo Castle. These were circles open to no Southern white men of the time. To his own race he preached "patience, forbearance, and self-control in the midst of trying conditions." From 1895 to his death in 1915 his philosophy, so thoroughly in tune with that of the dominant economic and political forces of his time, determined federal government and national policy in matters of race relations in labor, and in education.

What he really thought, and what he really sought, none may say with assurance. His policy did make for jobs for a people untrained, uneducated, and caught in the riptides of reaction and change. Carpenters, brickmakers and bricklayers, blacksmiths, harnessmakers, tinsmiths—these were trained at Tuskegee and there was work for all.

Challenge to the Washington philosophy came from W. E. B. DuBois of Massachusetts. Educated at Fisk and Harvard and in Berlin, he began teaching in Atlanta University in 1896. A brilliant writer, able to evoke mood and image, he bitterly challenged the "Tuskegee machine," demanding for the Negro "every single right that belongs to a freeborn American, political, civil, and social.[26]

But until his death in 1915, Booker T. Washington was unshaken. In 1913, after a half-century of emancipation, he pointed to the record as justifying his philosophy. There were, in that year, 128,557 Negro farm owners in the South, 38,000 Negro business enterprises, and 550,000 Negro homeowners. The national wealth of the Negro was estimated to be $700,000,000.

But DuBois was then in New York, an officer of the newly organized National Association for the Advancement of Colored People, an organization fated not to become really well known to the average American until after May 1954 and the Supreme Court decision of that year which reversed the one of 1896 that had followed so closely on the heels of Dr. Washington's great "Compromise."

---

[26]See McGill on DuBois in *Southern Encounters*; Danny Champion, "Booker T. Washington Versus W. E. B. DuBois: A Study in Rhetorical Contrasts," in Braden, ed., *Oratory in the New South*, 174-203.

In the year of 1913 all the Southern states, save North Carolina which acted two years later, had adopted the direct-primary system. In the one-party states of the South this was equivalent to election. The Democratic party elected to limit these primaries to white voters. This eliminated the Negro, but also took its toll of white voters. This entirely frustrated the aim of those Midwestern progressives who had urged the direct primary on the nation as a means of restoring popular control of government.

Slowly, powerfully, full of contradictions, baffling to itself and to the rest of the nation as well, the South moved. It was glacier-like in its speed—but it moved. Education, assisted by the great philanthropists, improved. The farmers of cotton and tobacco erupted now and then in violence against the trusts. Sometimes it was political revolt. Sometimes it was expressed through night-riding barn-burnings of those who refused to join. Tenancy and sharecropping increased.

After the century was well turned, the new generation which had grown up in the post-Reconstruction years slowly began to take over. Theirs had been a youth lived, one might say, on bread alone. There had been neither leisure for the arts nor money for travel. But this was a generation which included those who were aware of this. The South began then its first self-examination. In literature Ellen Glasgow led the revolt against the falsely sentimental and affected style of Southern writing.

The universities, too, began to demand attention. In the scholastic year 1900-1901 the Universities of Kentucky, Mississippi, and Tennessee had reported no state appropriation at all. The University of Alabama received $10,000. Of eighteen American institutions with endowments of $1,500,000 or more in that year, none were in the South. Of thirty with as much as $1,000,000, two were in the South—Tulane of New Orleans and Vanderbilt of Nashville.

But for the first time there were men and women in education and politics who not merely were aware of the debased standards but were willing to proclaim them and fling the facts in the faces of the people. The old defense mechanism of fiercely defending everything Southern no longer functioned as before.

In addition to novelists, the Southern historians began to write. Young, eager sociologists examined into the ruins of the old plantation and slave economy and wrote of its effects.

It was not easy. In education the day of the "broken-down-clergyman teaching profession" was dying, but the force represented by that phrase fought back. The battle for education and educational freedom is never done, but it always is fierce at the beginning of the fight to release the bonds of spirit and mind. The South shook with sound of combat.

By 1910 the new generation felt it had almost attained that "New South" so often prophesied three decades before. They and their fathers had suffered and endured much of humiliation, sorrow, toil and frustration. They both had learned to take a half loaf when there was no whole one; the crumbs when there was not a half. Yet they had recovered a considerable portion of their lost agricultural and commercial power and some of the industrial.

But none of the old political glory and dominance had returned. For nearly fifty of the seventy-two years, beginning with Washington and continuing through Buchanan, whose term ended in the spring of 1861, Southerners had been in the White House. For sixty years chief justices of the Supreme Court had been Southern. In the same period an almost incredible twenty of the thirty-five justices of the Supreme Court had come from the South. Almost half the cabinet members, thirteen of the twenty-three Speakers of the House, and more than half the major diplomats were from that same region. The shift of political power brought about by the War Between the States was profound in fact and effect. Nowhere in history is there a comparable shift in regional power.

When Grover Cleveland won in 1884, the first Democrat since the War Between the States, Editor Henry Grady of Atlanta rushed into the House chamber of the Georgia legislature with the news of it, seized the gavel, and declared an adjournment to celebrate. But there was no reform during the Cleveland years that alleviated the agricultural distress. By the time of his second election in 1892, Cleveland was regarded by Populists as a tool of the trusts.

It was Woodrow Wilson's victory and administration which effectively united the Democratic party. It had been suspicious and divided through the convention which nominated Wilson. Some of the old Populists, including the then embittered leader Tom Watson, supported Teddy Roosevelt's Bull Moose party. But even more important than unity was the fact that the stern Calvinist prophet enabled the South to regain much of its old political pride and prestige. Three of his cabinet were Southerners—Josephus Daniels, Albert S. Burleson, and David F.

Houston. Walter Hines Page and Thomas Nelson Page were, respectively, ambassadors to the Court of St. James and to Italy. Colonel Edward M. House, of Texas, was Wilson's closest adviser. Thomas S. Martin of Virginia was majority leader of the Senate; Oscar W. Underwood, of Alabama, in the House. Southerners presided as chairmen over a majority of the major committees in House and Senate.[27]

Happy days were here again.

But the problems of tenancy, of cotton, of abused soil, agricultural credit and debt were still unsettled. The boll weevil, which had left Mexico in 1892, had somehow managed to do what everyone said it could not do. It had crossed the Mississippi. And in the Balkans, events were moving toward a bridge in Sarajevo.

War came to Europe—and to the South. The 1914 cotton crop was the largest ever harvested—sixteen million bales. That November, cotton, with the export market demoralized, was selling at 5.5 cents per pound. When America entered the war in 1917 cotton boomed with all other commodities.

The war brought boom times. The fifteen-dollar silk shirts, which all shipyard workers were supposed to wear, and the five-dollar neckties were symbols of it. There was a surge of patriotism, and the South took great pride in the divisions which included its guards, volunteers, and draftees.

Southern shipyards boomed, too, and the training camps were bonanzas to the towns and cities nearest them.

When the Kaiser was defeated and the war done, the shipyards shut down and the barracks emptied. But in 1919 cotton went to thirty-five cents and some of the longer-staple varieties brought thirty-six and thirty-seven. It was the year of the two-billion-dollar cotton crop. Tobacco kept it company. The cigaret had come into its own with the war, winning a place in the literature—poetry, ballads, and the stories of the men who had fought in it.

But in the delirium of those boom years not much attention was paid to the fact that some farmers had made less than half a crop of cotton. The boll weevil had arrived.

---

[27]See McGill on Wilson in *Southern Encounters*.

"Sometimes," said a sad, weary and beaten man, in 1922, "it seems to me the farmer is always being hammered on the anvil of bad luck."

In Louisiana the cotton crop was reduced two-thirds in two years. In Mississippi it was more than halved. All the Sea Island cotton disappeared. In Georgia, farms which had made one thousand bales in 1919 made two hundred in 1920 with the same expenditure of seed, toil, and sweat. Banks failed. There were tens of thousands of foreclosures. Bankruptcies were many. Homes, lost to mortgage holders, were abandoned. The pine trees began to grow where fields had been since the 1840s and before.

The 1930 census reported a ten-year decline in Negro farm population and a smaller but substantial one for whites.

It was on top of this disaster that the Great Depression came. Old men talked of the harsh and hopeless days of the Reconstruction years and those that followed.

Tariff rates went up, reaching their peak in 1930 in the Hawley-Smoot Act. The agricultural South, like all agricultural areas, needed markets. It got tariffs. The cotton South, which had lived largely on exports, suffered most as prices collapsed when European nations sought other cotton.

The South, already impoverished and battered by ten years and more of the boll weevil, was severely tried by the depression. Its capital reserves and savings were almost nonexistent. It had always offered the fewest jobs. In 1932 the New England states alone paid a little more than thirty million dollars in federal income taxes. This was about twice as much as those paid by the Southern states. The schools suffered as did the people and the land. But with a fortitude born out of so many years of the locust, with a grim humor springing from so many generations contending with austerity and trouble, they tightened their belts and lasted it out.

March 4, 1933, began the first one hundred days of the New Deal and Franklin D. Roosevelt.

"So desperate was the crisis," wrote Arthur S. Lenk in *The American Epoch*, "and so frightened were congressmen and the people that Roosevelt possessed a power unprecedented in American peacetime history.

Had he harbored imperial ambitions he probably could have attained dictatorial powers from the Congress. . . ."[28]

By May 6, 1933, "Triple A" legislation was adopted. There began then the historic and never-solved battle to control and regulate production—to raise farm income, to conserve the soil, to cushion the farmer against the gamble of weather and crop disaster. The Southeast, with two-thirds of the nation's farms, and perhaps the sickest, turned to New Deal with an almost emotional fervor.

A president's committee, named to examine into the South's depressed status, noted the too many people on the land, the underemployment, the lack of capital and managerial skills, the abuse of some resources and the neglect of others. In its report in 1938 it referred to the South, struggling out of the great world depression which had been piled on top of the boll-weevil disaster, as the nation's "Number One Economic Problem."[29]

The South began an amazing self-study, led by universities, newspapers, and local study and forum groups. If the region was the number-one economic problem, then the other side of the coin was number-one opportunity. Results began to appear in the legislation introduced in state legislatures and in the debates therein. Out of the Congress and the White House in 1933 came the Tennessee Valley Authority (TVA). America had wasted the natural resources across all its dynamic years. But nowhere had that process gone on as thoroughly as in the South. The TVA built dams to control floods and produce electricity. Soil was reclaimed and cheaper fertilizers produced. The Tennessee Valley covers an area of 49,910 square miles. It is about four-fifths the size of New England. The river valley includes parts of seven states: Tennessee, Kentucky, Virginia, North Carolina, Georgia, Alabama, and Mississippi. The effect was immediate. The inspiration of it everywhere encouraged conservation. Phosphate fertilizers developed by the TVA program were tested and used in more than half the states of the Union. River shipping grew. The power generated provided a great national

---

[28]Lenk, *American Epoch*, 393.

[29]See Frank Burt Freidel, *F.D.R. and The South* (Baton Rouge: Louisiana State University Press, 1965); Paul E. Mertz, *New Deal Policy and Southern Rural Poverty* (Baton Rouge: Louisiana State University Press, 1978).

impetus to greater use of electricity and appliances. It inspired the creation of the Rural Electrification Administration of 1936 which brought power to the nation's farms. Millions of trees were planted and recreational lakes spawned fish and new business in boats and fishing.

By the time the TVA had helped America out of the depression, Europe was at war, and the TVA's power was a godsend in the war plants. Before that war was done, the TVA was to make possible the crash program of the atomic bomb.

Farm prices went up in demand, and lend-lease defense plants were pleading for workers. The exodus from the South began to speed up. But even before the Japanese attack on Pearl Harbor, there had begun a great emigration of troops to Southern training camps and air bases, hacked out of the piney woods or spread on the coastal and wire-grass plains. This was accelerated until the South seemed almost one great base for training soldiers and pilots.

Plants came, too, as they had not in 1917-1918. Bombers and fighter craft rolled off Southern assembly lines. Metal fabrication plants multiplied. Subcontractors reached into the small-town factories to find makers of parts. The timber business boomed. Service industries came into being to absorb the payroll demands. Retail shops of all kinds, dry cleaners, tailors, filling stations, drug stores, cafes—all of these, and more, made the smallest towns boom. They glowed late with the splendor of neon red, green, and blue.

War had boomed life for the Negro, too. The demand for manpower was so great that thousands of Negroes found industrial jobs in their own region and demonstrated they could as quickly be trained to skills as anyone else. Stirrings of the national conscience and the need to mobilize all possible production workers brought from the White House an executive decree against discrimination in employment because of race or religion by any employer working on federal contracts. Out of this developed a Fair Employment Practices Commission which simply, by focusing attention on discrimination and by holding hearings in more flagrant cases, brought about considerable reform and an improvement in attitude, even though all states in the South refused to write it into legislation.

It was a wary South which emerged from the capitulations in Europe and Japan. The prosperity of the First World War had not caught on. It had been a rich diet but it had not stuck to the economic ribs.

But by 1946 it was once again a new South. Now at last came a prosperity to match that which the prophets of bygone years had seen in their visions.[30]

Nor was the material evidence the whole story. There was a new South, too, in the intangibles. There was a new confidence, a new and increasing enthusiasm. One of the greatest lacks of the post-Civil War South had been that of managerial skills. The World War II years had produced managers and administrators. Literally hundreds of the young and middle-aged executives who had come South to help manage war production plants stayed on to augment the local supply. Capital, too, had put down roots.

The South began to enjoy the heady wine of being able to finance sizable projects through its own banks which, in turn, did not need to obtain credit in the East to handle them. Service businesses sprang up as the GI's returned. And this time not even all the shipyards closed. Cotton consumption declined. By 1954 it was down to the 1935-1939 level. But there were plants making synthetic fibers and cotton itself steadily was moving westward out of the rolling terrain of the Piedmont and the Appalachian slopes.

Mechanization needs flatter lands and fewer hands. In the West, irrigation and drier climates meant higher yields and less boll weevil infestation. In the South beef cattle and dairy herds began to graze on new pastures where for a hundred years only cotton had grown. Small grains and hybrid corn suited to Southern climes came out of the experiment research stations. Even in the rich loam of the Mississippi Delta grain elevators began to rise out of the level landscape and by 1950 tourists were startled to see cattle grazing in pastures hard by the cotton. The commercial broiler and chicken industry boomed higher and higher.

There is water in the South, and the new industries in chemicals, synthetics, pulp, paper, and the nuclear plants are great drinkers of water. The assembly plants came, too. Furniture, metals, equipment, and machinery were all part of the changing structure of the new industrial South.

---

[30]See Charles Pearce Roland, *Improbable Era: The South Since World War II* (Lexington: University Press of Kentucky, 1975); Jack Bass and Walter DeVries, *Transformation of Southern Politics: Social Change and Political Consequence Since 1945* (New York: New American Library, 1976).

Wages, too, were changing. In 1929 the average wage was equal to 36.6 percent of the value added per worker. By 1947 it was above 40 percent. In 1957 it was nearing 50 percent.

The industrial growth in the South that was evolving in the last half of the twentieth century could be measured in both absolute and relative terms. During the decade of the depression, for example, the region barely held its own in absolute terms but made gains in relation to the rest of the country. From 1939 to 1950 the South's labor force, released from the farms being mechanized, merged, and abandoned, increased by 50 percent. This was slightly less than the increase in the rest of the nation. But in wages paid, and value added by manufacturing, the increases respectively were 274 percent and 244 percent. These were considerably higher than corresponding increases in other regions.

For the first time, too, the region began to attain an industrial structure which had balance. The textile mills had by far the smallest rate increase of production workers of any major group of manufacturers between 1939 and 1950. Other relatively low-pay groups had smaller rates of increase during and after the war years. Conversely, industry groups which employed fewest workers in 1939 and which generally paid higher workers had the highest percentage increase. There were geographic shifts, too, as the states with more hydroelectric power, water, and raw materials marshaled their resources with planning and promotion.

As 1957 drew to a close the U.S. Department of Commerce, through its Atlanta office, reported that the states of the Southeastern area had surpassed the average rate of advancement for the nation as a whole in many divisions of its economy. These included salaries, wages paid in manufacturing, gross and per capita personal income, expenditures for new plants and equipment, electric energy produced, telephones in operation, amount of life insurance in force, retail and wholesale sales, beef cattle on farms, chickens hatched commercially, industrial and commercial firms in business, and others.

In the field of race relations the South also was in a period of accelerated transition. Because this was concerned with human beings and not with economic statistics, the action was, and is, and for sometime will be, surcharged with emotion. The South did have a way of life which made it unique among the regions. It was based on the Negro's acceptance of a secondary position in the economy and of a segregated existence in all the public life of the region. The affirmation of this status by Booker T. Washington and his long years of national dominance in the field of race relations helped fix this secondary status both in the law, customs, and traditions of the region. The nation conveniently turned its back during this period as the South created this subordinate status. The Jim Crow laws did not appear on the statute books until some thirty years after the Civil War.

But all the while the South, like the nation, was evolving, though its rate was slower. For some years after the agony of the Reconstruction years, it was not well understood by the South that as the region reached eagerly for industry and the payrolls, with them would come unions, a sharing in the gain by the Negro, and an inevitable erosion of the foundation on which the so-called way of life was based.

The First World War and the years of the boll weevil had accelerated the agricultural revolution. The Great Depression not merely revealed the economic and spiritual misery of the submarginal farms and the families that worked them; it exposed, too, the greater woes of the tenants and sharecroppers. And in so doing, it focused attention on the sociological features of the South and the position of the poor white and Negro.

Political and economic gains came to both out of the Roosevelt years. And out of them came, too, a slowly developing regional sense of guilt insofar as the separate but equal status of the Negro was concerned. There was a separation, rigidly enforced, but nowhere was there equality of schools, transportation, housing, parks, recreational facilities, or economic opportunity. Almost nowhere was there equality of medical and hospital care. And, worse, rare was the city where the Negro could feel confident of equality before the law insofar as police, sheriffs, deputies, and the minor courts were concerned.

By the late thirties it could be seen that the South's unique way of life, based as it was on a permanent subordinate position for the Negro, beset by moral, economic, and political forces, was doomed. The United States Supreme Court began to hand down rulings which required Southern states to admit Negroes to graduate schools where the states did not offer separate but equal classes in graduate work. It was obvious the Court was saying, when it had opportunity, that in American the Fourteenth Amendment did not permit any discrimination or second-class citizenship because of color. There began then what was a confession of guilt in the form of a building program to equalize teachers' salaries and the schools which, since 1896, had been legally separate only on the presumption they were in every respect equal. The Second World War interrupted, but by the time the 1954 Court decision declaring compulsory segregation on the basis of color to be unconstitutional, every state in the Southeast was engaged in an almost feverish building campaign and some political speeches noted these new schools were often superior to those for white children."

There was a brief lull after the Court decision of May 1954, but resistance soon hardened. Quite inevitably it was most extreme in the Deep South. The old pattern was there more deeply etched. There also was most of the Negro population, and the largest percentage of it was in agriculture in areas where there was most of the old-plantation-type economy. In the Deep South, too, was a long history of radical, often violent, exploitation of race for political ends. Almost all the more notorious racial demagogues had come from four Deep South states.[31]

Slowly, the South once more began to demonstrate that it is many Souths. The border state of Missouri began to obey the Court. Within three years after the Court decision, Kentucky's schools were eighty-five percent desegregated. Beginnings had been made, not without mass violence participated in by outside agitators, in Arkansas and Tennessee. North Carolina alone inaugurated her program without disorder.

In September 1957 Little Rock's school system planned to inaugurate a well-advertised ten-year program of desegregation. The governor, who had offered no opposition to the plan, suddenly, in what generally was accepted to be part of a plan for a political campaign for reelection, called out state troops on the morning the schools were to open and halted the plans.

He later asked for and received an invitation to talk with President Dwight D. Eisenhower. Emerging from this meeting the governor of Arkansas declared he accepted the Supreme Court decision as law and the people of his state were law abiding. Returning home, he did not comply but maintained his troops to defy the Court. President Eisen-

---

[31]See Numan V. Bartley, *Rise of Massive Resistance: Race and Politics in the South During the 1950's* (Baton Rouge: Louisiana State University Press, 1969); Numan V. Bartley and Hugh D. Graham, *Southern Politics and the Second Reconstruction* (Baltimore: Johns Hopkins University Press, 1975); V. O. Key, Jr., *Southern Politics in State and Nation* (New York: Vintage Books, 1949).

hower, confronted with open defiance of federal authority, had no other recourse save to federalize the state guard and send in additional troops of the regular forces to see that the Court order was carried out.

It was, of course, a historic decision. And while the immediate effect was further to harden resistance in the Deep South, it had the necessary catalyst effect of demonstrating that the 1954 decision was not, as some of the wishful-thinking politicians had been saying, merely a political gesture which would never be enforced. Deep South states, joined somewhat surprisingly by Virginia, made plans for closing their public schools rather than comply. No local board was permitted any autonomy. Since all political machinery was in the hands of those pledged to abolishing schools, the Deep South, not surprisingly, was facing another indeterminable period of travail and disorder such as it had known in the days of Reconstruction, of Populist revolt, and of depression. Its children were certain to pay a price in the quality of their education. What the cost would be in the loss of teachers and economic progress was for the future to determine. The Supreme Court decision, while a blow to a way of life based on a subordinate economic and political position for the Negro, was merely a part of the overall panorama of change. History had moved on. Time and morality were on the side of the Negro. That the far-reaching social and economic changes going on all over the world also were at work in the South was not obvious to many. But they were. And time was at work.

But as one must look back now and then to the past to understand the future, it is plain to see that there is yet another "New South" in the making. And that South, possessing its share of great and wonderful people of both races, as well as economic assets for vast development, will not be fatefully unique in that it possesses a way of life based on a subordinate position for any of its people. It will be fully in the mainstream of American life. It will have come a long, hard road, but along the way it has never lost its best human qualities. And possessing these, and rid of the old burdens, it may very well match the dream of its most optimistic prophets.

Constantine Chapter, C. S. A.

It was spring in Georgia. And it was the spring of 1864. The dogwood bloomed, splashing the hills with its whiteness. But the
sweating, swearing teamsters on the muddy clay roads did not see
it, except perhaps briefly and with a nostalgic wistfulness. And the
tired, marching men did not see it. It rained much that spring. And the
rifles were heavy.

In Chattanooga William Tecumseh Sherman, grim-lipped and dis-
liking the whole business very much, said: "Forward."

From that day onward, though none of the men knew it, every road
led toward Appomattox. But the long agony and the long dying was
ahead.

There was feverish activity in the South. The trains rolled out of
Atlanta. And the roads were choked with teams and men and guns.

There was one muddy road they used more than any other. And
today—

Today they call it the Dixie Highway. You may ride it for a thousand
miles or more. The tourist cars use it in an annual parade down and up.
Sitting back in the upholstery one may glance out at the little towns and

Reprinted from *The Magazine of Sigma Chi*, February 1938, by permission of
Mrs. Ralph McGill and Sigma Chi. The Constantine Chapter was organized 17 September 1864 "in the vicinity of and a few miles southwest of Atlanta, Georgia."

their most curious names. Lost Mountain, New Hope Church, Ezra Church—and finally Calhoun and Cartersville and Marietta and Kennesaw Mountain. The land rises sharply on the right going south.

And then—in 1864—

It was a dark mass of hill and tree and rock. And the white dogwood that had bloomed there in the early spring was gone. And there was to be red on the hills soon, staining the leaves and rocks.

Joe Johnston and his men were there—on Kennesaw.

The Generals in Blue who opposed him said they never felt so worried as when Joe Johnston was in front of them.

And they never felt so alarmed as when they had him retreating. He was a stubborn man to fight. In retreat he was a running wolf.

But there he was on Kennesaw. His men were behind breastworks of logs and rock. He had retreated slowly, taking a heavy toll. And they never dislodged him until their flanks (they almost doubled him in numbers) were about to pinch behind him.

And while he held, Nathan Bedford Forrest ("Get ther the fustest with the mostest men" was his formula for victory) slashed at the Blue flanks and raided outposts. He didn't have the mostest men. Not then.

The 28th Mississippi Volunteer Cavalry was there with the Army of Tennessee.

And with them rode a young man in a faded uniform. On it gleamed a curious badge. A silver dollar had been carved and hammered into the shape of a white cross.[32]

His name was Harry St. John Dixon. He was twenty. Behind him were three years of war. The University of Virginia and his chapter of the Sigma Chi Fraternity seemed farther back than just three years. There was a growing something in the air, the rush of brazen, invisible hoofs and somehow, though it was hot that summer, there was a chill now and then.

You may see his picture. His eyes look out from a face that is young. But even in the old picture there is something about the eyes which says they have seen men die and live. And they have seen defeat and victory. And they have gone back to the job when it was all over.

---

[32]Harry St. John Dixon, "Recollections of a Rebel Private," *Sigma Chi Quarterly* 16 (February 1897): 207.

But that day before Kennesaw he was thinking. A few days before he had seen another Sigma Chi. He hadn't time to get his name. There was a deal of fighting. And there was hurry. They had clasped hands at Cassville and he wondered what had become of him. He and Hal Yerger, a Sigma Chi from Eta at Mississippi, had talked things over.

It was curious to them. They didn't hate the men on the other side. They knew there must be Sigma Chis there. But it was curious to see the old flag, the Stars and Stripes, flying over men who invaded their states. It was something to puzzle about. But they reckoned that every man who did his duty as he saw it was right—no matter if he wore Blue or Gray. Meanwhile there was the fighting.

There was a long try at Kennesaw. The Blue lines charged many times there and fell back, cursing and grim, leaving their dead to carpet the hillside. The hail of lead from the barricades was too much.

And so, at last, William Tecumseh Sherman shook his head and muttered something about Joe Johnston. And he gave orders.

From the mountain Joe Johnston watched. He knew what it meant. He saw the troops move out. And next day his scouts brought the information he knew was coming. Sherman was opening his pincers again. The Blue jaws were opening wide. And the nut they would surround and crack would be Kennesaw. So, the next morning the Federal troops inspected the deserted ditches on the mountain. Joe Johnston was gone.

The boy of twenty was at Ezra Church. He was there with the silver cross on his breast on 28 July. They were holding a hill with a thin line. Both flanks were turned and a terrible barrage of fire turned on them. But they clung there. They poured their ammunition on the ground and so did not have to reach for their pouches to load. They were relieved at last. And he wrote in his diary:[33] "Which brigade relieved us I never knew; but I can never forget how it acted. I never saw a body of men more precise on dress parade. They came at [a] double-quick from our rear, and at that step and by the regiments that formed, cast[ing] away their blankets as they moved into line, under [a] fire that seemed like

---

[33]Harry St. John Dixon, "Recollections of a Rebel Private," *Sigma Chi Quarterly* 6 (February 1887): 148-49. Dixon actually wrote the following words: "forget now it acted"; "like the fury of hell"; and "a carnival."

fury from Hell to us, and went on to the carnival of death beyond. . . ."

(He was twenty years old. And he wrote like that. And reading it, and the rest he wrote, one may understand why "Sigma Chi endured in the South.")

Joe Johnston was gone. Atlanta was gone. Hood was in command. And the troops, wishing for Joe Johnston, were near Jonesboro, some twenty miles south of Atlanta. The last chapter of Sherman's march to the sea was about to be written.

The tired armies rested, like tired prizefighters on their stools in their corners between rounds of a long, hard fight.

And that night Yerger and Dixon talked.

They felt, somehow, the end was inevitable. There were many more months of the long agony, but they wanted to do something. The colleges were closed. There was no telling what might happen if they met defeat. Sigma Chis had been killed. The fraternity in the South must be kept alive. There was no authority to which to turn. They would form a chapter in their regiment. Writing of it, after the war, he said: [34]

> The death of many comrades, and the constant danger of being taken pris-
> oner, a fate we thought worse than death, ripened an idea long in my mind. We
> felt cut off from all communication with the rest of the world, hemmed in and
> fighting for life. Every college in the South was closed. In the ruin at hand
> my sentiment was to preserve the white cross. There was no means of outer
> communication. There was no central place to rally. I knew I had no authority
> to establish a chapter of Sigma Chi outside a college, or at all; but, isolated as
> we were, all of us in the army doubtless of Southern blood, I thought to raise
> the standard and fix a rallying point, which would preserve the existence of the
> order, whether we failed or not in our struggle for independence, as an insti-
> tution in which we as Southern soldiers had participated, in order not only to
> subserve private benefit, but in order to have means of communicating with
> our brethren of the North, all of them, no doubt, in arms against us.

(Remember—he was a boy of twenty.)
On the night of 17 September 1864, they met.

---

[34]Ibid., 220-21. Dixon actually wrote: "preserve the lofty principles typified by the white cross."

They found an old log cabin. Dixon writes that it was in a fearful state of dilapidation. There were cobwebs and dirt, but he wrote: "The spirit was there and shone brightly."[35]

There was not much time. They slipped away from camp without permission.

And there, with the light of one guttering candle, they gathered. On the rude benches sat the candidates. Not far away were the restless sounds of the camp. Dixon sent out a man to see no one was near this cabin. It was on the edge of a lonely field with branches and vines half covering it. He came back and shook his head.

Dixon was elected consul. Yerger was pro consul. They named their organization the Constantine Chapter. Reuben T. Pollard, of Mississippi, was there. He was Eta '61. Evan J. Shelby, Eta '62, had helped make Dixon a Sigma Chi at Virginia. William H. Bolton, of the original Sigma, was there in the cabin. Thomas N. Fowler and A. B. Raffington, of Company D, were there to be initiated. The latter did not live long in Sigma Chi. He fell in battle. Fowler survived. But that was later.

Before a crudely fashioned altar, oaths were taken, the Charge was improvised, the mysteries explained. They clasped hands with the newly-made brothers, fingers finding the grip, and closing tightly. They put out the candle, the poor one of tallow. But they had lit new lights that would go on and light more lights to make an immortal light in the lives of thousands of men.[36]

That was the scene. The silent night and the lonely cabin, the solemn young men, dedicated to a great principle, standing there with the noise of battle still in their ears, bringing men to Sigma Chi that the great light in their lives might be transmitted to other men—that Sigma Chi should not perish in the Southland.

The shadows danced on the walls of rough logs, the September wind that moved the vines and the pines behind them made a sound like surf far off—

[35]Ibid., 221.

[36]Ibid.; and Dixon, *Sigma Chi Quarterly* 16 (February 1897): 89.

That candle light, flickering there in the lonely cabin that night in the autumn of 1864, comes down to us yet, stronger and stronger through the years.

A white light—a white cross in the Heavens—*By This Sign Conquer*—

As nearly as is possible the site of the cabin has been located.

It is perhaps significant and no mere coincidence that it is located on land which has long been in the family of Sigma Chis and is today in their hands.

It is a great nursery, one of the nation's greatest, and there bloom fields of flowers and evergreen shrubs and things of beauty.

And it is there that land will be dedicated to Sigma Chi, and a great white cross shall be built to remain through eternity in memory of that one candle that burned there near three-quarters of a century ago, in memory of Harry St. John Dixon, and his comrades of the Constantine Chapter.

3

This Is Our Georgia

The Spanish came first. Then the French. There was marching of troops across the land, the Spanish being settled at Pensacola. The French came. The Carolina traders came across the Savannah for trading. There followed, in the vast Georgia wilderness, war extending to outposts on the St. Mary's and St. John's.

The Carolinians wanted the territory about what is now Savannah, settled and colonized. Two efforts failed. The Southern border, where the English and Spanish forces clashed, was the most dangerous border in the New World. There were attacks on St. Augustine. And counterattacks.

In England there was a depression. There was tremendous unemployment. Even members of the more privileged classes were getting into debt. Since the law allowed imprisonment for debt, the jails were filled.

James Edward Oglethorpe, student, soldier, and member of Parliament, was named on a committee to investigate the prisons. In 1729 and

Reprinted from John Temple Graves II et al., eds., *A Book of the South* (Southern Editors Association, The Jas. O. Jones Company, 1940) 54-56, by permission of Mrs. Ralph McGill. In the foreword McGill wrote: "This book is a newspaper reference book . . . to be distributed to newspapers throughout the South and to leading newspapers of the United States. It is not in any sense a 'publicity' book. . . . It will prevent publication of inaccurate information and be a very real service."

1730 more than ten thousand prisoners were liberated because of the report.

There were no jobs for those released. England was crowded with unemployed. Petitions were made to set up a new colony for the relief of the unemployed. The British Crown liked the idea because it would relieve the home situation, and it would provide a great market for the homeland and at the same time produce raw materials.

The limits of that new colony today would include Little Rock and Los Angeles. It was a vast territory, for even then they had little idea of the greatness of that territory. They drew a line to the "South seas."

The new colony was given a different setup from that of any other colony. It was to be ruled by a board of trustees. The British government was, perhaps, a bit more interested in imperial advancement. The trustees were interested in a philanthropic and social experiment.

England became excited over the venture. Seeds and tools, together with some money, were subscribed. Some debtors were to be allowed to come. A commission was appointed to visit the men and select the most likely pioneers. The histories show that it was announced people would be received:

> of reputable families, and of liberal, or at least, easy education; some undone
> by guardians, some by lawsuits, some by accidents in commerce, some by
> stocks and bubbles and some by suretyship. These are the people who may re-
> lieve themselves and strengthen Georgia by resorting thither, and Great Brit-
> ain by their departure.

By the autumn of 1732 more than one hundred persons had been accepted and the *Anne*, a ship of two hundred tons, was ready to sail. They reached Charleston on 3 January 1733, and the next day moved on to Beaufort. The Carolinians were delighted at the new help which had arrived.

William Bull, a South Carolinian, accompanied Oglethorpe and they ascended the Savannah river, and about eighteen miles from the mouth came upon a bluff where he decided to make his settlement.

The Indians were friendly and the city soon was laid out. Georgia early was a refuge for persecuted people. The Lutherans were the first to arrive, sailing eleven months after Oglethorpe, and being given a settlement six miles away. Within six years after it was settled the colony was one of varied peoples, there being represented English, Swiss, Salzburgers, Moravians, Germans, Jews, Scotch Highlanders and Piedmontese.

It was this colony which at last decided whether this section of the New World should be Spanish or English. Oglethorpe and his small force defeated a superior Spanish force at Bloody Marsh and turned the tide for England.

Because the new colony was an experiment in philanthropy and a new social order for the New World, slavery was prohibited. Wines and beers were permitted but Georgia had the first prohibition law, prohibiting rum, whisky and brandy.

An effort was made to make of the new colony a great silk-producing section. Mulberry trees, descendants of which flourish today, were planted. Some cities, notably Canton, took their names in anticipation of rivaling China as producers of silk. Some silk actually was produced but it soon became apparent Georgia was to be a great farming section.

Later, the laws against rum, brandy and whisky became impossible to enforce and were abandoned by being unenforced. In that respect, at least, the utopia was a failure.

Time went on. The new colony grew. King George II made of it a royal colony. It was not until 1755 that the first assembly met under the new royal governor, John Reynolds. [37]

Discontent began to rise in the colony, as it did in the others, as more and more taxes were imposed. England was at war. The new generation didn't care about it. They began to draw away. In 1770 there was open discontent and threatened rebellion. By July 1775, the Georgians had begun to capture British ships off the coast, as had the Carolinians. And finally, when independence was voted, three Georgia delegates were there to sign the document: Button Gwinnett, Lyman Hall, and George Walton.

Not many battles were fought in Georgia during the Revolution but in few colonies was there as much devastation. There was a bitter civil war between the Loyalists and the Revolutionists. It was not until after three years of war that real fighting reached Georgia.

---

[37] See Kenneth Coleman, *The American Revolution of Georgia, 1763-1789* (Athens: University of Georgia Press, 1958); Kenneth Coleman, *Colonial Georgia: A History* (New York: Charles Scribner, 1976).

Georgia came under the control of the British troops at all the coastal cities while in the interior civil war and outlaws spread terror. Charleston fell and things looked dark. British power was located in Savannah.

By 1782 the tide again turned. General "Mad Anthony" Wayne was in Georgia with regulars. In July, the British were defeated in the East and marched out of Savannah.

There followed land speculation and settlements; wars with the Indians, a near clash with the United States government over the Indian treaties.

The state began to develop tremendously in agriculture and industry. By 1832 the boom of growth and development was in full force.

Roads, canals, turnpikes and railroads came. By 1860 Georgia had made remarkable railroad progress. All principal cities were connected with railroads.

Cotton was king but in 1860 Georgia raised more than thirty million bushels of corn, more than two million bushels of wheat, a million and a half bushels of oats, more than fifty million pounds of rice, almost a million pounds of tobacco and almost a million bales of cotton.

In addition she produced a million bushels of sweet potatoes, floods of molasses, honey, butter and other products of the farm. There was a vast amount of cattle, sheep and hogs. It was a rich state and already being called "The Empire State of the South."

Schools began to develop. The educational system was one of the first requisites of government.

Then came the clouds of war. Alexander H. Stephens, Benjamin H. Hill and Herschel Johnson led the fight to keep down secession but when it came they went with their state.

Georgia supplied many of the Southern leaders. The brilliant Howell Cobb was president of the convention. Thomas R. R. Cobb wrote the Southern constitution in all its essential details.

The great Robert Toombs almost became president. He was made secretary of state. Stephens was made vice-president and could have had the presidency had he been willing to fire the first shot and thus hurry the border states into the Confederacy.

The war came. Sherman came. The end came. Georgia troops had earned much glory. General John B. Gordon, protecting General Robert E. Lee's army on its last desperate retreat, was one of the great heroes of the war. There were others. But the war was lost.

Reconstruction was a terrible ordeal. "The Age of Hate" was a bitter one in Georgia as the military and carpetbagger governments exacted their toll in human misery and economic wreckage.

The *Atlanta Constitution* was founded to help bring back constitutional government to Georgia. Bob Toombs and Charles J. Jenkins organized a new convention. The fight went on. Constitutional government was obtained.

There followed the new prophets. Henry W. Grady, one of the nation's most brilliant editors and orators, was to do much toward "loving the nation into peace" before he died at the age of thirty-nine, already an international figure. Joel Chandler Harris's voice was added to his.[38]

By 1910 Atlanta had become such a manufacturing center that its productions were greater than that of the whole state combined in 1870.

Georgia stood third in the production of cotton. Largely because of Grady's editorials and speeches, the state began to diversify.

Following the world war, in which Georgians did their part, Georgia experienced the prosperity which all the nation enjoyed.

The boll weevil came in 1921 to ruin cotton. In 1929 came the depression. Because of the boll weevil Georgia had been in a state of deflation and therefore felt the depression less keenly.

In the "reconstruction" after the depression, Georgia took the lead in slum clearance and other forward-looking social improvements. The state accepted the challenge of the second economic challenge.

In 1940 Georgia's people were working toward building up a great agricultural empire of diversified crops. Livestock had become a great industry and was but in its beginnings.

Manufacturing was exceeding the wealth of the annual agricultural crops. Political problems remained, as well as social ones. But in 1940 Georgia can look forward to the future with confidence. Behind her are more than two centuries of life. Ahead of her are many more centuries.[39]

---

[38]See Joel Chandler Harris, ed., *Life of Henry W. Grady Including His Writings and Speeches* (New York: Cassell Publishing Co., 1890).

[39]See McGill's "Something of Georgia," "My Georgia," "Give me Georgia," "Introduction to *The Old South*," and articles on Atlanta, in volumes 1 and 2.

4

Something of Georgia

One of the original thirteen colonies with a land area much larger than that of today, Georgia still is the largest state east of the Mississippi river, the twentieth in size among all the states.

Her 59,265 square miles of territory is but a trifle less than all of New England. Bordered by five states: Florida on the South, Alabama on the west, North Carolina and Tennessee on the north, and South Carolina on the northeast, Georgia still has 126 miles of coast line offering excellent harbors. From the coastal plains Georgia moves northward, offering upland, tablelands and then mountains. These mountains were, in the earlier days, natural barriers to trade and settlement. Yet the pioneers settled them. Through Rabun Gap and the Ellijay valley came the supplies and the men who followed the Indian trails into the mountains.

The Blue Ridge mountains and the Allegheny chain send their peaks and ridges into Georgia. Thus Georgia offers all varieties of terrain from the famous islands along her coast, across the coastal plains, to the

Reprinted from John Temple Graves II et al., eds., *A Book of the South* (Southern Editors Association, The Jas. O. Jones Co., 1940) 50-53, by permission of Mrs. Ralph McGill.

uplands and thence to the mountains where there are summer resorts to match those of winter along the coast.

The state offers a wide variety of fishing in its many lakes. Deer and bear may be hunted in season. So may other game of which the quail is the most famous. Georgia, especially the territory in and near Albany, Georgia, has become known as the bird dog capital of the world.

The Okefenokee swamp, one of the greatest phenomena of nature, remains untouched. Here game and fish and an abundance of trees, flowers, and shrubs grow and are protected. The famous swamp is near Waycross, Georgia, extending southward about 5 miles out of that city with an area of about 600 square miles. It is not a stagnant swamp, but a series of many waterways which converge to form the famed Suwannee river.

As with her terrain, Georgia offers a variety of climate. The state is located in the temperate zone. There is subtropical climate. In certain sections of the coastal plains oranges and tropical plants are grown. In the northern part of the state a temperature of zero has been recorded. The growing season averages from 275 days along the coast to 185 days in the northern sections.

Ores of various kinds, including gold, have been found in Georgia since the days of the Indians. In late 1939 rich gold finds were reported in the old mines at Dahlonega where once the slaves of John C. Calhoun brought out ores which made a fortune for that famous South Carolinian. Limestone, granite, marble, sand, feldspar, manganese, ocher, talc, baryte, pyrite, coal, some iron, slate, and many other ores and minerals are to be found.

Georgia is one of the leading marble-producing states in the nation, and Georgia marble has been used in famous buildings and monuments the world over. The state capitol at St. Paul, Minnesota, the Stock Exchange at New York, and many other buildings have been constructed entirely of Georgia marble. The belt of marble is about 60 miles long and from 1 to 3 miles wide in the northern section of the state. Cherokee and Pickens Counties have the largest deposits.

Cement rock, clay, Fuller's earth, kaolin, yellow ocher, and baryte are mined profitably. Brick plants and others for the production of clay products have been in operation for many years. In the past year production in the kaolin belt of South Georgia, one of the world's finest, has begun. Baryte, found in large amounts near Cartersville, also is found in five other counties. The Cartersville mines are the largest in the United States.

Gold, previously mentioned, has played a part in the state's history. Once it almost led to open revolt by Georgia against the United States government. The removal of the Cherokee nation grew out of the development of the gold fields.

By 1838 the United States had established a mint at Dahlonega, and it continued in operation until 1861 when the War Between the States began. The mint coined more than six millions of dollars. Mining was resumed after the war but fell off to almost nothing in 1922. Recent developments and the reported discovery of a profitable vein have revived interest in the Dahlonega section.

Despite the fact the value of its manufactured products are greater than those of its farms, Georgia remains an agricultural state. The climate, the variety of soils and the long growing season caused farming to be the inevitable major industry of the state.

Cotton, tobacco, corn and peanuts are the major crops. Many grains, rye, wheat, oats; fruits of variety and abundance; watermelons, cantaloupes, sugar cane, nuts, sweet potatoes, truck produce—all come from the farms of Georgia. Peaches and apples are among the more famous fruits with the Georgia watermelon, whether fruit or vegetable, ranking with them in importance.[40]

Georgia's farm problems are acute. Loss of the foreign markets has depressed the cotton crop. Loss of soil through erosion and row crops has become a problem occupying the best minds of the state. Progress is being made.

Perhaps the most progress is being made in the improvement and substitution of livestock as a money crop for cotton. The state still imports beef, pork, and poultry to meet its consumer demands but great reductions have been made in these imports. The quality of beef annually is improving. Georgia is the largest pork-producing state in the South.

Work of the state agricultural school and the many vocational agricultural schools throughout the state augur well for the future.

---

[40]See Kenneth Coleman, ed., *A History of Georgia* (Athens: University of Georgia Press, 1977).

Georgia was the educational leader in the original colonies, issuing the first charter for a state university and making education one of the chief interests of the state.[41] Since the War Between the States, education has suffered through lack of adequate appropriations by the legislature and, as often has been the case, failure to provide the money appropriated. This explains the state's illiteracy problem which is about that of other Southern states. The number of illiterates annually is being reduced.

Timber is one of the great "crops" of the state. Care now is being taken to educate the people to protect the timber so it may not be ruthlessly cut and destroyed.

A new era in this industry has been indicated by the discoveries of the late Dr. Charles E. Herty. It was this Georgian who discovered a method of making newsprint out of the slash pine of Georgia and the South. This industry will be added to the ever expanding kraft paper industry which already exists.

Georgia, like other Southern states, has suffered in industrial and agricultural development because of the tariffs and the discriminatory freight rates imposed by an industrial East on the South and West.

Despite the fact the South was, after the end of the war, a battlefield on which property, homes, and field had been destroyed as much as those in France during the World War of 1914-1918; and despite the fact the South returned to a broken economic system, great progress has been made. Georgia has become one of the great states of the nation just as it was a great colony in the earlier days of the New World.[42]

---

[41]See Kenneth Coleman, *Colonial Georgia: A History* (New York: Charles Scribner, 1976).

[42]See McGill's "This is Our Georgia," "My Georgia," "Introduction to *The Old South*," and articles on Atlanta, in volumes 1 and 2.

5

My Georgia

Each of us has "his Georgia."
For some it is the wire grass of the coastal plains, for others the great forests of pine with highways cutting through them, the rough brown trunks and the aromatic green boughs endless on either side, save where the dark rivers cross.

For others "their Georgia" is the coast, with its beaches and its maze of islands and marshes, where the flocks of white herons fly, and where when tides are high, one may take a boat and ride out and kill the brown marsh hens to be cooked in earthen pots with bay leaf and green peppers. For some it is fishing in the surf, or going out to search for the telltale flight of small birds feeding where the Spanish mackerel are running, ravenous and fast. For others it is casting in the dark tidal rivers, brackish and strong, for the big black bass which hide by the lilly pads and in the edge of salt grass.

For many "Georgia" is the mountains, the last southward thrust of the ancient and oft-folded Appalachians. Here a few trickles become a mountain creek which rushes swiftly to join with others to become a river—the Chattahoochee, the Tugalo, the Tallulah. Here are the

Manuscript provided by Mrs. Ralph McGill from the McGill papers, now at Emory University, Atlanta. No date. Written for the *Atlanta Constitution*, and published by permission of Atlanta Newspapers, Inc.

heights. It is a long way there, from the sands of the coast, up through the wire grass, the piney woods, the Piedmont, the mountains called the Blue Ridges, but it is all Georgia.

Others see only the land, a farm, and give their lives to it, making its soil better, planting, reaping, tending cattle, growing chickens, selling eggs, joining a co-op dairy. Their lives are a part of the earth, and when they return to it, the minister stands in the quiet church, or by the grave side, and says, "This was his Georgia."

Yet others like only the city, finding their lives in tune with the noises a city makes, the municipal sound of traffic, the never ending echo of feet and voices.

A great poet, Stephen Vincent Benét, said it better than any one else, writing of the old South, and the Georgia before the great war of division. A young Georgian, riding back to the pillared manor house, stops his horse and looks at his land. And the poet says:

> This was his Georgia, this his share
> Of pine and river and sleepy air,
> Of summer thunder and winter rain
> That spills bright tears on the window-pane
> With the slight, fierce passion of young men's grief,
> Of the mockingbird and the mulberry-leaf.
> For, wherever the winds of Georgia run,
> It smells of peaches long in the sun,
> And the white wolf-winter, hungry and frore,
> Can prowl the North by a frozen door
> But here we have fed him on bacon-fat
> And he sleeps by the stove like a lazy cat.
> Here Christmas stops at everyone's house
> With a jug of molasses and green, young boughs,
> And the little New Year, the weakling one,
> Can lie outdoors in the noonday sun,
> Blowing the fluff from a turkey-wing
> At skies already haunted with Spring—
> Oh, Georgia . . . Georgia . . . the careless yield!
> The watermelons ripe in the field!
> The mist in the bottoms that tastes of fever
> And the yellow river rolling forever. . . .[43]

[43]"John Brown's Body," in *Selected Works of Stephen Vincent Benét* (Holt, Rinehart & Winston). Copyright renewed 1955, 1956 by Rosemary Carr Benét. Reprinted by permission of Brandt & Brandt Literary Agents, Inc.

That is an eloquent picture of the old Georgia—the old South. And "The New South?" Men and women have always had dreams of the South. And that is a good thing. If dreams ever stop, life dies.

Ben Hill, one of the truly great of Georgia, was the first to speak of the new South. In one of his moving orations he said: "There was a South of slavery and secession—that South is dead. There is a South of union and freedom—that South, thank God, is living, breathing, growing every hour."[44]

It was this sentiment of Hill's, one of Henry Grady's heroes, which so excited and thrilled the young editor, who was to leave his mark and name on so much of Georgia and the South. He saw there must be factories staining the pastoral skies of the South if that new South was to thrive and prosper and become economically strong. He knew cotton and tobacco were not enough. And, so he dreamed dreams of that "New South." He could see it plain. He said, in one of his best speeches, made at the great Texas Fair in Dallas:

> The South, under the rapid diversification of crops and diversification of industries, is thrilling with new life. As this new prosperity comes to us, it will bring no sweeter thought to me, and to you, my countrymen, I am sure, than that it adds not only to the comfort and happiness of our neighbors, but that it makes broader the glory and deeper the majesty, and more enduring the strength, of the Union which reigns supreme in our hearts. . . .
> As I think of it, a vision of surpassing beauty unfolds to my eyes. I see a South, the home of fifty millions of people, who rise up every day to call from blessed cities, vast hives of industry and of thrift; her countrysides the treasures from which their resources are drawn; her streams vocal with whirring spindles; her valleys tranquil in the white and gold of the harvest; her mountains showering down the music of bells, as her slow-moving flocks and herds go forth from their folds; her rulers honest and her people loving, and her homes happy and their hearthstones bright, and their waters still, and their pastures green, and her conscience clear; her wealth diffused and poor-houses

---

[44]Soon after the Civil War began Ben Hill warned Southerners of "native traitors and immigrant spies," believing patriots should again be "willing to fight and die for their rights." Later Hill argued that "we will join our Northern brethren." *Columbus Daily Times*, 22 February 1865; *Atlanta Constitution*, 29 December 1870 and 24 February 1872; Benjamin H. Hill, Jr., ed., *Senator Benjamin H. Hill of Georgia: His Life, Speeches and Writings* (Atlanta: T. H. P. Bloodworth, 1893) 308-19, 428-31; *New York Times*, 1 September 1877.

empty, her churches earnest and all creeds lost in the gospel. Peace and sobriety walking hand in hand through her borders; honor in her homes; uprightness in her midst; plenty in her fields; straight and simple faith in the hearts of her sons and daughters; her two races walking together in peace and contentment; sunshine everywhere and all the time, and night falling on her generally as from the wings of the unseen dove.[45]

It was a good dream. Grady worked to make it come true. It was his inspiration which brought new factories south. He sparked the Cotton States Exposition and, when the show was done, thrilled to see cotton machinery move into the buildings. "His Georgia" was a balanced one—of industry and agriculture. It was a sound dream.

Many prophets after him proclaimed a "New South." All the while, by fits and starts, by trial and error, a new South was developing—and is developing. The industries come. The cities grow. The farms prosper. Problems come, cities and counties all struggle with the chores which growth brings. We have learned, too, that progress does not mean driving an automobile four times as fast as one of twenty years ago; producing ten times as much goods as did our fathers, or having twice as much population in our cities as a quarter century ago. There must be more than that.

So the South, and Georgia, have maintained an emphasis on the growth of their churches and of the religious life of the people. There are new churches and new factories, new people, new schools.

The Chattahoochee River, too, had its poet—and its dream.[46] Sidney Lanier, in his beautiful and prophetic "Song of the Chattahoochee," looked into the future and saw it turning the wheels of industry.[47] It has come true, that dream of his.

The new South is never done—because it is always a-building. There are the dreamers and planners of today. "Their Georgia," when they achieve it, as they will, assuredly will make the one of today seem primitive and small, as does that struggling Georgia of the days when

---

[45]Joel Chandler Harris, ed., *Life of Henry W. Grady Including His Writings and Speeches* (New York: Cassell Publishing Co., 1890) 115, 120.

[46]See McGill's "Chattahoochee River," in volume 2.

[47]*Poems of Sidney Lanier*, ed. Mary Day Lanier (Athens: University of Georgia Press, 1981) 24-25.

Hill and Grady, watching a new South rise out of the ashes of the old one, fiercely began to proclaim it, and to encourage it on.

The New South? It is here—and equally as true does it lie in the years ahead. And it will always require dreamers, poets, and prophets, along with its material growth.[48]

---

[48]See McGill's "Something of Georgia," "Give Me Georgia," "Introduction to *The Old South*," and articles on Atlanta, in volumes 1 and 2.

6

It Has Happened Here

James Peters, typical, mild-looking, successful rural banker from Manchester, Georgia was speaking.

He stood on the clerk's rostrum in the House of Representatives in Georgia's state capitol. Immediately below him sat the governor of Georgia, Eugene Talmadge. His scowling face was clamped about a long unlit cigar.

He sat near the head of a table. About it sat fifteen men, members of the board of regents of the state's university system. Days before it had been purged of three members who had refused to vote with the governor in a previous meeting. The new members were somewhat nervous and belligerent.

Regent Peters was one of the new members. Customarily, on that board, the new member is quiet for a period of time. On this day which was, of all days, Bastille Day, Regent Peters, sworn in a brief hour before, was running the show.

Before him where semi-annually sit the members of Georgia's House of Representatives, the seats were filled. Above him, in the gallery, the seats were filled.

Reprinted by permission of Mrs. Ralph McGill from *Survey Graphic* 30 (September 1941): 449-53.

The crowd knew what had happened. Also, what would happen. It was history how the governor twice had tried to have Walter D. Cocking, dean of the school of education at the University of Georgia, fired on the charge he had advocated a campus where graduate white and colored students would study the state's educational problems. The statement was alleged to have been made almost two years before at a faculty meeting. One teacher, dismissed from that school and employed in another, had made the charge. More than thirty others, attending the same meeting, did not hear the statement. The dean had denied it.

The governor had tried twice and failed twice. Three regents had been removed. The last vote was eight to seven. On Bastille Day they had come with the three new ones and new "evidence."

The state knew, too, of affidavits made in the last days before the "trial." A representative of the state's gasoline tax department, said one affidavit, had asked a photographer to fake a photograph showing Dean Cocking sitting with Negroes. Another affidavit from Dean Cocking's Negro house servant and yard boy said that he, the boy, had been taken to a tourist camp and told he was in the headquarters of the Ku Klux Klan. There he had been offered a bribe to steal papers from the dean which might have been written by Negro teachers. Or to let them into the house with his key. Finally, he swore, he had been told to sign a typewritten statement which was not given to him to read. A pistol was on a nearby bureau. He signed.

No one ever denied this. None of it appeared in the trial.

On this day Dean Cocking was on trial for the third time. This time the jurors had been changed. With him, also on trial, was Dr. Marvin S. Pittman, president of the South Georgia Teachers' College. The original charge against him had been undue political activity, but that charge was shelved; instead, it was said he, along with Cocking, had sought to promote racial equality.

Hatton Lovejoy, Georgia attorney, appearing for alumni groups of the state university, defended. He asked for time for the gathering of new evidence since the witnesses at the former trial of Dean Cocking had not been called. He had not thought they would be necessary.

The first vote had come. Regent Peters had consulted a typewritten sheet of paper and made the motion that each side would have one hour. The vote was ten to five. The five remaining from the original group of eight to seven were to stand many times that day. No one else was to join them. Always it was ten to five that day.

(All that the crowd knew before it began.)

Regent Peters had begun to speak.

Most of the evidence was from two books, *Brown America*, by Edwin R. Embree, of the Rosenwald Fund, and *Calling America*, a symposium published in the magazine *Survey Graphic* and later republished by Harper.[49]

It has been charged that at Dr. Pittman's school the book *Calling America* was required reading. Dr. Pittman had said he did not know it was in the library and it was not required reading. It heatedly was said to be communistic and to encourage racial equality.

Of *Brown America* it was said that it proposed not merely social equality but intermarriage and the creating of a brown America. Dean Cocking, not at all connected with the Rosenwald Fund, was puzzled as to how it could be evidence against him. The book did not advocate what was charged, but there was no time for discussion. The typewritten schedule was rather exact.

Regent Peters went on.

"Pretty soon the Negro will be wanting to sit in the same seats with us, eat at the same tables with us, and ride in the same train cars with us," declared Regent Peters.

He paused and, looking down at the governor, waited.

"They ain't a-gonna do it," shouted the governor.

The crowd cheered.

Regent Peters went on. The politicians in the crowd were watching him closely, cynically. They knew he was being shown to the crowd, without wraps, as a possible candidate for governor in the event the governor should choose, in 1942, to run for the United States Senate.

Regent Peters slowed down a bit.

"Hit the chair and holler," said the governor.

---

[49]Edwin Rogers Embree, *Brown America: The Story of a New Race* (New York: Viking Press, 1931); Embree, *Brown Americans: The Story of a Tenth of the Nation* (New York: Viking Press, 1943); *Calling America: The Challenge of Democracy Reaches Over Here* (New York: Harper and Brothers, 1939).

It went on and on. The crowd was about divided, shocked, angry, and partisan.

Regent Peters hesitated, fumbling for a word.

"Go ahead, they are listening," said the governor.

The show went on.

Now and then there was testimony of a sort. Witnesses came. The president of the university, Harmon Caldwell, stood with his men. Willis Sutton, superintendent of Atlanta's city schools, testified for Dr. Pittman, saying that if the state of Georgia did not want men like him it was in a bad way.

It was a bit ironic. There had been a flurry by the governor in the weeks before this Bastille Day hearing in which "furriners" had been castigated by the governor. Cocking, from Iowa, was a "furriner." Pittman, from Mississippi, and the son of a Confederate veteran, also was damned as a "furriner" and as promoting a meeting at which whites and colored had met together. The Rosenwald Fund and anyone even remotely connected with it, were damned as favoring "equality."

They came and went. It was not a tense meeting. News reporters had seen the schedule in Regent Peters's hand. It had been known for days what the verdict would be. The governor had announced what it would be ten days before the "trial."

It would have been a pleasant farce, if one could fail to note and feel the vicious undertones. It would have been downright humorous if one could have forgot that it was not just a hearing about the jobs of two men. One might have laughed out loud at it had one not known that this was not just the trial of two men on charges which had no sustaining evidence. It might have been dismissed as political had it not gone so deep.

It was, viewed from one angle, a sort of Gilbert and Sullivan opera, yet from another angle it was a dirty cloud on the skies. It was ironically humorous, even to the defendants, to know that on the night before the hearing a caucus dinner had been held. From that had come the typewritten schedule for the majority to follow.

There was to be, later on, loud laughter. That was when Regent L. W. (Chip) Robert, former assistant secretary of the United States Treasury, stood up and from his pocket produced a typewritten resolution of thanks to the governor for ridding the university of the two men.

Before that act there was some more of "Nigger! Nigger!" some more of the threat to white supremacy, some more talk about your daughter going to school on the same campus as a Negro. No one had advocated all this. It was the old familiar, phoney formula, used for almost half a century by Tom Heflin and others to maintain themselves in office.

It was not all one way on the floor. Part of the crowd cheered the five regents who kept standing up each time the typewritten resolution called for a vote. Now and then this caused a bit of a row. The people saw then, for the first time, the state's new secret police. Men in plain clothes, officers, tried to quiet some of the demonstrations.

Cocking and Pittman were allowed a brief denial and a brief affirmation of and a plea for democracy.

But, at last, Regent Peters had hit the chair for the last time and hollered for the last time. For the last time, that day at least, the vote had been ten to five.

The last line on the typewritten sheet had been reached.

Regent Robert arose, somewhat sheepishly, assuming dignity, and read his resolution praising a verdict arrived at before the hearing. The big-business man, holding millions in government contracts, and with a large state bill collected, had come through.

The two men were dismissed from the university system.

What an almost unanimous roll call of the state's newspapers was to call a "legal lynching," had been accomplished. The newspapers were to keep it up, too, to the great surprise of many. That so many of the weekly newspapers took it up was to cause some worry at the capitol. It was to bring forth a radio speech from the governor and inflammatory editions of his personal political publication.

Three more men were fired from the university system a day later. It was easy then. They were fired for three casual reasons. The governor didn't need reasons.

The whole show was, as everyone knew, not just the trial of two teachers. The farcical trial, the unsupported, unrelated evidence, the typewritten sheet of paper, the deliberate arousing of racial prejudices in a state which had been working hard at cooperation and which had been getting results—all the show sprang from something deeper. The attack on the Rosenwald Fund and the indiscriminate slurs on any who had received one of its fellowships was not merely because it had given money to Negro education in the South. (And more to white education.) It was also an expression of poorly concealed anti-Semitism.[50]

All of them were the chills, the fever, the rash, the high blood pressure, the coated tongue, the sore throat which the doctor finds in sick patients. All were symptoms.

It is best always to begin at the beginning. But, here, it is not easy to find the beginning.

It is easy enough to find the beginnings of the actual "lynching." But it goes deeper.

Before the dictator can strut his not always brief hour upon the stage, someone must build the stage.

Among the ghostly hands which pulled the rope at the lynching were those that had written the freight rates and the tariffs which were to keep the South a tributary section.

The rest of the nation has been very tolerant and easy about the South. They have laughed at the Scopes trial in Dayton, at Heflin, at Bilbo, at Talmadge. They were immensely amused by Huey Long.

Those who work in the South; those who have fought all these men and all they stand for, have long been disturbed by this carefree attitude of the rest of the nation where the South is concerned. The newspaper men and the honest business and professional men of Louisiana knew Huey Long was no clown long before the rest of the nation learned it. They know that the nation which has kept the South a tributary section helped create the lacks and wants which make up the soil in which fascism flourishes. They all are children of the nation, these Heflins, Bilbos, Talmadges, Longs.[51]

Those who work in the South, who work for the South, know that all these things, racial lynchings, chasing off after promises, all this cruelty, spring from the same soil, economic fear. The black man crowds

---

[50]In 1937, because of a series of articles on farm tenancy and sharecropping, McGill won a Rosenwald fellowship that enabled him to "go to Scandinavia where I diligently visited, lived with, and wrote about the farm marketing problems and methods of small farmers." *Atlanta Constitution*, 9 June 1948. Racists criticized McGill for receiving this fellowship.

[51]See Cal M. Logue and Howard Dorgan, eds., *The Oratory of Southern Demagogues* (Baton Rouge: Louisiana State University Press, 1981).

the white man. The eroded fields of small farms give up their boys and girls to come to town and to crowd those who already work there. The poor whites and the poor Negroes resent one another, both wanting the same jobs and food.

One cannot blame them for listening to promises. They have so little.

One cannot be puzzled at their following a Talmadge.[52]

Hitler, like Talmadge, Long, Bilbo, and all the others, arose out of economic failures and poverty, and out of a people with the lacks and wants, despair and doubt, which they produce.

We know it can happen here. The people of Louisiana, of Georgia, and other states, know it has happened here. In Louisiana they already tremble lest the hungry, dispossessed ones fed by Huey Long's hand, turn back to the apostles of Long yet out of jail. There are signs that they may.

The reform moves do not meet the problem. The Talmadges, the Longs, the Bilbos are so much more resourceful and, usually, much more courageous than their foes.

So, Georgia has seen it happen here. And Georgia moves on. There are courageous newspapers, courageous teachers, writers, citizens. They are frightened, now and then, by the ruthless determination of the forces loose in the South and the nation. They wonder how much of a national tie-up there is, how deep go these movements of the demagogues in the South and of all the others in the nation who suppress education, who would burn books, who use slander and smears; who whisper or shout openly anti-Semitic propaganda; who foster a revival of the Klan as a political instrument? How close is the tie-up and who backs them?

No one takes enough time with the red-necked sharecropper, moving his pitiful family and his pitiful belongings each year, going to hear brother Norris preach the good, old-time religion, seeking a better cabin, a better crop, a better landlord, wishing all the while for something easy, something better; looking up to be fed. He has courage and

---

[52]See William Anderson, *The Wild Man From Sugar Creek: The Political Career of Eugene Talmadge* (Baton Rouge: Louisiana State University Press, 1975).

he has convictions. They are often dangerous convictions. But he has them. All this tribe—Bilbo, Long—all had handy convictions.

It is not difficult to understand this soul sickness which listens to promises. Deep-seated, long-standing political and social inequities have created a soul-sickness which no one has solved.

The stage, on which a dictator may strut and from which he may promise food and a surcease from this sickness brought on by lacks and poverty, is plain to see. Its every plank may be named.

The gallows on which Cocking and Pittman were hanged is stark and clear.

Georgia, with other Southern states, remains one of the raw product states, with the accompanying low income which raw product production produces.

The state's per capita income and property values are about half those of the nation.

About two-thirds of the population of Georgia earns its living from the soil, including the timber which grows from it. About two-thirds of that population owns no land. About half that landless two-thirds lacks any tenancy contracts and moves each year.

The average annual income of this farm and lumber group is, across a period of years, about one hundred dollars less than the average individual farm income in the United States. If there are five in a family, and it is interesting to note how often there are five or more, this means there is a family income five hundred dollars less than that of the average farm family of five in the nation.

There are few doctors in the rural section. The politicians fret with proposals such as refusing to admit any student from out of state or with promoting another medical school. They never think that the graduates will keep on leaving the state and leaving the depressed rural areas alone because they, too, must eat and the free samples of vitamins they receive are not enough.

They never think that the reason the depressed rural areas have no doctor is because the people aren't able to pay for them and won't be, no matter if they build a medical school in each section of the state.

Annually there is deploring in all southern states that so many of her young men and women, educated in state universities at the expense of the state, leave the state for work. The legislatures worry themselves with futile thinking about some plan to make them stay at home even though there be no jobs.

The men with skills do the same thing. They leave, going to states with greater industrial developments.

According to the 1930 census almost a million Georgians had left their native state. Only 300,071 had moved in.

The result of all this has been that Georgia, and other southern states, long have found themselves with two high-dependency groups: young people who must be educated and old people who must be supported. Coupled with this are low incomes and low property values.

This has produced another plank in the platform, another prop on the gallows.

Revenue is sorely needed, always. The South is faithful to education. It spends, on education, a larger proportionate share of its income than any other state. It has so little to spend. Today education costs more. And no one can be politically elected who does not promise more and more generous old-age pensions. Business concerns—successful business concerns—literally have been forced into politics.

There must be more and more revenue. The business concerns which are well managed and which produce profits are the targets. They have been forced, and the realist cannot blame them, to buy protection by contributing to political campaigns. They obtain a political, financial interest in people elected to office. It is their only chance for survival. They take it. A poll tax, which is retroactive up to fifteen dollars, is a stumbling block to voting among the low-income farm groups, and also among the low- and medium-income city groups.

The summer political campaigns, especially the campaigns for governor (after 1942 to come only every four years), are the social seasons for the poorest ones of the state. For a whole summer they are given barbecues, free barbecues. The speakers lambaste one another. Names are called. Characters cheerfully and gleefully are blackened. The smear campaigns grow in intensity, the crowds love it.

The landless, hungry, shiftless, half-sick ones become important in the summer campaigns. Many have their poll taxes paid. They suddenly find themselves in front of men standing on platforms promising—promising—the land flowing with milk and honey. A politician might seek to interpret this as saying these people are "bums." This is not to be so interpreted. These are good people, of good stock. If they are landless, hungry, and half sick, it is because the system has made them so. The Farm Security Administration has shown in the few hundred cases it has been able to reach that they have the initiative and the ability to rehabilitate themselves. Only a few have had the opportunity.

If they lift up their eyes who can blame them?

(Does it still seem easy to say that all one must do is to say to this curious South that really, it must quit lynching Negroes, quit disfranchising voters? That it really, after all, must come to its senses and get rid of its foolish demagogues? Does the problem still seem that simple?)

Now and then they provide some entertainment during the off-season.

Georgia's governor brought down to Georgia Dr. Frank Norris. Now and then Georgia's governor goes up to Detroit "to do a little preaching" for Dr. Norris. Dr. Norris denies any pro-KKK connection. He merely goes about preaching the Lord's word in the old-fashioned way.

Georgia's governor had him down recently, preaching in each district. The governor sat on the pulpit platform and listened while the laborer in the Lord's vineyard told the crowd they'd nail the hides of newspaper editors to the fence; assured them they must defend their heritages. It was the old-fashioned religion. The governor wrote about how pleased it made him to hear "the great truths of the Bible expounded in the good, old-fashioned way which our fathers knew."

Georgia's governor has aspirations. He is no fool. He is smart and he is shrewd. He was an ardent admirer of Huey Long. He obtains the support of businessmen because he promises them—and delivers to them—a balanced budget and no new taxes. And how he can promise and sway the ones who love him best—the "wool-hat boys"—eternally waiting for political promises, bigger and better!

He found the state in debt after four years of administration by his predecessor who gave to the state a progressive program but lacked the ability to finance and to direct, and whose friends helped destroy him and his program.

Georgia's governor, elected not without opposition, but with the support of business and almost all county machines, forced through the legislature a finance plan which allowed him to do what no other governor has been empowered to do—take money from the rich highway department, or from any other department with a surplus, and use it where he willed. The gasoline taxes, heretofore sacrosanct, enabled him to make a really fine showing in paying off the teachers and reducing indebtedness. His predecessor could have financed his program with similar power and with banishment of his "friends."

The point is that Georgia's governor, like others before him and like others who will come after him in the South and in any other states where there are landless, dispossessed farmers and depressed city groups, rose to unusual power out of a state plagued by debt, by despair, and by doubt and confusion.

Only twelve percent of the adult population elected him, eighteen percent of the white adults.

The average Georgia child leaves school in the fourth grade.

More than half the state's farm population are tenants and share-croppers; of which half are landless, moving from year to year in futile and pitiful search for a better cabin, a better crop, a better landlord.

All this has happened in a state which once was a leader in progress. In this state was established the first Sunday School and the first orphan asylum in the United States. In it was chartered the first state university. In it was established the first women's college in the world, Wesleyan. A graduate of its state university was the first to use ether as an anaesthetic. It was the first state to adopt legislation permitting and allowing married women to own and control their own property, a shockingly progressive piece of legislation at the time of its passing. It was a glowing, gallant history.

When the Civil War was fought and done, there arose the voices of democracy. Henry Grady died, as they said, "literally loving the nation into peace." General John B. Gordon, the general who had covered Robert E. Lee's last retreat, campaigned for governor with a plank for Negro education in his platform. There were voices speaking out.

Even as they spoke the planners of economic inequality were busy building fences. For seventy-five years that inequality has persisted and, as the South well knows, political democracy has been a mockery. It is almost impossible to convince the rest of the nation, even today, that the tributary South is sick because of roots which go back to the writing of freight rates and the tariff laws for a conquered section of the nation. But it is so. The roots go back.

7

Hate
at Cut Rates

C ertainly the Confederate dames were in a tizzy.
And while there likely was no truth in it, a late passerby at the
state capitol grounds said that he distinctly saw the bronze jowls
of General John B. Gordon quivering, while just a few yards away the
iron figure of the late huckster of hate, Tom Watson, was applauding
vigorously.[53] But, if the sheeted dead were not out of their grates gib-
bering in the streets, it was a fact that the unreluctant grand dragon,
Doc Sam Green, of the Ku Klux Klan, was up on his feet, rocking back
and forth on his rounded heels, speaking out loud for tolerance and the
Christian ideal.

If it had not been so sordid, and if there hadn't been the usual
amount of frustrated fear which is the corrosive element watering down
Southern community action, it would have been downright humorous.

But it wasn't.

Atlanta, Georgia, and the somewhat startled citizens of the city and
state suddenly found themselves in the middle of a cut-rate war in the
hate racket, in which a license to hate could be bought for three dollars

---

Manuscript provided by Mrs. Ralph McGill, from the McGill papers, now at
Emory University, Atlanta, probably written in 1946.

[53]See McGill's essay on Watson in *Southern Encounters: Southerners of Note in Ralph
McGill's South*, ed. Calvin M. Logue (Macon GA: Mercer University Press, 1983).

cash—and of this, mind you, under the flag of the late Confederacy with a drunken thunderbolt design sewed right in the middle of the Stars and Bars.

It is believed that it was the cutting of the hate rate from the Ku Klux fee of ten dollars to a mere pittance of three dollars, which brought Doc Green rushing out of his klavern screaming for tolerance and the abolition of sin, but this is an age of cynicism.

What had happened was that an organization, chartered last August by an uninquisitive secretary of state as "The Columbians" explosively was out in a frank imitation of Hitler's brownshirt uniforms, publicly mauling innocent and terrified Negroes around and saying the Jews were next. Not only that, but they had as their platform the taking over of the Atlanta city government, by political organization and intimidation, in six months, and the United States government within two years. (Today we fly against England—tomorrow the world.)

The brown-shirted street fighters were their police force and the Atlanta police force had best mind its manners, said Fuehrers Homer Loomis, late of Park Avenue, and Emory Burke, Montgomery, Alabama born, but more lately of the German Bund affiliates in New York. This was just too much, just as Doc Green had said, and so the confused police force finally took down four of the brownshirts, with their thunderbolt emblem on each shoulder. They posed for pictures, mugging with the hard Hitler-stare, and the resemblance to the clean-cut bully boys who used to be seen in the Berlin newsreels of 1938-1939 was startling.[54]

The arrest had taken place on Garibaldi Street, in a section of Atlanta once "nice," but now just a frowzy and down-at-the-heel slum in which a lot of persons whose luck had run out held on to homes in which they had lived for thirty years, watching the neighborhood deteriorate. It already had become a mixed section. That is to say, Negroes had bought and rented some of the houses. But, along this block of Garibaldi Street there were no Negroes.

On this afternoon a Negro man and his wife, bearing the Anglo-Saxon name of Mr. and Mrs. Frank Jones, arrived in Garibaldi Street

---

[54]In April 1938 McGill heard Hitler speak in Vienna in a railway station.

with a truckload of poor furniture and high hopes. A white man had sold them a house, telling them it was in a Negro neighborhood.

They found a placard on the door with the red thunderbolt design in the center and a warning from the Columbian organization that it was a white neighborhood. It wasn't, but that didn't matter to the Columbians.

True to the Nazi blueprint, there had been block organizations, and in front of the house was R. L. Whitman, block leader, who carried his 16-month-old daughter who also was in uniform with the thunderbolt patch on her shoulder. Three others waited while Whitman badgered the Negroes.

Notified by an anonymous source, police arrived on the scene, led by Chief M. A. Hornsby and Captain of Detectives Buck Weaver, arrived on the scene. Chief Hornsby walked up to the nearest Columbian, Jack Price, former prizefighter and wrestler, and asked: "What are you doing here?"

"Protecting white people."

"What business is that of yours?"

"The police won't do it. The people asked us to help them."

The four were pretty tough and Buck Weaver finally blurted out, "Are they going to police the town or us?" That did it. The four were arrested.

"Move on in," said the chief to the frightened Negroes.

"We don't want to bother nobody," said Jones, glancing about, scared in the presence of the two chief fears of the average Southern Negro—"The Law" which he knows is so often quite careless with a Negro's rights, and "The Ku Klux," under which he lists any, and all, orders which make a profession of "hating niggers."

"I was livin' in two rooms on Davis street," Jones said. "My boy, Eddie, he come home from the army and moved in with his wife and baby on me. I had to move and this white man sold me this place sayin' it was all right." Chief Hornsby, who teaches Sunday School, expressed an un-Sunday School opinion of the white real estate man.

The sordid side of the whole business was the exploitation of poor whites and colored by unscrupulous real estate men, some of them believed to be working with, and through, the Columbian leaders, providing a financial "cut-back." The illiterate poor always have grievances, many of them just. And they almost never have anyone to whom they can go.

The housing shortage, which has even Homer Loomis "Privileged Rich" speaking in querulous tones, has brewed more bitterness and resentment in the white-collar class than anything that has happened to it before. For the illiterate poor, driven back to the worst of the slums, there is no place to go and no one with an answer. Until the Columbians, or similar organizations, come along saying it is all the fault of the "nigger." And the rich, especially the rich Jews.

The racket worked in the housing had all the moral ethics of a man-eating shark. A poor, illiterate family, with a small, shabby house, half paid for across long years of pinching quarters and dimes for the monthly payments, would be approached and told that a Negro had bought the house next to them. "It was just like the damned, black bastards, but that's the way they were." That made the white man's house worthless, but they'd be glad to pay him a sum, or put it down as a first payment on another, and more costly house, just as a favor, of course, as one loyal Anglo-Saxon to another.

No Negro had bought the house next door, but if their scheme worked, a Negro would be sold the one just obtained and they would then be set to work the scheme on the rest of the neighborhood. Once a sale or two was made and Negroes had put up cash, or a large down payment, and were ready to move in, the Columbians would go to work. When the Negro family arrived the Columbians would be on hand. The neighbors would be stirred up. "Things" would happen, at night, if the family moved in. A little touch of dynamite worked well here and there, according to confessions of those who later turned state's evidence. The terrorized Negro would then be approached by the white real estate dealer who would, as a favor, buy the house back at—of course—a much less figure than the Negro had paid for it. The chief's un-Sunday School remark was in order.

Meanwhile, the patrol loaded in the four brownshirts and departed amid jeers by the occupants. At the Columbian headquarters, 82 Bartow Street, handsome Homer Loomis was excited and busy calling up extra "police" or street fighters. He had a file of members. On the wall was his "battle map," a map of Atlanta showing "infiltration" by Negroes.[55] "We're not a secret order," said Loomis to reporters.

> We're open and political. We're a national movement, rising up to speak for the masses, and to organize them and show them how they can take control. The masses are held down by the privileged rich. They work and slave all week for the bare essentials of life, and maybe a beer or two on Saturday night.
>
> We are putting on a show to help tell them their own story, that they, the white, Anglo-Saxon people, are the best people on earth and entitled to the best on earth. We are political. We are going to show them how to take control of the government—first, a neighborhood, then the whole city, then the state government, and finally, the national government.
>
> Two races can't live together in this country. We've got to send the Negro back to Africa, get every one of them out of America. As for the Jews, they are never Americans, always Jews. They are not God's chosen people. The Anglo-Saxons are that. Exterminate them or send them out of the country. Palestine isn't big enough. But we must find a place. The damned liberals are always fighting for the Negroes and the Jews. We must send them out, too.
>
> Any mass movement must use mass tactics. Hitler appealed to the little people; so does our movement. Most of them lead dull lives, work, sleep, and work. But they have a lust for power if you can awaken it. That's what we are going to do. We have appeals from all over this country and we will set up extra units as soon as this one is organized. You've got to build up their egos. So many of them don't want to share.

Emory Burke, a better rabble-rouser than Loomis whose two terms at Princeton, 1932 and 1933, where he was dropped for failure to attend classes, made him a little too pedantic, sat by and kept nodding his head. "We are not the Ku Klux Klan," said Burke, "We are not even members, although I once was a member. We are going to be forty times worse, or more aggressive, than the Klan. It's political and wants to get fat on local graft. We are political, but we are a national movement for the masses. We aim to rid America of the Jews and Negroes and to put the rich in their places. This country belongs to the people.[56]

---

[55]For a related discussion of the "Atlanta wall" between black and white neighborhoods, see interview with McGill concerning his 1963 trip to Africa, in volume 2.

[56]See John Bartlow Martin, *The Deep South Says "Never"* (New York: Ballantine Books, 1957); Neil R. McMillen, *The Citizens' Council* (Urbana: University of Illinois Press, 1971).

Loomis, breaking in with his hysterical falsetto voice and slight lisp, walked up and down like a ham Shakespearean actor, half-shouting:

There are only two solutions to the nigger question—separation or amal-gamation (this is the title of [Theodore] Bilbo's book). . . . The niggers are making one advance after another. . . . Pretty soon our children will have to go to school with the little black devils. . . . If you give the nigger political equality, over one-third of our state legislature will be nigger and then they will do away with the Jim Crow laws. . . . This very night white men are in bed with colored women, bringing on more mulattoes. . . . The rich people are trying to hold you down. . . . They try to tell you there are two sides to this question. The Columbian Party will see to it that we have separation. The Columbian Party is a white man's party working for the interest of the white men of the nation. . . . We'll fight for a greater share of things for the masses. . . . The Jew movies are teaching our kids to be gangsters and to drink. . . . The Commies in the U.S. are represented by the niggers and Jews. . . . The Jew Reds are trying to get us to mix our white blood with nigger blood in order to weaken us. They call us a hate movement, but the truth is they haven't the guts to use the word *hate* themselves. They are the real haters. . . . We say there are some things which ought to be hated.

The rich power company forces you to ride on street cars where big, fat, stinkin' niggers force themselves between you and your wife. . . . The dollar and the newspapers will control you only so long as you let them. . . . The rich men's ideas are opposed to yours. . . . "The dear nigger has a side," they say. But in the U.S. there are only about 25,000 Jews and 5,000 rich people, whereas there are between 150 to 200 million other people, and it is votes that count. If they will listen to us, you can control America completely in six months. If we get on the streets in our uniforms and get into a fight with the police, niggers, and Jews, and they start slugging back, taking away our rights and putting us in jail, you'll know we are fighting.

A psychologist, or a research psychiatrist, would without doubt greet the Columbians with all the glee of an archæologist stumbling upon the lost mines of Solomon. The two leaders, Burke and Loomis, will do for illustration, although most of the members, recruited from behind the counters of hamburger heavens and pearl-diving jobs in cheap restaurants; picked up from the wandering, discontended kids waiting for the draft to get them; attracted from the ranks of veterans of the recent war who just somehow can't buckle down to work, or who have delusions of persecution and mistreatment, offer a rich field of research.

To the query, "How do they get that way?", one may answer that all obviously arrive through the same psychological channels of lack of self-confidence, frustration, and what the mental scientists refer to as "transfer of blame." Burke, born of a poor family in Alabama, became embittered in high school when he couldn't go on to college and saw that some of his rich classmates could. That many other classmates went on and did jobs of waiting on tables, delivering laundry, and other chores to pay for a college education, didn't seem to come within his ken. One feature of all of them is an almost total lack of first-hand knowledge about a job of work.

Walling Keith, now editor of the Cleveland (Tennessee) *Daily Banner*, recalls Burke from his old days on the *Montgomery Advertiser.* "Burke," he wrote in a personal column on 7 December, "was regarded as a screwball. He used to visit the offices of the *Advertiser* when I worked there and sing the praises of Benito Mussolini and Adolf Hitler. That was back in the Hoover depression era. He was a young 'intellectual' then, and fanatically devoted to what was a new rod for most of us on the paper—Fascism."

Burke wandered the country in the depression days, going from one New Deal transient camp to another, and for a time, joining up with one or two vaguely remembered Fascist organizations in California. "Commercialism, commercialism," he says of those days. "I hated seeing money values put on men. It tore my soul. In those days, though," he says, "I had some Jewish friends."

Loomis, now thirty-two, was a New York playboy good enough to rate the gossip columns. Son of Homer Loomis, Sr., with a Park Avenue residence, a Wall Street law office, and an interesting credit rating which makes some cynical persons believe the money Junior receives comes from someone other than papa, Homer was a card, as they say. Back in 1935 Homer says he went on a bender during a wedding and woke up next morning married to a girl he didn't know, a Miss Laura Hampton Hover. Laura had the marriage annulled. In her papers she said that on their one-day honeymoon Homer had her sit in bed, with all the lights out but one, and read a horror story in which a lunatic murders his wife.

In 1937 Homer was in the saloon gossip notes. He and some friends staged a sit-down strike at the Club Bali, wearing pajamas. That same year Homer went to the altar again, this time with Miss Mary Ellen

Plaintiff, daughter of a well-known family, the Gaston Plaintiffs, an association of Henry Ford's.

Now a resident of Florida, and divorced, Mrs. Loomis wants to forget it all. She lives quietly, recalling that Homer lived off her money, never had a job, boozed a lot, abused his two children and gave them lessons in his atheism.

Homer, after his past was revealed by the *Atlanta Constitution*, tried to explain it to a Columbian meeting. Some of the poor female members who had borne four or five kids, washed clothes, scrubbed, cooked, and nursed for them and a husband, stared at Homer as if he were a resident of Mars when he said, in his mild falsetto: "I used to tell my wife that we must dismiss the governess and get close to the children." But, he wowed them when he spoke of the idle rich, living in luxury and eating tons of rich food, while they, the masses, the real Anglo-Saxon inheritors of the earth, starved and toiled for little money.

Burke and Loomis obviously sopped up some of the flood of Nazi propaganda which was flooding the country in the thirties. "Hitler had a lot of good ideas," says Loomis.

Loomis, who served with the Second Armored Division, refuses to talk about it. It is something he will not go into, although he declares he has an honorable discharge. "You know," he said, once, in his one brief departure from refusal to talk about his service, "the Jews aren't afraid. I saw some who fought well." His second wife says, in the divorce proceedings, that he joined the army in 1944 to postpone or avoid a lawsuit brought by her against him.

Loomis's attempts to affect a Southern accent were good for a laugh on occasion. But he could be tough and members feared him more than Burke. Burke apparently admired him, but never quite trusted him. Loomis was "rich." "I had to fight my way up from the bottom," he said. He is, incidentally, the same age as Loomis. It is known he was associated with Ernest Elmhurst and other bundists and fascists.

It was, finally, the war and God, which and who, got the organization into trouble. Pounding in and out of their headquarters were a number of young men in storm-trooper uniforms, but of the lot two were favorites of the fuehrers. One was seventeen-year-old Ralph Childers, who was given a medal for attacking a Negro on assignment. The other was Lanier Waller, twenty-one. Childers had quit school at thirteen. Working at a hamburger joint, he heard Columbians talking and joined. Waller, raised in an orphan's home in Sherman, Texas, ran away at fourteen and joined the Marines. He fought well at Guadalcanal and Bougaineville. He came out of the war with malaria and nervous fatigue.

It was Loomis's talk against God and his admiration for Hitler which began to turn these two. Waller was willing to hate "niggers," as part of his Texas background, but he didn't even know any Jews. Childers didn't either. Waller was proud of his war record, but Loomis kept insisting he would have done better to be on the other side.

One day Waller asked Loomis to swear to how money had been expended. "Swear on this Bible," said Waller, picking up a Bible which in some manner was in the headquarters.

"I'd rather swear on a telephone book," Loomis told him. "It has truer names in it."

Waller was fearful of a heavenly bolt.

By this time, in the life of the Columbians, there were investigators and newspaper men who had managed to get in under assumed names. Some of these persuaded Waller and Childers that Loomis was taking the Columbians the wrong way. Waller and Childers left them and later made sworn statements involving, and turning up, an old well digger who had sold dynamite for use in bombing "nigger houses." Indictments and arrests followed.

Some members began to leave, many of them turning state's evidence, and revealing all the plans to take over government, to hang, or at least "beat up" the editor of the *Atlanta Constitution* and an assistant state's attorney general, Dan Duke, and to "take over" the government of Atlanta. Some of the members are convinced they meant to reveal all anyhow, had not their plans been exposed. They still hate "niggers," but Loomis and Burke being against God was too much. God's attitude on the race question apparently remains unknown.

Both Burke and Loomis are disappointed in Governor Eugene Talmadge of Georgia, who was waiting to take office when their tribulations began. They both admit they came to Georgia because of his election in which his racial position and his anti-Negro platform was paramount. They expected to be welcome. They sent out feelers, which went unanswered. Governor Talmadge has never been anti-Jewish, and he is not in favor of sending the Negroes to Africa, not with farm labor needed as it is. Also he does not at all wish to exterminate the rich, idle or otherwise. Governor Talmadge always has refused to condemn the Ku Klux Klan and it earnestly supported him. He has never joined because of three Catholic friends, but he approves it.

Therefore, the Columbians had their feelers rebuffed, although they cling to a hope things may be different later on. They won't be. Talmadge wants no part of them for several reasons, one of them being their psychopathic violence. Their avowed intention to be "forty times worse than the Klan" did not endear them to the Klan or its friends. So, they will have no influence in the Talmadge administration.

The Columbians have come upon lean days.

They attracted national attention and, for a time, had there been any depression, discontent might have become a threat. But there wasn't. Loomis and Burke insist they have only begun to fight.

They have, meanwhile, served again to expose the real threat—the existence of poor, inarticulate, and uneducated people with legitimate grievances and no agency or persons to whom to go; the growing pressure on the Southern Negro who still is at the end of the line in housing, education, health, and plain simple justice. Until something is done about all of this, there will always be, not merely in Georgia, but the whole country, a field for the hate racketeers to harvest.

8

How It Happened Down in Georgia

tlanta—it was well before dawn on the morning of Tuesday, January 14, when the first old car rattled up and parked on a side street near the state capitol. Its occupants climbed out, stiff from a four-hour ride. They joined a shadowy group waiting near the steps. By then, other lights from arriving cars began to pierce the foggy mountain mists of the four converging streets.

Herman had sent for them. They liked Herman all right. He was a good boy. But they had come because of the thin-faced man with the unruly lock of hair whom they had seen lying in state beneath the rotunda of the capitol on December 22 and had buried on a hilltop near his farm in McRae, Georgia, the following day. Ten thousand of them had trudged past his coffin where he lay in the neat blue suit that was to have been his inaugural garment for a fourth term as Governor of Georgia. Hundreds of them had gone on to the funeral the next day. Curious crowds had watched that cortege pass, with the snarling, shrilling sirens of the highway patrol escort providing a threnody that rose and fell among the hills and valleys along the way.

It was for him they had come, for old Gene, even though the word had come from Herman. Herman Talmadge was all right. He showed

Reprinted by permission of Mrs. Ralph McGill and the *New Republic*, 27 January 1947. Copyright 1947, Harrison-Blaine of New Jersey, Inc.

all the signs of growing up to be a fine man like his papa, they said, talking there in the morning. But it was for Eugene Talmadge, his thin lips set in cold smile down beneath the soil at McRae, that they had left their beds and walked or driven, many of them for great distances, to Atlanta to see that Herman didn't get mistreated.[57]

The legislature was going to elect Herman governor in his papa's place. And that was, they argued, right and proper. They had voted for old Gene, but since the Lord, in his infinite wisdom, had called him to glory, Herman would do.

They didn't quite understand it. There was a legal argument. That was for the lawyers they reckoned. They stood around talking as a cold, damp, gray broke over the square, beading the iron face of Tom Watson's statue with dew. The drops clung as the sweat once did when he had that right arm flung up and the words rushing through the frothy lips like a torrent over rocks. But, they allowed, there were lawyers on their side to match anything the other side had. Except, of course, the other side had the sweet-talking, Philadelphia-lawyer type who could rob you blind and yet give you a sugar tit to make you satisfied until it was too late to be otherwise.

They came for the next two hours. They walked from the slum sections and the boardinghouse areas in the city. They came from farm and town. They were to fill the galleries as soon as the capitol opened. They were to stand about the corridors when there were no more seats, spitting, talking, arguing, ready to fight if Herman sent word he was being robbed.

They were to stay there for almost 24 hours, until in the late watches of the next morning a weary, harassed, confused legislature, sitting in joint session, had elected Herman Talmadge—the only son of the late Eugene Talmadge—governor of Georgia in a scene which was a mixture of legal red tape and Graustarkian drama, a coup d'etat out of a fiction-writer's plot.

Old Gene had won in the first primary election in which Negroes had voted in Georgia, having boldly announced at the outset that he did not want, and would not have, a Negro vote. He counted on the

---

[57]See William Anderson, *The Wild Man From Sugar Creek: The Political Career of Eugene Talmadge* (Baton Rouge: Louisiana State University Press).

[county] unit system to nominate him and he beamed his campaign on the rural counties, which was his custom. He used to boast he never wanted to carry a county with a streetcar in it. But this time he beamed it even more heavily and he set out to pick up what other votes he could from those who feared that white supremacy was in the balance.[58]

He knew he would get two-thirds of the industrialists. He knew that with the CIO against him, the older and more politically potent AFL group would help. He knew the Negro issue would fetch the textile workers to him, even though they hated him after he broke their AFL-supported strike in 1936.

He was an Ishmael, with his hand against that of every man who disagreed with him. But most of all he counted on the rural counties. The backbone of his strength was by no means all wool-hat boys. There were plenty of smalltown bankers, warehouse keepers and owners and big farmers who had always been with him. And there were others who came with him for the first time because they had Negro majorities in their counties. And they saw these Negroes organized and instructed and they knew it would be a bloc vote, just as old Gene was telling them on the radio. No amount of newspaper argument that supremacy, white or otherwise, could be maintained only on a basis of justice and fairness was able to stand against what they could see.

But it was the wool-hat boys who were his darlings and his lambs. They would follow him to hell, or march off a towering cliff if he ordered it, even as legend had it the dark soldiers of Christophe did in faraway Haiti. The phrase *wool-hat* comes from the pioneer days when a man could take a square of felt, soak it well and then pull and shape it about his head. Dried in the sun and trimmed with the sheep shears, it became a hat.

The wool-hat boys are a part not merely of Georgia politics, but of every Southern state's politics. There is something of China and her problem about the deep, cotton South. Feudalism is not quite gone from wide reaches of it. Nor was it ever the dreamy idyll of enchanting acres

---

[58]See Cal M. Logue and Howard Dorgan, *The Oratory of Southern Demagogues* (Baton Rouge: Louisiana State University Press, 1981).

and perpetual afternoon, of magnolias and mint juleps stirred with a silver spoon.[59]

The industrial revolution has come but slowly, being greatly resisted in some regions and towns. Since 1865 there have always been hunger and not enough jobs. There has always been too much pressure on the land. A feudal slavery was exchanged for a feudal cropper and tenant system. For generations the crowded hillsides have been giving up their young men and women, who come into the mills suspicious and afraid, knowing there are more young men and women from the other fields waiting to take the jobs.

Cotton has been in retreat, and the pace is stepping up. Even with the price of cotton what it is, hardly a small or medium-sized farm is having anything new put on it that isn't paid for by income derived elsewhere. There has been a dramatic turn to livestock, but it has been made by men who earn the money somewhere else.

What the good governors and the reformers and the better element, so-called, always forgot was that nothing very much ever reached down to the wool-hat boy, whether he moved to town or stayed in the country.

The new courthouses, the new main highways, the new hospitals for the insane, the new jails, didn't patch his pants or teach him how to market his small crop. Those improvements didn't make his slab-sided school any better and didn't feed his kids any more. And they didn't build a hospital or put a doctor within his reach.

And when Ellis Arnall came to the capitol and made one of the finest governors Georgia ever had, even he didn't reach them.[60] He reformed the prison system and eliminated the chain gang. He took educational boards out of politics by making them constitutional. He eliminated the pardon racket with a constitutional pardon and parole board. He brought dignity to the office of governor and he astounded the citizens by being very good indeed on the best radio forums.

But the wool-hat boy rarely listened to the radio forums. School reforms at the university didn't feed his hogs, and the feed had gone

---

[59]See Jack Bass and Walter DeVries, *The Transformation of Southern Politics: Social Change and Political Consequence Since 1945* (New York: New American Library, 1977) 136-57.

[60]McGill helped with the Arnall campaign.

higher than a cat's back during the war. The innovations didn't provide any help, and the Negroes had all gone off to the war camps and not worth a damn when they came back, wanting wages on the farm like those they got in town. If his boy got into trouble and went to jail, it was still jail and reform didn't make it home. Also, it was a good deal harder to spring him. The constitutional board was too tough. The reforms didn't reach down. Not many persons say that they didn't, but old Gene did—he saw it plain.

"They talk about the state," he would tell them. "You are the state as much as the sweet-talking big shots in the town, as much as the newspaper columnists talking about democracy and good government. You can't feed your kids democracy and you can't buy pig and chicken feed with it. The newspapers talk like you can put all that fine talk in your kid's lunch box and let him get fat on it. They ain't done nothing for you." And the sad fact was that no one had.

To make matters worse, the foreign devils were taking a hand. And what business was it of theirs anyhow? One of the worst was Henry Wallace, him that killed all the pigs and plowed them under. Imagine that now, and him talking about being a farmer. Not only that, but Henry Wallace and the Yankee magazines are all sold out to the Communists and the Pinks. They are down here telling us what to do and making fun of us for being ignorant as dirt. Why don't they let us alone and clean up the gang killings and the stealing and the poverty in their own backyards? And the same for the newspapermen who try to get compliments from the big-city writers by fouling their own nest.

So, it went on and when the votes were counted Eugene Talmadge had won a great majority of the white votes. While he had got only a few hundred votes from the Negroes who were not fooled by Communist money and who knew their place, and while his total vote was short of his opponent's, he had more than enough county-unit ballots to give him the governorship.

Then on October 19, on vacation at Jacksonville, Florida, a vein hemorrhaged in old Gene's esophagus. Five weeks later, in Atlanta, he was well enough to go home with the knowledge that if he would be quiet and keep a Spartan regime, he would be cured a good while. But there was too much Ishmael in him, or as he said it, "too much Talmadge," and he died early in the morning of December 21. His fourth-term inauguration was set for January 14.

The Talmadge-faction leaders long before had found that in Ellis Arnall's rewriting of the state constitution, much of the old text remained unchanged. One paragraph of the new part said that the governor should serve four years and until his successor was elected and qualified. Another, lifted from the constitution of the old days when the legislature and not the people elected the governor, said that, in the event no person had a majority of the whole vote, the legislature should elect from the two men having the highest number, which two persons should be in life and willing to serve. With Talmadge sick and, as they said, the first man who ever had everyone in the state praying—half that he'd get well and half that he'd die—they worked out a plan. Just as protection they would instruct some of their friends to have a few hundred write-in votes for Herman. And sure enough, as old Gene himself said a few days before the dark messenger came for him, "you boys planned better than you knew."

Son Herman could present to Georgians a good, moral sort of record. He was born at home at dawn on August 9, 1913. He grew up on the farm through high-school years. He was a good boy, his mother says, and learned to shoot and ride and swim. He graduated from the University of Georgia where the Sigma Nu social fraternity received him. He was a better than average student and active in debating. Following his graduation with a law degree from the university, the youngest Talmadge was admitted to the Georgia Bar.

He was married in 1937 to Kathryne Williams, whom he met while both were attending the university. The ceremony was performed in "The Little Church Around the Corner" in New York City. Three years later, Kathryne Talmadge obtained a divorce from the then governor's son on the grounds that he smoked smelly cigars in the house and went away to political meetings when she didn't want him to go. She also charged that her husband nagged her about money and was "cold and indifferent" and fond of sitting at home reading the newspaper. Young Talmadge filed an answer which was withdrawn and stricken from the record the day before the first decree was granted, February 5, 1941.

The following Christmas Eve, Talmadge, then an ensign in the Navy, and blonde Leila Elizabeth Shingler, a University of Georgia sophomore, were married at the Executive Mansion. Young Talmadge was granted a three-day leave for the ceremony. The Talmadges have two children, Herman Eugene, four, and Robert Shingler, ten-months old.

Talmadge spent thirty-two months with the Navy in the Southwest Pacific and was discharged in November 1945, with the rank of lieutenant commander. He served with the Sixth Naval District Charleston and the Third Naval District in New York until February 1942, when he applied for sea duty and was ordered to the Midshipmen's School at Northwestern University. He participated in the invasion of Guadalcanal aboard the USS *Tryon* and served as flag secretary to the commandant of naval forces in New Zealand from June 1943 to April 1944. He was ordered to the USS *Dauphin* as executive officer and participated in various engagements with the Japanese fleet and in the battle of Okinawa. He entered Tokyo Bay on V-J Day. This was the heir apparent and the only one with a war record.

9

Will the South Ditch Truman?

I n revolt, the Democratic party in the South is in somewhat the same state of mind as old Ely Lanier, rural undertaker in South Georgia, the time a tornado blew him, his house and a small stock of caskets into the air.

"It sure didn't comfort me none," he said later, when he had been picked up in a nearby field and his battered frame placed upon a neighbor's feather bed, "to have them three coffins flyin' along with me."

President Harry Truman blew the leadership of the Southern Democrats into the air with his February message to Congress in which he recommended specific civil-rights legislation. But even as these Southerners whirl about in their political tornado, they can see flying along with them certain seemingly inescapable facts which cast shadows on the revolt and that resemble old man Lanier's caskets and are no more comforting. Chief among these interment-suggesting shades is probable defeat in November by the Republican nominee and a Congress committed to even more substantial civil rights legislation than offered by Mr. Truman.

In its inception the revolt was directionless and was confined largely to the discussion of Harry S. Truman in terms profane and exaggerated.

Reprinted by permission of Mrs. Ralph McGill and the *Saturday Evening Post* 220 (22 May 1948): 15-17, 88-90.

But, after a few days of breast-beating calisthenics, the revolt took on direction. A determined and unreasoning effect began to prevent Harry Truman from becoming the party nominee in the July convention.[61]

The fight will be carried to the convention floor. And the Southern Democrats are of a temper to offer to lick any Truman man in the house, in the manner of the late John L. Sullivan, even though they don't have his punch.

If Truman stays in the running all the way to the convention and isn't forced out beforehand—as might happen if certain Northern party groups and the more restive labor organizations join the angry Southerners—there will be at least four Southern states that probably will withhold their electoral votes from him. Mississippi, South Carolina, Alabama and Virginia have gone too far to retreat from their position, unless they find the Republican platform even more distasteful, as they may.

Almost every Southern state will go to Philadelphia with a favorite son to nominate or with uninstructed delegates to employ in the most effective anti-Truman strategy that can be devised. Even though it should mean sure national defeat, state politicians in the South ghoulishly are willing to accept that fact and use any means whatever to defeat Truman in convention.

But should Truman emerge from the convention with the nomination, at least half, and perhaps three-fourths, of the Southern states will reluctantly give him their electoral votes. At the moment, they don't believe they will have to do a thing so repugnant. Southerners count cynically, but nonetheless heavily, on help from the big-city Democratic machines in the North. They know these machines, such as Kelly's old organization in Cook County, Hague's in New Jersey, Ed Flynn's in New York, and others of lesser infamy, are up against a dilemma. State machines, especially those in the competitive two-party business, are interested in the presidency only as it can help them with their state tickets.

They believe local chances will be nil with Truman. This is a situation which causes Southern politicians to wear large oily smiles, even though they do not expect the big-state machines to make their positions

[61]See Emile Bertrand Ader, *The Dixiecrat Movement: Its Role in Third Party Politics* (Washington DC: Public Affairs Press, 1955).

known before convention time. The machines doubtless will play it safe until the final moment, even to the point of having a spokesman announce for Truman—with fingers crossed. A high-ranking federal district judge might die, or some other high patronage position might be made vacant between now and convention time, to be filled by White House appointment. But once the gavel falls to open the convention or perhaps in those traditional, smoke-filled rooms on the eve of the convention, the South believes the Northern machines will as ruthlessly throw Harry Truman on the political scrap heap as they did Henry Wallace in 1944. Having seen how right they were to get rid of Henry, the South trusts them to proceed in like manner with Harry. The Southerners anticipate that the heave-ho of Harry by the Northern machines will be put on some high moral ground, probably that of party unity.

This same cold political pragmatism is at work in an occasional Southern state. With his civil rights recommendations, President Truman gave many Southern senators who rather nervously had remained "Administration men" a chance to go whooping off the reservation. They, too, had their eyes on local politics and were not interested in the presidency if support of Truman was to prove so unpopular as to let greedy and unworthy pigs break through political fences at home.

Alabama offers the best illustration of those who dropped the pledge to Truman before it fell on their political toes. In the Yellowhammer State, Big Jim Folsom is the bull elephant in his own circus. What with kissing gals here and there, having kind words to say about the benisons of bourbon, and being glamorized by a paternity suit, Big Jim is hot. He recently whooped it up at "the branch heads" of Alabama's rural sections and scattered his foes at the polls. Big Jim has his eye on the 1950 senatorial race, when Senator Hill runs again. He is feuding with Truman and hollering about "dumping money in the laps of them foreign kings and queens." All this gives Sen. Lister Hill the ague. One day, after prayer and meditation, Hill suddenly gave the startled Mr. Truman the back of his hand and went over to the insurgents with a blast which, loud as it was, still failed to scare the Folsom pigs out of the senator's pea patch.

Sen. John Sparkman had beaten him to the exit by a few weeks. Both soon found themselves unhappy. They had not gained very much. The anti-Truman forces welcomed them, but coldly and with indifference.

Senators Hill and Sparkman soon discovered what other Southern political observers know—namely, that the same forces which fought Roosevelt in 1940 and 1944 are again the leaders in fanning the Southern revolt. They are the same forces which spent large sums trying to defeat Administration Southern senators up for reelection in 1944, with special emphasis on Hill and Claude Pepper. Both Sparkman and Hill have, in effect, joined their enemies.

Southern observers know, too, that every absentee, corporative landlord is pulling strings attached to Southern politicians. These strings have had various persons around the South leaping up and demanding that conferences which have gathered to push the revolt consider also the tidelands-oil controversy, which now seems to be a grave insult to Southern womanhood and states' rights. The same old anti-Roosevelt crowd has stepped into the new opportunity with renewed hope of sabotaging the Democratic party. Their chances are pretty good, Southern anger being what it is.

This makes the revolt the more disturbing to progressive Southerners who can see some distressing parallels between 1948 and 1856-1860. One of these is the poverty of leadership in the Democratic party, a weakness which contributed to the debacle of 1860. While the Republicans are embarrassed by too many candidates, the Democrats are bankrupt with only the harassed Truman. The Southerners have their favorite sons, in whose praise they will light the Philadelphia skies with glittering words, but they know no man from south of the Mason and Dixon's line can get the nomination.

One of the illogical, face-destroying positions of the extreme Southern wing is that it will go to the convention seeking to offer a "Southern platform" which will exclude even the planks to which it subscribed in 1944. In the effort to escape reality, it is insisting that no attention be paid to the protestations of Gen. Dwight Eisenhower that he will not be a candidate and thinks no soldier should be. The extreme Southern thinking is that he be nominated by the Democrats and the nomination then be put in his lap on the high ground of "patriotism."[62]

---

[62]See McGill, "Dwight D. Eisenhower" and "Dwight Eisenhower and the South," in this volume.

If all plans fail and Harry Truman is nominated, much of the Southern leadership is prepared to slay itself with the jawbones of the asses who have talked them into their psychological trap. They are determined to make a Truman nomination as worthless as Confederate bonds. However ridiculous and illogical some of the aspects of this Southern position may be, there are those who are sure to exhibit no common sense at all.

Basically, there is nothing new in this present tempest. It first came into the open in 1937, when some of the South's most distinguished senators so dissented from the Roosevelt program that they were put on the black list. Then, Mr. Roosevelt himself rode into the South to purge them with the fire and sword of his oratory and magnetic persuasion. He blunted both on the stubborn rocks of Southern political mores, the very stones which now are bruising the bones of Harry Truman.

The senatorial dissent in 1937 reflected an uneasiness which is endemic in Southern politics, based as it is on the one-party system. This system, born and bred in the bitterness of the Reconstruction years, is of necessity a neurotic, fearful one. The opposition of 1937 continued on through the war years, with loud and angry laments over the federal administrative practices which were striking, as the party's leaders said in the South, at the fundamentals of Southern traditions. Typical was the action of Alabama's Gov. Frank Dixon in 1942. He refused to sign a federal contract for manufacture of cloth, even though the plant involved was the state prison, because of the contractual clause against racial discrimination in employment.

There were filibusters at war's end against antilynch and poll-tax legislation, and against a permanent fair-employment-practice act. There was evidence of increasing fear and irritation. So, when President Truman, long believed to entertain sympathy for the Southern problem, himself let fly with a set of barbs, the Southern half of the Democratic donkey—and no rude comments, please—reacted very violently indeed.

The average Southerner has felt, with some justification, that he and his section are making real progress in the field of racial problems. His feeling that the problem is his, that it is not fully understood by others, and that only he and the Negro working together can solve it, caused him to receive the president's recommendations with an immediate growing anger.

He also regarded them as a gratuitous slap at a section faithfully Democratic, for reasons purely political. There was a consequent stubborn refusal to regard the Truman message as a mild and generally unobjectionable proposal for action in the field of civil rights. Instead, it was widely damned as a political scheme to turn over a white majority to a Negro minority, and to destroy with federal legislation the complex tradition and social pattern covered by the shibboleth "white supremacy," merely to salvage votes which otherwise might go to Henry Wallace's Communist-dominated party.

Therefore, in the first white heat of the boiling anger felt generally by the average Southerners—few of whom had read the message—it was not rare to see usually responsible persons come forward with grim and radical suggestions. Among them was a proposal, still seriously advanced, to abolish the public school systems in the Southern states and substitute privately supported schools, leaving the Negro to do the same.

The most fabulous rumors ran like fevers through rural communities and towns: Truman had come out for intermarriage; Truman was for compulsory mixing of the races at dances, dinners and swimming pools. Knots of men on courthouse lawns, before country hardware and drug stores, discussed the rumors as Truman's words. Many weekly rural newspapers and some dailies commented wildly and irresponsibly, saying the South's way of life was in danger.

Since the Truman recommendations were, in essence, contained in the 1944 Democratic platform, and had each been proposed by the late Franklin D. Roosevelt, the wonder grows that Truman should have touched off the loudest political pyrotechnics since 1860. The answer seems to be that Roosevelt was more adroit. There also was the paradoxical fact that in all controversies of a racial nature during Mr. Roosevelt's years, it was Mrs. Eleanor Roosevelt at whom all the dead cats were flung. But the chief reason is that control of Congress now has passed to Republican hands. There now is a very real likelihood of at least some of the recommendations becoming law.

But among the Southerners who remained calm there is a general belief that even the Republican Congress will go slowly about the job of pressing legislation in the field of civil rights, taking first the less controversial ones.

Of the ten recommendations by the president, the South is concerned with but five. One urges elimination of segregation in interstate travel. Mr. Truman here has but reaffirmed something already done in 1946 by the Supreme Court. Another asks that the residents of the District of Columbia be allowed the ballot, so as to remove, if they wish, inequalities within the pattern of segregation. All honest Southerners will admit that there are gross inequalities within that pattern. The three other recommendations deal with the poll tax, lynching and a fair-employment-practice commission.

Few respectable persons today defend the poll tax per se, though there are those who insist that its status is a matter for the states. Seven states, all in the South, retain it; Virginia, one of the seven, has initiated machinery to abolish it. The poll tax was never a vehicle to bar only the Negro from the polls. The fabulous Huey Long assured himself of political dominance by abolishing it in Louisiana because it had disfranchised thousands of whites who wanted to vote for him. The late Eugene Talmadge gave support to its abolition in Georgia and would not have been nominated in 1946 had he not done so. Even the late Theodore Bilbo had a kind word for poll-tax abolition. It remains largely a defense mechanism for those politicians who are afraid of their own people. It is no coincidence that nowhere else in the South is the revolt so furious as in the poll-tax states.

Many Southerners today regard lynchings as more or less an academic question. They point to the fact that it is the only crime which is being reduced, and that it has about disappeared as a growing public opinion prevents lynchings. These believe a lynching law would not be useful in preventing lynchings. But here again there is no great objection from the people, though some politicians make it seem so.

The FEPC, enforced by a federal "police force," already called a "Gestapo," is anathema. The demagogues and the race-baiters interpret it in terms of: "Do you want a nigger foreman in the mills?" Textile organizers for the CIO report that they can persuade their people to go along with antipoll-tax and antilynch legislation, but they can't push FEPC because of the racial angle.[63]

---

[63]For McGill's changing view on Fair Employment Practices Commission see the editor's introduction.

There is other opposition to FEPC, which is free of any racial prejudice. Many Southerners with progressive reputations hard-won in political and social fields regard the proposal for a permanent FEPC as new evidence of a national sickness which tends to regard federal authority as a cure-all for every ill. These Southerners feel that in opposition to an FEPC they should be joined by citizens in all regions who believe there is danger in a completely centralized government. They fear that in seeking further centralization of federal power to supervise employment for protection of minorities, we might create one of those Boris Karloff creatures which eventually could destroy the civil rights of the majority, and incidentally deprive the employer of his civil rights as well. They further argue that a job cannot be classified as a civil right; that to argue on to the logical conclusion, we would have to set up another agency to protect applicants at banks against discrimination in getting loans.

It is this attitude which caused lifelong Democrats to speak of Republican Senators Taft and Ball, who opposed the FEPC measure in hearings before the Labor Committee, as princes among men. Each said he believed the legislation would do the Negro's economic cause more harm than good. The more pleased Southern editorial writers dusted off their best adjectives, and both Taft and Ball were described in terms usually reserved for Robert E. Lee and Jefferson Davis.

Examination reveals the Truman recommendations, aside from the FEPC, to be relatively mild. It is highly probably that had not the South reacted so immediately and with such violence, Negro leaders and organizations would have protested the proposals as weak and mealymouthed.

That a segregation measure handed down by the Supreme Court in 1946 and since then observed in plane and Pullman travel—but largely ignored in bus transportation—should have been interpreted as a recommendation to overthrow the entire Southern pattern is evidence of the political neuroses always present in the Southern one-party system.

The emotions of the Southern Democrats were forged in the rebirth of the party in the years of Reconstruction and the exploitation era of "The New South." Party discipline was, and is, feudal, not democratic. It was based upon fear, and it has so continued. There are the fears of the Negro "menace"; of a return of federal bayonets to the ballot box; of a second disfranchisement; of scalawags—and there are other fears, including some imaginary ones.[64]

This discipline of feudal loyalty means that white men dare not divide at the ballot box on lines of class interest. Nor may differences over issues or the party's nominee be reflected at the polls. Corruption, fraud and unfit candidates all have been tolerated. To do otherwise, runs the watchword, is to endanger the white race, to encourage "mongrelization." The white primary, limiting primary voting to white persons, was the lock put on the door. National issues in a one-party system are relatively meaningless. Politics becomes the business of the few. The paradoxes of Southern politics frequently drive sensitive Southerners to nail biting or a mournful reliance on the soothing effects of bourbon.

With the Negro effectively reduced to second-rate citizenship by the white-primary mechanism, the average Southerner long has typed him in general terms. There are the "good niggers"—the smiling "yassuh-boss" type, who really are good Negroes who have somehow attained a philosophic rationalization of their lot. They will work hard for less than the average wage scale, and will live in shacks which go unrepaired year in and year out. This patient, exploited type usually is found in agriculture as tenant or cropper. This one the white man will get out of jail, pay his doctor bills, and in general treat with paternalistic consideration and kindness. At times, warm personal relationships develop, and genuine affection. But it never escapes from that pattern.

A second "type" creation is that of the "biggety nigger." This type the average Southerner describes as being partially educated and thereby unfitted for honest work and not to be trusted. Unable to rationalize himself with the problems about him, such a Negro usually is unwilling to work for below-standard wages and actually is, by his small amount of education, psychologically unfitted for stability.

The third type is the "bad nigger." The folkways description of him is that of a sullen, often drunk, knife-carrying, killing-scrape, chain-gang Negro likely to commit any crime, whose probable end is the gang or the lynching rope.

---

[64]See Numan V. Bartley and Hugh D. Graham, *Southern Politics and the Second Reconstruction* (Baltimore: Johns Hopkins University Press, 1975).

White juries aid the caste typing by dealing lightly with the "good Negro" before them and giving harsher sentences to "biggety" and "bad" Negroes, though the crimes charged be the same. Negro murder of another Negro is treated rather casually as "just another Negro killing," with the result that Negro crime against Negro is shockingly high in almost every Southern city.

This habit of the average Southerner in thinking of all Negroes as being more or less typed has excluded the intellectual Negro, who, if considered at all, is regarded as sort of a curiosity. There is almost no opportunity for the cultured, educated Negro to get to know cultured, educated white people, even on the nonsocial terms of professional or artistic interests.

The Hydra-headed phrase *social equality* is a barrier which frightens and confuses both races. For the average Southerner, the phrase has many meanings. To one person it may mean simply equal pay for Negroes. To another it may mean allowing a Negro to work at a job customarily held by white persons. A white clerk may fit shoes on a Negro customer, practically kneeling at the Negro's feet as part of the job, but will resent furiously a suggestion of abandoning segregation on buses. Another clerk will cheerfully fit gloves on a colored hand, but would be incensed at a suggestion of sitting beside the customer at a soda fountain. They will shop side by side, but to sit side by side in a trolley would be "social equality."

The average Negro is not so much concerned with social equality as with political equality. He knows he will not really attain his civil rights until he can obtain them with the ballot. Today he is closer to a free ballot than any previous time since the Civil War. With the white primary and the subterfuge variation attempted in South Carolina both nullified, more Negroes will vote this year in all the Solid South than ever before.

In Georgia, for example, the Talmadge faction, which in January 1947 sought to impose the soon-to-be-outlawed South Carolina white-primary plan, in March of 1948 moved to drop all white-primary tactics.

In the light of the Supreme Court ruling, the blind, clamorous party revolt against civil rights recommendations and the furious plans to remove Harry Truman's political head and carry it on a charger before the rejoicing throngs seems curiously out of keeping with the facts of life and politics. The truth is the Supreme Court has already smashed the old political pattern. No amount of feudal party loyalty will put it back together again. The old status quo has had a great fall, yet few seem to comprehend its meaning.

There will be more years of seeking for stratagems to prevent many of the genuinely qualified Negroes from voting. But the years cannot be many before fair and equitable qualification laws will be in effect.

The more astute local politicians in the South already have seen the handwriting on the walls of the old one-party banquet hall. If the Negro is going to vote—and he is—they want his vote and will seek it. They will offer benefits in citizenship in return.

There are a few politicians who still regard the Ku Klux Klan as a rock in a weary land. It isn't. The Negro no longer generally is afraid of the Klan . . . as the Klan itself is learning. Early in March, Grand Dragon Sam Greene, of Georgia, stood before two hundred of his sheeted Kluxers at Wrightsville, Johnson County, Georgia. His sad, somewhat wistful face was lit by the crackling flames of a cross which spread its burned-gasoline stink over the scene. The wistful dragon talked of blood in the streets, and next day no Negro voted in the county primary. But that was the only victory. At Jeffersonville, Georgia, a short time later, the Klan burned two crosses, one on Saturday, and another on Sunday night before a Tuesday primary. On that Tuesday, two-thirds of the registered Negroes voted. The trend has continued in primary after primary.

The free ballot is a surer road toward citizenship rights than federal legislation, which many Southerners of good will have been saying for years as they sought to end the poll tax and the white primary. But their voices have been largely lost in the contests between the all-or-nothing elements of both races.

In the phase just now beginning there will be occasional violence, and more demagogues will appear. It will be a period of change as the stubborn mores of the South, cemented with something of the same bitterness as those in India and Palestine, give way.

In the first week of the Democratic party revolt, the world's first production-line mechanical cotton picker rolled off the line and got a one column head on an inside page of most newspapers. Yet it was more meaningful than the revolt. It will shift greater population to the cities and will further hasten the breakdown of the one-party system and the establishment of the two-party competition in the South.

How fast the two-party trend develops depends largely upon the Republican party. In the past, it has not wanted a party in the South. It has permitted and sustained local Republican organizations through the South that, with but few exceptions, are disreputable. Republicans coming South invariably are shocked on meeting the Southern Republican organizations.[65]

But here, too, is change. An example is Wilson Williams, a successful businessman of Columbus, Georgia. Son of a Confederate soldier, Williams went into the Republican party in 1919 in an effort to assist in establishing it as a competing state party. He is now National Republican Committeeman for Georgia. Joe Martin, Speaker of the House and one of the most influential Republicans, has promised cooperation in building a better Republican organization in the South.

There are thousands in the South who want a change in politics and in attitudes. At many colleges, students have shaken the old political leaders with their views. Churches, veterans and many civic organizations are denying the old feudal demands of political loyalty so long unquestioned. There is open admiration for several Republican leaders. Perhaps the most widely respected member of the United States Senate in Southern estimation is Michigan's Arthur H. Vandenberg.

Wearied of the revolt, long wanting a change, thousands of Southerners this year will vote the Republican ticket, unless the GOP comes bumbling out of Philadelphia with another Mark Hanna product. They will do so even though grandpa, peering down over the ramparts of that Valhalla from which the old Confederates watch us as we cast our ballots, faints at the sight and spills his ectoplasmic julep.

The revolt really has no place to go. The South has.[66]

---

[65]See V. O. Key, Jr., *Southern Politics in State and Nation* (New York: Vintage Books, 1949); Jack Bass and Walter DeVries, *The Transformation of Southern Politics: Social Change and Political Consequences Since 1945* (New York: New American Library, 1977).

[66]See McGill's "Common Sense Can Save Both," in volume 1.

10

The Housing Challenge

H ousing, as a word, has many meanings. It means the trees in the forest being felled, trimmed, loaded and sent to the whirring blades of the saw; the whining scrape of the planing mills. It means train loads and truck loads of manufactured lumber, all in movement toward some building site. It means the juncture there of other materials, bricks, stone, tile, bags of cement, roofing, kegs of nails, frames, windows, doors—

It means, too, the putting together of these materials; the sound of hammering, sawing, of grunting bulldozers moving earth; of men at work as the apartment building or house takes shape and becomes a place to live.

But, away from the site itself, there are other meanings to the word *housing*. Back of "housing" are deeds, permits, loans, mortgages, interest rates, attorneys' fees, taxes, contracts as to rents, and so on.

Thousands of men have worked in mines for iron ore; dug in pits of clay; fired kilns, moved trains, assembled motors and truck bodies; cut

A pamphlet published by the Atlanta Housing Authority, May 1948, and reprinted with permission of Mrs. Ralph McGill and the Atlanta Housing Authority. In a letter to the editor on 4 March 1983, Atlanta's Mayor Andrew Young wrote, ". . . the AHA is delighted to permit you to use this article. It turns out that the AHA did not have a copy of the pamphlet in its library and we are grateful to you for bringing it to our attention."

down trees, floated them down streams or dragged them out to be loaded on flat cars; toiled in saw mills and finishing mills; handled the red-hot flow of a snakey, seemingly endless pencil of steel that goes clattering into a machine to emerge as nails; fabricated angle iron and beams.

Housing has many meanings. These are the material meanings.

But history has shown us that every time we have tried to separate the meaning of things and follow only the dictates of the material, we have come upon grief and failure. There must also be given full consideration to the spiritual, or human meaning of our way of life. It is especially true of housing. It is possible to say that the meaning of housing is the meaning of our civilization and culture; or as the phrasing of today has it, our way of life.

When a man thinks of his country he thinks of his home, the place where he lives; his home city and his house, or home, in it. He does not think in the greater terms of its economy or its politics, but in terms of his own home. His whole attitude toward his government, city or national, is conditioned by his home. A great many persons have written of this, in philosophy, in prose and poetry.

One of the world's greatest men, with a feeling for humanity, was Britain's great prime minister, Benjamin Disraeli. In a speech made a good many years ago, in 1874, he said:

> The best security for civilization is the dwelling, and upon proper and becoming dwelling depends more than anything else the improvement of mankind. Such dwellings are the nursery of all domestic virtues, and without a becoming home the exercise of these virtues is impossible.

One of our own great poets, Walt Whitman, wrote in his "Notes" as early as 1888:

> The final culmination of this vast and varied republic will be the production and perennial establishment of millions of comfortable city homesteads and moderate sized farms . . . healthy and independent . . . life in them complete but cheap, within reach of all.

Discussion of housing, now so much a part of our lives because of the great shortage and the inequitable distribution of new housing, is not itself new. There long has been discussion and study of housing, but, as always, those who saw the human and spiritual side of it have been in advance of the dominant thinking and the economic integrity of their time.

It is fair and conservative to say at this time, with much of the world destroyed by a world revolution of which the Second World War was a part, that we who have been relatively less touched by its forces nevertheless have not escaped them and must continue to contend with them.

People expect services from their government. And they think of services chiefly in terms of their health and their housing. We who believe in a concept of individual opportunity, and who have built our government on that concept, must see that to maintain it our system must be resilient and flexible. Among the world powers, capitalism, which has shown the world that it is the most efficient productive system ever devised, must become an even more intelligent capitalism to bring its people along with it and conquer the great and hostile forces loosed in the world.

That being so, as thoughtful men will not deny, we must agree with Disraeli and Whitman, and with many others of the past and of our own day, that "the best security for civilization is the dwelling, and upon proper and becoming dwellings depends more than anything else, the improvement of mankind."

Neither housing nor houses can remain static. Architects continually improve and change the concept of the house or the multi-unit dwelling. We laugh today at the old "gingerbread" horrors of the eighties and nineties. We revere the purity of line left us by the Greeks and Romans. And we try in our modern dwellings to give them both beauty and utility. There always is change, to meet new developments in heating, cooking, living and custom.

Neither may the philosophy, the legal, nor the spiritual status of housing become static. As a weapon of intelligent capitalism it can be the bulwark against which the hostile forces loose in the world will break. It can be the house built on a rock. Or, if greed-induced blindness and a refusal to consider housing in terms of national security have their way, we will live to see the hostile waves undermine much of what we want to keep.

We have come a long way in our thinking and action, when one considers that it was in 1933, a mere fifteen years ago, that the first action was taken. In those years the opposition contained some of the arguments still to be found today against public assistance in housing the one-third of the nation which is ill-housed. But, in fifteen years many of the old arguments have been proved false and some proved ridiculous, as time will prove those remaining to be ill-founded and conceived largely in lack of understanding, not wholly in hostility.

Fortune magazine, of, for, and by big business, is intelligent and factual, and conservative within the true meaning of that word, now one of many words greatly abused and distorted. In the depression of the thirties, the first approach to housing was that of "make-work," as *Fortune* magazine reports. The idea was to encourage the building of homes. *Fortune* says:

> What happened was this—and it is not without its irony. The purpose of Congress had been to *make work* by encouraging the construction of houses. That purpose had been blocked by the protests of invested capital which claimed that if new houses were constructed its investment would be destroyed. It was therefore capitalism which gave the program (of public housing) its first shove in the new direction. Complying with these protests, the Housing Division had turned its face toward the housing of the poorer one third of the population of the country. Down to the summer of 1933 there did not exist in the United States one single instance of the replacement of a slum with new housing capable of occupancy by the families which had occupied the old quarters. But all those having to do with the Housing Division knew, as Great Britain had already discovered before them, that the clearance of slums and the provision of decent housing was more important to the maintenance of a stable social order than any other gesture.

So concluded *Fortune*. It is worth noting that when the Conservative government was replaced with a Labor government in Britain, the chief weapon used by the Labor candidates was the failure of the Conservative government to meet the housing problem of Great Britain before the war, and the belief that it could not meet the greatly exaggerated problem of war-destroyed housing by the methods of the past. It was chiefly on the basis of their housing failure that the Conservatives fell, and this fact explains why a government which had won the war, nonetheless failed of reelection.

This country may well be disturbed by the present problem. Behind us are the foolish babblings of fifteen years ago—that the slum people like slums; that they will ruin new housing; that they will keep coal in the bathtubs; that rents will be defaulted; that only the middle-income groups will benefit, and so on.

But, there remain the objections of the greedy and the stupid, who would call even Senator Robert Taft a Communist because of his advocacy of a public housing bill. And there remains the even greater hurdle of the apathetic opposition of those who are not informed and who do not take the trouble to inform themselves about their local conditions and needs.

Housing needs differ regionally. Before World War II, an approximate ten-and-a-half-million persons lived in the South. In every region there are people in poor housing. But the Federal Bureau of Census reports show more persons in the South living in poor housing than in any other region. In the rest of the nation, one of every three dwelling units falls short of minimum standards. In the South two out of every three are so designated.

That was the situation in 1940 as compiled by the Bureau of Census reports for that year. They are made every year. So, we find that the 1947 reports show a slight improvement nationally. Housing has improved, least in the South and especially in the South's cities and towns.

There is a reason for this. We have been, and are, predominantly a rural region. Since 1880 our country has been witnessing a shift of farm population from farms to the cities and towns. Now the nation has a majority of its people in cities, called urban regions.

That movement has been slowest in the South. World War I stepped it up. The depression slowed it down. World War II greatly accelerated it. Now we are witnessing the movement of industry into the South and at least fifty percent of it, on the average, is moving into the cities with less than 50,000 population, some of it into cities with populations of 1,500 and 2,000. More and more people will move to our cities and towns where the housing is not merely inadequate but below standard. The larger industries, which demand thousands of employees, still must move to the larger cities, or to their outskirts.

Let us go back to the census reports. They tell us that in 1930 about thirty percent of the South's total number of dwelling units were in urban centers of population from 2,500 on up to the largest cities. By 1940, just ten years, forty percent of the South's dwelling units were in these urban centers. By 1947 this had grown to forty-five percent. Is an urban, or city house, a big one?

No, the census shows that even in big cities in the South, like Atlanta, Memphis, and New Orleans, most of the houses and apartments are of three or four rooms.

Now, what are these "minimum standards?"

According to the listings a dwelling unit of minimum standards meets these requirements:

1. It is not in need of major repair work.

2. It has an adequate supply of water, piped into the house if in town or city, or within fifty feet of the house on a farm. (These are minimum. Farm houses with piped water are desirable).

3. A flush toilet in a town or city, and on a farm an outside privy properly kept. (Keep in mind these are minimum standards.)

4. Electricity.

5. As many rooms as people living in it. This does not mean as many bedrooms as people living in it, but simply as many rooms.

Many more things are desirable. These are the minimum for health and decent living.

Now, what are some of the conditions in our South, including Atlanta, Georgia, where within the city limits there are hundreds of houses with outdoor toilets, not too well kept, and even schools without indoor flush toilets?

In 1940 almost half the dwellings in the urban South fell short of the minimum standards. (The same is true for farm houses.)

One out of six of every urban house had no running water piped into the houses. Sixteen percent of the city houses had no electricity. Seventeen percent were so in need of major repairs as to be considered dangerous to live in.

The census for 1947 shows little change. Indeed, in some phases it was worse. Our contrast with the rest of the country is bad. Our Southern housing picture shows us to be below the national average on running water, toilets, crowded conditions, repairs, and other standards.

The South has the most Negroes. But, wherever the Negro is in America, he is the worst housed.[67]

Here in the South we need to know the facts. We need to know what our actual needs are. Then we need to apply the remedies. We must face the fact of national planning to do something about housing for the millions for whom the system of competitive enterprise cannot act. And we

---

[67]For McGill's support for adequate housing for blacks, see the editor's introduction to this volume.

need to learn not to be afraid of that fact or to be deceived by shibboleths. The lesson of history is pretty clear, even to modern history in Britain where failure to solve the housing problem, before war came, had created a great dissatisfaction with the existing government.

The regional picture is part of the national picture. Let us examine that.

In 1948 we are using more building material, in all forms of construction, than ever before in our peacetime history, but the bald and paradoxical fact is that we are a long way from any startling change for the better in housing for those who need it most.

How far we are from real improvements may be seen by the fact that in 1947 the government estimated 1,000,000 new homes were begun. These included temporary quarters, much of it on campuses for colleges. An approximate 850,000 permanent new homes were started.

There were, in 1947, about 900,000 new marriages which, with few exceptions, do, and should, create demands for new housing. We hardly held our own in potential demand.

The president and the building industry have envisioned 1,000,000 new homes this year. This is a tremendous figure because, if our inflation should break, construction would halt for a substantial period of time.

But, if we get them, we will get almost that many new marriages and we will also not take care of the accumulated backlog demand for housing from persons who long have been living "doubled up" or "quadrupled up," or who are living in houses badly in need of repair and unsuited for habitation.

There are thousands of veterans still living in "temporary" barracks. Millions of Americans, living in crowded rooms, weary of the inevitable friction between relatives and in-laws compelled by lack of housing to seek cover under the same roof, want housing. They have been pretty patient about it. And there are those millions who cannot be rescued from slums unless there is a program of public housing. There also are several million thrifty, hardworking people of low income who want low-cost housing and low-rent housing which meets at least minimum standards and who cannot pay for it unless there is some governmental participation.

Out of the problem seem to emerge two phases of the problem which will be apparent to all.

1. There is an immediate and urgent problem of overcoming the pressing lack of room caused by the lack of building during the war which was precipitated into extremely abnormal shortage of space by the slow rate of building in the years before the war.

2. There is also a long-range problem concerning the replacement of old dwellings which have become, and others which soon will become, unsanitary, and even unsafe. The minimum such old buildings already in need of replacement is set at about 5,000,000. Estimates have gone as high as 12,000,000.

As millions of veterans and others know, problem number one has not been solved. In 1946 the administrator of the National Housing Agency announced that it was believed possible to build a maximum number of 2,700,000 temporary and permanent homes. This was not set as the number needed, but as the number that might be built. With these built, it was estimated there would still be 2,000,000 families— families, not persons—still "doubled" or "tripled up" when these were completed by January 1948. The goal was not nearly reached.

As a result, the census figures for 1946 showed about 2,500,000 married families crowded in with other families, in addition to the other housing needs. This was a fifty-percent increase over the figures for 1940. The census figures for April 1947 showed 2,754,000 married couples sharing rooms with other families. And everyone knows that even a large house is crowded with two families in it. Indeed, the Chinese have a saying that no house can be large enough for two families.

The present state of affairs, in which we are using more building materials than ever before, serves only to emphasize the failure. A proper use of building materials should provide the kinds of housing people need in ratio to these various needs. It should include rental units as well as units for sale. It should provide dwelling units, in apartments or houses, for low- and middle-income needs as well as from the higher-income groups. It should be proportioned in city and suburb.

Every person who goes about his community knows there are houses standing empty—for sale. We all know the emphasis has been on homes for sale, largely in suburbs or even beyond them, instead of rental units in the cities and suburbs—they being the most badly needed.

In our country about sixty percent of the population normally rents their dwellings. In 1947 only about ten percent of the permanent new construction was built as rental property.[68]

Another failure, and one which has a long-range danger, is that most of the new dwelling units, apartments and homes, are the "birth control units," in dollhouse effect, with no necessary space to take care of the arrival of children.

President Truman, in his housing message to Congress, touched on three reasons for our housing failure. Chief among them was cost.

The conservative people in the low- and middle-income ranges make up the greater part of our population. They are our great bulwark against radical change. Yet it is they whom we have punished by our housing failure. The inflated costs have put new housing out of reach of most of these people. Costs have also "scared" both builder and buyer.

A second factor is scarcity. We are producing most building material in greater quantities than we believed likely by this time. Yet scarcities still are reported in some materials: nails, mill work, soil pipe, some fixtures, gypsum-lath and steel. The result has been a slow sort of piece-by-piece building.

The third factor is fear of a collapse in the economy which would catch both purchasers, renters, and builders.

But anyone who studies the problem comes also upon other factors. There are conflicting, and often obsolete, building codes which delay building, and often prevent it. Building goes on furiously, but there is still lack of building to meet the needs of various groups.

Actually, there is very little free enterprise, or competitive building in the mass construction going on. It is somewhat ironic that many builders furiously oppose any federal housing subsidy, yet eagerly avail themselves of Title 6 of FHA, by insuring ninety-percent mortgage loans and thereby providing themselves more liberal financing. Almost no rental property is being constructed today in urban centers save under this form of federal subsidy in which the taxpayer is the final owner of any property which might not pay out. And also the final loser. Never-

---

[68]For more by McGill on housing, see article on Peter Knox in McGill, *Southern Encounters: Southerners of Note in Ralph McGill's South*, ed. Calvin M. Logue (Macon GA: Mercer University Press, 1983).

theless, this is an excellent plan, and its facts merely illustrate the hypocrisy of opposing other ventures by the government in providing housing for those who cannot be reached by this subsidy to private builders.

Whatever the plan, it is folly to exclude from it a permanent public housing provision of flexible provisions. The builder with ninety percent of his mortgage guaranteed by the taxpayers cannot with good face refuse to agree that for persons of low income decent minimum housing can be provided only by some form of subsidy. The veterans who were promised so much are by no means the only ones who need this sort of aid or subsidy to make up for the difference between present costs and rentals and what they can afford to pay.

What we must face, honestly and without hypocrisy, is that the program, proposed under the Taft-Ellender-Wagner bill is flexible enough to meet the demands of the years and the nation. It should be passed by the Congress if we are to do the job of intelligently sustaining our capitalistic system by maintaining its tap root—the domesticity of our culture and our traditions. Public housing for low-income families is the keystone to the arch. "As the homes, so the state."[69]

---

[69]For more by McGill on Atlanta see "Why I Live in Atlanta," "Georgia Tech: Lighthouse to the Postwar South," and "She Sifted the Ashes and Built a City," in volumes 1 and 2.

11

Common Sense
Can Save Both

There is a rumor going around, and very well substantiated, too, that when the delegates from Mississippi and a part of those from Alabama walked out of the 1948 Democratic Convention at Philadelphia, the shade of John C. Calhoun arose at the toddy table in the political Valhalla and said, "It's too damned late." John C. Calhoun was always the pessimist. His last words, as he lay dying, were, "The South, the poor South, God knows what will become of her."

Those words echo yet, in these days of states' rights and civil rights controversies which have brought on at least a partial political secession and political war between some of the states. Not even the South is united and, as usual, those who make the least sense make the most noise. But there is a case to be made. And, actually, it is not the South's case, but the nation's.

The tragedy of it is that it has become the South's case. Because, in so becoming, the basic and important factor of states' rights has be-

---

Manuscript provided by Mrs. Ralph McGill from the McGill papers, now at Emory University, Atlanta. When the piece was rejected by *American Mercury*, McGill responded on 19 August 1948: "I don't have time to rewrite."

come fouled with the filth of the late Theodore Bilbo and by all the racial hate spewed up by his spiritual kin in the South's politics.[70]

There were, for example, many genuine friends of states' rights in the Democratic delegations at Philadelphia which voted against the Southern position as presented by Mississippi, South Carolina, Texas, Georgia and Tennessee—namely, that the convention merely reiterate its historic position that the Constitution of the United States specifically reserves certain rights for the states. There also had been friends of states' rights at the Republican Convention, but they, too, were impotent.

Neither they nor the Democrats could vote for states' rights because of the obvious fact that, with certain exceptions, many of those who were demanding the acceptance of the principle of states' rights, were doing so to condone and, in a sense, give status to state wrongs.[71]

To have voted for states' rights as presented at the Democratic Convention would have been to put the stamp of approval on the use of the poll tax, which may turn out to be unconstitutional, and which bars as many, if not more, white persons as it does Negroes. It also would have meant accepting the worst discriminations against the Negro in housing, jobs, education, recreation, and in the courts, had the convention appeased the Southern position.

This was a tragic fact—and the word *tragic* belongs to this discussion and is an inevitable part of it—impossible to avoid. Not all the speakers who spoke there on that final, steaming afternoon when the platform committee's report was overridden and the minority report demanding an endorsement of a broader civil rights platform accepted, were seeking to sustain or gloss over ancient wrongs. Cecil Sims, of Tennessee, for example, was not speaking in behalf of states' wrongs when he presented the Tennessee delegation's request for a reiteration of the states' rights principle. Nor, for that matter—and this may surprise some—

---

[70]See Cal M. Logue and Howard Dorgan, eds., *Oratory of Southern Demagogues* (Baton Rouge: Louisiana State University Press, 1981).

[71]See V. O. Key, Jr., *Southern Politics in State and Nation* (New York: Vintage Books, 1949); and Jack Bass and Walter DeVries, *The Transformation of Southern Politics: Social Change and Political Consequences Since 1945* (New York: New American Library, 1977).

was Georgia's Charlie Bloch so speaking. He had led in Georgia the fight to have Georgia's politicians recognize the right of the Negro to vote under the same fairly administered qualifications as white voters, and had helped kill the Georgia poll tax.

But, there was no escaping the fact that the whole Southern position, including the sincere element of it, was damned from the start by the facts of discrimination; was sicklied o'er by the slime left by Bilbo, Rankin and all. . . . [One page is missing from this manuscript from the McGill papers.][72] [States'] rights [were used by some persons] as a cloak for wrong, lies—and this will be ironical to some—in the American "Bill of Rights."

It is the Tenth Amendment to the Constitution of the United States, one of the vital ten as urged by Jefferson and others who were opposed to the Hamilton theory of centralization of federal power, and it reads:

> Article 10—Powers not delegated, reserved to states and peoples respectively.—The powers not delegated by the United States by the Constitution, nor prohibited by it to the States, are reserved to the States respectively, or to the people.

That is plain enough. And it is on this rock, as yet unbroken by the Supreme Court, that stand many Southerners and many Americans, who have been in the forefront of those progressives and liberals seeking to give to the Negro full and complete citizenship and all the privileges thereof.

They are Americans who want every Negro who meets proper voting qualifications (such as New York's, for example) to have the right to vote. They are those who, in the South, have led the fight to abolish the poll tax, as Georgia recently did, and who applauded the decision abolishing the white primary.[73]

They are those who have fought for equal rights, justice and opportunity for the Negro and all other minority-group Americans. They have headed the fight against lynching, against the Ku Klux Klan, against all the hate organizations. They still do. But, they stand for

---

[72]According to Ms. Grace Lundy, McGill's secretary, McGill would remove a page from a previously prepared manuscript when writing a new piece.

[73]For McGill's campaign for civil rights for blacks and his changing views on voting qualifications, see the editor's introduction to this volume.

states' rights as defined in the Tenth Amendment to the Constitution, believing that the only lasting rights are those given and not coerced.

Today their position is distorted in the public mind with that of Bilbo and confused with the tenets of the Ku Klux Klan. And that is a pity. There is the chance that, in our understandable and proper zeal to establish minority rights, we might, in haste, damage the rights of all.

The Jeffersonian principle of democracy was that of local self-government. Our federal government has never become a stiff, inflexible bureaucracy because it has been composed, even down to the bureaus it has developed, of men and women who have graduated from local governments, precinct, county, municipal, and state. Congressmen, senators, cabinet members, many of the judiciary, have carried with them to their federal positions the experience and the philosophy of local government. This explains our great reservoir of national strength, the muscle of our government, as well as the awkward and often inefficient use of that strength.

Tragically, the entire system of local, self-government is endangered because of the failure of the South, and the nation, to end discriminations against minorities. The Dixiecrat movement, which is a splinter party in revolt from the Democratic party, is a movement supported by fear, not principles, and motivated by forces and money which for years have supported every reactionary trend in the South.[74] It hastily donned the robe of states' rights when it saw opportunity to sabotage the Democratic party with the fear aroused by the fact that the Democratic party had now joined with the Republicans to see which could be first to legislate in the field of Southern race relations.

They do not represent the South. They are a minority's minority. But they do represent many Southern fears. Their movement is strongest in Mississippi. It has its next largest followings in South Carolina and Alabama.

These states have, per capita of white population, the largest Negro population and, by and large, they are the most reactionary in regard to giving the Negro what the generally-ignored Southern segregation laws have always required—equal but separate rights.

---

[74]See Emile Bertrand Ader, *The Dixiecrat Movement: Its Role in Third Party Politics* (Washington DC: Public Affairs Press, 1955).

Every year more and more Southerners have been made ashamed by the obvious hypocrisies in the segregation system. The facilities of education, travel, justice, housing, and so on were separate. But they were not equal. Every year more and more persons worked at making them equal. The progress was most obvious in the cities, with perhaps Atlanta, Georgia, doing more within the shortest span of time to at least put in motion a program to equalize the school opportunities. But the hypocrisy remained and was always the most articulate.

The white primary, which was the vehicle barring Negroes from participation in the only elections the one-party states had, is gone with the wind of the Supreme Court decisions. The Supreme Court support of the Gaines case in higher education has put upon the states the necessity of immediately providing approximately equal schools of higher education, but it is significant that the Supreme Court did not go into the field of segregation in the schools. These changes have come—not out of new legislation, but out of the Constitution itself.

There are greater changes already on the horizon, and not dimly so. On the morning of 8 August 1948, the United States Bureau of the Census released some startling figures, even though they were not unexpected. The South, alone of all the regions, is still losing population by migration. Some of the Southern states, including Mississippi, Arkansas and Oklahoma, had a net loss of population because of migration. In Georgia, excess births over deaths gave the state a net gain of only fifteen thousand since 1840. In Alabama, the net gain was a bare one thousand. As farm machinery increases and as the cotton picker further dislocates farm labor in the great cotton states, the migration from the South will go on. It is not all Negro migration, although an estimated one million Negroes have left the South since war's end.

The Southern migration, of whites and colored, has gone on since the reconstruction days, but it got its first big impetus in the First World War. The boll weevil greatly speeded it up in the early twenties, and the Second World War set it going at an astonishingly rapid pace. The South's greatest export has long been some of its best brains, white and colored. Every school superintendent and almost every small town knows what happens to its best young high school graduates. They depart.

So, in the midst of great change, the almost fanatical zeal with which the "civil rights" measures are pushed seems to be somewhat out of date. The poll tax was not at all an anti-Negro measure, as the white primary was. The Negro is voting in increasing numbers in the seven remaining poll-tax states.

The proposed poll-tax legislation by Congress probably is unconstitutional. The Constitution seems plainly to give to the states the rights to establish qualifications for the electorate. At any rate, it is, at most, one of the minor restrictions on voting.

The Southerner feels that gang killings are as bad as lynchings and resents the casual treatment of these killings as matters for local government and the insistence of federal laws to cover lynchings—only one of which occurred last year. There is no escaping the fact that local pride in preventing lynchings has been built up to where lynchings have about disappeared. Twenty-seven attempted lynchings were prevented last year by local officers. Proponents of a federal law overlook the fact that the proposed law is probably unconstitutional. Even if it is not, a federal law would not produce different juries and new types of witnesses. It might destroy local determination and create an attitude of "Let the FBI do it."

The South has never had enough jobs, and still hasn't enough—as witness the steady migration to industrial "job" centers. The average Negro has been and still is discriminated against in hiring and firing. On the other hand, thousands in each state have managed—and this fact is largely overlooked—to become owners of property, to build businesses worth millions, and to enter fields of enterprise almost entirely barred them in the East and West, because he is segregated. But, the South views the proposed FEPC as an attempt to legislate "social mixing" of the races, and few there are who see anything good in it.[75] The Southerner who sees in it the beginning of a great federal bureaucracy reaching into every phase of business, is embarrassed by the facts of his region's economics. An FEPC to investigate, conciliate and negotiate would receive wide Southern support. The FEPC as proposed, with a federal policeman, will be greeted with mass defiance.

The realistic Southerner long has known that as long as a third or fourth of his population is restricted to menial jobs and menial wages,

---

[75]For McGill's changing attitude toward the federal Fair Employment Practices Commission see the editor's introduction.

the South can never attain the nation's economic par. He knows the Negro must be admitted to economic equality.

That already is changing, but with discouraging slowness. If the average Southerner could believe that the federal government would not attempt to force him to open his schools, his restaurants, his churches, his residential areas, theaters, public swimming pools, dance floors, his hotels to Negroes, almost all opposition to other legislation would disappear. The Southerner who travels in the East and West knows he sees few, if any Negroes, in the hotels, restaurants, residential areas, beaches, swimming pools, churches, and schools that he visits. He sees the huge Negro ghettos of the big Eastern cities and comes away convinced of his argument that segregation is best for both races and that the antisegregation policy of Northern politicians is a fraud.

Finally, the South has a case—for all its failure and all its guilt complex—in that there has been built up an anti-South complex, which ignores the steady and orderly process of change and improvement, the many dramatic Negro gains with full public support, and creates a false picture of "the South." This drives the most liberal Southerner to occasional anger and near despair.

The Southerner of intelligence sees what so few in the East see—that every day the Negro grows less and less important to the Southern economy—that every day racial tensions increase in the Eastern and Western cities; that the problem of race, long national, within a few years will be more of a problem in the East and West than the South.

Therefore, such a Southerner believes he has a case in arguing that the emphasis is all wrong—that since segregation isn't now going to be anywhere entirely eliminated by legislation or troops, the lot of the Negro and the Negro problem could best be served by federal legislation aiding education; making it possible for the many good Negro farmers now landless to own land; for those with farms to have credit to mechanize and carry out soil improvement practices; for credit to shift from cotton to cattle and pigs; to remove freight and tariff barriers making it easier for the South to industrialize and produce more jobs; to come through with more slum clearance projects and credit for low-cost housing. All these would do more to solve the Negro question than all the "civil liberty" laws put together.

It is fair, too, to ask how the lot of the Negro in the crowded slums of Chicago, New York, Cleveland, Los Angeles, Pittsburgh, or Georgia is going to be helped by eliminating the poll tax or passing an antilynching law. The proposed "policeman" FEPC doesn't create the know-how for skills and makes no jobs. An FEPC to investigate and negotiate would make sense.

And, there is the Constitution, and the decision about local government and centralization. It is by no means as simple as it seems when the attack is on the picture that anti-Southern bias has painted, even though the South's case is blighted by the disease of Bilbo and kindred fungus. States' rights and human rights have been maneuvered, by politics, into opposition. Common sense can save both.[76]

---

[76]See McGill's "Will the South Ditch Truman?" in volume 1.

12

Give Me Georgia

The Georgian contemplating his realm of sea and plain, of mountain and pine, of river and hill, has a mighty pride in the state, so that even Texans have been known to retreat from argument about it. His quick pride, which sometimes intensely and stubbornly defends even that of which it is not proud, is not all the defensive mechanism of an isolated people sprung from the same seed stock.

Georgia began as a refuge for the oppressed and for those seeking freedom of religion. To his Britannic Majesty's government of 1733 and to certain of her shrewder merchants, this new colony might have been planned to serve as a buffer against the Spanish and the French. But to the excited people of Britain, it meant a haven for those persecuted because of their religion, a utopia that might conceivably establish a pattern for a new world. In Britain, there was a fervor of raising money for the new settlement. Noblemen and yeomen, clerics and laymen, Gentiles and Jews all worked tirelessly to raise money and gather gifts. Seeds and plants, herbs and vines, guns and powder, swords and drums, religious tracts and books were dutifully donated in a great outpouring of enthusiasm. One of the trustees, a certain Hales, even wrote a special gift tract entitled "A Friendly Admonition to the Drinkers of Gin, Brandy

Reprinted by permission of Mrs. Ralph McGill and *House and Garden* from *House and Garden*, March 1949. Copyright 1949 by The Condé Nast Publications, Inc.

and Other Spirituous Liquors," to go with those who founded the new colony.

It was only natural that the new utopia should attract a diversity of peoples. The first ship, the *Anne*, arrived on 12 February 1733. Soon after came "a group of 40 Hebrews," who were to provide doctors, as well as loyalty and devotion, to the new colony. Within the first year there came also the Lutheran Salzburgers, fleeing persecution. Soon came the Moravians, for the same reason, but finding the atmosphere not to their liking, they moved on to Pennsylvania. Calvinistic Scottish Highlanders came, as did some Huguenots. These stayed, and their names still linger in Georgia towns and in many of the families in them. From the very beginning there have been Scottish, German, Irish, French, Spanish and many other foreign names whose owners are honored as Georgians. Independence of mind is one of their qualities; not even in the smallest farm tenant's house will you find servility.

Georgians are basically conservative people, as persons with a rural background are likely to be. This conservatism is based on regard for the solid, old-fashioned virtues, and is never willful reaction.

Georgia was ready early for the break with Britain, on questions of principle, but the colony moved slowly to an outright war with established authority, despite the urgings of the Liberty Boys, of whom she had her proper share. Years later, she moved even more slowly to leave the Union. Many of her greatest leaders opposed the move, though they unhesitatingly joined their state when the dreaded secession was voted.[77]

Georgia had no liking for war for war's sake. War twice had devastated her coasts and cities and made her sparsely settled inland regions a hell of guerrilla fighting.

After the Civil War, in a condition of defeat, her economic and social systems destroyed, there developed an inevitable defensive attitude. It took on, in the earlier days, a peculiar resentment against interference and "outsiders." There was an occasion when a citizens' committee at Washington, Georgia, approached General Robert Toombs, former sec-

---

[77]See Kenneth Coleman, *American Revolution in Georgia, 1763-1789* (Athens: University of Georgia Press, 1958); Coleman, *Colonial Georgia: A History* (New York: Scribner, 1976).

retary of state of the Confederacy, suggesting wistfully that they'd like
to build a hotel to catch the trade deposited there by the new railroad.
The general considered it, then decided, "We don't need a hotel. If
a gentleman comes to town, he can stay at my house. If he isn't a gentleman, we don't want him here overnight."

Today, Washington, Georgia, mourns that attitude, and it, with
other small cities in Georgia, is busy catching up with the industrial and
commercial development which has swept the state. All the way across
the coastal plains into the hills of Habersham, there is a great foment of
planning and doing. There is also an intellectual foment. During the
decade when her income more than doubled, she has almost tripled the
millions she spends on education. Travelers come now not merely to look
at magnolias and camellias, at sharecroppers and the race problem, but
also to interview Georgia authors and to buy Georgia paintings.

Margaret Mitchell is almost as much of a legend as her novel, *Gone
With the Wind* (which the USSR has seen fit to ban in all its satellite
countries because of its resistance-movement sentiment). New books
come out of Georgia every year by such writers as Nedra Tyre, Carson
McCullers, Barry Fleming, Edison Marshall, Calder Willingham and
the former-governor-turned-author, Ellis Arnall.[78]

Over in Wrens and Louisville, Georgia, near which ran the
short stretch of road known as "Tobacco Road," there are hundreds who
remember with deep affection the tall old Presbyterian minister, Ira
Sylvester Caldwell, whose work with the poverty-ridden dwellers in that
section gave his son, Erskine, a chance to write a book. When the road-
show version of his book came to Augusta, Doctor Caldwell took the
chief characters his son had portrayed to see the production. They re-
joiced mightily at the play, were saddened only by the fact that Jeeter Les-
ter had died the year before and couldn't see himself on the stage.[79]

---

[78]For more by McGill on Mitchell and McCullers, see essays in McGill, *Southern
Encounters: Southerners of Note in Ralph McGill's South*, ed. Calvin M. Logue (Macon
GA: Mercer University Press, 1983).

[79]For books by Erskine Caldwell see *Certain Women* (Boston: Little, Brown,
1957); *Close to Home* (New York: Farrar, Straus and Cudahy, 1962); *God's Little Acre*
(New York: Farrar, Straus and Cudahy, 1962); *Georgia Boy* (New York: New American
Library, ca. 1970); *Deep South: Memory and Observation* (Athens: University of Georgia Press, ca. 1980).

"Wouldn't old Jeeter hev pure enjoyed it?" they asked happily of one another.

Lamar Dodd has given impetus to a school of painters from Athens and Atlanta University.[80] There also is good sculpture being done in Rome and Savannah and Atlanta.

Strangers are welcomed in Georgia, even Republicans. It was at Thomasville, Georgia, that Mark Hanna came with William Mc-Kinley in 1895 to plan a campaign that was to put McKinley in the White House. There is a colony of Eastern-owned plantations there now, and Georgia has so attracted many of these owners they have foresworn all else and cling to her. Thomasville is in the heart of the great quail-hunting kingdom, the finest in the world, where native quail offer the best upland shooting in America.

Eugene O'Neill lived at Sea Island, Georgia, for a number of productive literary years.[81] The coastal islands, the legendary Golden Islands of Georgia, annually attract numerous visitors, many of whom buy land and stay on. Many soldiers, GI's and officers, trained in the state during the late war, have come back now to take jobs and to settle down.

Thus, Georgia is to me a state of perpetually unfolding promise. I like to live in it, to travel it, to have my share of its physical and spiritual self. I have seen its farmers and their families, with no outside income and only their pioneer courage and strength, depart from the slavery of cotton, take worn-out fields and make of them green lands of oats and wheat and hybrid corn. I have seen good cattle come; watched towns change from sleepy, slattern cotton villages, living on one busy sales period a year, to prosperous towns interested in building new buildings, in creating something to hold their young people. I have seen new machines give to more and more acres the curving beauty of terraces that

---

[80]Dodd was head of the art department, University of Georgia, and actively retired at this time.

[81]See Barrett Harper O'Neill, *Eugene O'Neill: The Man and His Plays*, rev. ed. (New York: Dover Publications, 1947); John Henry Raleigh, *Plays of Eugene O'Neill* (Carbondale: Southern Illinois University Press, 1965); Louis Sheaffer, *O'Neill: Son and Artist* (Boston: Little, Brown, 1973).

hold water and the soil. I have seen factories rise out of cities and on rural hills and plains where twenty years ago there were only cotton fields.

I like the coast and the Golden Isles where old ghosts walk; where Fanny Kemble Butler lived and hated slavery and wrote of it so compellingly; where today old houses and old ironwork remain.[82]

In deepest winter, there is South Georgia with maybe a hint of frost but always the sun warm by day and the fields eager for hunting dogs, for shooting of field trials, and always the promise of spring. The mountains are there for summer or winter. There the winter snows fall light, never a matter of three or four inches. I have known bright winter days when all one needed for a walk through the valleys that the Cherokees knew was a light coat-sweater.

In summer, the lakes are good for bass or boating, and the air is soft and cooled with gentle breezes that blow from the mysterious distances where weather is made.

There is a vitality to Georgians, a desire to build a better state, to keep moving onward with the constantly unfolding promise. I have come to know this by knowing them, by visiting and living with them in their homes and on their farms. They have learned the lesson of self-examination, and they have the courage to apply the lessons they have learned. To me, they are the basic stuff of which America and the American dream are made. They have triumphed over the destruction, the bitterness and losses of wars which saw their land, homes and possessions destroyed. They have survived much, but most of them have gone on patiently building some of their warmth and their hopes into the bricks and timbers of their homes and institutions, even while intolerant clamor and recrimination might seem to deny this.

I would not want to leave this state. It is young and strong, and it is just beginning to find its own strength. Not always is it given anyone to be a part of such a force. I would not want to miss it.[83]

---

[82]See Frances Anne Kemble, *Journal of a Residence on a Georgian Plantation in 1838-1839*, ed. John A. Scott (New York: Alfred A. Knopf, 1961).

[83]For more by McGill on Georgia see "My Georgia," "Something of Georgia," "Introduction to *The Old South*," and articles on Atlanta, in volumes 1 and 2; also Kenneth Coleman, ed., *A History of Georgia* (Athens: University of Georgia Press, 1977).

13

A Northerner
Looks at the South:
Review of Ray Sprigle's
In the Land of Jim Crow

L ast summer Ray Sprigle of the *Pittsburgh Post Gazette,* disguised as a Negro, spent four weeks traveling the South. It should be said at the outset that Mr. Sprigle's newspaper stories, on which this book is based, were written honestly and without undue attempt at sensational effect. It would have been easy for Sprigle to cast his material in more lurid form.

What Mr. Sprigle sought to accomplish is less plain. As he himself says, he first conceived of the idea merely as a source for good newspaper copy. He also admits that he sought out the worst aspects of the Negro problem and ignored the progress made and the obvious changes. Changes are taking place in the minds of both Negro and white citizens of the South. Fear, which Mr. Sprigle emphasized, is much less general than he reports. Indeed, one of the most significant facts about the Negro in the South today is that he has lost his fear. Even an election-day killing in one of the more remote of the old-plantation regions of Georgia served not to intimidate but to make Negroes more determined than

Review of Ray Sprigle, *In the Land of Jim Crow* (New York: Simon and Schuster, 1949). Reprinted from *New York Times Book Review,* 5 June 1949, by permission of the *New York Times* and Mrs. Ralph McGill. Copyright 1949 by The New York Times Company. An earlier draft of this review is in the McGill papers, now at Emory University, Atlanta.

ever to vote. Equally important, more white persons moved to help
them do so.

Mr. Sprigle traveled a little too fast. Four weeks is a short time. He
was well directed and well supplied with information. But his book remains, somehow, for all its basic honesty, a sort of journalistic quickie in
blackface.

This reviewer has the feeling, too, that Mr. Sprigle was quite understandably excited by the melodrama of his disguise. He found, after
all, that he was not arrested when he used the white entrance to a railway
station in Atlanta. He should have tried it again, somewhere. Also, the
new Atlanta Negro police are armed and have been since the first day of
official duty. The melodrama of his situation led him to some extreme
statements, which are illuminating to Southerners, colored and white.
But each of these as well as other similar statements, whatever their
grain of truth, is at best an exaggeration.

Mr. Sprigle's generalizations are too sweeping. Consequently they
will not prick the conscience of the white South, which knows the ini-
quities of Jim Crow, but which will find in such generalizations and errors an opportunity to employ the specious argument that many of the
discriminations noted are practiced in the North.

The *Atlanta Daily World*, an aggressive and intelligent Negro daily
which ardently supports NAACP policies, reviewed Mr. Springle's articles in an editorial headed "No Help to Our Cause." The editorial said
in part:

> In utter frankness, we see nothing uncovered in Mr. Sprigle's series which
> all Americans, certainly white and colored Southerners, did not already know.
> In a broad sense it would be fair to say that the series not only do not present
> any new angle or thought on the race problem in the South, but will give flesh
> and substance to the cause of Dixiecrats, who are seeking by every means, both
> honorable and discredited, to set back the cause of mutual advancement be-
> tween the races.
>
> Moreover, we believe Mr. Sprigle is guilty of the common blunder of a
> great number of other Northern whites. A white man who is sincerely inter-
> ested in promoting the advancement of the Negro in the South need not make
> any apology for being white. There are hundreds upon hundreds of Southern
> white liberals who make no pretense of being friendly to the cause of the Ne-
> gro. They are making a great and lasting contribution to this cause. And never
> once have we heard of them having to change their racial identity in order to
> accomplish their desired ends. They work in season and out of season to achieve
> harmony, and not just thirty days under disguise.

It would be helpful, I think, if Mr. Sprigle came back as a white man and visited the Negroes, as Southern white men frequently do. The South needs assistance and criticism, and the South knows that joint endeavors and the exchange of ideas are essential to a solution of a nation-wide problem.

14

Civil Rights
for the Negro

The problem of race relations is a national one. Continued immigration will increasingly emphasize this fact. But the case for civil rights and the present dilemma of Negro-white relationships are largely the problems of the South because of the vis à vis fact of population.

The fight for civil rights should be concentrated on one phase of the problem—that of voting. As I see it, democracy consists basically in every citizen's having equality before the law and in every qualified person's having the right to participate in choosing the officials who will govern him. This right to vote is the basic civil right. All the others are a part of its mosaic structure. In this civil right is the specific for the ills of all other rights.

For example, the poll tax as a prerequisite for voting remains as a restriction on the electorate in seven states. It is slowly disappearing. It will disappear last where the racial population figures are most nearly equal. It is natural this should be so. But the poll tax was never merely

Reprinted by permission of Mrs. Ralph McGill and the *Atlantic Monthly* 184 (November 1949): 64-66. Copyright 1949 by The Atlantic Monthly Company. Reprinted in *Negro Digest*, March 1950.

a barrier against the Negro ballot. It kept as many, if not more, white persons from the voting booth. It will disappear as soon as other discriminations against the ballot are removed. And they are much easier to eliminate.

The Supreme Court of the United States has abolished the white primary, which was the real anti-Negro barrier, withholding from him the status of full citizenship. If the full weight, advice, and assistance of the Justice Department could be thrown into the measure so that all the various camouflaged imitations of the white primary may be brought quickly into federal courts and found to be against the letter and spirit of the Constitution of the United States, the victory for civil rights would be won much easier than through the slow, tedious procedure of Congressional legislation.

In 1948 the Negro vote in the old South was an impressive six hundred percent larger than in 1940, with a total of a little more than seven hundred thousand registered. Three years hence there should be two million. With five million Negroes of voting age in the former Confederate states, there could be more than twice that many if the various limitations of the white primary system were ruled out in time.

Competition for the Negro vote is already a fact in the states of the old Confederacy, and the Negro knows it. Competition for that vote is an open sesame to rights. Competition for that vote has already paved ugly streets, put Negro police in uniform, established Negro fire stations, put Negroes in minor elective offices, equalized some school salaries, built new schools, and constructed parks and playgrounds.

In some of our municipal elections this year, that competition was keen. It was true of all Southern cities. In Atlanta there were four candidates for the Democratic nomination for mayor, a nomination equivalent to election. All four attended Negro ward meetings, spoke in Negro churches, heard appeals for a fire station, more Negro police, more schools, and so on.

The Southern politician, when he goes to a Negro political meeting seeking Negro votes, is made aware of—and is sometimes shocked by—the fact that the Negro's rights have been neglected for so long that the Negro is in a strong strategic position to ask a great deal from politicians. And he is asking. Out loud. In public. Unafraid.

The regular Democrats, as the Philadelphia convention so starkly revealed, are forced to fight the emotional onslaught of tradition, which varies with the states, but they will make, and indeed already are making, more and more concessions. The Republicans, having lost the Negro vote in 1930, eye the growing number of voters as a field ripe for the harvest of recruiting. They, too, will make concessions.

When sheriffs, county commissioners, mayors, and governors compete for votes and seek new votes from the continually increasing total of Negro voters, then indeed will they begin to do what some so flagrantly fail to do—prevent violence and lynchings. Those of us who insist that the states properly, and even constitutionally, are responsible for law enforcement ceased to argue the point long ago in the face of cynical, even farcical, trials and the brutal callousness which simply ignored some lynchings. Federal legislation in this field may be unconstitutional, but we say let's adopt a bill and see. The people are far ahead of the Congress on this issue.

While there was sound and fury from Southern congressmen concerning the poll tax and the antilynching legislation, this was merely the emotional onslaught of a dubious tradition. There never was much opposition from the people. The only real furor was caused by the proposed Fair Employment Practices Act and the several bills introduced. Indeed, one of the troubles has been that civil rights, in the minds of many persons, have been confused with specific pieces of legislation, to the detriment of civil rights.[84]

There was much distortion of the meaning of the Fair Employment Practices Act. It sifted down to the crossroads as meaning social equality; as forced social mixing of the races; as a prelude to compulsory intermarriage and worse. It had police in it—as indeed one of the bills did—and it had courts and jails as its coercive weapons. It was never possible to discuss the bill in any climate of the will to hear. It isn't now possible.

To be honest, most of the Southern progressives have opposed some of the proposed Fair Employment Practices legislation. They would favor an act which would produce investigation, conciliation, and recommendations. But we do not regard it as a field where fiat will replace the admittedly slower processes of education and attempts by the people

---

[84]See V. O. Key, Jr., *Southern Politics in State and Nation* (New York: Vintage Books, 1949).

of both races to conciliate. We think a bill with the coercive powers of police and court and jail is a load which might prove too heavy. Such a coercive act is regarded by many of us as questionable democracy. It seems to us more of an effort to legislate in the field of morals and social doctrine. We keep thinking of prohibition enforcement. And we ask one another, "If one bureau is given its enforcement police, why will not another and yet another ask and receive?"[85]

A recent study by a faculty committee at Tuskegee Institute, discussing not the FEPC but the historic problem of employment and the relationship of Negro colleges to it, said:

> The confusing ferment of opinions with which the daily press and the Negro weeklies, the periodicals, and the current output of the book publishers are confronted suggests that the examination of the race relationships is a continuing process. These relationships won't be made adequate by one-sided solutions or sugar-coated panaceas. Our nation, in spite of partial knowledge and much confusion, persists in its endeavor to improve race relationships in terms of the democratic concept. As it does so, a survey of the facts indicates that most issues arise only incidentally from race, but rather, directly from those factors which govern all human relationships.
>
> One of the unsolved problems of the South is too many people and too few resources. The Negro problem cannot be isolated and treated separately from the overpopulation of the South.
>
> Efforts have been too much on the moral-legalistic side, and not enough on the sustenance side. Populations get grouped into communities according to the function they perform in keeping the communities alive. Historically, the function of the Negro in the South has been that of an unskilled laborer. As soon as technology advanced far enough to perform the function of the skilled worker he was no longer needed for the efficient operation of the community. The South in particular, and the nation in general, have been unwilling to accept the Negro in any other category of community life. The reason for this is fairly simple. There have never been enough skilled and professional jobs in the South for the white population. It is not likely that groups in power, without a compelling motivation of the importance and soundness of democratic participation, would willingly give up favored positions to less advantaged groups.
>
> Unless we can implement our ideals of fair play by finding a way through the cooperative efforts of capital, technology, and educational institutions to create enough job opportunities in the nation to fully employ the whole labor

---

[85]For McGill's evolving position on the FEPC see the editor's introduction.

force, we cannot expect too much progress in securing for Negroes a larger measure of opportunity.

Before advocating action programs for dealing with the race problem we suggest that Negro colleges, in cooperation with other colleges, make a scientific investigation of the following areas:

Population. . . . We need to know how many people the resources of the South can support. We need to know how much capital and technological wealth is necessary to develop these resources to their fullest and most efficient use.

Migration. We need to know what skills we will need to import from areas outside the South to develop our resources, and we need to know the job needs of areas outside the South so that we can train our excess population for these jobs. Negro colleges, in particular, may explore the migration possibilities to other regions, and courses of study to train Negroes for these jobs outside the region.

Techniques of Minorities. There is the possibility that the race problem in the South has much in common with the problem of minority peoples in other parts of the world, and the immigrants to America from other parts of the world. A study of how these groups adjusted, and the barriers they had to encounter, may lead to fruitful techniques of handling the problem here.

Desirable as it is to preach and legislate evils out of society this method seldom, if ever, works. Negroes and many of the whites in the South are being affected by the forces of declining farm opportunities, and increasing farm mechanization and livestock pasture farming. Unfortunately displaced agricultural workers fail to become absorbed in industrial jobs as fast as they are being pushed off the farm. The solution of the human problem of the South is too intricate and involved to be left to people of good intention but who lack the necessary knowledge to deal with the issues involved. Fortunately colleges serving both white and Negro youth may share substantially in reaching solutions through the development of leadership and in the conduct of continuing studies on the problems listed in this statement.

That is a fairly lengthy quote, but I regard it as most pertinent. We are a region which has never had enough jobs. As industry comes, and as more Negroes come to the ballot box, this economic and social condition will change. But jobs by fiat in a region historically short of jobs would not work out. The laws would be unenforceable. I believe we are correct in saying a majority of Southern Negroes, while wanting an FEPC, prefer one of investigation, arbitration, conciliation, and not one with coercive police powers.

There is a great deal of misunderstanding about segregation, which in varying degrees is a national institution. In the South, the pattern called segregation is deeply written in social custom and heavily written in law. In the North, it is not the law, although it has found its way into custom in by no means negligible quantity, as may be seen by any who choose to look.

Segregation is a broad and fluid term. All its students and all its practitioners are agreed as to its unpredictability and flexibility at its fringes. It changes as society changes. Various forces work to make its maintenance more difficult. Universal education and universal segregation are uneasy bedfellows. The complexity of the industrial economy and of the growing administrative services which accompany modern society has brought into being wide areas of life even in the South in which the institution breaks down. One Southern state, it is true, by law requires the segregation of operatives in mills so that white people alone must work in a weaving room and colored people alone must work in a picker room; but it is significant that this statute, now many decades old, has not been copied.[86]

With the growth of the Negro vote, a good many signs appear that in state and local administration, as well as in the federal government, Negro views are being sought on policy matters. There have been some significant recent appointments of Negroes to boards and commissions, in Southern states, which govern the expenditure of important amounts of public money.

When public education was a matter of one-room schools, two such schools in each neighborhood were no great drain on the public purse. When a consolidated school building costs several hundred thousand dollars and its technical and vocational equipment is expensive too, here and there ways will be found to reduce the rigidity of school segregation. The states which maintain segregation in education are face to face with the cost of providing entirely equal if separate facilities. The changing pattern in the graduate education in states around the Southern borders undoubtedly foreshadows further modification in colleges and, at a later stage, in secondary education.

There is a more obscure factor, too. The customs of a segregated society were formed at a time when the two peoples, living side by side,

---

[86]See C. Vann Woodward, *Strange Career of Jim Crow*, 3d. rev. ed. (New York: Oxford University Press, 1974).

were widely different in their cultural inheritance. That gap closes every year. The educated South, long ago, found ways in which to work on matters of common interest with colored people of equal attainments, in a courtesy that bears only vestigial traces of the separateness beneath. That area of common understanding and common courtesy broadens as to the number of persons it includes and as to the fields which it invades. It broadens now into the whole field of trade-unionism and into organizations of farmers.[87]

It is against this background that the forces of reform, progress, reaction, and violence are at work. The Klan activity is vicious, but it is local in influence; and its violence—also local, directed by no central authority—is a part of the struggle to slow down the breaking up of the old patterns. There are sadistic, evil men in the various Klans. There are even a few good, well-meaning persons who are not informed but are easily led and made afraid. There are also the cynical phonies who make the profits. But the Klan is finished, although its philosophy and methods will endure here and there in the old-plantation counties where cotton and timber are gone, the economy is poor, and a few men control the politics.

As Booker T. Washington sensibly advised, we are letting down our buckets where we are.

We earnestly believe the bucket which will draw up the most water of success is that of the ballot. The best rights come from it. The barriers before it are by no means iron curtains. They are pushovers, if really tested by the Constitution.[88]

---

[87]See Wilma Dykeman and James Stokely, *Seeds of Southern Change: The Life of Will Alexander* (Chicago: University of Chicago Press, 1962).

[88]See John Hope Franklin and Isidore Starr, eds., *Negro in Twentieth-Century America: A Reader on the Struggle for Civil Rights* (New York: Vintage Books, 1967); John Hope Franklin, *From Slavery to Freedom: A History of Negro Americans*, 5th ed. (New York: A. A. Knopf, 1980).

15

Demagoguery
State by State:
Review of V. O. Key's
Southern Politics

F
ailure rarely receives that criticism of judgment which success always commands, and the politically unhappy South and its political failure until now have lacked an overall dispassionate critical analysis.

There have been many studies of the demagogues. Memphis's Boss Ed Crump has been subjected to almost microscopic examination, but not until the appearance of *Southern Politics* has the whole complex picture and story of failure been put between the covers of a book. It is a really magnificent accomplishment, the errors and unsound conclusions in it being so few as to detract not at all from the net result.

The study was first conceived as one which would deal with the poll tax. The then governor of Georgia, Ellis Arnall, agreed to assist the originators of the idea, Roscoe C. Martin, director of the Bureau of Public Administration at the University of Alabama, and his associates. Soon after the original decision Governor Arnall was able to have the state legislature abolish the poll tax and, since only seven states were left with that iniquitous device, the study was, fortunately for all students of politics, changed to research into the political structure of nine Southern

V. O. Key, Jr., *Southern Politics in State and Nation* (New York: Vintage Books, 1949). Reprinted from *Saturday Review*, 3 December 1949, by permission of Mrs. Ralph McGill and *Saturday Review*. Copyright 1949, The Saturday Review Associates, Inc.

states. Funds were obtained from the Rockefeller Foundation. Dr. V. O. Key, native of Texas and professor of political science at Johns Hopkins, happily, was selected to direct the research. Three years were spent gathering the material.

It will be most helpful to the nation's understanding of the South if all commentators of air and pen will learn from Dr. Key that Southern politics have no regional unity per se but are factional, each state conforming to its own folkways and mores. Thus, four states could go Dixiecrat last November, not for any real belief in states' rights by those who led the movement, but because to do so would enable them to seize control of the party machinery within the state. In still other Southern states, Georgia for example, the will to join the Dixiecrats was present, but since there was no rival group seeking to take over the party machinery the safest course seemed to be to stay in the party, although at no time was there ever even lip service paid the Democratic party platform.

It is the Negro, of course, who remains in his inevitable role of a black Nemesis. The political chorus of shibboleths is the same in every state, racial superiority being the loudest and most frequent. Here again it is well to recognize that the ratio of Negro population to white determines the degree of demagoguery.[89] Thus, as the state-by-state survey reveals, there is a vast difference, for example, between the politics of Virginia and Mississippi, of North Carolina and Georgia. Dr. Key noted, for example, that in Georgia the two newspapers in Atlanta, long in opposition to Talmadgeism, while by no means supporting Herman Talmadge, did not oppose him. He missed the real decadent depths the factionalism at times attain. A sad situation had developed. A majority of Georgians knew, as did the papers, that the men who would take over the state in the event of a victory by the anti-Talmadge candidate would have been more corrupt and damaging than those who would serve under the son of "Old Gene." There was no Republican party ticket. Thousands refused to vote at all. The state-by-state study is, to a Southerner at least, the most fascinating feature of the book.[90]

---

[89]See Cal M. Logue and Howard Dorgan, eds., *The Oratory of Southern Demagogues* (Baton Rouge: Louisiana State University Press, 1981).

[90]See "How It Happened Down in Georgia," in this volume.

Dr. Key sees hope for the South, as indeed there is. Banishment of the white primary and the knock-down of all imitations of it are bringing the Negro to the polls. The number of registered Negroes increased an amazing six hundred percent from 1940 to 1948. There are an estimated 5,500,000 Negroes of voting age in the states of the old Confederacy, and their increasing appearance at the polls is going to bring civil rights long before legislative fiat can do the job.

It is a depressing picture of a South politically isolated from national realities—not actually connected to the Democratic party save by name, and not yet aware of the steady growth of its urban centers and their inevitable influence on affairs political, an influence which, as of now, is merely casting a foretelling shadow. The book, while dismaying, is not an indictment. It is a document so basically sound it may hurry the political reformation. And certainly it is a valuable book to all interested in the future of American democracy.[91]

---

[91]For a follow-up study to Key's work, see Jack Bass and Walter DeVries, *The Transformation of Southern Politics: Social Change and Political Consequence Since 1945* (New York: New American Library, 1976).

16

Weighing a Dixie Dilemma: Review of Hodding Carter's *Southern Legacy*

ooks on the South are almost as numerous as those on the Soviet Union. They stem, too, from almost the same diverse motives: to justify, explain away, to pillory, to arouse hatred against, to gloss over, and so on. Like those about Russia, the enthusiastic justification and the hatred largely are uncritical.

The critical truth is rarely come by in books about either. Jonathan Daniels did an excellent job of reporting and observation some years ago in *A Southerner Discovers the South*. Virginius Dabney has made scholarly and valuable contributions in *Below the Potomac* and other publications. W. J. Cash was the first to go boldly and deeply into the "why" of the South in his *Mind of the South*. Howard Odum's *Southern Regions* remains the basic source book and his sociological studies have been and are necessary readings.

Hodding Carter's *Southern Legacy* takes its place beside these. Excluding historical and biographical contributions, I can think of no previous book on the South which so carefully hews to the line of truth, avoiding all save that for which the author personally may vouch. It is

Hodding Carter, *Southern Legacy* (Baton Rouge: Louisiana State University Press, 1950). Reprinted from *Saturday Review*, 4 February 1950, by permission of Mrs. Ralph McGill and *Saturday Review*. Copyright 1950, The Saturday Review Associates, Inc.

an account of the experience of a very human, clear-seeing, wise, courageous scholar and reporter in singularly plain terms. He relates much of it to human beings and their lives. More than any other person who has written on the "why" of the South, I believe he has come closest to an answer which can be understood and accepted as true and reasonable by all save the unreasonable.

Here, in *Southern Legacy*, is the South which, after all the years of talking about a "New South," is suffering the first real labor pains of the long prophesied new being.

In the South the race problem is so interwoven with all that is the South that it may not be dissected out and examined as one may examine an inflamed appendix. Carter is the first to do so clear a job of demonstrating this. Carter reveals and demonstrates that fact. There are fourteen chapters in *Southern Legacy*, and the problem is in all of them, woven there as part of the fabric of the South.[92]

The initial chapter is titled "The Broadsword Virtues." It was these virtues which made it possible for Hodding Carter to establish himself in Greenville, Mississippi, and publish there a newspaper which disturbed and annoyed the status quo from the day of its first issue. It is the strength of these virtues which enabled him to absorb his newspaper competition and to become one of the most progressive voices in the South, one of the most forthright spokesmen for full citizenship for the Negro in the state with the largest Negro population, and therefore, with the most fear and resistance.

On concluding reading the book, I found myself hoping it would have a large readership—South, North, East and West. Also, I found myself wishing especially that three of the chapters—"The Case of Eddie Mack," "Clint Ate Corn Pone," and "Just Leave Us Alone"—might somehow be "must" reading for every literate person with the slightest curiosity about the South.

Hodding Carter is the first of those writing a book on "the South" to give full force to the folkways and folklore of the South. Yet, it is the folkways and folklore of a nation or region that best explain its resistance to or acceptance of laws, decrees, ideas, government, or force.

---

[92]McGill wrote the foreword to Carter's *Southern Legacy* when that book was reissued in 1965; it is reprinted in volume 2.

In his chapter "Just Leave Us Alone" Mr. Carter reveals the hypocrisy which is behind much of the Southern resentment against distant criticism. He reveals that same hypocritical quality in the states' rights movement, too. But he says, with great truth:

> The white South does have a historic and present-day basis for suspicion and fear. The Southern contradiction of democracy is the only one in the nation against which an aggressive demand for full, abrupt, and forcible revision is continuously directed. Ours is the only region in which an ethnologically distinct, repressed, and culturally retarded people are constantly told, through every available medium of communication, that the dominant majority is unqualifiedly evil in its behavior. . . . Certainly this majority is too reluctant to give ground. No one is more aware of this reluctance than the mounting numbers of Southerners who are determined upon absolute justice for the Negro. But they are equally aware that justice and equality and democracy are absolute nowhere in the United States, that the battle line is nationwide, and that violent propulsion toward the ideal precipitates violent reaction.

Certainly Hodding Carter and others who stand with him, as well as those who were earlier in the fight, are asking for no let-us-alone period, nor any relenting in the struggle to remove the contradiction of democracy. They are saying, "It is not true that we must be let alone, but that we must not be set apart as an incomprehensible, stubborn contradiction."

I believe the most unrelenting critic of the South's failures and injustices will be impressed with the honesty of this book. It is an aggressive book, which will offend the Southern Bourbons, cause the hypocritical and dishonest states' rights leaders to wail, and encourage those Southerners who love their region enough to be dissatisfied with it until it is "more perfect and secure."[93]

---

[93]Other works by Carter are *South Strikes Back* (Garden City NY: Doubleday, 1959); *Angry Scar: The Story of Reconstruction* (Garden City NY: Doubleday, 1959); *First Person Rural* (Garden City NY: Doubleday, 1963).

17

The Real Reconstruction
Begins

"You been noticing all them lone chimneys and fallin'-in shacks out in the fields?" he asked as we drove along.

"Yes," I said. "They always look lonely, and even now, with vines growing on them or bushes almost hiding them, they still seem sad."

"Boll-weevil monuments," he said. "Inside, in front of them chimneys one night, some poor, hungry devil of a nigger or a white feller, tenant or 'cropper, waited until his kids was asleep and then sat there and talked it out with his wife. They got out. They left maybe in the dead of night with a quilt or so and a few pots and pans in an old pickup truck or a jalopy, with their woke-up young 'uns whimpering and afraid. Or, they just left by day, bold-like, and to hell with it. They was hard days there in the early twenties, when land that had growed a bale to the acre maybe turned out a bale to ten. Sometimes they set the house afire. A few did. But usually it was later that some tramp or roamin' kids set 'em just for fun. Now most that wasn't burned has fell in.

"They pulled out for Detroit and Akron. They went to Pittsburgh and to Chicago. But they went. And not many come back."

Reprinted from the *Reporter*, 28 March 1950, by permission of Mrs. Ralph McGill and the *Reporter.* Copyright 1950, by Fortnightly Publishing Company.

We crossed a new concrete bridge, and off to the right, a hundred feet or more from the road in a small grove of trees, stood a small church, its windows broken, its doors swinging drunkenly, the shingles gone from a section of its roof.

"See that?" my driver said. "You see more and more of them. Plantation churches. Now they're monuments, too. The tractors and the cotton pickers closed 'em. There ain't nobody to go to 'em no more. Most of the cabins is empty, with cotton growing right up to the doors. In another year or two, they'll be gone. She's a-changin', this here South is."

I had hired this man to drive me on a trip to see the mechanization at work on cotton farms in Georgia, Alabama, and Mississippi. He was no better or worse an observer than any other Southerner who goes out and looks at his region today.

The South *is* changing—fast. It is in a period of transition, in which people are leaving the land faster than jobs are opening up in the new industries.[94] Too many Southerners are still going to Detroit, Pittsburgh, and Chicago. But the destinations are becoming more varied. California is no longer too far away. Of course, the great industrial centers of the nation are drawing people from the land not only in the South, bu also in the Dakotas, Nebraska, and other agricultural states where machines are taking over, and hand laborers are not needed in anything like the numbers they were ten years ago.

In Memphis, Nashville, and Columbia, Tennessee, in Louisville, and Atlanta, the once-great mule markets are still operating, but many of the stalls are vacant, and the lots where the long-eared hybrids brayed are often empty, or filled with beef cattle or yearling calves.

In Cleveland, Georgia, Jim Davidson, soldier of the First World War and editor of the Cleveland *Courier*, talks and writes about the new life in the Appalachians, where once corn whiskey and a few hogs and sheep were the only crops, and the burden of making a living was hard, and comforts few. Even the mountains are changing. Rural electrifica-

[94]The changing South was a recurring theme in McGill's writings and speeches, as evidenced by essays in this volume and by "The South in Transition" speech, 1965, in *Ralph McGill: Editor and Publisher*, ed. Calvin McLeod Logue (Durham: Moore Publishing Company, 1969) 2:348-60.

tion has come—and still is coming. The mountaineers are planting clovers and grasses and hybrid corn. They are marketing millions of broilers each year. They are creating new, small dairies, and the big cheese firms are becoming interested.

"The mountains had it hard," Jim Davidson says. "We had small fields and couldn't compete with the big ones. Now, with hybrid corn and with grasses that will grow in our valleys and along our slopes to hold soil, we can build, and are building, a new and solid economy. There are pumps in the wells and water in the houses now. We've just begun. But we are on the way."

One of the reasons the South has punished its land so severely has been its almost necessary devotion to row crops. Added to that was the fact that the land had to support so many people. There was never money enough to carry out scientific farm practices, such as crop rotation and planting of cover crops.[95]

Now small factories are coming. At least one member of almost every family lives at home but works at a mill. This prosperity is reflected in painted houses and barns, in new farm machinery and washing machines. It is evidenced, too, by many small, new houses for young people who have married and built on family land.

In the South ten years ago, a green field in January was an oddity. Today all over the South are rich meadows on which cattle can graze the year around. The livestock population has more than tripled, and there is almost a distinct cult of farmers who favor the new grasses and legumes that keep fields green in winter: serecia, lespedeza, ladino, white Dutch, Manganese, and crimson clovers; Kentucky 31 fescue, and its rival from Oregon, kudzu—the miracle plant that heals land wounds that time alone will not heal, but worsen. Cattlemen from Nebraska, Kansas, and Illinois come to look, and some even to stay. There is also a trend toward small grains. Many a farmer, quitting cotton, has started planting oats and wheat, and found them rewarding.

"I felt like I had got out of jail when I quit cotton," one farmer told me last June, as we rode on the combine which was harvesting his oats.

---

[95]See Thomas Dionysius Clark, *Three Paths to the Modern South: Education, Agriculture, and Conservation* (Athens: University of Georgia Press, 1965); Timothy Thomas Fortune, *Black and White: Land, Labor, and Politics in the South* (Chicago: Johnson Publishing Company, 1970).

His wife, who once picked cotton, was happy in her newly electrified kitchen.

I spend a lot of time traveling around the South by airplane and automobile. When I do, I cannot help recalling the South that I saw in 1928 when I came down from Tennessee to work in the cotton region; and that I saw in 1938, on a special tour with the presidential committee that called the South the nation's economic problem number one. Today from an airplane I see the greens of new pastures, the geometric curves of contour plowing, both signalizing the disappearance of the old washed, galled land, crisscrossed with gullies.

The towns, too, have grown and improved. Finally, there are the people, whose faces don't look as they did ten and twenty years ago.

But the South has by no means caught up. Measured by absolutes, it still lags in many details. Measured by the past, however, the gains have been dramatic. The South today has a feeling it is out of the woods. It still has its frustrations, and its infections, like the Ku Klux Klan, and the demagoguery of some of its politicians, but even these plagues are not as virulent as they used to be.[96] The talk today is not so much of the two lynchings last year, but of the more than twenty that were prevented by forthright action of local law-enforcement officers. As for the Klan, it is an almost impotent organization, unfeared save in the few remote rural regions where population is sparse and frustration and poverty worst. Even in such areas, the Klan is growing less resolute.

There is no question about the improvement in race relations. It will be a long time before segregation breaks down to the degree that it has in Chicago, New York, or Philadelphia. But it has broken down at the edges enough for the two races to get together and work at solving their problems.[97] It is easing, too, in the fields of graduate and professional

---

[96]See Cal M. Logue and Howard Dorgan, eds., *Oratory of Southern Demagogues* (Baton Rouge: Louisiana State University Press, 1981).

[97]See C. Vann Woodward, *The Strange Career of Jim Crow*, 3d. rev. ed. (New York: Oxford University Press, 1966); Thomas Jackson Woofter, *Southern Race Progress: The Wavering Color Line* (Washington DC: Public Affairs Press, 1957); Raymond W. Mack, ed., *Changing South* (Chicago: Aldine Publishing Company, 1970); Charles Pearce Roland, *The Improbable Era: The South Since World War II* (Lexington: University Press of Kentucky, 1975).

education and travel. There is still a struggle going on between the old and the new attitudes, and nothing reflects it better than recent action in the Dixiecrat state of Mississippi, where the Dixiecrat governor took the lead in appropriating money to equalize educational facilities in the state, both as to equipment and pay. There are many lesser, but still important, illustrations of change and improvement in race relations, and of the corresponding increases in human dignity.

It is only lately that Southerners have come to realize that, while there are as many differences in politics, economics, and attitudes as there are states, and while the South has never been a separate entity, there are two distinct physical Souths. One is the Piedmont South. The other is the old plantation South.

The Piedmont curves, roughly like a scimitar, from the edges of New Jersey to the eastern boundary of Mississippi. Rivers run across it and along it. Roads and rail lines follow it. It saw the first power development, and the first industrialization, when cotton manufacturers began moving from New England to North Carolina more than thirty years ago. Today, most industry is clustered on the Piedmont. It has begun to wander off into some of the old plantation towns, where roads, rails, and labor supply make it possible, but in the main, it is the Piedmont South where one finds better wages, more impressive advances in working conditions, improved schools, housing, and living standards, and, importantly, superior relations between the races.

It is the old plantation South which still lags. In its most poverty-stricken counties, where the land is worn out, where the timber is used up, where for years the best young people have gotten their high school diplomas and left, one finds the most hidebound political thinking, the most corrupt county government and justice, the most friction and race violence, and much of the drag on the South's general progress.

The First World War quickened the emigration from the South, and the second accelerated it beyond expectations. It has not really slowed down yet. A few people are returning, but there are many others going north and west.

The man with the mule, the plow, and the wagon is finished as an economic unit. He died of gasoline, and especially of tractors, one of which can do the work of seven mules. There are a few one-mule farms left but they are pitiful, as all starving and dying things are pitiful.

There is one danger in the inexorable transition—that farming may become a monopoly of the relatively few who can afford it. A good pasture cannot be made in a year's time. For some, three years will do, but poor soil really needs five to be rebuilt so that it will support good sod and mineral-rich grasses. There is a saying that a man ought to be in the cattle or dairy business five years before he gets his first animal. A cotton farmer without capital and with little or no income can't condition, fertilize, and grow grass for three to five years and then buy cattle to put on it. The South knows there must be a change in the farm-credit system, and it knows too, that it has waited almost too long to agitate for one.

But, for the first time since the Civil War, the South has some capital of its own, and can see light ahead. It is surer of the road. It has more confidence in its own ability to work things out. There is a ferment of change, enthusiasm, hope, and determination that even the casual quick-tripper is made to feel.

It was in 1938 that President Roosevelt made public the study by a group of Southerners which proved the South to be the nation's chief economic problem. In 1938 the New Deal was five years old.[98] The TVA was almost completed. Huey Long had been dead three years. The Scottsboro case was seven years old. The average per capita income in the South was $315, as against the national average of $509. The average textile wage was only 37.5 cents an hour.

Since 1938 the South's population has increased by more than three million, despite the heavy emigration. Wages are higher, farm income is greater, and agricultural practices are much improved and diversified. There are five million more cattle. New industries have been established and more continue to come. Yet the South still receives only about a fifth of the nation's income, and still buys most of the nation's fertilizer.

In 1938, available figures show, the South mined one-tenth of the nation's iron ore, but produced only seven percent of the nation's pig iron. By 1948, the South was producing about thirteen percent of U.S. pig iron. In 1938, the South had twenty-seven percent of the nation's

---

[98]See Frank Burt Freidel, *F.D.R. and the South* (Baton Rouge: Louisiana State University Press, 1975); Paul E. Mertz, *New Deal Policy and Southern Rural Poverty* (Baton Rouge: Louisiana State University Press, 1978).

installed hydroelectric generating capacity and a production of twenty-one percent of the nation's total power. Today it is estimated that the South has about thirty percent of the generating capacity and produces about twenty-eight percent of the national total.

With more than half the nation's farmers in 1938, the South had less than a fifth of the nation's farm machinery and implements. In 1948, with about forty-eight percent of America's farmers, the South had about twenty-two percent of its farm implements. In 1938, fifty-three percent of its farmers were tenants. By 1940 the percentage was forty, and the figure was estimated at only thirty-eight percent in 1948. High land prices will probably hold the figure at about that level in 1950. Southern farms continue to be the smallest in the nation, but their average size has increased from seventy-one to ninety-four acres. In housing, the South has made its greatest advance in rural areas. Urban housing has generally been improved only slightly.[99]

Recent application of the 75-cent-an-hour wage law has raised the Southern average, but certainly its full effect will not be measurable for at least another year. This law was particularly important for the South, which has long been cursed not merely with low wages but with a curious psychology, explained by the long job-hunger, which made the South willing to accept lower wages as a sort of old Southern tradition. The textile wage has almost tripled since 1938, but is still below the national average. Only the UAW has succeeded in wiping out the North-South differential.

Since the South has the most children and the least income, education is perhaps the region's major problem. Progress is being made. Georgia, for example, which had one of the most impoverished school systems, has increased its state school appropriations from $14,457,132 in 1938 to $50,875,000 in 1950. Such increased budgets are more or less the rule all over the South. Yet measured against the national figures, they still reveal a serious lag.

---

[99]See Edgar Streeter Dunn, *Recent Southern Economic Development as Revealed by the Changing Structure of Employment* (Gainesville: University of Florida Press, 1962); Brian Rungeling et al., *Employment, Income, and Welfare in the Rural South* (New York: Praeger, 1977); Arthur M. Ford, *Political Economics of Rural Poverty in the South* (Cambridge: Ballinger Publishing Company, 1973).

Perhaps the greatest improvement has been in public health, although even here the national figures reveal how far the South has yet to go. Malaria, once the worst plague, has been greatly reduced, and in many areas eliminated. The doctor shortage is most severe in the South.[100]

According to a study made at the University of Georgia in 1935, the South's percentage of the nation's industry in 1930 was almost exactly that of 1865. It is against this background that one must measure the progress—and the tremendous lag which remains. Migration to the cities emphasizes the fact that, while there has been improvement in the farm and industrial economy, training for service industries is not receiving enough attention. These must, eventually, absorb much of the increase in urban populations.

Certainly the nation must see, as the thoughtful Southerner does, that the South's backwardness, and its influences on migration, politics, and the national economy are national problems—not regional ones.

Few in the South believe in the filibusterers, the demagogues, the Klan. But what often seems to the South almost a national policy of hostile criticism and suspicion, in which misrepresentation and error are not uncommon, makes for a stubborn defense of leaders and policies for which the South actually has only contempt. This is one of the great frustrations of the South—it must so often defend its wrongs.

Something of Lincoln's spirit and of Roosevelt's policy of aid to the South would be helpful now, because, as nearly always, fears outweigh realities.

But even so, 1950 finds the South with more courage, more willingness to subject itself to self-examination, with more money and enthusiasm, and more determination to work and sacrifice for the needs of a region which firmly continues to hold the affection of most of its people.

---

[100]For more by McGill on malaria see "Robert Winship Woodruff," in McGill, *Southern Encounters: Southerners of Note in Ralph McGill's South*, ed. Calvin M. Logue (Macon GA: Mercer University Press, 1983).

For a generation now the South has talked and written of "a New South." The birth pains are at last beginning.[101]

---

[101]See John Hope Franklin and Isidore Starr, eds., *Negro in Twentieth-Century America: A Reader on the Struggle for Civil Rights* (New York: Vintage Books, 1967); John Hope Franklin, *From Slavery to Freedom: A History of Negro Americans*, 5th ed. (New York: A. A. Knopf, 1980).

18

Why I Live in Atlanta

From the Georgia seacoast inward for about 150 miles lies her coastal plain, hardly 500 feet above sea level. This plain ends at the old fall line, where once the first sea was, and here the waters from the mountains and the Piedmont highlands step down to the flat and slow their movement toward the sea.

From this ancient shore line, the Piedmont climbs swiftly to highlands of 1,000 and 1,500 feet through which the Chattahoochee River cuts its deep valleys, and then, almost suddenly, meets with the great ridges and reaches of the Blue Ridge Mountains.

On the plateau of the highlands sits Atlanta, a comfortable six hours' drive from quiet beaches and the historic Golden Isles, a brief two-hour journey from cool mountain slopes more than 3,000 feet above sea level.

That's my town—Atlanta. And I like it.

I like it first of all because it is an American city, with a great cross-section of Americans who have been attracted to it and who leaven well the really native-born who make up about twenty-five percent of its total population. Now and then the envious call it a Yankee city. It is—and yet it isn't. The Yankees come, full of great plans—and for a time they move

Reprinted from *Pageant* 5 (April 1950): 114-17, by permission of Mrs. Ralph McGill. A typed draft of this piece in the McGill papers now at Emory University, Atlanta, is entitled, "That's My Town—Atlanta, And I Like It."

as if they expected to fulfill them in a single day. But then, they learn. They discover that, though the plans still are good and important, there also is time for living and for play, and that somehow one may live and play and yet get things done. So, the blending of the Yankee and Southern tempo creates for Atlanta a faster pace perhaps than other Southern cities but one still comfortable and easy.

The capital city of one of the Deep South states, Atlanta still is not a city of magnolias and moonlight—and what is more, it never was. It is not an old city. Indians were living just north of the town site until 1837 and it was only in 1846 that its name was changed from Marthasville to Atlanta. An executive of the Western and Atlantic Railroad, which had its southern terminus in the town, picked the name Atlanta, which he said was the feminine for Atlantic. Perhaps it is.

When the Civil War came, Atlanta was a bustling railroad city not far from frontier status. General William T. Sherman burned the city in November 1864. Of 3,800 buildings, 400 escaped the flames.

I like Atlanta because of its courage. It was a city wise and brave enough to bury its hatred and emotions in the ruins of war and to direct its strength toward recuperation rather than revenge and wistful wishing about the past. The city has never looked backward but always toward the future. It is not frustrated, but confident.[102]

I like it, too, because it is a town with integrity and character, and it is not afraid to value those qualities. Atlanta escapes being puritanical, yet it has never been an "open" town with an entrenched underworld, organized gambling, and vice. It is a good city in which to bring up children. Its public schools are excellent, and it also supports splendid private schools for both white and Negro students.

I like Atlanta because while too much of the South was saying merely "Give us time," and doing nothing about its racial problem, Atlanta was doing much to equalize opportunity for all its citizens. Its Negro teachers now receive equal pay for equal training and experience, as do those in the county of which Atlanta is the county seat. Atlanta has Negro police officers and is adding others. It has a Negro bank which is a member of the Federal Reserve System and many other successful Negro busi-

---

[102]See McGill's "The Housing Challenge," "Lighthouse to the Postwar South," and "She Sifted the Ashes and Built a City," in volumes 1 and 2.

nesses with high ranking in Dun and Bradstreet. Atlanta is the largest center of Negro university education in the world, supports the only Negro daily newspaper in America, and I believe, the only radio station entirely Negro-owned and operated.

It is a city which makes errors but which has never been ashamed to admit them as it seeks earnestly to remove injustices. The stupidities of the Ku Klux Klan no longer have any following other than dupes for promoters and prejudiced neurotics. The building which housed Klan officials in the 1920s is now a rectory of the Catholic Church Cathedral of Christ the King.

And I like Atlanta because of its churches. They are many, but because most of them understand the mission of the church and religion, Atlanta escapes being "church-ridden" or oppressed by the bigoted.

My town pleases me, too, because it is a cosmopolitan one, with a very substantial Greek and Syrian community and lesser numbers of other nationality groups. They are among the city's best assets, and we all get along together well.

Atlanta has no decaying, stately mansions of the antebellum period, but it does have residential sections of beauty and charm. It has slums, but they are decreasing and they are less brutal than those of, say, Washington DC, or Pittsburgh or Chicago. Atlanta had the first slum clearance projects in the nation—and they were for both white and colored races. The program continues, with a new project costing thirty million dollars begun this year.

Atlanta is a city with no past-due bills. It has excellent credit and a tax rate which is comparatively low. It is a city with a growing metropolitan district population of about six hundred thousand, though its city limits, unmoved in about forty years, restrict the city proper to about four hundred thousand.

I'm proud of Atlanta because it has been a leader in the transition of the South from an agricultural region tied to cotton and row-crop poverty to one in which an agriculture based on pastures, cattle, dairying, poultry, pigs, tobacco, peanuts, and some cotton is being balanced with industrial jobs. Ford and General Motors have built huge assembly plants in Atlanta to add to long-established Chevrolet and Fisher Body plants. It is the financial, wholesale, and transportation capital of the Southeast. Within another twenty years, it may confound some of its critics in old Savannah who have been heard to say that, if Atlanta could suck as hard as it can blow, it would pull the Atlantic Ocean to its door. A channel is now being planned from the sea to Atlanta by way of the Chattahoochee River.

Atlanta is a city of department stores and many shops. Last year two stores alone did a combined business of almost one hundred million dollars. They enable the "Peaches on Peachtree Street," famed for their beauty, to be listed among the best-dressed women in America.

Because its streets grew almost casually, however, Atlanta's traffic situation is pretty bad. Famous Five Points, the heart of the city's business district, was originally the site of an artesian well and a large spring. All paths led there and streets took on the pattern of the paths. But we are doing something about the problem. A bond issue of many millions is already at work building super highways. When these are done, other jobs will be initiated, such as opening dead-end streets and building additional access streets.

Atlanta is becoming a great medical center, built around Emory University Hospital. The Public Health Service has just announced a research laboratory in tropical and communicable diseases to be established in Atlanta, its buildings and equipment to cost ten million dollars, making it the finest laboratory of its type in the world. The city's Grady Hospital is being enlarged through an endowment built up by some of her more thoughtful citizens. A contract also has been let to build a new Negro hospital at a cost of about two million dollars.

I like Atlanta because its people are sports-minded. A big football game weekend at Georgia Tech turns the city into an overgrown college town with all the trimmings. Baseball fans are treated to Class AA ball by the Atlanta Crackers of the Southern Association. The excellence of our golf courses has brought on a parade of champions probably unmatched by any other city in the country—headed, of course, by the incomparable Bobby Jones.

Atlanta has its own symphony orchestra, assembled from its own musicians, and last year over-subscribed. It has a civic ballet and an opera company. Its High Museum of Art is growing steadily, and it is a city that can be counted on to sell out any concert performances of merit.

Atlanta rivals New Orleans itself as a city of good food, although, admittedly, the best Southern cooking is in its private homes—a fact generally true over the South, where citizens join to warn the unwary of the average Bar-B-Q or fried chicken shack located along the highways.

My town is always going somewhere, and it seems always to know where it is going. It does so in no precipitate rush but steadily, never forgetting to retain a tempo which permits gracious living, friendship, and pride in being a part of life.

There is a zest to my town, and yet a feeling of warmth and the best meanings of life. To me, Atlanta combines best the pleasant virtues of a small city with those of a large one. I like it.[103]

---

[103]See Kenneth Coleman, ed., *A History of Georgia* (Athens: University of Georgia Press, 1977).

19

History in a President's Letters: Review of *F.D.R.: His Personal Letters, 1929-1945*

On 12 November 1928, Franklin D. Roosevelt, governor of New York, sent a telegram from Warm Springs, Georgia, to Louis M. Howe, initiating plans to rebuild the Democratic party, shattered in the elections of that year.[104] On 9 April 1945, from the same address, Franklin D. Roosevelt, four times president of the United States, wrote a brief note to Supreme Court Justice Frank Murphy, saying that he planned to attend the United Nations Conference in San Francisco and therefore would be unable to see him for several weeks.[105] Three days later Roosevelt died at the Little White House.

The two messages open and close what is one of the most fascinating books of our time: *F.D.R.: His Personal Letters, 1928-1945*. The entries are arranged chronologically, and as they march through the years the

Reprinted from *New Republic*, 18 December 1950, by permission of Mrs. Ralph McGill and *New Republic*. Copyright 1950, by Harrison-Blaine of New Jersey, Inc. A draft of this review is in the McGill papers, now at Emory University, Atlanta. Review of *F.D.R.: His Personal Letters, 1929-1945*, ed. Elliot Roosevelt, 2 vols. (New York: Duell, Sloan and Pearce, 1950).

[104]*F.D.R.: His Personal Letters*, 1:7.

[105]Ibid., 1:1581.

reader is pulled along with them. It is almost as if one were given a seat inside FDR's mind. They reveal his astonishing background of knowledge and information. They let us see how great projects began and developed. They allow us to understand his genius for getting along with people. They permit one to know, and not merely surmise, that he had a gift of intuition. And, finally, they present to the reader the picture of one of the most versatile, active, and hard-working presidents we have had. Only Lincoln's years of labor can match Roosevelt's and his were cut short by murder.

Letters that would involve national security or international relationships and those containing the more candid of his comments about political figures still living are omitted. Like the Lincoln letters, they must remain for the future. As Mrs. Roosevelt says in a foreword, the chief value of the letters has been

> to show the preparation and development which equipped Franklin Delano Roosevelt to deal with the responsibilities and circumstances of his life. Whether in your opinion he did well or ill, it is still interesting to see the background that formed his character and the influences which shaped his actions for the future.[106]

All the great, and many of the small, personalities of those years are in these letters; he wrote to kings, queens, emperors, dictators, prime ministers, generals, and hundreds of plain, average persons who touched his life. To any but the most closed of minds, these letters give the lie to many rumors, assumptions and charges made by his enemies. The reasons he did certain things in certain ways are revealed in his correspondence. And certainly his mind was clear and strong and his zest for life great to the last moment of it. The letters demonstrate that the image the people formed of FDR in the years of his presidency was the true one. There was no plotting for a third term. Roosevelt indicates at every turn his determination to open the government to more, rather than less, participation by the people. There was no sinister plan to draw Japan into an attack upon us.

His hopes were high after Yalta. He felt, he wrote his wife, a little exhausted, but "am really all right." But he was not blind to events. He noted, in a letter of 16 March, the first instance of Soviet violation of

---

[106]Ibid., 2:xvii.

the Yalta agreement when Russia insisted that the Lublin government, consisting only of Communists, represent Poland at San Francisco.[107] On 24 March, he sent a personal message to Stalin urging that Molotov be sent to the San Francisco conference, stating frankly that his absence would be interpreted as Soviet lack of interest in the great objectives to be outlined there.[108]

In the light of U.S.-Soviet relationships today, his hopes appear ill-founded, but the letters show the grounds on which they were developed. In a letter to Thomas W. Lamont in 1942 he tells a story "never yet committed to paper," as follows:[109]

> In the Autumn of 1933, when I initiated with Stalin the question of renewing diplomatic relations, Litvinoff was sent over and we had a four- or five-day drag-down and knock-out fight in regard to a number of things, including the right to have American priests, ministers and rabbis look after the spiritual needs of Americans in Russia.
>
> Finally, after further objections on Litvinoff's part, I threw up my hands and said to him, "What is the use of all this anyway? Your people and my people are as far apart as the poles."
>
> Litvinoff's answer is worthy of an eventual place in history. He said, "I hope you will not feel that way, Mr. President, because I do not. In 1920, we were as far apart as you say. At that time you were one hundred percent capitalistic and we were at the other extreme—zero. In these thirteen years we have risen in the scale to, let us say, a position of twenty. You Americans, especially since last March, have gone to a position of eighty. It is my real belief that in the next twenty years we will go to forty and you will come down to sixty. I do not believe the rapprochement will get closer than that. And while it is difficult for nations to confer with and understand each other with a difference between twenty and eighty, it is wholly possible for them to do so if the difference is only between forty and sixty."

It is obvious that this comment, among other things of like nature, was in his mind as all through the war he sought to work out a program with the Russians, and, as later, he believed it possible to make them a cooperating partner in the UN.

There are, of course, letters on reforestation, on the TVA, on soil conservation, and on many of his other reforms that now are firmly

---

[107]Letter to John G. Winant, London, ibid., 2:1575.

[108]Letter to Joseph Stalin, *F.D.R.: His Personal Letters*, 2:1577.

[109]*F.D.R.: His Personal Letters*, 2:1365-66.

written into the laws and the thinking of all Americans. The wide range of his interests is amazing. He wrote about stamps, history, ships, books, paintings, the family, Harvard, Groton, a wartime gift of English gin, movies, and sports.

He liked jokes, and he had fun making small bets on horses whose names intrigued him. Once he won seventy cents on a horse called Naval Cadet. Anything having to do with the Navy attracted him and the letters show how close a check he kept on its development.

Small personal joys and sorrows, triumphs and failures leaven the letters. All husbands will appreciate his note of 7 October 1942, to his wife, in which he calls her attention to the reduction in their income which the new income-tax law would mean and asks her to take steps to reduce the food bill. He suggests cutting down portions served, and notes that one egg is enough for breakfast.[110]

The letters are prepared by Elliott Roosevelt with the assistance of Joseph P. Lash; the job of selection and of editing, especially the addition of clarifying footnotes, was excellently done. The letters must be read by those who would understand the Roosevelt years; but, apart from their historical importance, they are absorbing in their own right.[111]

---

[110]Letter to Eleanor Roosevelt, ibid., 2:1352.

[111]See McGill's "Memories of Bellamy and FDR" in this volume.

20

Yellow Fever Experiment

I n Charleston, South Carolina, which is the only Southern city with
no secret social envy of Richmond, I learned that one of the nation's
unknown but genuine heroes was yet very much alive in Orangeburg. Elliott Wannamaker flew over to fetch me to his city. We drove
to the hero's home. He was out. Wannamaker said J. B. Bryant, attorney and state senator, knew what street corner each citizen stood on, so
we went to his office. Senator Bryant went to a window and hollered real
loud to a man on the courthouse steps.

"Bill," he bellowed, "will you go tell Jim Hanberry to come here?"

So that was how I met James Leonard Hanberry, one of the three
men living of those who answered Dr. Walter Reed's call for volunteers
in the yellow fever experiments at Camp Columbia, Havana, Cuba, half
a century ago. Seventy-five years old, arrow-straight, hard and healthy
as a pine knot, Jim Hanberry recalled those fear-ridden days when soldiers and civilians were dying of Yellow Jack, and death carts went about
the streets, the drivers calling, "Bring forth your dead."

Apparently submitted to *Colliers* magazine, but not published by that source.
Manuscript provided by Mrs. Ralph McGill from the McGill papers, now at Emory
University, Atlanta. Notes on the manuscript indicate McGill's correspondence with
William A. Emerson, Jr., associate editor of *Colliers*, 1950 and 1951.

"I was in the Hospital Corps—they call it Medical Corps now—with Charley Soontag, both of us farm boys from Denmark, South Carolina. The yellow fever was bad, and I had learned one thing about it by looking on. That was that a booze fighter died quick.

"There was always mosquitos about, but you just slapped or cussed them. There was a Cuban doctor (Dr. Carlos Finlay) who had been saying for years that mosquitoes caused it, but not 'til Dr. Reed took over would anyone listen to him.

"It has been so long, but I recall that thirteen of us and five Cubans volunteered. There was three of us from South Carolina, Soontag and me and Levi Folk. He was from Newberry. All of us recovered, but they died years later. I don't think the fever had anything to do with it.

"I am the only living one who took both tests—mosquitoes and bedclothes. I took the bedclothes first. They built a tight-screened house and placed a stove in it to make it good and hot. They brought in a lot of bloody, vomit-stained sheets, towels, mattresses, and pillows that men had died in, and put them on our cots. The smell was awful bad. We slept in that stuff for twenty-one straight nights. None of us caught the fever. That made Reed mighty happy.

"Could we sleep in all that? Son, a young soldier can sleep anywhere.

"After that I took the mosquito test. I remember watching that hungry mosquito in that tube-contraption biting on my arm. I took it all right. A headache comes first. Then fever. At the end of about five days you get over it or you develop the black vomit and you go down the road. My fever went to 105. But I overed it.

"All we got was water. I lost forty pounds in nine days. On the ninth day, a soldier nurse came to me and said, 'I got some rice and chicken for you, South Carolina boy,' and he stuck the spout of a little pitcher in my mouth and began to pour in chicken broth. I was so mad I'd have knocked it away if I hadn't been so weak.

"Walter Reed was sure happy when they had proved the case on mosquitoes. He was a great man—a really fine man, too. I'll always be grateful to the fellow that nursed me, Gus Lambert. He lives in Chicago. Dr. Robert Cook, who took the bedclothes test, is still living in North Carolina. John Moran lives in Cuba. He had the fever bad."

Jim Hanberry, holder of the Congressional Medal of Honor, serves as a bailiff in the Orangeburg County Court. He has one other job. The man who volunteered for death lives next door to the Orangeburg cemetery. Every Sunday morning Jim Hanberry unlocks the gates. At sundown he closes them. He goes to bed early and no ghosts bother him. Old soldiers sleep well, too.

21

A Word Portrait: Review of James Howell Street's Article on Atlanta

I t has been almost a century since William T. Sherman moved from Atlanta to the sea, through the rich pine-fat heart of the land, along the red clay roads which finally ran out into the sand of the coastal plain. Any of his troopers who cared to look back could see for two whole days of marching the smoke of the burning capital staining the November skies.

Since that time, many writers have striven unsuccessfully to picture the civic soul and personality of the city which arose from those ashes. A few months ago, the old girl sat for her picture, and now James Street has finished it and it is across some half-dozen pages and in a good five thousand words in the January issue of *Holiday* magazine, on sale this week.

Mr. Street is one of the nation's better writers—*My Father's House, Tap Roots, By Valour and Arms, The Gauntlet*—these are but a few of the better known.[112] He is himself out of the South. He knows the sound of

---

James Howell Street, "Atlanta," *Holiday* 9 (January 1951): 26-37, 106-11. Manuscript provided by Mrs. Ralph McGill from the McGill papers now at Emory University, Atlanta. In his article, Street lists McGill with other well-known newspapermen (pp. 36, 106).

[112]See Street's *In My Father's House* (New York: Dial Press, 1941); *Tap Roots* (New York: Dial Press, 1942); *By Valor and Arms* (New York: Dial Press, 1944); *The Gauntlet* (Garden City NY: Doubleday, Doran & Co., Inc., 1945).

a hound dog baying, the harvest moon, the taste of cornbread and greens. But he is no provincial, and so great is his affection for his native land he has a mighty distaste for anything but the truth about her.

Atlanta's patron saint, he says in the beginning, is Scarlett O'Hara, and the town's just like her—shrewd, proud, and full of gumption, "her Confederate slip showing under a Yankee mink coat."

He is the first man to write of us who has seen and felt the great vitality of the city which has kept her growing, not merely in building but in matters of the soul and spirit. Behind us are the race riots, the [Leo] Frank case and the heyday of the Klan; and today a Jew is hailed as our leading citizen of the year, and a Papal Knight is head of the University Regents. Street saw, too, that our town is not a Southern city at all, but an American city, proud of her state and region but with a vision not cramped by mean or narrow horizons.

He has put it all down, our beginnings, our history, our growth, and our spirit. He has caught the real character of our city, the softness of its heart and the toughness of its strength. We are lucky to have had Jimmy Street apply the rasp of his great personal and literary honesty to us. I recommend it—*Holiday* for January and the word portrait of Atlanta.[113]

---

[113]See McGill's "The Housing Challenge," "Why I Live in Atlanta," "Georgia Tech: Lighthouse to the Postwar South," and "She Sifted the Ashes and Built a City," in volumes 1 and 2.

22

Georgia's Stake in the Democratic National Convention 1952

On the morning of 21 July, in the great livestock coliseum in Chicago's sprawling, aromatic stockyards area, "The Star-Spangled Banner" will be sung to the standing delegates of the Democratic party, prayer will be said, a gavel will fall, and the quadrennial search for a party ticket will begin.

It is a fateful convention. The Democrats are fat and lazy after twenty years of power, a span second only to the Republican stretch from 1860 to 1884, which was twenty-four years of special privilege and corruption. The Democrats face the tragedy of a split. If it comes, the GOP is assured of victory. If they break the party to bits it could wander in the political wilderness for a generation. If they find unity, they may win.

As usual—when the convention is in Chicago—Georgia will have a direct interest far beyond party affiliation. This year it is the fact of Senator Richard Brevard Russell, native son candidate for the presidential nomination, and also a power, because of the Southern delegates pledged to him, in the construction of the party's platform.

Senator Russell is the first Georgian in our times to be a serious contender for his party's highest award. An able, popular and efficient pub-

Reprinted from the *Atlanta Journal and Constitution Sunday Magazine*, 20 July 1952, by permission of Mrs. Ralph McGill and Atlanta Newspapers, Inc.

lic servant, he is handicapped by the party's division over civil rights legislation, but in the event of a common-sense compromise in that field, he will be in a really strong position. He is admired and respected by all.

The first Democratic convention held in Chicago was in 1864 and Georgia had a direct interest in it, even though no Georgian or Southerner was there. The leading candidate was Gen. George B. McClellan, who entertained a bitter dislike for Abraham Lincoln. Old Abe had removed him from command of the Army of the Potomac, and McClellan became an implacable foe not merely of Lincoln, but of the president's war policy. The Democratic party in 1864 was a "peace party" pledged to bring an end to the war if its candidate was elected to office. The war had dragged on at great cost in lives and money, and all over the North there were voices in high places demanding the South be allowed to depart and a way found to end the fighting, and to develop cooperation between the two regions. The hammer blows by U. S. Grant had brought no victories and the casualty lists had horrified the North, already sick of war. The Confederate states, also weary, were hopeful of McClellan's victory. It seemed likely.

Lincoln himself rather thought he would be defeated—and he probably would have been had it not been for a hasty decision by Jefferson Davis. Urged on by the embittered Braxton Bragg, President Davis relieved Gen. Joe Johnston of his command in Atlanta and gave it to Gen. John Hood of Texas. In his memoirs, General Grant said he thought Joe Johnston had been right in his tactics, which were delaying the war even though Johnston was winning no battles. Grant believed Johnston might have forced a peace. But Hood smashed his exhausted, outnumbered troops against General William T. Sherman's battle-toughened victory-inspired veterans and was defeated. He was soon thereafter maneuvered out of Atlanta and proceeded on to Tennessee where his army was almost annihilated. It was the capture of the Georgia capital city which turned the political tide and gave the jubilant Republicans victory over McClellan. "The capture of Atlanta knocked the bottom out of the peace talk that might have elected McClellan," said Lincoln's manager.[114]

---

[114]See Emory M. Thomas, *The American War and Peace, 1860-1877* (Englewood Cliffs NJ: Prentice Hall, 1973); Emory M. Thomas, *The Confederate Nation, 1861-1865* (New York: Harper and Row, 1979).

It was July 1884 before the Democratic hosts met again in Chicago. That was the year the name of the peerless Grover Cleveland was on every hopeful citizen's lips. The long-entrenched Republican party, fat and lazy, graft-ridden, corrupt, and arrogant, had for a long time kept down any opposition. But the people, especially the farmers, the middle class and the more thoughtful men of whatever status, wanted reform and turned to the Democrats. Georgia, one of the more fervently Democratic states, was especially interested because Cleveland had promised to name a Southerner to his cabinet. He did, too. In fact, he named two, and both were Georgians. The first was the gallant Lucius Q. C. Lamar, and the second was the able and highly esteemed Hoke Smith. They each held the position of secretary of the interior. Cleveland was both times nominated in Chicago conventions.

William Jennings Bryan was selected there in 1896, but was defeated in November. Here, too, the Southern interest was direct. Bryan also accepted the nomination of the Populist party with Georgia's fiery Tom Watson as the choice for the vice-presidency on that ticket. The Democrats did not again return to the city on the great lake until 1932, when Franklin D. Roosevelt, whose second home was in Georgia, was nominated in the historic convention which once again elevated the Democrats to power after a long political drought.

So overwhelming were the Roosevelt victories, and for so many years was he the world's greatest political name, that we have forgotten that his nomination was not easily won. The fight was intense, the more so because the party sensed the nation was sick unto death of the bankrupt Republican rule and the depression which had followed as a direct result of the repudiation of Woodrow Wilson's League of Nations and his policy of foreign aid and trade.

In the first roll call Franklin Roosevelt had a large lead—666 1/4 votes, more than a majority, but not enough to win. (The two-thirds rule then applied.) In the second roll call he picked up only 11 votes and in the third but 5. The Roosevelt momentum seemed at an end. It was a critical moment. There were other eager seekers of the nomination. Chief among them was Alfred E. Smith, John N. Garner, Newton D. Baker and a number lesser known. Party leaders seemed to believe the best chance for victory lay with Roosevelt. So, as the convention seemed about to deadlock, James A. Farley, manager of the Roosevelt forces, sought out his old friend, the present Speaker of the House, Sam Rayburn of Texas. Farley was in a hurry. If Roosevelt could have the Texas votes, going for Garner, then Garner would receive the Roosevelt votes for the vice-presidency. Rayburn telephoned Garner, then Speaker, and the Texan released his votes. Roosevelt was nominated for the presidency and the next day the convention roared its approval of Garner by unanimously naming him to second place on what was to become a historic ticket.

The Democrats were back at Chicago for the 1940 convention, the one of 1936 having been held in Philadelphia. This also was one of the more historic meetings in America's political history. It was Roosevelt for a precedent-breaking third term. It was a decision which caused Jim Farley to break with Roosevelt and to allow his own name to be offered in opposition as a matter of principle. Many other Democrats bolted. But Roosevelt was easily nominated and in November won a great victory over the late Wendell Willkie, who nonetheless received a record-breaking total of Republican votes.

It was Chicago again in 1944 for the fourth nomination for Roosevelt. Had the war not been on there would have been more serious opposition. But we were in the great conflict and the tides of it were beginning to run strongly in our direction. A majority of Americans wanted to retain the leadership which was fashioning a victory. It was almost perfunctory.

In 1948 Harry S. Truman was nominated by a convention which did not expect victory. It was stirred only by the keynote speech by Kentucky's Alben Barkley, who lifted them with a magnificent oration which won him the vice-presidency. None expected the November defeat of Dewey by Harry S. Truman, unless it was Truman himself.

So, in 1952 the Democrats are back again in Chicago—and once again the Georgia interest is high. She has her own candidate. And there is also the added speculation as to whether the Democratic party will split over the platform and nominee, with some of the Southern states withdrawing.

But, whatever happens—the conventions are always dramas on which the nation hangs. This year millions of Americans will see a convention for the first time—via the magic of television. Both NBC and CBS will carry all the deliberations, the parades, the demonstrations, the speeches and the debates as the Democrats meet in a time of great decision.

The conventions as we know them today really began with those of 1856. For most of the elections before 1832, presidential candidates were nominated by a Congressional caucus. The first Democratic convention was held in May of 1832 to name a vice-president to run with Andrew Jackson, and Van Buren was the choice. The Whig party held a number of conventions, and the Democrats met in Baltimore a number of times. But the great national conventions began in 1856 and have grown in interest ever since. Certainly, with millions watching television, and with the huge coliseum packed, 1952 is the greatest convention year in history.[115]

---

[115]See McGill's articles on Adlai Stevenson and Dwight Eisenhower, in volume 1.

23

Dwight D. Eisenhower

Seven years ago, when a great war had been won in which the United States supplied one of the great geniuses and commanders of the victory in Dwight D. Eisenhower, the suggestion was made to the general that his country might some day call on him politically. "It's silly to talk about me in politics," he said, with his famous grin testifying to the sincerity of that remark.

He had led the vast Allied army in a very literal "Crusade in Europe." The invasion of Europe across the channel will remain as one of the Herculean masterpieces of military history. Perhaps he was able to do a superlative job because he does not possess merely a war-machine mind. It is much more than that.

In 1948 he took off his uniform and began to make sense in his new capacity as president of Columbia University, one of the nation's largest and more notable educational institutions. About two years later he was called back to uniform by the challenge of a job which vitally affects the future of all of us and our children—the creation and organization of a

Essay provided by Mrs. Ralph McGill from the Ralph McGill papers, now at Emory University, Atlanta. This piece was written after the Republican convention in Chicago, July 1952, had ended.

vast European and international army to enable Europe to have some measure of protection against Communist, Soviet aggression.

Now, he has begun his campaign for the presidency of the United States, following his nomination by the Republican party in a historic July convention at Chicago in which the will of the people managed to break through and thwart that of political bosses.[116] It was a session which because of television and the issues interested millions never before really attracted to the doings of politicians.

Further, and equally important, it was one in which not surprisingly, the name of Eisenhower came to be linked with morality, integrity and character in politics, as the name has always been associated in military and civil affairs. He was the nation's number one citizen before politicians ever began to consider him in the role of the country's chief executive. In a sense, the key to his advancement in both fields has been the same—there was a need for him. And those who were seeking to fill the need had respect and confidence in him.

He was appointed as a cadet to West Point during the administration of William Howard Taft, an ironic corollary to the fact that it was the son of that president whom he defeated for the GOP nomination. He received his chief advancements during the terms of Calvin Cooledge, Herbert Hoover, and of course, Franklin D. Roosevelt. It was Roosevelt who, acting on the advice of Gen. George Marshall, advanced the young officer several grades in order to make use of his talents in the national emergency.[117] At no time, of course, did Roosevelt ask about Eisenhower's politics. There was a war on, a war of survival, a crusade for freedom. And Eisenhower was a soldier. The nation needed the best.

As the army advanced him upward on merit, so has politics. Both parties offered him the nomination in 1948. He turned them down with the remarkably statesmanlike explanation that, in his opinion, no man whose whole life had been military, should consider himself fit for public service until he had spent some years as a civilian.

His political victory will certainly have a place in all the political science classroom books of the future. It was January of this year before General Eisenhower, with an eye on the big job to which he had com-

---

[116]Eisenhower won the nomination over Robert A. Taft of Ohio.

[117]See McGill's review of *F.D.R.: His Personal Letters* in volume 1.

mitted himself, agreed even to say he would accept the nomination if the American people decided they wanted him to have it—but he would not campaign for it nor ask for it. Meanwhile, his chief rival, Sen. Robert A. Taft of Ohio, had been hard at work since the early autumn.

There then began to develop one of the most unusual of American campaigns—friends went to work in behalf of the man who would not seek the nomination and who was busy with another task in Europe. In March, in the first primary, General Eisenhower won in New Hampshire. But from that time on, his campaign failed to generate any real steam. It went along. But it did not race. The American people were again demonstrating that they prize the highest office within their gift, and were saying, by their refusal to stampede to the Eisenhower banner, that they wanted a man to ask for the job.

But, it was June before General Eisenhower determined he could resign the job in Europe and come home and ask for it. But things then went worse. He would not compromise himself. He would not attack the foreign policy in which he believed. He frankly said he was no expert on domestic affairs. Meanwhile, his opponent had a huge lead in delegates. The convention was a little more than a month away. Eisenhower's few speeches merely proved he was a political amateur. Taft seemed unbeatable.

Then, just two weeks before the convention began, there seemed to be, and was as we later learned, a new direction and strength in the Eisenhower campaign. It seized suddenly on the issue "Thou Shalt Not Steal" and beamed it at the Taft-controlled committee which had thrown out Southern delegations that had been elected pledged to the general. The other delegates and the public began to get arguments such as this— "We have insisted Taft can't win. How can Taft win if he goes before the people with his own nomination achieved by corrupt acts? Can corruption throw corruption out of Washington?" Gov. Tom Dewey, of New York, had lent his advice.

But in Chicago, the Old Guard committee, with what observers called "typical Old Guard astigmatism," voted Taft's way and then capped the climax by barring television. Protests came from owners of television sets, from the television networks, and from station owners, as well as from the general public. The Old Guard, perhaps unwittingly, had lent strength to the "steal" charge by its apparent unwillingness to allow the people to see the proceedings.

The second big break came, oddly enough, and for the Taft people unexpectedly, from Houston, Texas. There, twenty-three Republic governors, fearing the impact of the "Southern Steal" in their own states, sent something new to the National Republican committee—a manifesto asking for a fair play attitude. The Taft people were willing to compromise on Sunday night before the convention opened on Monday. But the Eisenhower strategists decided that if their opposition was frightened, they could be defeated, and that they, the Eisenhower group, could not afford to compromise a moral issue.

Once the convention began, it seemed to reporters, broadcasters and telecasters to go on without ceasing. When the great meeting hall at the Chicago stockyards greeted the delegates on their first day, the tension was electric. It was known that the Eisenhower forces would try to jam through a "fair play amendment" to allow the dispossessed Southern delegations another hearing. The Taft forces were defeated 658 to 548, and Eisenhower had scored a great psychological victory. The hearings went on into the third day, and while the majority Taft forces on the credential committee made an exception of Louisiana, they again gave Georgia and Texas, the two principal states in the dispute, to the Ohio senator. They were obviously nettled and worried by the "steal" label so successfully applied to them.

On the evening of the third day, tempers were at the breaking point. Fists flew. One delegate suffered a heart attack. Senator [Everett] Dirkson, of Illinois, made a bitter, personal attack on Gov. [Thomas] E. Dewey, who was supporting Eisenhower. But the strategists behind the general brought the issue to the floor.

Georgia was the first state to be voted on, and again the Eisenhower strength was enough. The disputed Georgia delegation which had been thrown out was seated amid the cheers of the suddenly hopeful supporters of the general. "Imagine," said a disgusted Ohio delegate, "the cotton state of Georgia deciding a Republican convention—especially on a moral issue." Once Georgia was seated, the forlorn Taft forces surrendered Texas by a voice vote.[118] General Eisenhower was in front.

On Friday morning the balloting began. When it was done, General Eisenhower had 595 votes, nine short of a majority, and Taft had 500.

---

[118]See McGill's "Dwight Eisenhower and the South," in volume 1.

But immediately Minnesota's delegation demanded and received recognition. Nineteen of its votes, previously cast for Governor Stassen, went to General Eisenhower, and that was the nomination.

In an impulsive gesture of decency and sportsmanship, the general immediately went across the street from the Blackstone Hotel to the Conrad Hilton to Taft's headquarters on the ninth floor "to speak to and greet a very great American." Senator Taft, in the best tradition of American politics, pledged his support.

That afternoon the party submitted only one name to the convention for the vice-presidency—Richard Nixon, junior senator from California, the man who as a member of the House Un-American Affairs Committee had broken the Alger Hiss case. He was chosen by acclamation.

The ticket is one that fits the American legend and dream that in the United States, every boy has a chance to become president. Dwight D. Eisenhower was born in Texas, but the father, a small, unsuccessful farmer, soon thereafter moved his family to Abilene, Kansas. There he farmed and worked in a dairy. He was almost a religious mystic, of a sect related to the Mennonites and Lutherans. All the Eisenhower boys had to work hard to help keep the family going. They knew poverty and need, but they received a strict, moral upbringing.

Richard Nixon's father was a streetcar motorman, later a filling station operator, and still later, a small business man. Young Nixon, too, knew hard work as a boy and worked his way through school. His fiber also is conditioned by the religious training received as a boy and by the discipline of hard work. These are the men whom the Republican party looks to attract enough votes to end the twenty-year GOP drought and to restore the party to power and the White House.[119]

---

[119]See Dean Albertson, *Eisenhower as President* (New York: Hill and Wang, 1963); William Bragg Ewald, *Eisenhower the President: Crucial Days, 1951-1960* (Englewood Cliffs NJ: Prentice-Hall, 1981).

24

Report
on Adlai E. Stevenson

Some of his party associates blushed, drawing away from him as he struck out the praise of General [George] Marshall which he had written into his Milwaukee speech.

Hope of peace in Korea would aid political victory in the United States and [Dwight D.] Eisenhower, who knows the truth about Korea and the fighting there, offered an impossible hope to American wives and mothers, knowing it was impossible as he spoke it. Nothing he has done is so unworthy of the great soldier as this personal betrayal of the women of America who put their faith in his military utterances.

On political issues, Eisenhower has taken the side most pleasing to that section of the country in which, on that particular day, he happened to be speaking.

In Illinois and Wisconsin, home of [Everett] Dirksen and [Joseph] McCarthy, where isolationism controls the vote, Eisenhower attacked the international policies which he himself helped to form and so valiantly had put into practice.

In the North, Eisenhower satisfied the advocates of a national FEPC [Federal Employment Practices Commission], yet in the South he spoke his burning faith in states' rights.

Reprinted from the *Atlanta Journal and Constitution Magazine*, 2 November 1952, by permission of Mrs. Ralph McGill and the Atlanta Newspapers, Inc.

In Tennessee he was for the TVA [Tennessee Valley Authority]. In the state of Washington, where the Columbia Valley Authority is a bitter issue, he questioned such a plan. There, reversing his Tennessee declaration, he insisted that the government "keep its long nose out of private enterprise."

In Wyoming one morning he said he was no politician and would make no promises. In New Orleans that night he made eight.

He speaks of himself repeatedly as a leader of a great crusade, out to end corruption in government. At first it seemed he intended to demand a cleaning of his own party, even to rejection of his running mate. Then [Robert Taft] spoke and Arthur Summerfield spoke and Eisenhower hurried to surrender. Mingling his fears with those of Richard Nixon, he drew the errant young man to his breast.

The old soldier has become a civilian, the civilian a politician. As a politician, Eisenhower now believes he is essential to the political salvation of his country. Having accepted this belief, he regards all trimming, all vacillation, all surrenders as incidental to his election.

He takes his orders from the masters of the party and has become so obedient that, if elected, he will continue subservient. The shrewd politicians, now controlling him, will maintain control.

All this is written in no immediate criticism of any man who aligns himself with other men whose sole creed and purpose is to win, to get elected. Nor is this piece to be construed as praise for, or even implied approval of, Mr. Truman, Mr. Stevenson, or the current Democratic party. This piece is not concerned with them to the slightest.

It is written solely about Dwight Eisenhower. It is written that the voters may know for whom they vote when they mark the name of Eisenhower for president.

Ninety-two autumns have come to the lovely valley of the Sangamon since a man waited there for the November election returns. For almost a hundred years the summers have merged slowly into fall; the green corn has slowly turned brown and the prairie winds have come to make elfin music with the sawing and swaying of its dried spear-like blades, while the old ghosts of the Sangamon who gathered there with Abraham Lincoln to receive the returns of 1860 have waited patiently for another night like that one when they sat with their friend, feeling the foundations of the Union trembling beneath them.

And now, on Tuesday night another will wait there, almost within sight of where the Rail Splitter and others gathered to read the sparse news which the nation's few slender telegraph wires would bring. Lincoln was to lose his own county that day, and he was to receive a minority of the votes cast, but he won because the Democratic party was foolishly divided.

On Tuesday night in Sangamon Valley, where crisp, tart-sweet apples grow, a man whose words have been like golden apples in pictures of silver, such as Proverbs commends, will wait for what the amazing communications of our time will present to his eyes and ears.

Adlai Stevenson, the Democratic nominee, is given but a fighting chance. Against him is the great military hero of our time, Gen. Dwight D. Eisenhower. He is to our time what Generals Robert E. Lee, U. S. Grant, and W. T. Sherman were to theirs. Against him, too, is the most prodigious amount of money ever spent on a political campaign. The Republicans, lean and hungry from twenty years out of office, have determined to have this one at all costs.[120]

So, the odds are against the man who waits by the Sangamon—Adlai Stevenson. But, win or lose, he will remain in the public eye for generations to come as the most refreshing candidate in our time and one of the most able.

He brought to the political campaign a freshness which the weary hustings had not known since the days when there were giants in the land who knew their mother tongue, the language of Shakespeare, Milton, Jefferson, and Webster. He had something to say, and he could say it without using the tired old clichés of today's politics.

He comes from a long line of public-spirited, active citizens. His forebears, Scotch Presbyterians, came from North Ireland to Pennsylvania in 1748. One of them pushed on into Kentucky, and his son moved on into Illinois, his family with him. One of the babies was Adlai Stevenson who became vice-president under the great Democrat Grover Cleveland, whose election in 1884 so thrilled the South—he was the first Democrat to become president since the War Between the States.

---

[120]See William Bragg Ewald, *Eisenhower the President: Crucial Days, 1951-1960* (Englewood Cliffs NJ: Prentice-Hall, 1981); Dean Albertson, *Eisenhower as President* (New York: Hill and Wang, 1963).

In Georgia Henry Grady, editor of the *Atlanta Constitution*, receiving the news on the day after the election, rushed from the newspaper office to the state capitol where the legislature was in session, seized the gavel from the Speaker of the House, and declared the legislature adjourned to celebrate. Vice-President Stevenson's wife, whose ancestors had fought with Washington in the wilderness of the West, was an early and active member of the Daughters of the American Revolution, the Colonial Dames, the Women's Clubs of America and an organizer of the forerunner of the Parent-Teachers' Association. Their son, Lewis Green Stevenson, was the father of the Democratic nominee of today—Adlai Ewing Stevenson. He comes from a line of able men and women.[121]

He was drafted for the Democratic nomination at Chicago. This is an unvarnished fact. The Republicans have said the nomination was "dictated" by the city bosses and Truman. This is not true. It was a genuine draft. The Stevensons are not the dependent type. They stand on their own two feet.

He did clean up Illinois. Certainly he did not make it as innocent as Eden. He did not clean it up completely. It had long been under corrupt Republican rule, and he has had to combat a hostile Republican majority in the legislature. But he did expose and correct the worst and most scandalous of graft, chiefly in construction, where by cutting out the rackets he gave Illinois construction at a reduction of about five to ten percent when it was everywhere going up.

In state purchasing he brought about tremendous reform.

In the mental institution he brought about modern care and treatment. This policy of modernization was carried out in all the welfare program.

At the time he was elected governor of Illinois the welfare department was regarded as one of the worst in the nation. Today it is one of the best.

The legislature fought him all the way, but he won great victories and vetoed more than 125 appropriation measures passed by the Republican legislators.

There is more to the story. These are its highlights.

---

[121]See McGill's "How Adlai Stevenson Won Georgia's Heart All Over Again" and "Adlai Stevenson and the Democratic South," in volume 1.

Stevenson is a frugal man, both in his own affairs and in government. The Mansion is kept clean and neat, but it is not luxuriously appointed or staffed. He, himself, has a habit of turning off lights left burning by others to help the taxpayers of Illinois with their electric light bill.

His office is plain. On the walls are paintings of his grandfather, his father, and an old lithograph. Recently newsmen were invited to a reception at the Mansion. Some ventured into the governor's bedroom. On a table by his bed was a copy of the new version of the Bible, a book of essays, and a collection of poems.

People have asked about his wife's obtaining a divorce. His statement was all-inclusive. He said: "I am deeply distressed that due to the incompatability of our lives, Mrs. Stevenson feels a separation is necessary. Although I don't believe in divorce I will not contest it. We have separated with the highest mutual regard." There was no accusation made which in any manner involved character. Stevenson was crushed. But he met it honestly.

He is a man of great candor. He thinks things through in a hardheaded manner. He works hard and never spares himself.

Should the Republicans win, with their wartime hero, there will be millions unwilling to forget Stevenson. In Illinois many persons say they have "time and enthusiasm invested in Adlai Stevenson and are willing to invest more."

Today, almost on the eve of the election, millions more on the prairies, in the Western states, the Midwest, the South, and all the regions, great and small, feel that same way.

Thousands of Southerners have come to share that feeling—and it is the South which may decide the election. Stevenson is the best friend the South could have obtained at the convention. He is a reasonable man who has paid high tribute to the South's contribution to the party and has said he will, if elected, lean on Southern leaders for advice and counsel. Despite this, a few Southern Democratic leaders, out of some inexplicable pique, have not made any real effort to assist the party and the Eisenhower vote will be large in the South. In the balance are the newly "doubtful" states of Texas, Florida, Virginia and Louisiana.

Sometimes the underdog wins. And if Stevenson does it will mean a great change in ideals and ethics.[122]

---

[122]See Kenneth Sydney Davis, *A Prophet in His Own Country: The Triumphs and Defeats of Adlai E. Stevenson* (Garden City NY: Doubleday, 1957); Stuart Gerry Brown, *Conscience in Politics: Adlai E. Stevenson in the 1950's* (Syracuse: Syracuse University Press, 1961); Stuart Gerry Brown, *Adlai E. Stevenson, a Short Biography: The Conscience of the Country* (Woodbury NY: Woodbury Press, 1965).

25

How Adlai Stevenson Won Georgia's Heart All Over Again

Adlai Ewing Stevenson, who shares a Revolutionary War ancestor with Georgia's Senator Richard B. Russell, and whose "kinfolks" are scattered throughout Tennessee and North Carolina as well, won the hearts of Georgia, Alabama, and the South on his first Southern tour since the 1952 presidential campaign when he was the Democratic nominee.

He arrived in Atlanta on 23 November and when he departed on the afternoon of 24 November for Montgomery and a visit with Governor Gordon Persons, he had charmed even his most reluctant and implacable critics of 1952 and further heightened the enthusiasm of many who had greeted him a year ago as a fresh and courageous voice in national politics.

Somehow an open car failed to arrive at the Atlanta Municipal Airport, and those who gathered along the way to see him were disappointed that he was in a closed car—but at historic Five Points he got out of the car to greet the large crowd gathered there.

It was at the Henry Grady Hotel—where a loud speaker was ready—that he began to charm them. It was something of a coincidence that on the same day President Dwight D. Eisenhower was arriving in Augusta, Georgia for a weekend of golf.

Reprinted from the *Atlanta Journal and Constitution Magazine*, 27 December 1953, by permission of Mrs. Ralph McGill and Atlanta Newspapers, Inc.

"If I'd known Atlanta would offer such perfect weather I'd have brought my golf sticks," he said, "but Democrats aren't interested in breaking 90—we are interested in 108—out in '52 and back in '56."

He had lunch; he met all afternoon with delegations and Georgia political figures of note—all without their hatchets. Former Governor Ellis Arnall and former Acting Governor M. E. Thompson were among the factional figures who called. Senators Walter George and Richard B. Russell along with congressmen Carl Vinson, Paul Brown, Henderson Lanham, J. L. Pilcher, and Don Wheeler participated in the greetings and luncheons. Mayor Hartsfield also had a full share in it.

Here as the house guest of Governor and Mrs. Herman Talmadge, Stevenson was guest of the legislature at the speaking—with Lt. Gov. Marvin Griffin, Speaker of the House Fred Hand, State Committee Chairman James S. Peters, and others of the official family joined to welcome him.

His address before the legislature and a huge crowd gathered about the special platform prepared for the occasion, went out on a state radio hookup and on television stations WSB and WLW-A. It was a major address, receiving generous space in newspapers over the nation.[123]

He called for unity in the party; he denounced those who put their special interests ahead of the party which is "an umbrella covering many groups." He decried the attempt of the Republicans to charge the Democratic party as the party of disloyalty as they did in the Reconstruction and later years after the War Between the States when they waved the "Bloody Shirt" and now use the same dividing tactics by waving the Red Shirt. It was a magnificent speech, enthusiastically received.

He toured the city—saw the Cyclorama, visited four schools, ate country ham and grits, made his speech, and got off to Montgomery on time—leaving everyone wondering if in 1956 the Democratic nominee ought not to be Adlai Stevenson.[124]

---

[123]See McGill's "Report on Adlai E. Stevenson" and "Adlai Stevenson and the Democratic South," in volume 1.

[124]See Kenneth Sydney Davis, *A Prophet in His Own Country: The Triumphs and Defeats of Adlai E. Stevenson* (Garden City NY: Doubleday, 1957); Stuart Gerry Brown, *Conscience in Politics: Adlai E. Stevenson in the 1950's* (Syracuse: Syracuse University Press, 1961); Stuart Gerry Brown, *Adlai E. Stevenson, a Short Biography: The Conscience of the Country* (Woodbury NY: Woodbury Press, 1965).

26

At the Threshold

On 1 January 1954, the Department of Records at Tuskegee Institute issued its annual report on lynchings during the previous year.

There were none. Nor had there been one in 1952.

Indeed, the department announced that this form of racial violence had ceased to become a valid index of race relations. It had lost its significance as a yardstick of race relations because of changes in the status of the Negro and the development of other extra-legal means of control such as bombings, incendiarism (in housing disputes), threats, and intimidations.

"We believe that a new standard for measuring race relations is needed," said Tuskegee president, Dr. L. H. Foster. "This can and should be as objective and as factual as were the lynching reports.

"This standard, we think, can best be established in such areas as employment and other economic conditions; in political participation; in education; in law and legislation; in health and perhaps other fields. We propose, then, in future annual releases, to issue a statement with in-

Reprinted from *Confluence* 3 (March 1954): 93-100, sponsored by Harvard University Summer School of Arts and Sciences, by permission of Mrs. Ralph McGill and *Confluence*.

formation as significant for the present times as was the lynching letter in the past."

Elaborating, Dr. Foster, who has been Tuskegee's president only a few months, said the study probably will make a comparison of white and Negro standards in four categories.

1. Income relationship.
2. Voter participation.
3. Education and the per pupil cost.
4. Employment; comparative conditions in certain jobs.

Dr. Foster's conclusion required no confirmation, but there was a sentence or so in it which supplied all the necessary buttressing. There had been no lynchings. Indeed, three attempts at such violence had been prevented by law-enforcement officers. The listing of these became familiar enough with Alabama. But the next one skipped to Willcox, Arizona, and the third such rescue of a colored person from lynching in 1953 was in New York City. The old criteria of race relations truly are no longer valid because of a slow process of education in hardening public opinion against it; because of federal civil rights laws which were frequently applied, especially during the period from 1940 to 1950, in cases involving law-enforcement officers in the more rural regions of the South where those guilty of violence had long been secure from fear of local sheriffs, judges and juries dependent on local votes and business; and also because, as a result of federal decisions, the Negro increasingly has been coming to the ballot box.

There is yet another reason why new criteria are needed. It is industrialization. It has been only in the past thirty-five years, and particularly in the past ten, that the industrial society really began to overhaul that of the old-plantation pattern. The plantation economy began to lose the battle shortly before the turn of the century when the first of several "New Souths" brought industry to the curving crescent of the Piedmont where water power was available. The economy of the man, the mule, the bent back and the skilled hands of cotton pickers, gave way slowly before the cogwheels and the steam engines; the cotton looms and the furniture plant tools. Within a few years, as industrial wages and the ameliorating effects of urban society began to have an effect, a sort of truism began to develop, though to be sure it was not without its exceptions. It was that race relations were best where industry had come; worst in those areas where most of the old-plantation economy remained.

In the past ten years, industrialization has come with such a rush that in 1951-1953, the Southern region added one new multi-million dollar factory for each working day of each five-day week. As more and more of it comes, and as trade unionism increases, the educational and civil rights gulf between two races, seemingly so rigidly fixed under a plantation economy, steadily narrows.

In the past fifteen years the white primary disappeared, the poll tax was abolished in all but six Southern states, and the number of Negro voters increased from 200,000 to 1,100,000. In the same period 6500 Negroes obtained employment in professional and clerical fields in Southern municipalities. One hundred and twenty-eight Southern cities and towns used 718 uniformed police officers. Ten cities have elected one or more Negroes to their city councils. Two states and seven cities have elected one or more to school boards. In forty-three of the forty-eight states, as 1954 began, Negroes were admitted fully to the school systems or, as in some Southern states, only to the professional and graduate schools. It was obvious that as the industrial society inexorably pushed more and more of the old-plantation economy from the scene, as the cities grew and mechanization in agriculture increased, the gulf would narrow still more steadily.

Trained economists, looking at the American scene, estimate the United States still has about one million farmers too many. In 1939 those fourteen years and older, gainfully employed on the nation's farms, totaled roughly nine million. These now are down to about seven million and in the nonpeak seasons go as low as six. Economists believe elimination of the inefficient farm, still going along with the more or less hopeless competitive power unit of the mule, would be a healthy economic result—always providing the government understands the need to undergird the transition to avoid any suffering. Since the South has most of the nation's small farms, and most of the remaining mule-and-hand labor, it is estimated that perhaps thirty percent of the reduction in the number of farmers and agricultural workers should, and will, take place in the South. Of this thirty percent a good half would be Negro.[125]

---

[125]See Jay R. Mandle, *Roots of Black Poverty: The Southern Plantation Economy After the Civil War* (Durham: Duke University Press, 1978); Paul E. Mertz, *New*

For a good many years now travelers through the South have grown used to seeing the lonely chimneys in abandoned fields, or pastures where once cotton grew. They are monuments to the old economy. Men and women in the 1920s made up their minds to go to "Dee-troit" when the automobile industry began to burgeon and talked bitterly of devastation done by the boll weevil, which did more to accelerate Negro migration than the First World War. There are still a few of the old cabins left, leaning drunkenly, their windows long gone, their doors torn away. Cattle graze where, until a few years ago, cotton had grown for a century. Persons looking at them speak of the "old days" though it was but relatively few years ago that they were occupied.

Change and transition are apparent in agriculture, the cities, the economy—and in politics. Especially in politics. Once I talked, years ago, with Uncle Cade Worley, ninety-one, in his mountain home on a spur of the Blue Ridges where they make the last thrust of the Appalachians into the South. "Son," he said, "you don't ever solve a real problem. You ameliorate it out of existence. That is true of the South's basic sociological and racial problem.

Negro-white relations are a national problem, complex and trying. But for all the migration and change they remain largely the problem of the South. Thus, the Negro's national welfare continues to be bound up in the welfare of the South—the whole South.[126] Since 1940 an estimated two million Negroes have left the South. Seven Northern urban areas alone, Baltimore, Chicago, Detroit, New York, New Jersey, Philadelphia, and Washington DC, have gained one million in colored population. The West Coast has received a heavy migration. But somewhere around nine of the thirteen million Negroes remain. Indeed, in the intellectual field, teachers and professional men, especially doctors, have been coming back South for more opportunity, and also because, "here

---

Deal Policy and Southern Rural Poverty (Baton Rouge: Louisiana State University Press, 1978).

[126]See McGill's discussion of migration in speeches in *Ralph McGill: Editor and Publisher,* ed. Calvin McLeod Logue, 2 vols. (Durham: Moore Publishing Company, 1969).

I feel I am doing something for my people and my country. In the South
I live where the future is."

Perhaps the most important factor of Negro nationalism just now is
being generally recognized. It is nationalism unique. In all other nations where a race has developed a nationalism it has sought to become
separate, to demand special recognition as a race, to call for exclusive
racial privileges and "rights." Negro nationalism seeks not to be more
separate, but less; not to withdraw from America, but to be more
merged in America.

To understand the background of race relations in the South one
must remember two great facts of history. One is that in the nineteenth
century the South came to a historic crossroads and took the fork away
from industry and democracy, choosing instead plantation agriculture
based on slavery. The second is that after Lincoln's murder the nation
gave over to the radicals in the Congress, "at the moment of opportunity," the destiny of both the South and the Negro. They abandoned Lincoln's formula of a unified nation, peacefully reconstructed, for one of
a conquered province status for the South.[127]

The problem of the South ever since has been of "catching up" in
democracy and industry. The past ten years have seen a lot of ground
gained. And now, in 1954, the South and the nation wait on a decision
from the Supreme Court in Washington which again will test the South
and the nation in whether it will, at a great moment of decision, turn to
radicals and hotheads for leadership. If, to the fear and suspicion created
among Americans by what has come to be called McCarthyism, be
added racial hatred and violence, the load would be indeed heavy to bear.

As the South waits, there are those who are embattled. It is an interesting substantiation of the old truism about the forces of resistance
to change being greatest where most of the old-plantation economy remains, that it is in Georgia, South Carolina, Alabama, and Mississippi,
plus the cotton and/or rice areas of Arkansas, Louisiana, and North Carolina, where there is the most violent and inflammatory political exploitation of the probably "adverse" Supreme Court decision. Yet, there
are, even in those states, enough persons of Christian-and-social-mo-

---

[127]See Robert Haws, *Age of Segregation: Race Relations in the South, 1890-1945*
(Jackson: University Press of Mississippi, 1978).

rality conviction, upon whom to build a rational acceptance of a possible elimination of segregation. It is for this reason that Southerners who long ago realized that segregation no longer fits today's world, hope the Supreme Court will provide a reasonable, supervised transition period. There is a historic background in this hope.

At all times, before and during the War Between the States, there was strong sentiment for the Union in the South. In most Southern states, support of secession had been given reluctantly, sorrowfully. Only the hotheads urged it. Lincoln was aware of this fact and wished to use it to build the unity of the nation. In the South there were many of a like mind, notable among them being Alexander Stephens, vice-president of the Confederacy. Their hopes were drowned in the floods of radicalism and political opportunism. This "Old-Whig" tradition survived the war as was demonstrated years later when the Old Whigs, operating within the Democratic party into which they had been forced by the extremes of the Reconstruction period, joined with Republicans to steal a recount election for Rutherford B. Hayes.

Many Southerners do not even now realize that the wounds which throb today, the cult of "supremacy" and other "traditions," came not from the war itself, but from the tragedy of reconstruction abuses. It was this folly which solidified resentment against the Negro and produced the theory of white supremacy, which drove every person of whatever previous political faith into the Democratic party and made the word *Republican* an epithet. The spirit of the South was not defeated. It was magnificent. But abuses warped and distorted it. That is why a period of transition is hoped for by most of the thoughtful colored and white leadership. There are those upon whom a working acceptance can be built.

It is possible, if reasonableness has a chance to be heard in the transition period, that the South might be able, through the next twenty years, to produce not merely the best race relations, but a superior political climate. An odd feature of race relations is that the thousands of thoughtful Negroes who have made careers in the South are proud of being "Southern." In the political North, for example, there are many types of votes. There are Polish-American voters, Italian-American ballots, German-American interests, Labor-American pressures, Jewish-American votes, and Negro-American votes. To date, unless a candidate in the South has a known anti-Negro record, or has been a fellow-traveler of the old Ku Klux Klan philosophy, the Negro has been voting as a voter. He hasn't been "voted." He resisted the Henry Wallace party blandishments and he ignored the Communists.

The transition will not be easy.[128] There will be a period of resistance as in Georgia and the South, where, for example, plans are presently being made to abolish the public school system and to provide each school child with a sum of money with which to attend any available private school. The idea is preposterous in essence, yet it almost surely will be attempted, leaving for later administrations a financial and educational burden which will be costly for generations to come. With great luck this may be avoided, but if so, it will be an almost miraculous escape. In the border states, where less of the old-plantation economy and social pattern remains, there will be travail and bitterness but not a mass educational suicide as planned in the hard core of resisting states.

The Negro who expects a favorable Supreme Court decision to bring about an end to all discrimination and prejudice is, of course, due for a rude awakening. Not many do expect such deliverance. But, for all there will be a great soul-stirring lifting of the spirit. To have lived all these years legally barred from full citizenship has been, of course, a corroding experience for the spirit and mind. Even those adults who have rationalized it as a struggle to be won only with the passing of time, have known bitterness and sorrow.

As William Gordon, managing editor of the Atlanta *World*, said to me one day, "I can explain segregation to everyone save my eight-year-old boy."

So today the Negro in the South stands at the threshold of full citizenship. It seems that the legal stamp of "second-class citizen" is about to be removed from his person. The hard way he has come to this threshold has been, by and large, a path of honor and law. All the way he has been saying, "I want to be more American, not less." It has been a slow progress, and the Negro's patience has been enormous. He will

---

[128]See "South in Transition" speech, in *Ralph McGill: Editor and Publisher,* 2: 348-60.

need more of it. There will be more resistance and there may be sordid incidents of violence.[129]

But when the legal barrier to first-class citizenship is removed, the nation, whatever happens by way of reaction, will for the first time be able to lift its head the more honestly to reveal the real heart of this country and its promise—a government of free and equal citizens.

And the South, once it has been through whatever agony the transition period brings, will find itself spiritually lifted, being free of the old guilt complex and the uneasy sense of being an accomplice of injustice. The Southerner is not, and has not been, a person of ill will. He, too, has been caught and his region fated to many unnecessary second-class conditions. The South, too, stands at the new threshold.

---

[129]See John Hope Franklin and Isidore Starr, eds., *Negro in Twentieth-Century America: A Reader on the Struggle for Civil Rights* (New York: Vintage Books, 1967); John Hope Franklin, *From Slavery to Freedom: A History of Negro Americans*, 5th ed. (New York: A. A. Knopf, 1980).

Is the Federal Government Running Our Lives?

*A*nnouncer: "Town Meeting" tonight originates from the Jai Alai Fronton in Tampa, Florida, under the auspices of the local Optimists Clubs and in tribute to Tampa's Centennial Year. . . .

Mr. [James F.] Murray: . . . One of the most complex problems of government in the United States, particularly since the turn of the century, has been the maintenance of a sound balance in federal and state relations. During the election campaign of 1952, many Americans expressed themselves as being hostile to overcentralization of power in Washington and as such they eagerly endorsed General Eisenhower's pledge to establish a "businessman's administration" as a possible first step in reduction of federal control and restoration of rights to local governments.

And yet despite the Republican transition of the past two years the debate still continues. Many see disaster in transferring to the states responsibilities which the states may be unable to accept. Others feel that there is too much "big government" even under the Republican administration; while still others maintain that increasing federal power can be

"America's Town Meeting of the Air," 3 November 1954, 842d broadcast. Broadcast by 310 stations of the ABC Radio Network. Reprinted from *Town Meeting*, 3 November 1954, vol. 20, no. 27, by permission of Town Hall and Mrs. Ralph McGill.

halted only by the states themselves; proving once more that they can govern honestly and well in periods of crises as well as in normal times.

Now in the wake of the significant nationwide elections of Tuesday, "Town Meeting" tonight discusses this problem by seeking the answer to the question: "Is the Federal Government Running Our Lives?"

Congressman John Bell Williams, Democrat of Mississippi, is our first guest and he feels that the federal government is running our lives. Welcome to "Town Meeting," Congressman Williams.

Cong. [John Bell] Williams: Mr. Murray, in taking the affirmative side of this question, I would remind the public that this nation was created by men and women seeking refuge from the tyranny of oppressive government. The framers of our Constitution—the authors of American liberty—deliberately strove to write safeguards into that document that would guarantee a maximum of individual freedom to our citizens with a minimum of governmental interference. They sought to eliminate forever the dangers inherent in overconcentration of power into the hands of the few.

Specifically, they placed rigid limitations on the authority to be exercised by the central governing body and—with the Tenth Amendment—distributed the remaining powers to the states or to the people.

The system of checks and balances exercised by each branch of our government against the others, and the division of authority between federal and state governments has served, until recent years, to maintain and preserve the freedoms which our Founding Fathers deemed to be inalienable.

It is not so today. Our personal liberties are under attack, not only from a predatory enemy abroad, but also from those within our borders, who, for various reasons, would prefer to make government the master and not the servant of the people.

Through subtle but highly effective attrition, based on the false premise that the federal government should be all things to all people, more and more personal freedoms have been bartered in return for temporary material gratuities, and a will-o'-the-wisp thing called "security."!

Thus, we have permitted the federal government to invade fields of jurisdiction properly belonging to the states. The judiciary has taken it upon themselves to usurp the functions of the Congress—to create new laws in the absence of legislation. The executive branch, chiefly through abuse of its appointive power, has deliberately thrown out of balance the checks of one branch against the other. All this has been directed toward the concentration of authority into the hands of the few—which, if allowed to be followed to its ultimate conclusion, will lead to nothing else than eventual despotism with its attendant enslavement of the great masses of our people.

Murray: Thank you, Congressman John Bell Williams. Now on the opposite side of tonight's question, believing that the federal government does not run our lives, the distinguished editor of the *Atlanta Constitution*, Mr. Ralph E. McGill.

Mr. [Ralph] McGill: As I see it, the real genius of the American system of government, so carefully devised with its system of checks and balances, is that it makes impossible any running of our lives. It seems to me quite plain that our government does a magnificent job of preventing private economic or political interests from running our lives, and that, in essence, is what our government in part was designed to do. All of us are familiar with the great agricultural protests of the 1880s and '90s, out of which grew the Populist party. This was a protest against exorbitant credit regulations and exploitations through economic means. Out of this protest came William Jennings Bryan, Grover Cleveland, and many others, and out of them came the Sherman Antitrust Laws. These laws prevented great concentration of economic power from running our lives. They had about destroyed the farmers of America and the average wage earner of America. Surely there is no one who would, for example, say the antitrust laws are an imposition of government. Quite the contrary obviously is true.

My honored friend—I note from his excellent record—has voted consistently for farm-support prices, yet I do not think he is attempting to run my life or yours. My honored friend also has supported minimum-wage laws adopted by our government and I do not think he is trying to run our lives, but, instead, is trying to prevent economic greed from exploiting the American wage earner—especially those in the lower brackets.

Who is there who would like to remove from our legislation unemployment insurance, old age pensions, the laws relating to public health, the laws requiring free public schools, the laws requiring the stock exchange to be more honest than it was before October 1929? We could go on and on in this field, and what it adds up to is not government interference in our lives, but protection of our liberty and personal dignity by our government enabling us to live our own lives.

Murray: Thank you, Mr. McGill. And there, gentlemen, you have the opening statements of position, but perhaps now to sharpen the debate somewhat, may I ask you, Congressman Williams, if you would care to enumerate perhaps for us some specific instances of why you feel that the government is running our lives, and perhaps tell us why you object to those decisions?

Williams: First let me say this, Mr. Murray. After hearing Mr. McGill's opening statement, I am inclined to think that there is not too large an area of disagreement between us.

Murray: I trust you're wrong because then we'll have less interesting debate.

Williams: There will be areas of disagreement, of course. But philosophically and basically, I don't think there is too much area for disagreement. Mr. McGill mentioned my having voted for unemployment insurance, old-age pensions, minimum wage, laws relating to public health, and so forth. In that, he is correct to a certain extent and in another way he is wrong. I did not vote for those when they were originally enacted because I was not in Congress, but I have voted for amendments to those acts because I felt that the act as it stood perhaps needed amending. Now I am one of those who must find himself in agreement with the old Jeffersonian philosophy of government which says, "I believe that the best government, is the least government."

I believe that it is the purpose of government to guarantee insofar as possible the dignity of the individual citizen, and not to take him like a drop in a bucket of water, drop him in that bucket, and let him lose his identity. Of course, a lot of the things that the government has done are desirable, but the most specific example that I can think of at the moment of government interference into the lives of our citizens is the compulsion in our Social Security Act and the limitation placed upon income earned by Social Security annuities.

McGill: Well, of course, on that particular point, the Congress recently has made a change permitting persons drawing Social Security to earn more money. That came about by public opinion and there again is a fine example of government not running your lives, but in passing a law which enables you to run it better. You're going to have these continued large concentrations of people. We long ago ceased to be a rural nation. Whether we like it or not—and a lot of us don't like it and I wish it weren't true—but, we're an urban nation now. We're an industrialized nation. We're going to be more so when atomic energy comes into industry. We're going to have more and more crowded cities and it's just necessary that the government not run our lives, but that the government make regulations which enable us to live and run our lives without being victimized by the great pressures which grow up in huge concentrations of industry and people.

Williams: I might mention that another case of government interference in the lives of our people occurred on May 17 of this year when a political Supreme Court took it upon themselves to legislate into law, illegally, that which the Congress had down through the years refused to do. And that is to destroy our states' segregated public school system.

McGill: If the Congressman will pardon me, may I suggest that he is entirely incorrect and that the Supreme Court has done no such thing. All the Supreme Court has done is lay down a principle. It has not attempted in any way to enforce it. It has not even heard argument on the cases before it—that is, final argument. It has heard earlier arguments on two occasions, to be sure, but on December 6 it will hear arguments. We don't know what sort of enforcement the Supreme Court will hand down and even if they do hand down specific decisions, in most cases, it still is possible for any community that wishes to have a mutual agreement as to separate schools, and I believe very firmly in letting the local communities working it out—not in having state action on it. And I suggest that I am absolutely correct in that the Supreme Court has not at all destroyed any of the school systems. It has laid down only a broad principle—an American principle that we have had all along—that we can't discriminate on the basis of color, religion, race, or any previous condition of servitude, to drag in the long part of it. The Supreme Court has done nothing except lay down a principle. It hasn't destroyed a thing.[130]

---

[130]Until the late 1940s McGill generally advocated equal opportunity and equal (but separate) facilities for blacks, believing this to be the best strategy for that period.

Williams: There is some doubt in my mind as to whether the Supreme Court has laid down a principle or has destroyed a time-honored principle. Certainly there was no constitutional basis for the Supreme Court's decision. And as for me, I will accept as my theory of government the words of Thomas Jefferson, who said, in enumerating the powers which he believed the Constitution was intended to delegate to the states and to the federal government. He said this:

> Let the National Government be entrusted with the defense of the Nation and its foreign and federal relations, the state government with the Civil Right Laws and police and the administration of what concerns the state generally; and the counties with the local concerns of the counties until it ends in the administration of every man strong by himself.

I would say that I think the real basis of American freedom has always been in a community's account as a state right for local self-determination. Historically, that has been the real strength of the American government and free people everywhere in this world. Every government which has become overcentralized has eventually destroyed itself.

McGill: I submit again that I can't quite agree. If you restore the country which Jefferson had, namely a small stretch of population along the Atlantic Coast—a few million persons—and Jefferson's concept of government—he hated cities and I sometimes agree with him, although, I like nice cities like Tampa to be sure—but Jefferson said many times that he wanted this country to remain an agricultural country without any great cities, nothing but villages. He wanted home industries. He often said—he said on two occasions—that cities were to government what sores are to the body of a sick man. Now I submit first that I stand in great awe and respect of Thomas Jefferson. I have a great affection for him, his principles and his integrity; but he was talking about a small country of about ten or twelve million persons in which trappers and farmers and a few merchants made up the whole population. And you just can't deal with a hundred and sixty-two million and a population predicted to two hundred million by 1970 in any such fashion.

From the late 1940s to the early 1950s McGill attempted to prepare Southerners for changes he knew the Supreme Court would require. This public statement is an excellent example of the strategy McGill employed after the 1954 Supreme Court desegregation ruling to convince Southerners to be more receptive to social change. See the editor's introduction to this volume.

Williams: I am sure that Mr. McGill will agree with me in this. I will agree with Mr. McGill in that changing times require changing conditions and changing laws, but I would say that, like the Ten Commandments, basic fundamental principles transcend the onslaughts of time, and, like the Ten Commandments, our American Constitution is still the best vehicle for government ever conceived in the minds of man, and I don't believe in construing that Constitution lightly.

McGill: I agree with that Constitution. We've amended it many times, though. I certainly hold up the Constitution as the greatest document ever devised for government, but we amended it many times. We'll do it again.

Murray: Gentlemen, I have a question from the audience. . . .

Questioner: I would like to ask Mr. McGill—How do you think a social change can be brought about overnight by a judicial decision such as the one on desegregation?

McGill: I don't think it can be brought about overnight, and I am very hopeful that the Supreme Court won't think so. What I object to is so many persons insisting that the Supreme Court has already handed down its specific decision, and it has done nothing of the sort. It's not said what you've got to do or when you've got to do it. Maybe the Supreme Court won't say you've got to do it overnight.

Questioner: Why are we getting that interpretation from the order . . . of the Court?

McGill: I don't know, sir. It isn't in the Court's order—if you've read it. I don't know what you've been reading or to whom you've been listening, but somebody hasn't been giving you the correct facts.

Questioner: Well, everything I read in the papers down here leads me to believe that it has been pushed on us and we might just as well accept it because it has been pushed on us.

McGill: Well, sir, they don't begin argument until December 6 and nobody knows what sort of decision or when the Court will say the compliance must be had or in what fashion. We won't know that until next spring sometime.

Murray: Thank you, sir, for your question, and thank you, Mr. McGill.

Gentlemen, while on that same point that you were discussing about the urbanization trend in our nation, what is your feeling about the additional complexities of modern civilization producing a greater centralization at the federal level of government? What are your feelings on that? Congressman Williams, do you think that that attributes to a trend toward centralization?

Williams: Undoubtedly that presents many complex problems, but problems which, I believe, can be worked out within the framework of our Constitution and without destroying the states' sovereignty and individual freedoms.

McGill: I certainly wouldn't even suggest destroying the states' sovereignty and I don't believe that the Congressman thinks that any of Mississippi's sovereignty has been destroyed. But I suggest—

Williams: I disagree with that.

McGill: But, I suggest that, as our population grows, and as our urban areas increase and industrial populations increase with a great many persons renting homes—more and more owning small homes—that you simply must have federal participation. Now let's be honest about it. We've had a great drought—and it was a tragic thing. But what happened? When the farmers needed hay, did these people who were always talking about states' rights let us alone and let us take care of our own people? Where did they go? They were running to Washington for free hay. They didn't try to do it themselves, not one, not a single one of the forty-eight states attempted to do anything for its own drought-stricken people. They ran to Washington. You hear about states' rights at the national convention every four years.

Williams: I would not condone the idea of the states running to Washington, and I must admit, of course, that on occasion they have been guilty of doing that very thing. But it should be remembered that for the last twenty years the federal government has encouraged the states to look to Washington as the source of the solution to all of their problems, particularly their financial problems, and that also the federal government has invaded every possible field wherein the states might obtain some revenue. Now if the federal government were to return some of those fields of taxation—those sources of revenue to the state—I am sure that there would not be such a great clamoring for federal aid in every field.

Questioner: Mr. Williams, what would happen to our aged citizens if the federal government did not match dollar for dollar what the state appropriated?

Williams: I believe you asked the question: what would happen to the aged, that is, the old-age assistance program, if the federal government did not match the money put up by the state. Well, I assume that they would receive just the amount put up by the state or perhaps the states would attempt to increase theirs. But, as I said a minute ago, it should be remembered that the federal government has usurped practically every source of revenue that the states have, and, therefore, it is necessary for the states to request that the federal government assist them in carrying out their program; the federal government having taken away from them the money that rightfully belonged to the states.

Questioner: I don't think the federal government is running our lives when we ask them to help us.

Williams: Well, of course, the federal government's not running our lives when we ask them to help us. But the federal government moved in on the states' areas of taxation and the state being a part of the federal government and having the programs that it considered necessary for the welfare of its own citizens—being unable to finance it because the federal government has taken its money—had to ask the federal government to return some of it and, therefore, the matching program.

Murray: Thank you, Congressman. While on that same field of taxation, many are wondering whether or not the enormous new global commitment of our nation, to contribute to an increase in the centralization, is the question of our foreign aid. Would you care to give us your opinion, Congressman and Mr. McGill, as to whether or not this process should be continued?

McGill: The enormous program of which you speak, sir, has been substantially reduced and will be even further reduced come next year, but I submit that, for the first time in the history of this troubled world, we have a situation in which two great ideologies and two divergent forces—one of tyranny and one of individual freedom—are facing each other, and I just can't help it; I believe this program of Marshall aid has restored the economy and trade of France and Italy, possibly Belgium and Holland, from Communism. I believe it's been worth every nickel we've paid and I think that if we hadn't done it—and if we don't continue foreign aid on a basis of need—that we're going to wake up and find that the bill of fighting Russia is going to cost a great deal more. I'm all for foreign aid where needed and on a basis of need.

Williams: The question of whether the fifty-odd billions of dollars that we have spent all over the world has kept these various countries from going Communist is, of course, a moot question. Perhaps they would not have gone Communist anyway, perhaps they would have. I don't know. But it's a question that nobody in the world can answer. Now, frankly, I have asked the question on the floor of the House of members of the Foreign Affairs Committee where the constitutional basis for foreign aid is to be found inasmuch as Congress is limited—the powers of Congress are limited in taxation to promoting the general welfare of the national defense—and that question has not yet been answered, nor has it been tested by the courts. Now I might say this further, as far as this program entering into our private lives, I consider your tax money and my tax money that goes into the foreign aid program to be money confiscated by the federal government for the general welfare of peoples abroad, and I can't find any constitutional basis for this.

McGill: Well, Congressman, I don't, if you'll pardon me, sir. By the same token, I don't believe that you can find any constitutional basis prohibiting it. You get back to the same situation you had when Jefferson brought off the Louisiana Purchase. Both of us agreed we admired Jefferson and he was subjected to tremendous attack because he did it without any constitutional basis. But heaven help us if he hadn't done it.

Murray: Gentlemen, tonight's listener question . . . is directed to you both. "As the federal government grows, does this tend to decrease or increase individual rights and freedoms?" Congressman Williams.

Williams: I would say that the answer to that question depends upon the rate at which the federal government grows in proportion to the growth of the population. I would say this and point this out as an interesting fact—not necessarily a part of my argument—but the per capita federal tax, that is the tax imposed on the individual in the United States, increased 2,420 percent between 1933 and 1954. And if you want to find out whether individual freedom has been curtailed between 1933 and 1954, just ask any businessman in the United States who has to cope with all of these rules, regulations, forms, and red tape.

McGill: I might point out to ask those same businessmen if it isn't true that their net profit over the past years hasn't been greater than ever before in the history of this country—and, of course, it has. . . .

Murray: We have a question now from the audience.

Questioner: Congressman Williams, congratulations for being elected again. Do you believe that the abolition of public schools in favor of private schools is the solution to the desegregation problem? I probably should say *a* solution to the problem.

Williams: Well, of course, it is a solution. I would certainly hate to see that done, but if there is no other answer, then I think that is the only solution.

Questioner: I'd like to ask Mr. McGill how do you reconcile compulsory labor arbitration with your position that the government is not interfering in our lives?

McGill: Compulsory labor legislation is not general. It exists only in a few industries and in a few states which agree to it. Isn't that correct, sir?

Questioner: Did you say arbitration or legislation?

McGill: There hasn't been any federal compulsory arbitration law except in a few industries which have voluntarily agreed to it. The railroads, for example, who else? If you'll pardon me, sir, I don't think the question applies generally. It's done voluntarily. The government doesn't force you to agree with it.

Questioner: In the steel industry when both sides reach a deadlock, then the federal arbitrator comes into the picture, correct?

McGill: Only by request.

Questioner: And when he makes a decision, it covers not only one plant, but an industry. Correct?

McGill: Only if the industry agrees. In other words, the government isn't sending him there unless he is requested to come, and I don't think it's logical, sir, to assume that if you are requested to come, the government's running your life.

Questioner: Well, sometimes in management one possibility outweighs another and the possibility that you may not even be able to reopen your business because labor shuts you; therefore, you will agree with most anything, even compulsory arbitration.

McGill: It isn't compulsory, sir, if you agree to it.

Murray: Gentlemen: I think we've cleared that up to the satisfaction of neither party, perhaps, but at least we've gone into it. May I have the next question, please?

Questioner: Mr. Williams, if you only voted for the amendments to the antitrust laws, farm-support prices, minimum-wage laws, Social Security, and so forth because you felt they needed change, would you abolish these laws?

Williams: Not under our present conditions, no.

Questioner: From your position then do you consider this to be an intrusion on states' rights?

Williams: I do.

Questioner: And you would not abolish them?

Williams: No sir, I would not abolish them because conditions are such that the country cannot abolish these things at this particular time. I would like to see this federal interference end through the states' sovereignties—the states' fields of jurisdiction—reduced in the same manner that it was built up and that is through an attritional method, step by step, perhaps taking a bit of the compulsion out of each one of these laws and then eventually eliminating that law as conditions and circumstances permit.

Questioner: Sir, you now do not think they should be abolished because they are necessary. I would assume from that, then, the federal government is not running our lives.

Williams: Well, now let me say this. These laws are necessary, individually, because the pattern has been set in that direction. And if we take one of these laws away, that's going to leave that group without any protection. That's the basis, of course, of our farm-support prices. It's because practically every other segment of our economy is being supported and protected by government. We can't afford to leave the farmer unprotected.

Questioner: Then these laws are for the protection of the people.

Williams: Although, I might say this, that the farmer would be the first to say take the government out of everything.

Questioner: Mr. McGill, we know that the federal expansion comes from requests from the people. How can the people be shown that when they make requests that they must be paid for?

McGill: I think that's a matter that you and I ought to be interested in. Both of us work for newspapers. I would suggest that newspapers, radio, television, public forums, businesses themselves, employers—a great many employers are already making that plain when they pay your wage indicating how much tax is taken out. Congressman Williams and I were talking about that at dinner tonight. I think a great many of the telephone companies are now sending out their bills on which they indicate the tax. It's simply a matter of the public education, but I don't go along too much on that because it comes down to the business that all of us have a little larceny in us. We'd all very much like to buy wholesale and sell retail. And we're always ready for the other fellow to pay the tax. And I say that if you have these services, then stand up like a man and be happy you can pay the tax. There's nothing wrong with the tax if it provides adequate goods and services for which the taxes are designed, in my opinion.

Williams: There, I think that the questioner has pointed to one of the fine examples of government interference into our lives. Every wage earner is compelled, by law, to have deducted from his salary his taxes by the month. The taxes which are deducted from his January salary he loses the use of throughout the year, yet he receives no interest from the government for the use of his money. And yet, he has no alternative other than to pay that tax. I would think that if the average wage earner in the United States—and he comprises the great body of our people—could just be made conscious of the tremendous amount of taxes that are deducted from his salary, I believe that he would be the first to be asking that the government get out of our lives as much as possible because it's costing too doggone much.

Questioner: I'd like to ask Mr. McGill if he doesn't think it might be a good idea to have some of the hidden taxes more brought out into the light?

McGill: I'd be all for that. Most of the hidden taxes are state taxes.

Questioner: Mr. Williams, I understand that the percentage of big business that is owned by the federal government, at this time, is startling. I wonder if you could tell me just what percentage of big business is owned by the federal government.

Williams: I'm afraid that you've asked a question that I'm not prepared to answer. But I would say that a rather large portion of business is controlled by the government. The government is the largest lending agency in the world, if you'll take that as an example.

Questioner: This is a question on segregation for either of the speakers. We have friends who, if desegregation comes about, plan to have their children removed from the white schools. I do not plan to remove my children in that event. Now what kind of argument can we give these friends of ours?

McGill: I don't know your friend, and I don't like to advise persons I know very well, let alone a perfect stranger, but it seems to me, that feeling as you do you might well argue that in the state of Texas there are several hundred Negroes at the college level and there's been no friction.[131] There's been none of the fear of mongrelization or social mixing.[132] The schools have been going on pretty successfully in many of the Eastern and Western states on an elementary school basis. I'm not familiar with them. I'm not prepared to say I've experienced [them] but

---

[131]McGill stated that "when I was made executive editor in 1938, on the very first day I came in the office I sent down instructions that the word *Negro* should be spelled with a capital *N* because this was proper according to the rules of English usage."; see "A Conversation with Ralph McGill," in volume 2.

[132]Throughout his campaign for civil rights for blacks, McGill confronted the fear of racially mixed marriages; see the vocal response of a member of the audience during McGill's "Editors View the South" speech at Emory University, Atlanta, in 1957; *Ralph McGill: Editor and Publisher,* ed. Calvin McLeod Logue, 2 vols. (Durham: Moore Publishing Company, 1969) 1:159-60; "An Interview on Race and the Church" and "Radio 'Conversation Piece,' " in volume 2.

they have been going on. There's been no bad effect that I've heard of. It's a matter of personal opinion, but if he wants to take them out, the government isn't going to run his life. He can take them out.

Questioner: Congressman Williams, is it possible to preserve the original concepts of the sovereignty of the states in the light of modern social and economic situations peculiar to the national interests?

Williams: I think so, yes. I would say as Washington said in his farewell address—that if the Constitution be wrong in any respects, then let it be changed in the manner that the Constitution provides by submission and by the approval of the people.

Questioner: Congressman Williams, a minute ago you stated that . . . government was growing in proportion to the population growth—in that case I wonder if you could tell me if the socialistic trend is growing in the same proportion?

Williams: I can answer that by saying that I think definitely so. In one word, yes.

Murray: May I take this occasion to thank you, Congressman John Bell Williams of Mississippi and Ralph E. McGill, editor of the *Atlanta Constitution*, for your contribution to our discussion this evening. . . .

28

New Truth
in a New Nation:
Review
of Jay Saunders Redding's
An American in India

S aunders Redding, distinguished teacher and writer, has written a book out of a disturbing experience in India, courageously and intelligently endured, which frightens as it inspires. It is inspiring in that it is one of those rare human documents in which a man learns something new about himself and rationalizes it to find strength and a new truth.

The book is *An American in India*. It begins almost serenely. A calm and detached man, to whom the final result of his American experience had been "to force me to depersonalize myself," set out for India under state-department auspices to tell "the clinical truth" about his country. He found in India that Communist propaganda had gone a long way toward equating "Western" with "white." This, plus the sensitive nationalism of the Indians produced a color consciousness perhaps as intense as that in South Africa and in its overall aspects more disturbing even than that in the United States. At the outset of his journey Mr. Redding

Jay Saunders Redding, *An American in India: A Personal Report on the Indian Dilemma and the Nature of Her Conflicts* (Indianapolis: Bobbs-Merrill, 1954). Review reprinted by permission of Mrs. Ralph McGill and *Saturday Review.* Copyright 1954, The Saturday Review Associates, Inc. From *Saturday Review* 37 (25 December 1954).

was made aware of this fact by a sign in his first Indian hotel which read "No White South Africans Allowed" and by meeting in his first social group a beautiful, cultured, and intelligent young Indian woman who had never married because she was "too dark." From these beginnings the experiences were more complex, more shocking.

Mr. Redding produces new and irrefutable evidence of a fact which too many Americans, especially too many Southern political leaders, do not comprehend—namely, that "colonialism" in Asia and the Orient is a revolt of colored peoples demanding status and that the problem of race in the United States is on the same umbilical cord of the birth of this revolution.

It was a path constantly beset by harassment which Mr. Redding faithfully followed up and down India, insulted and bedeviled by the dialectics and rudeness of the Communists, and frustrated by the sensitiveness of those Indians who retreat from what is pragmatic in their problem into an escapist shell of Hindu philosophy.

Out of wartime and postwar visits, all too brief, to India's villages, I found her urban intellectuals readily approving a conclusion that the Indian peasants, or villagers, were magnificent people, kindly and good. But they were immediately hostile if one talked of their backwardness and the primitive status of their economy; the barrenness of their lives (theirs, through no fault of their own), and what could be done about it. Their sensitiveness and their pride in the new nationalism may easily be understood. But it also must be faced.

His conclusions seem to me, on the basis of my own inadequate visits to India, entirely valid. There is a hard core of Communism in India. And it is harbored by the intellectual segment of the nation—professors, writers, journalists, politicians, and students "who will soon be professors." It was chiefly for this reason, it appeared to me, that if Nehru should die or be assassinated India would find the problem of replacing him and maintaining his policy an impossible task. Communist power, supported by so many of the intellectual class, would be strong enough to make it so.

Communist propaganda, as Mr. Redding says, has persuaded India that America is imperialistic; that Point Four and various other American organizations, the Rockefeller and Ford Foundations and the Fulbright Student Exchange Program, are tools of a giant imperialistic conspiracy.

Mr. Redding offers a plan; to continue to bombard them with truth and with sincere visitors and friends. He proposes a concentration on two groups, the professional groups, who should be sought out and helped in a spirit of complete equality and friendship, and the indecisive masses, who should be shown more films, magazines, books, "and the like." The Communists have done this while we have provided Mickey Spillane.[133] The shortsighted "penney-wise, pound-foolish" attitude of our Congress on appropriations and the poor planning of American countermeasures are starkly illustrated by this book.

It is a good book, of a man of courage and democratic spirit. It merits wide reading. That the author should have found it necessary to send out, after the early reviews, a statement clarifying what should have been plain from the reading of his book—namely, that while former Ambassador Bowles wanted a neutral India, he did not endorse the Indian theory of "neutralism"—is a significant illustration of how difficult it is to present the complex story of that country's political dialectics and problems. I hope there is some way to have it reach India's intellectuals and professional and college-educated men and women.[134]

---

[133] Author of popular mysteries.

[134] See Ralph Emerson McGill, *Report On India*, newspaper columns, 21 November 1951 to 8 January 1952, *Atlanta Constitution*.

29

Adlai Stevenson
and the Democratic South

I t is very likely that Adlai Stevenson, Chicago attorney, may take a
Deep South vacation this summer. If he is to have a decision as to
his presidential candidacy ready for November release, he must
spend some time in the South looking and listening and putting an ear
to the sun-baked earth.

It will not be an easy diagnosis. Southern politics includes within its
bloodstream the chills and fevers of various and curious malarias. A
state may go to bed at night with a normal temperature, and for no common-sense reason, wake up in the morning alternately sweating and
chilling in an emotional seizure. There is just no telling what the emotional content of the Deep South will be when the next national election
arrives.

This might be the time to say those conventional few words about
the state, and the state of mind, called Texas. National Democratic
Chairman Paul M. Butler, a quiet, friendly man, recently made a six-
day peace tour through that state and was harassed with war-whoops and
raids, even though constantly he bore aloft an olive branch. Gov. Allan

Reprinted from the *New Republic*, 27 June 1955, by permission of Mrs. Ralph
McGill and the *New Republic*. Copyright 1955, Harrison-Blaine of New Jersey, Inc.
In the McGill papers there is a typed version of this piece entitled "Refusing the
Thirty Pieces of Silver," now at Emory University, Atlanta.

Shivers led Texas into the Republican column in 1952. He is politically beholden to the industrial strength of the state, which strongly backs the present administration. This includes the vast oil and associated chemical developments which have made the Lone Star State one of the really great industrial regions of the nation. Its industries are worth more than its traditional cows. Like many Southern politicians caught in this unhappy, uncertain time of transition in the South, Governor Shivers can't quite make up his mind. He says he is still a Democrat, but he has his own definition. If he doesn't like the party's nominee or the platform adopted by the party's delegates, then he isn't a Democrat. He objected to the 1952 Democratic platform on tideland oils.

Candidate Adlai Stevenson, typically refusing the thirty pieces of silver so often urged upon him during that long campaign, declined to compromise a single plank in the platform. He spoke in Texas against the tideland oil grab, though he knew it meant almost certain loss of that state, as it did. He did the same thing in Louisiana where the issue was at the boiling point. There he lost merely the governor. [135]

At any rate, Chairman Butler learned that Governor Shivers felt slighted because the chairman could not attend a luncheon the governor belatedly organized. The Texas State Democratic Chairman and the National Committeewoman also felt that Chairman Butler had not recognized their importance and retaliated by attending none of the meetings scheduled for him. Mr. Butler toured the plains on a program arranged by the Texas Democratic Advisory Council, which is composed of men and women who remained loyal in 1952 when Shivers went over to the Republican party.

It would be equally easy to stir up similar childish, though serious, political angers in almost any of the Southern states. All of them presently are troubled, nervous, suspicious, alarmed, and suffering enormously from growing pains. Most of them now are paying very little attention to state government as such. They are devoting most of their thinking and planning toward postponing, as long as possible, the recent school decision of the Supreme Court.

---

[135]See "Report on Adlai E. Stevenson" and "How Adlai Stevenson Won Georgia's Heart All Over Again," in volume 1.

Nearly all of them have tax systems which specifically were created for agricultural states. Not a single one of them has moved to establish a new tax system geared to the industrial and population growths of the present and future. Without exception, they have kept patching up and adding to obsolete systems. The result is that the tax burden falls unequally and is in constant need of further patching.

None of them has enough physical plants adequately to house all the children who will be going to school next fall. Their salary scales to university, grade, and high school teachers are below the national average. The programs for building the separate-but-equal school systems have been enormously expensive and have loaded them all with extra debts.

In not a single state is there any evidence that the leaders comprehend the complex political and social meaning of "urbanization" as reflected in the great growth of their cities and the decrease in farm population. There already are deep, uncharted political currents running through these populations.

It is some of these currents which have brought about the split in Texas. They are present in each of the Southern states and will evidence themselves in one way or another as the great political and social issues of the future arise.

The truth is that the so-called cotton South is likely, for a long time, to be an "agin-the-White-House" region. It already is learning to its distress and consternation, that neither the Democratic nor Republican party can, or is willing, to give it what it wants. Much of the Democrats-for-Eisenhower strength, for example, stemmed from Candidate Eisenhower's frequent statements that he believed in allowing the states to have as much latitude in government as possible and in withdrawing the federal government from participation in state affairs.

As they turned against Franklin Roosevelt in his last years in the White House, so did they become bitterly antagonistic to Harry Truman. Now again they are "against the White House."

In addition to the endemic political malaria, which makes for instability and brings prophets to grief, there are other factors at work. Florida is the first Southern state to develop Republican strength by virtue of new population and the conservatism of the "retired class." It still is Democratic, but there is a right-wing independent vote in the state which has maintained its organization since the 1952 Eisenhower campaign. In all Southern states there is an increase in the middle-class population and in organized labor. Texas with a large Republican vote, is still normally Democratic. But politics nowhere in the South are "normal" anymore.

Under the circumstances, Stevenson's greatest asset is that he now is in fact the middle-of-the-road Democratic candidate. We earnestly suggest to Attorney Stevenson that when he does come South, he bring all the latest listening devices, and if possible, a political univac contraption too.[136]

---

[136]See Kenneth Sydney Davis, *A Prophet in His Own Country: The Triumphs and Defeats of Adlai E. Stevenson* (Garden City NY: Doubleday, 1957); Stuart Gerry Brown, *Conscience in Politics: Adlai E. Stevenson in the 1950s* (Syracuse: Syracuse University Press, 1961); Stuart Gerry Brown, *Adlai E. Stevenson, Short Biography: The Conscience of the Country* (Woodbury NY: Woodbury Press, 1965).

30

The Angry South
1956

Southerners trying to be fair are confronted daily with the many and frustrating complexities of the racial problem in its most aggressive form. The newspaper man or woman in the Deep South who, as carefully and as objectively as his or her talents permit, produces critical opinion experiences an immediacy of thermal reaction. To some he has fouled his own nest, sold out to Yankee dollars, betrayed his people, and so on. A cross may be burned in his yard, or his windows broken by stones thrown in the night. He personally is pilloried, vigorously and libelously, by political demagogues. He encounters some support, and there is perhaps one constant satisfaction: he knows he is being read.

Now and then, he indulges in a Walter Mitty nostalgia for the old days as pictured in the literature of once-upon-a-time. There was a time when being a Southerner could be made into a pleasant semi-official profession if one rehearsed it a bit.

But not now. In May 1954, the trumpets of the nine black-robed justices in the Greek temple on the Potomac blew down the already weakened walls of political feudalism in the South. There long will be fighting in the ruins, but it will be guerrilla stuff and its denouement

Reprinted from the *Atlantic Monthly* 197 (April 1956): 31-34, by permission of Mrs. Ralph McGill and the *Atlantic Monthly*. Copyright 1956, by The Atlantic Monthly Company.

is sure. When the walls crumbled, the Humpty Dumpty of a conveni-
ent, oft-invoked regional concept of states' rights fell, too. Even if apostles of this doctrine, which was as malleable as sculptor's clay in the
hands of its many interpreters, were to put Humpty Dumpty back together again, there is no wall on which to set him. He fell with the
walls, not from them.

The South of myth, reality, and paradox was beginning noticeably
to change its internal structure in the mid-thirties. The region had not
at all recovered from the boll weevil plague when the world depression
came. The disaster of the weevil had been even worse. It was not so recognized nationally save by insurance companies which ended up holding
mortgages on as much as three-fourths of the property in some of the
major cotton counties. In these counties some two hundred bales were
produced in 1920 on plantations which a year or so before had produced
two thousand bales. Banks failed, and there was no government policy
to reopen them. Manor houses emptied. The ruins of many still stand,
never again occupied. The tenant and sharecropper cabins began to be
deserted. Their doors sagged with the passing years, and the winds blew
a requiem through them for the lost dreams of men and their families,
white and colored, who were gone to "Dee-troit" to the already burgeoning automobile plants, and to steel plants in "Shee-cargo" and Pittsburgh. On top of all this came the Great Depression.[137]

Even the more insensitive should have known that something was
amiss in the depression years. The cotton economy was wrecked and
would never return. Ahead was the need for new crops. Machines were
to replace the many hands and the slow-plodding mules. That would be
change enough. But there came, too, the many government agencies for
relief, for rehabilitation of soil, and for the construction of roads,
schools, bridges, and public buildings. In the rush for aid and the almost greedy acceptance of it by a region long short of capital, the
strength of states' rights politics was dissipated. In a sense, it was bartered away. In this period, too, the South abandoned the two-thirds rule

---

[137]See Harriet Laura Herring, *Passing of the Mill Village: Revolution in a Southern
Institution* (Chapel Hill: University of North Carolina Press, 1949); Paul E. Mertz,
New Deal Policy and Southern Rural Poverty (Baton Rouge: Louisiana State University
Press, 1978); and Brian Rungeling et al., *Employment, Income, and Welfare in the Rural
South* (New York: Praeger, 1977).

which had given it a veto on the doings of the national Democratic convention. This was given away—a fact which later caused great regret in
the smoke-filled rooms.

But the walls of states' rights regionalism were undermined most
energetically by those who now protest the most—the Deep South politicians at the state and local level who head up or support the Citizens'
and States' Rights Councils, and other variations on the theme. It was
they who most encouraged and accompanied the entrepreneurs who went
north by plane and train in search of new industry. Some tempted this
new industry with low taxes or no taxes, with free land or cheap land.
Others offered intelligently prepared blueprints of the water supply,
skilled labor, transportation, and pointed with pride to the stability of
their local governments.

So it was that change came slowly, yet steadily, as did the new industry. It was accelerated by a desire to decentralize; it was quickened
by war and by the further urge to disperse industrial concentrations once
the A- and H-bombs came into being; most of all, it was hastened by
the job hunger of a region long short of employment.

It was, and still is, a puzzling fact that most of those who headed,
or were members of, delegations seeking new enterprises never saw
themselves as carriers of the virus which was to destroy the status quo in
their towns and communities—and also, therefore, the old "way of life
in the South." They brought new payrolls to their towns. Businesses
boomed and new ones came. The delegations basked in the sun of progress. But still they fretted. "Things are not the same," they said, shaking
their puzzled heads. The organizers and unions came. The Negroes
were encouraged to register and vote. The PTA and the community
meetings began to hear new and protesting voices about the crowded
schools, the town's municipal services. The political contests began to
be less and less "sure" of result. All the while, though deploring the
change and declaring to visitors that things were not as they had been,
the delegations never saw themselves as makers of the revolution. They
sought with a kind of desperation to maintain the status quo—all the
while laboring to bring new industries and payrolls which could only
accelerate the changes.

Because much of the South is still rural, and legislators from agricultural communities still dominate most legislatures, the effect of ur-

banization has come much more slowly to Southern politics than to politics in the industrial East. But its influences may be seen and felt.

Southern politics perhaps has been more consistently lacking in idealistic or progressive imagination, and therefore has been more pragmatic, than politics elsewhere. Its leaders have more often said no than yes. The South joined the Populist movement but did not originate it. Woodrow Wilson, who was Southern-born, aroused some of Thomas Jefferson's liberalism and idealism. His own stern Calvinism matched the religious climate of most of the South, and his political morality became, in a sense, also religious morality. But it did not originate in the South. Southern politics chose to follow Grover Cleveland, Woodrow Wilson, and Franklin D. Roosevelt's New Deal. It rejected, or was indifferent to, Harry Truman's Fair Deal and Adlai Stevenson's candidacy. Despite the competence, even brilliance, of some of its senators and congressmen, the South, since the days of the Virginia dynasty and of Andrew Jackson, has not offered leadership which the nation has followed. It could not because it was committed to a hard-forged regionalism.

It was in the last of the Roosevelt years that politicians began to see that they would never be able to win national acceptance of their social and political theories. Some of what they believed was good and just. But they stubbornly and uncompromisingly offered a package. The nation would not buy it, either in the markets of the national conventions held by the two parties or in the Congress.[138]

Out of this refusal came the Dixiecrat revolt of 1948 in which Strom Thurmond, now U.S. Senator from South Carolina, carried four states. Some commentators compared it to Herbert Hoover's cracking of the so-called solid South in 1928. It was not at all related. Dwight D. Eisenhower carried five traditionally Democratic states. In part, he was able to do so because of a belief that he was, in considerable degree, a "states' rights man" in the Southern meaning of that oft-employed phrase. Many Southerners believed he would, in particular, leave the issue of segregation in education to the states. When, through the office of the attorney general of the United States, the Administration filed a

---

[138]See V. O. Key, Jr., *Southern Politics in State and Nation* (New York: Vintage Books, 1949).

brief before the Supreme Court asking an end to segregation, the disenchantment among the unyielding Southern political leaders was complete.[139]

But even before the Court's decision in May 1954, the diagnosticians of Southern political distemper could, with confidence, make one entry on their charts. It was that, for a long time to come, a very considerable portion of the South would be an "agin-the-White-House" political force. Since neither national party was willing, or indeed able to give this Southern leadership what it wanted, it would not greatly matter which party was in the mansion on Pennsylvania Avenue. The Deep South would, for the most part, be against the occupant.

The strength of these states will be used to bargain collectively at the national conventions with the threat of "an independent party" as alternative to rejection of their demands.

The Court's decision, which for the first time split the traditional solidarity of the South on the racial issue, assured this future aspect of the Deep South politics. The antisegregation issue was not, paradoxically enough, so much of a shock. In their secret hearts the most ardent advocates of the status quo knew that the Constitution of the United States could no longer be interpreted to mean one thing for one citizen and an opposite thing for another. Many had come to see, though they would admit it only privately, that if the Southern interpretation of states' rights meant such an inequality in citizenship, then that doctrine had no slight chance of winning national support. In 1954 any political device which could make one man less a citizen than another, or give one American child less opportunity than another, was not merely impotent, but was regarded by most Americans as politically immoral. States' rights remained firmly imbedded in the Constitution, but they no longer meant what some political leaders said they did—any more than they meant, in 1861, that there was a states' right of secession. All this would be granted in private by men who declared in public they would fight it to the death.

The more angry and defiant among Deep South politicians, being obsessed with politics of the past, had ignored what had been occurring

---

[139]See Emile Bertrand Ader, *The Dixiecrat Movement: Its Role in Third Party Politics* (Washington DC: Public Affairs Press, 1955).

in the South with the slow, steady change to an urbanized society. They also had missed the meaning of the fact that for years substantial numbers of Negroes had been attending the professional schools in Texas and Arkansas, and that in Tennessee and North Carolina there had been admission of one or two such students. They could not understand it when there was no immediate fusion of all the Southern states and a hedgehog regional opposition to the Court's edict. Tennessee's four-year plan for integration was denounced by the more angry as the sinister influence of politicians seeking the labor and Negro vote. And the more rabid elements from the town, not from the campus, have had their way at the University of Alabama.[140]

But many school districts in Missouri, Oklahoma, and West Virginia moved to desegregate, as did isolated communities in Arkansas. The University of South Carolina became the first Southern state university to admit Negroes to the undergraduate school, although a similar decision by the University of Louisville had preceded it. And when great Texas herself announced a plan for gradual compliance with the Court's decree, the reaction was one of furious incredulity. Immediately there was a quick hardening of opposition in the Deep South and in Virginia. Some of these states legislatively and emotionally are prepared to abolish their public school systems. They can count on support from a majority of unhappy but agreeable people.

Nor was this unexpected. Back of the cotton states in the Deep South is a history of generations of political exploitation of the racial issues and the closely associated fact of larger percentages of Negro population. Inflammatory and violent agitation of racial politics in the cotton South dates back to Pitchfork Ben Tillman of South Carolina and Tom Watson of Georgia, both of whom had really profound regional influence down to our present day. They have never lacked heirs and imitators. They and the cumulative effect of their successors are factors in the quick hardening of Deep South opposition. A region, like a nation or a man, is a product of its history and traditional environment. Deep in the instincts of many Southerners is a fear of what might happen "when the children all drink out of the same bucket." Many of these people are entirely sin-

---

[140]See Numan V. Bartley, *The Rise of Massive Resistance: Race and Politics in the South During the 1950s* (Baton Rouge: Louisiana State University Press, 1969).

cere when they say that nonsegregation means a "mongrelized" race. They will die before they will agree, they say. And they mean it.[141]

It must not be assumed that this position is an evasive device. It is honestly held. It does no good for a minister, a newsman, or an editor, seeking to discuss the problem objectively, to suggest that the North has had no segregation, save the considerable degree obtained by the geographic facts of residence and by some judicious gerrymandering of school districts, and that there has been no mongrelization. If it further be suggested that this is, in a sense, an affront to the Southern people in that it suggests that only separation maintains their racial integrity, the result is unreasoning anger. The sociologists say that while the number of interracial marriages is up because the population is, percentagewise the number is down. That there is much less miscegenation than there was twenty or thirty years ago is not denied. With increased education and opportunity the Negro has, like anyone else, developed more and more racial pride. But it is this one issue of the possibility of intermarriage which most concerns the Deep South. That the reasoning is not always sound does not at all detract from the strength of its belief or fear. When emotions dominate, reason plays little part. He who dismisses this attitude as a mere prejudice does neither himself nor the great American problem any good.

Northern editorialists may thunder at it and reason it away. But the Southern newspaper editor or writer of any sensitivity, who knows his people, will not, though he disagree with them, mock or denounce them. It is a part of his duty personally and professionally, since he knows the path his region has taken, to seek in every way to ameliorate the problem, knowing it cannot be "solved." Few great problems are solved. Persons of good will keep on ameliorating them until finally they cease to be major problems.

Yet another force in the present situation is that of religion. The South, long ago labeled the Bible Belt, has always been a strongly churchgoing region, with heavy Calvinist overtones. It has prided itself on being Christian. To some, that Christianity, like states' rights, occasionally took on strange interpretations. "Before the war," for example,

---

[141]See Cal M. Logue and Howard Dorgan, eds., *The Oratory of Southern Demagogues* (Baton Rouge: Louisiana State University Press, 1981).

many honestly persuaded themselves that Christianity endorsed and made slavery obligatory. Their spiritual descendants today declare that segregation is justified by Christian principles. The religious attitude of the average Citizens' Council member is perhaps well expressed by an apocryphal story. At a meeting of one of the newly formed Citizens' Council groups, to discuss the school segregation issue, a member proposed asking a well-known minister to advise them. "There ain't a bit of use sending for him," said the chairman. "All he will do is give you the Christian solution."[142]

Nonetheless, the Episcopal, Catholic, Presbyterian, Methodist, and Lutheran churches have proclaimed a Christian policy in support of desegregation. So have many Baptist congregations and ministers (this church has no central authority).[143]

The Southerner, looking objectively at his region, would be happy if he knew how many persons there are who are willing to give the Supreme Court's decision an honest try. He suspects, on the basis of his knowledge of his people and their Christian faith, that the number is considerable. He knows also that many of these would not willingly undergo a public display and testing of their feelings.

Another development which the Southern newspaper writer honestly seeking to portray his region must face is the demand that "our side" be vigorously presented. Many people insist that it is not. Some argue that the fact of determined and unmoved Deep South opposition is not known to the nation. "Tell them we will die rather than yield" is a somewhat common statement. "Don't they know there will be violence?" is another question which must be dealt with and not considered as the cry

---

[142]See John Bartlow Martin, *The Deep South Says "Never"* (New York: Ballantine Books, 1957); Neil R. McMillen, *The Citizens' Council* (Urbana: University of Illinois Press, 1971); Francis M. Wilhoit, *The Politics of Massive Resistance* (New York: George Braziller, 1973); William J. Simmons, *The Mid-West Hears the South's Story* (Greenwood MS: The Citizens' Councils, 1958); Thomas P. Brady, *A Review of Black Monday* (Winona MS: Association of Citizens' Councils of Mississippi, 1954); and James O. Eastland, *We've Reached Era of Judicial Tyranny* (Greenwood MS: Association of Citizens' Councils of Mississippi, 1955).

[143]See Charles Reagan Wilson, *Baptized in Blood: The Religion of the Lost Cause, 1865-1920* (Athens: University of Georgia Press, 1980); and Samuel S. Hill, *Religion and the Solid South* (Nashville: Abingdon Press, 1972).

of a crackpot. There may be some violence, but there are no signs it will be as bad as the more fearful or angry declare.

It is often asserted today that the former "excellent relations" between the races have deteriorated and will worsen. This is, in a general sense, true, but it is more applicable to the smaller cities and towns and the rural areas. And what the average Southerner honestly does not know is that even the average Negro thought there was much lacking and much that was unfair in the excellent relationships that did and do exist. Many a sincere, average, Deep South Southerner does not know, or refuses to admit, that world forces are at work in the American race problem as they are in Asia and Africa. Somehow, to him, his present harassments are all a sinister business brought on by an organization called the NAACP. He feels that a proper government would put it in jail or order it to go away, and then everything would again be as it was. One of the more unrewarding tasks of a responsible Southern journalist is to interpret local events, when he can, in terms of the world picture.

The plain and really sad truth is that it is difficult to put together "our side" as the more disturbed and angry Southerner means the phrase. The various forms of Citizens' Councils, which are largely secret, are at present committed to "every legal method" of blocking desegregation. This is the most concrete form of opposition. But as a matter of fact these deeply disturbed persons represent a great accumulation of resentments, of seeming injustices. They want an interpretation of the constitutional phrase about reserving to the states those rights not reserved to the federal government. They have a passionate conviction that Southern traditions are sound and right, and that the North is wrong. The average Southerner really believes that everyone at least privately thinks that separation of the races by law is best for both. His political leaders so often have assured him they would prevent all this from happening. Worse, they were positive it would never happen. Now that it has, they can do nothing to justify their failure except denounce the White House, the Court, and the "radicals." The Southerner wishes someone would put all this into compelling form as "our side." This average Southerner with a deep sense of injustice is not a "bad" man. He wants to be liked. He wants it understood he loves his country—and he does, as he has proved in war and peace. But at present he feels that his country does not love him. And he is sad, angry, resentful, and defiant.

Much of the reporting on the segregation issue and the variety of reaction in the South has contained elements of joylessness and the sense of guilt which occupies so many pages of Southern novelists. It is difficult to see the gleam of the other side of the metal, but it is there. Despite the deep anger, the ranting, the violence, and the pious circumvention, the Southerner who looks in love and hope at his region senses somehow that the great loyalties and deep friendships which the two races have known will bring his region through. There is evil, but there also is much good. And he does not feel Pollyannish in believing that there is more good than evil in the people of the South, colored and white, just as there is more good than evil in all peoples everywhere.[144]

He will continue in this hope, even though the sound of guerrilla fighting in the tumbled-down walls of the way of life and politics that was, all but drowns out his words.

---

[144]See Rosemary Daniell, *Fatal Flowers: On Sin, Sex, and Suicide in the Deep South* (New York: Holt, Rinehart, and Winston, 1980).

31

A Southerner
Talks with the South:
Review
of Robert Penn Warren's
Segregation

entucky-born Robert Penn Warren has done an admirable and
moving piece of research-writing in *Segregation*. It fills an increasingly evident void in the great amount of material published about the subject.

One may predict with considerable confidence the reception which
this volume will receive. There will be those who express disappointment because it provides no "answers," or formula for quick "solution."
And this is true. It does not because of the historically supported fact—
secular and sacred—that great moral issues carry their own built-in solutions. These may be delayed, sometimes indefinitely, by resistance
born of fear, misunderstanding, custom, tradition, greed, meanness,
honest conviction, and organized force. The moral issue of slavery had
been a divisive and deeply emotional force for years before the first gun
was fired at Fort Sumter.

Review of Robert Penn Warren, *Segregation: The Inner Conflict in the South* (New
York: Random House, 1956). Reprinted from the *New York Times*, 6 September 1956,
with permission of Mrs. Ralph McGill and The New York Times Company. Copyright, 1956, by The New York Times Company. An earlier draft of this review is in
the McGill papers, now at Emory University, Atlanta.

There can be no mathematical formula for solving moral problems. The solution comes about soon or late, depending on how many persons there are who work to soften the often harsh and brutal emotions, as well as the more difficult ones arising out of honest conviction, which arise out of social change and resistance to it. Problems are never "solved," but may be slowly ameliorated until they cease to be "problems." A moral issue, more especially a great one, therefore cannot be run through a univac machine for a formula, or answer. Nor can it be defeated, a fact implicit between the lines of Mr. Warren's book.

To the sensitive Southerners who read the book it will sound almost like a cry of anguish, as indeed it is. Mr. Warren has not sought to deal technically with the impact of the Court's decision. He employs instead, the familiar technique of putting down the conversations he had. They are not interviews—but the troubled, angry, hopeful, anxious talk of divided men and women. He had conversations with leaders of the Citizens' Councils, with Negro sharecroppers, and white farmers and operators of large plantations; with taxi drivers, NAACP organizers and workers, with the men who run the new industries of "The New South."

Being a Southerner, born and bred, and being himself tortured and troubled, he was able to draw out inarticulate people and to learn that most of them, too, like the rest of us, are engaged in soul-searching. Out of these conversations, for example, come some of the paradoxes which sometimes are so impossible of rationalization. A white clerk will sit at the feet of a Negro customer and fit shoes on colored feet, but the same clerk would define sitting beside the same customer on a bus as social equality. Taxis in one suburb will accept Negro passengers, while across town others won't. White and colored fishermen will sit along the bank of a commercial-operated lake in complete amity, but Negroes may not fish in the public lakes of the state parks.

Perhaps the most tortured of all is the sincere Christian. He knows that he must decide whether he is to operate his church as a private club or as a place where any who seek God may come to worship. It would be interesting to know how many Christians there are who would accept the Court's decision as to schools if it were not for the mores of the community and the fear they and their families might not then be accepted as before. There are a great many who otherwise would be willing. In Missouri and Oklahoma, which have much in them that is "Southern," there was no political agitation, and the "deliberate speed" of carrying out the Court's decree has proceeded without trouble or incident.

The demagogic have created a number of myths.[145] One is that the Court has decreed a general "mixing" in schools and out, and that it destroys one's ability to choose one's own friends and associates. Another myth is that the Court's decision was illegal. One would like to know what will happen when the politicians get through, and what would have happened had they not created a Frankenstein they must continually feed with the raw meat of agitation to prevent it from devouring them politically. Goodwill and common sense have not had too much opportunity to function. Mr. Warren manages to make clear how the myths work as well as the other factors involved.

With his job done, he reflected on what he had heard, feeling both the pull of it and that of his own past:

> Out of Memphis I lean back in my seat on the plane and watch the darkness slide by. I know what the Southerner feels going out of the South, the relief, the expanding vistas. I think of the new libel laws, of the academic pressures, of the Negro facing the shotgun blast, of the white men with a hard-built business being boycotted, of the college boy who said, "I'll just tell you, everybody is scairt."
>
> I feel the surge of relief. But I know what the relief really is. It is the relief from responsibility. Yes, you know what the relief is. It is the flight from the reality you were born to.
>
> But what is that reality . . . ? It is the fact of self-division. I do not mean division between man and man in society. That division is of course there. . . . But it is not as important in the long run as the division within the individual man.

This conclusion of his that the significant division is not that between man and man in society—but that within the individual man— is a true one. Mr. Warren's book fills a widening gulf because it reveals this, but also because it makes clear that the problem, and the resistance to social change, may not be oversimplified as race prejudice or "meanness." Prejudice there is and meanness, but there are other factors as strong. All this comes most eloquently from his pages.

He concludes with a final conversation—one with himself.

> "Q. Are you a gradualist on the matter of segregation?"

---

[145]For McGill's discussion of false Southern myths see the editor's introduction.

"A. If by gradualist you mean a person who would create delay for the sake of delay, then no. If by gradualist you mean a person who thinks it will take time . . . for an educational process, then yes. I mean a process of mutual education for whites and blacks. And part of this education should be the actual beginning of the process of desegregation. It's a silly question, anyway. History, like nature, knows no jumps. Except the jump backward, maybe."

"Q. Has the South any contribution to make to the national life?"

"A. It has made its share. It may again."

"Q. How?"

"A. If the South is really able to face up to itself and its situation, it may achieve identity, moral identity. Then in a country where moral identity is hard to come by, the South, because it has had to deal concretely with a moral problem, may offer some leadership. And we need any we can get. If we are to speak out of the national rhythm, the rhythm between complacency and panic."

The last paragraph is, I believe, prophetic of the South which, one of these days, will rise out of the ashes of the divisive forces which burn within our hearts and souls.

32

Dwight Eisenhower and the South

Preside nt Dwight Eisenhower's popularity, in general, continues at a high level with people in the Southeast. There have been defections. Many of the textile tycoons who supported him in 1952 were less enthusiastic in 1956 and by now are even more disenchanted.

The Southeast, while it has had increased industrialization and urban concentration, still reflects agricultural political opinion. By and large, the Southeast row-crop farmer believes the soil bank has been rigged against him. Taking land out of production also seriously has affected the economy in many small agricultural towns. Business is suffering because, with land deposited in the soil bank, there is a substantial reduction in the sale of fertilizers, seeds, and equipment. However, as far as one can determine, Secretary [Ezra] Benson seems to be bearing the brunt of this rather than the president.

The president's real strength lies in the fact that we are not in a shooting war. This was what elected him in 1952 and 1956. The people

Manuscript provided by Mrs. Ralph McGill from the McGill papers, now at Emory University, Atlanta. Reprinted by permission of the author, Mrs. Ralph McGill, and Newspaper Enterprise Association, Inc. Boyd Lewis wrote in a letter to the editor, 18 September 1969, that he could not recall the symposium to which McGill contributed this "appreciation of Dwight D. Eisenhower." The essay was written after 1956.

somehow disassociate him from failure of his administrators and so, in my opinion, they think his stewardship is good because he has kept us out of a hot war.[146]

With agriculture prices down, it is a truism that all agricultural areas are opposed to foreign aid. This is temporary, and if prices improve, opposition to foreign aid will decrease. As of now, there is considerable opposition and all congressmen and senators from the Southeast are being encouraged to cut the budget. This is, in my opinion, an irresponsible move and, without question, is sponsored in many localities by business organizations which, while they call for budget cuts, are at the same time lobbying for increased appropriations in their own special-interest pork-barrel projects. However, majority sentiment has been aroused in favor of a budget cut, although the president's second speech was effective in reducing this opposition.

There is only mild interest in the disarmament conference in London. [Harold] Stassen's popularity is at a low ebb, and there is a general inclination not to take too seriously anything which he heads up. There is a hard core of dedicated Eisenhower men in the Southeast, but the Southern business and commercial interests which flocked to Eisenhower in 1952 and 1956 still are more in the old Taft image and will remain so. The president's modern Republican policy is being sabotaged by the old line Dixie Republicans.

In Georgia, the Georgia Educational Association endorsed federal aid, although the top figures in state government, including the governor, opposed it. This is generally the picture in the Southeast. School people know they must have federal aid, but because they fear federal strings to federal aid might tend to break down segregation, the Deep South state administrations officially oppose federal aid, while privately they say they wish they could have it.

The Civil Rights bill generally has been presented to the people in a prejudiced, distorted manner, and there is very little understanding at

---

[146]See James C. Duram, *A Moderate Among Extremists: Dwight D. Eisenhower and the School Desegregation Crisis* (Chicago: Nelson-Hall, 1981); William Bragg Ewald, *Eisenhower the President: Crucial Days, 1951-1960* (Englewood Cliffs NJ: Prentice-Hall, 1981).

all, but without question, there is a great hue and cry against it, and almost no Southeastern representatives will support it. [147]

There is general apathy toward health insurance and not much interest in the issue of higher postal rates.

There seems to be no real objection to Ike's playing as much golf as he wishes, although there are those who object to his playing because they think it injurious to his health. [148]

---

[147]In supporting the Civil Rights Act of 1957, Eisenhower concluded that "suffrage, rather than school integration, was the legitimate subject for federal lawmaking"; Steven F. Lawson, *Black Ballots: Voting Rights in the South, 1944-1969* (New York: Columbia University Press, 1976) 165.

[148]See McGill's "Dwight D. Eisenhower," in volume 1.

33

Southern Politics: Won't Gamble Cushy Jobs

S outhern politics today is in a state inevitably attained when anger replaces reason: they are chaotic. There almost certainly will be some form of rebellion in 1960. But whether it will take the form of a third party or be merely a repeat of the old Dixiecrat movement none now can say.[149]

The principals themselves are in too turbulent a state to say. But they are all shaking their fists and threatening to do something. Exactly what it is they have not yet gotten around to deciding.

The Southern Democrat in the House or Senate has never liked the idea of a third party or split for obvious reasons—reasons, all very pragmatic.

The Dixie congressman or senator usually is accused of long continuity in office because of the one-party system. This builds up seniority for him. Southerners usually dominate important committee chairmanships when their party is in power. They are, by reason of seniority, influential, even when the GOP is in control of Congress. So, they have

---

Reprinted from the *Boston Globe*, 13 October 1957, by permission of Mrs. Ralph McGill and the *Boston Globe*. An earlier draft of this article is in the McGill papers, now at Emory University, Atlanta.

[149]See Emile Bertrand Ader, *The Dixiecrat Movement: Its Role in Third Party Politics* (Washington DC: Public Affairs Press, 1955).

always discouraged any third-party movement which would deprive them of prestige chairmanships and power.

It has been they who have seen to it that previous Southern revolts always were careful to retain the Democratic label, even though opposing the national nominees. The National Democratic Committee, seeking unity, never disciplined such bolters. They were allowed to retain all seniority rights even after the abortive 1948 Dixiecrat rebellion.

In the stormy condition of today there are, however, certain positive facts. One is that there is no Southern unity in either the segregation issue or the attempt to create third-party sentiment. The states of North Carolina, Tennessee, and Kentucky have begun a long plan of desegregation. Their governors have permitted and supported local school-board autonomy and decision. Even Governor Faubus had done this before he was bitten by the ambition to become first third-term governor of Arkansas since Reconstruction days and, from that vantage point, perhaps to take out after the scholarly Sen. Bill Fulbright.[150]

The upper tier of Southern states will not, therefore, join the Deep South in any third-party plans based on defiance of the Court. Deep South politicians already see this, and the private denunciations delivered against these governors by some of the politicians in Georgia, Alabama, Mississippi, South Carolina, and Louisiana have been known to curl and singe the hair of reporters.

Virginia, also adamant against segregation, presently is saying nothing because it has a gubernatorial race on. The Byrd machine is confident it will defeat the GOP challenge but wants really to pile up a huge majority. Virginia prefers to remain aloof and to make her decisions at the latest possible hour.

There is a paradox in the Southern political picture.[151]

Without question, the Southern Democrats are at their lowest ebb of influence in the Congress in our time. Yet it is quite likely there will be a Southern Democratic congressional gain in 1958. It will come from

---

[150]See Numan V. Bartley, *The Rise of Massive Resistance: Race and Politics in the South During the 1950's* (Baton Rouge: Louisiana State University Press, 1969).

[151]See Jack Bass and Walter DeVries, *The Transformation of Southern Politics: Social Change and Political Consequence Since 1945* (New York: New American Library, 1976).

the border states where, in 1952 and 1956, a few GOP congressmen were elected.

Some of these, perhaps most, would be defeated if the election were today.

The caloric emotions growing out of the Little Rock issue, distorted by a very considerable amount of irresponsible inflammatory journalism and equally heated denunciations by completely defiant political leaders, likely will maintain enough of this present climate to defeat border-state Republicans in 1958. But in so far as 1960 is concerned, the Republican party, as of today, has undoubtedly gained strength. The Northern and Western Democrats will have to carry the weight of Little Rock, and other violence which may occur, and this is no feather-like handicap.

All of it presently seems to be grist in the mill of Vice-President Richard M. Nixon, whom a sort of destiny seems to be assisting.[152]

---

[152]See McGill's articles on Adlai Stevenson and Dwight Eisenhower, in volume 1.

34

Review
of Winston S. Churchill's
The Age of Revolution

Winston Churchill was not a good student, a fact which may encourage parents of youngsters who are not on the dean's list. But he has told us in one of his memoirs that at Harrow he had a teacher of English who spent much time taking sentences apart and putting them back together again. This instructor used colored chalk, a different one for each part of the sentence. "I learned sentence structure," commented Churchill.

This sentence structure, plus his astonishing knowledge of history, added to his great feeling for things historical, draws one to any of his books, and keeps one there until the hour is late. His voice seems to come out of the pages. At hand now is *The Age of Revolution*, volume 3 of *A History of the English Speaking Peoples*. Many Americans wisely are adding these books to their library, both for their own pleasure and information, and as a sort of legacy to their children.

This book, which begins in 1688 with the flight of James II to France, and the crowning of Mary, married to William of Orange, clo-

Winston S. Churchill, *The Age of Revolution*, vol. 3 in *A History of the English-Speaking Peoples* (New York: Dodd, Mead, & Co., 1957). Manuscript provided by Mrs. Ralph McGill from the McGill papers, now at Emory University, Atlanta. Written for the *Atlanta Constitution* and *Journal*. Published by permission of Atlanta Newspapers, Inc.

ses with the Congress of Vienna, which had to do with settling up things after Napoleon's defeat.

Included between those years are, of course, the American Revolution and its second chapter, the War of 1812. It would be a good thing, we think, if American teachers of high school history would take this volume and read the American section to their students, or perhaps, assign it as required reading and examine them on it.

Most of us, out of our own histories, tend to think of our colonies as having taken on the might of Britain and humbled her. It gives us a distorted opinion of ourselves as well as of history. Americans, perhaps, from a century and a half of isolation, have less of a sense of history than most peoples. Historian Churchill paints the big picture. At the time of our revolution Britain was engaged in a world war and was without allies. She was taking on Spain, France, and Holland and then had to try to deal with the thirteen colonies.

He lets us see the divided opinion of that time in Britain and reminds us again that but for a foolish king and extremist ministers, the war might not have come. He traces the social and military background of the campaigns, many of which were, of course, in the Southern colonies.

He reveals an expected understanding and appreciation of the forces which shaped the Republic. He reminds us, too, that after the war of 1812, the British navies ruled the oceans and left the United States free from expense and threat of attack to work out their "continental destiny."

It is a magnificent history. We find ourselves in London; Calcutta; Charleston, South Carolina; Moscow; Trafalgar; Waterloo; Savannah, Georgia; and New Orleans . . . to mention just a few cities of the world.

We learn from his pages the evaluation of the demand for liberty and freedom. And he employs a quote from Edmund Burke, who was one of those who sought to prevent the colonial war, which has meaning in our own time: "The effect of liberty to individuals is that they may do as they please; we ought to see what it will please them to do before we risk congratulations."

The great heroes of the time—Clive, Wellington, Nelson, Hastings and others—come to life for us. We think better of Cornwallis, the general, after reading of his Southern campaign. We learn more as we see history, much of it our own, from the British viewpoint of events as interpreted by the Sir Winston's eyes and mind.[153]

---

[153]See McGill's review of Churchill, *The Great Democracies*, vol. 4, in this volume.

35

Review
of James McBride Dabbs's
Southern Heritage

A quietly contemplative South Carolina planter and business-man, James McBride Dabbs has examined his heritage and produced an excellent book about it. Mr. Dabbs is, among other things, an elder in the Presbyterian Church and president of the Southern Regional Council, a Southwide organization working inter-racially. Both affiliations have helped him in his examination.

As an active layman in his church he has seen at first hand the shock which has come to a great many Christians on realizing that the church, too, was segregated and operated, often, as almost a private club. He witnessed, too, the disturbing fact that some members of the Christian faith were willing to give up their church rather than segregation.

The Southern Regional Council, which is a highly respected and efficient organization, on no attorney general's list, and free from any taint of being any sort of "front," also gave Mr. Dabbs opportunity to see into the sociological and economic aspects of the problem. The council has been attacked strongly by the Klan groups and the White Citizens' Councils as being an instrument of desegregation. The men who signed

James McBridge Dabbs, *Southern Heritage* (New York: A. A. Knopf, 1958). Reprinted by permission of Mrs. Ralph McGill and the *New York Times*, 31 August 1958. Copyright 1958, by The New York Times Company.

its charter of incorporation, including a Methodist bishop and university teachers, have been harried and subject to abuse.

Through an excellent analysis Mr. Dabbs shows how an enormous
weight of cumulative guilt produced by the years of injustice done the
Negro by exploitations and discriminations, has fixed itself upon white
Southerners. Like many Southerners, perhaps most Southerners, he
bore the guilt lightly for many years. Some, of course, never face the
fact of this guilt, but it is there. It is inherent in some of the excesses of
sadistic crimes of beatings and worse.

Mr. Dabbs deals very skillfully with many of the inexplicable and
unreasonable paradoxes in Southern life. Other writers have noted the
insistence of extremists on "white supremacy" and the companion fear
that if there are not strict laws of separation there might be general intermarriage. Mr. Dabbs traces this curious conflict further. In his
small-town discussions he had listened to those who declare that God
himself, in his infinite wisdom, established segregation and that every
true Southerner knows "instinctively" that the races are meant to be separate. He has not endeared himself to them by asking why then, if this
be known, there must be strict Jim Crow laws. There is, of course, no
basis for declaring the Negro inferior as a human being. Mr. Dabbs's
satire will be devastating to those who think otherwise.

Other Southern writers have come to the same conclusion reached
by Mr. Dabbs, namely that in this great issue the South has made the
fatal error of committing itself on the wrong side of a moral issue and
to another "Lost Cause." He deduces that the slow, sometimes glacier-
like processes of law, plus industrialization, the democratic spirit, and
the Christian tradition are at work for elimination of racial discriminations and will enable the Negro to attain what he wants—to be more
American, not less.

Unhappily, almost all those who read this fine book will be persons
basically in agreement with Mr. Dabbs. Those who do not agree will,
with few exceptions, not read it at all. They will read a news story about
it, or a review of it, or they may simply hear that another Southerner has
fouled his nest by writing a book "to please the Yankees."

Nonetheless, the book will be helpful. It is a sincere eloquent testimony by a man of deep Christian and social convictions.[154] And he writes from a Deep South state out of a rich experience. It would be good if it could be distributed, as are the Gideon Bibles, in the localities that most need to read it.[155]

---

[154]See McGill's "Let's Lead Where We Lag," "The Agony of the Southern Minister," "Church in a Social Revolution," "Interview on Race and Church," and "Introduction to Robert McNeill's *God Wills Us Free*," in volumes 1 and 2.

[155]See McGill's speech for "Ministers Week," in *Ralph McGill: Editor and Publisher*, ed. Calvin McLeod Logue (Durham: Moore Publishing Company, 1969) 1: 163-79.

36

The Southern Moderates
Are Still There
1958

Afont fter four years of being storm tossed on the seas of segregation, with unusual turbulence and fog prevailing for the past twelve months, the Southern moderate now will be able to function more effectively by reason of the United States Supreme Court decision of Friday, 12 September, in the Little Rock case.[156]

The Court upheld the United States Circuit Court of Appeals in its reversal of Federal Judge Harry J. Lemley's order of June staying integration at Central High School in the Arkansas capital for two and one-half years. The Supreme Court decision had the immediate effect of restoring to the issue the sense of inevitability, which, with that of law, is the ingredient essential to rational thought on the subject.

For almost three years now, but more especially since Governor [Orval] Faubus began to dominate the Southern segregation scene,

---

Reprinted by permission of Mrs. Ralph McGill and The New York Times Company from the *New York Times Magazine*, 21 September 1958. Copyright 1958, by The New York Times Company.

[156]For more by McGill on Southern moderates see reviews in volumes 1 and 2 of Brooks Hays, *A Southern Moderate Speaks* (Chapel Hill: University of North Carolina Press, 1959); Hodding Carter, *Southern Legacy* (Baton Rouge: Louisiana State University Press, 1950); Frank E. Smith, *A Congressman From Mississippi: An Autobiography* (New York: Pantheon Books, 1964); Charles Morgan, Jr., *A Time To Speak* (New York: Harper and Row, 1964); see also, "The Case for the Southern Progressive," in volume 2, and the editor's introduction.

there has been a heavy attack on the legal image of inevitability. For a time it was blurred and befogged. It was precisely in this period that the Southern moderate seemed to some, at least, to have been submerged, or overwhelmed. And, in a sense, he was. But, being man, he endured.

The decision of 12 September provided a further dividend for the moderate. In addition to keeping alive the image of law and the supremacy of the high court in interpreting the Constitution of the United States, the Southern moderate had been hard at work creating a new image. It is one of the Negro as a citizen. It is a fact perhaps not well comprehended outside the South that many Southerners to this day have never considered the Negro as a citizen in the full meaning of the word. There is no image of such citizenship, for the good reason that it did not exist. It is only in very recent years that the white-primary laws and other barriers to citizenship have been declared unconstitutional.

The latest decision will greatly strengthen the picture of the Negro as a citizen, as well as renew the necessary sense of inevitability in the 1954 Supreme Court decision and its appeal to the moral and reasonable man. Because of this, the Southern moderate's real job has been to keep this sense alive in the mind of the practical man of his region.

It is the practical man who is so necessary to an emotionally stirred, disturbed and confused South. The Southern moderate is not the quiet, assured, often scholarly, detached liberal of the East. In the Deep South, ugly with reprisals, penalties, and abuses, where all the political controls are in the hands of men pledged to massive resistance, the moderate, like the liberal, learns that there is an immediacy of reaction, often violent, to anything he may say or write. From this he learns patience and acceptance of the fact that frustration is not defeat, though it can be almost as bitter.[157]

It will be the moderate and the practical man who will see the South through this period which is to many one of agonizing readjustment far

---

[157]See Thomas Dionysius Clark, *Three Paths to the Modern South: Education, Agriculture, and Conservation* (Athens: University of Georgia Press, 1965); Hugh C. Bailey, *Liberalism in the New South: Southern Social Reformers and the Progressive Movement* (Coral Gables: University of Miami Press, 1969); Thomas Jackson Woofter, *Southern Race Progress: The Wavering Color Line* (Washington DC: Public Affairs Press, 1957).

more acute than can be imagined by those whose liberal position is based entirely on principle without any corollary experience.

This practical man may be a leader on the vestry, a bishop, a clergyman, an executive of a great corporation, an editor, an attorney, or a person in some public position. With the sense of inevitability, this practical man can, and does, influence others in economic and professional positions to attain that image and to comprehend it and the ultimate meaning to his community.

It is this same image of inevitability that causes many a sincere Christian or Jew to say, "I don't like it, but I must either abandon my faith and its tenets or accept it, and so, with God's help, I will." And there are those who say, "I don't think the Court was right. I hate the decision. I wish it had never happened, but I love my country and I will accept decisions of its courts."[158]

Governor Faubus especially, and numerous other Southern political leaders—governors, United States senators and White Citizens' Council orators—had succeeded in greatly weakening this sense of the inevitable. They asserted over and over that the Supreme Court's decision was not legal or binding and was entirely unconstitutional.[159]

It was a commonplace experience of newspapermen to talk with a Southern political leader and hear him say, privately, he knew integration to be inevitable, and then, minutes later, hear the same man say to a whooping audience that the "left-wing Supreme Court" had acted unconstitutionally and that states' rights would emerge triumphant.

The Citizens' Councils urged their members to write their congressmen and senators. "Just stand up and make yourself heard," they

---

[158]For more on race and religion see McGill's "Let's Lead Where We Lag," "The Church in a Social Revolution," and "An Interview on Race and the Church," in volume 2. See also Charles Reagan Wilson, *Baptized in Blood: The Religion of the Lost Cause, 1865-1920* (Athens: University of Georgia Press, 1980); and Samuel S. Hill, *Religion and the Solid South* (Nashville: Abingdon Press, 1972).

[159]See Numan V. Bartley, *Rise of Massive Resistance: Race and Politics in the South During the 1950's* (Baton Rouge: Louisiana State University Press, 1969); John Bartlow Martin, *The Deep South Says "Never"* (New York: Ballantine Books, 1957); and Francis M. Wilhoit, *The Politics of Massive Resistance* (New York: George Braziller, 1973).

said, "and we'll win. We'll never surrender to those who would usurp our rights."

In addition, there were the fire-eaters who breathed defiance and slandered the Court, the president of the United States, and all who were not in agreement with them. Their text was "Never."

The effect of this, and the fact of it, were established before the Supreme Court by Richard C. Butler, the able attorney for the Little Rock School Board. The people of Little Rock, he told the Court, were confused about what was the law and did not accept the Court's decision as final, particularly since Governor Faubus "was repeatedly" telling them it was "not the law of the land."

It was not a good argument in a court of law, but it was a factual description of a state of mind widespread in the Deep South. There are even now literally thousands of good Southern people who believe the Court's action to be illegal and not applicable to them, because a governor, a senator, a congressman, an editor, or some other person of position has so said or written.

The Southern moderate, utterly destroyed insofar as any political influence in his state capital was concerned, was pushed out of the center of the picture by early 1955. He was chided and harassed. In some communities he was asked to resign from the vestry or board of deacons. Some teachers—a great many college teachers and some ministers—lost their jobs. There were businesses that warned employees not to "participate" in controversy. For a time various forms of coercions and reprisals flourished, mild and severe.

The Court decision shocked a great majority of the Southern people because their political leadership had failed utterly to prepare them for it. For some years the high court had been handing down decisions which clearly indicated that full citizenship was the right of all Americans.

Political leaders began a belated, almost frantic, drive to build schools and thereby comply with the long-neglected separate-but-equal Court ruling of 1896. There were those few who spoke out, saying that segregation was on the way out and plans should be made to live with such a decision. But, as people do, they looked to their leaders. And a great majority of these told them not to worry, the Court would not and could not so find.

When it did come there was a great shock. The political leaders soon regrouped and came charging back, crying betrayal. A number of urban school boards that tentatively, and sensibly, had begun to make plans to comply by gerrymandering school district lines and putting the fewest possible number of Negro children in school as a starter, abruptly were put in their place as legislatures hurried to write new laws and earn delay.

It was Virginia, with her pre-Civil War theory of interposition, that gave certain respectability and stature to these proceedings by throwing the great cloak of her history and tradition about total defiance.

In this period the national administration failed the cause of moderation. The Court had handed to the South, and some bordering states, a decision. But the executive department of justice failed utterly to provide any leadership or to offer any plans for, or assistance in, enforcement.

It is true that all governors and state officers, including judges, are sworn to support [the] Constitution of the United States. But in this period some imaginative national leadership and interposition between the moderate and the extremist might have made a different story. But it did not come.

However, the moderate was not as alone as he sometimes felt, or seemed to be. There were two elections, in particular, that refuted the belief that the Southern moderate had been driven from the scene.

In November 1957, Virginia went to the polls to elect a governor. Nominee of the Democrats was J. Lindsay Almond, pledged to support a state program of "massive resistance" to the Court decision. He had, of course, the full support of the Byrd organization. Senator Harry F. Byrd himself led the Almond campaign. In public speeches he called on the voters to crush the opposition and let the nation and the Court know how Virginia felt.

The opposition was Theodore R. Dalton, Republican. He had proposed a plan of limited integration. Thus, the sole, major issue was clearly drawn.

Almond won with, in round numbers, 300,000 votes to 188,000 for Dalton. Despite the heavy pressure by the Byrd organization, the emotionalism of the issue, and the fact that President Eisenhower's popularity was down, the Republican candidate and limited integration received almost 200,000 votes. An estimated 40,000 to 50,000 Negro votes were in this total. But of the white votes cast in a heated campaign pressed emotionally by one of the most efficient political organizations in the country, Dalton had a third.

More recent voting, that of the primary in which Governor Faubus won renomination, was one-sided. His two opponents were not well known. Neither had any following. Their efforts were not adequately financed. The governor's organizations went all out to round up the votes.

Governor Faubus received 264,346 votes. Yet, almost 120,000 moderates cast ballots in opposition. Of this vote perhaps seventeen percent was Negro. But in a superheated, almost hysterical campaign, about a third of the white voters stood for moderation and due process of law.

Other elections, too, were revealing of moderate strength. In Tennessee a richly financed primary campaign based on defiance of the Supreme Court failed as a move to unseat Senator Albert Gore, who was charged with being in favor of abiding by his oath to support the Constitution and the courts. A gubernatorial candidate who favored allowing communities to desegregate if they chose was given no chance to win. He came within a few votes of upsetting the favorite. The moderates in the state were the balance of power in the Gore race and they almost nominated a relative unknown for governor.

In Texas, liberal Senator Ralph W. Yarborough was renominated in a primary otherwise dominated by extreme conservatives.

There is no political campaign, even in the Deep South, where race is the only factor. The extremists seek always to make this the only issue.

In Georgia's primary of 10 September the three candidates were all profoundly pledged to defend segregation. The most qualified, Ernest Vandiver, campaigned on a program of reforming the state government to eliminate corrupt practices that had been exposed. A Baptist minister, who was one of the candidates, promptly and preposterously charged Mr. Vandiver with being "weak on segregation" and carried on a campaign of political abuse that shocked all but the most extreme. The Baptist minister was all but obliterated by the heavy vote for Vandiver.

There is one generality that largely explains the many paradoxes of the South. It is that the climate, or mood, in which the moderate lives and seeks to function reflects the leadership of his state and the background that produces it.

Why, for example, could North Carolina, Tennessee, Kentucky and Texas, all former members of the Confederacy, proceed with deliberate speed in school integration this fall while their neighbors in Virginia, Mississippi, South Carolina, Georgia, and Alabama were pledged to total, permanent defiance? They are all the same sort of people. Superficially their culture is the same. Why, then, the difference?

There is a very real explanation. Four states, Mississippi, South Carolina, Alabama, and Georgia, the heart of the Deep South, have had a continuity of political climate in which the race issue has been agitated in local and state campaigns. Some who have been most prominent in this form of campaigning have attained national reputations in that field. These same states have, on a percentage basis, the largest Negro populations. They also have remaining more of the old-plantation type of economy. Industrialization came last to them.

It is neither fair, nor is it helpful in the attempt at solution, to charge the people of these states with being willfully rebellious, mean, or perverse. Their political leaders are as pragmatic as those of other areas. They must first get elected. In a sense, they are captives of their past and of the leaders who before them set the pattern of violent racial agitation for political ends.

The Deep South has sent to Congress some of its ablest men. It has such men there today. Some of them have been, and are, fully qualified for the presidency. One of the most melancholy spectacles is to see such able, intelligent men barred from greater national recognition or from the presidency itself, not because they are Southern but because their region or state advocates a policy that jars with that of the forty-two other states. The frustration of such a situation leads some of them to bitterness of spirit and extremes of language and position that serve merely to add to their frustration.

In these states the political leader, or the moderate, practical, reasonable man who takes a stand and says, "Look, the only persons about to be hurt are our children; why can't we do what North Carolina or Tennessee has done—make a slow, token beginning?" is certain to be overwhelmed with abuse and charges of being a "nigger lover," a dangerous Leftist, or worse. If he is in one of the more rural areas of the Deep South he may well be in physical danger. The most preposterous charges are brought against him.

In the urban areas there are abusive telephone calls, threats, and slanderous mail, but there is less pressure for absolute conformity such as some rural areas demand. The moderate man, the reasonable, practical man, the Christian or Jew who stands on his religious tenets, the moral man of no religious affiliation, all these can, and do, take a stand.

In the elections referred to previously, the substantial opposition to extremes came from the cities. But, in general, in such a climate of complete political control, the powerlessness of reasonable men is difficult for those looking on from a distance and from an entirely different climate to believe or comprehend.

In contrast to the Deep South, North Carolina and Tennessee, for example, have no past history of reckless political exploitation of race. The leadership there led by the respective governors, Luther H. Hodges and Frank G. Clement, weighed the elements involved most carefully and with all deliberate speed. Once they had surveyed and discussed they assisted the school boards that wanted to go ahead and make a start at compliance. They assured them protection. They went on television and explained the plan to the people.

In North Carolina last year there was no trouble. In Tennessee there was. Prompt and effective police action ended it. This fall there were no incidents in a planned expansion of the program.

Neither this fact, nor the progress made in border states with a Southern flavor such as Kentucky, Oklahoma, and Missouri, has made any impression whatever in the Deep South save to produce harsh criticism of these states.

In candor, it must be said that in the Deep South the future will worsen. The region will continue to be an island of complete defiance while about it the deliberate speed of slow compliance continues. Arkansas, where five small cities have integrated schools, and Virginia, whose traditions and history make her a strange and unexpected companion of the old cotton states, are separate, if related, stories.

The melancholy fact is that in the Deep South the future will see more and more schools closed. One's heart goes out to the people who have not been told by their political leaders the terrible price they and their children must pay in this deliberate sacrifice of their school system. Nor have their leaders told them the truth about the private-school system that many propose.

Such a plan inevitably will be subject to injunctions and tests of its legality. If a state collects a school tax or provides money for tuition it can be said to be in the business of public education. The fact that such private schools would lack proper accreditation and that their high school graduates would find it very difficult to enter college was another truth not told. But candor also requires one to say that many, if told the truth, would not change their minds.

Certainly, the moderates in this area, used to daily wrestling with reality, know that the outlook is gloomy and will become more so. But they also know that reaction is certain.

Within days after the Supreme Court's recent ruling there were a few who were beginning to say that, much as they hated the idea, they would rather allow "a few" Negroes in the schools than to have no school at all. The moderate is aware that none can set a time limit on how long the chaos of closed schools and attempted, hopelessly inadequate private schools will last. It could be a long span of tragic years.

There is one thing for sure. When the reaction begins, and the bitterness of it wells up into politics, the moderate will be needed more than ever to help put the pieces together again.

In those states where the climate of leadership is more sure of itself and, therefore, more stable, the mood of the people is such that the practical man, the moral man, and the force of moderation will make continued progress. They will grow and prosper in comparison with their neighbors.

Not many new industries will come to a state where public education is in chaos. The young people of these states will go elsewhere seeking opportunity and schooling. That, too, is part of the price to be paid.

Meanwhile, more and more the clergy in all the South is making itself heard, if not heeded, in behalf of reasonableness and against destruction of the public school system. The Southern Regional Council continues a job of factual research and study. The Southern School News Reporting Service, a strictly objective monthly report of conditions state by state, is a continuing thorn in the flesh of extremist distortions of facts.

There are individuals, organizations, and newspapers that patiently, but firmly, point out that the question of whether one is for or against segregation is not relevant. The issue is the children, the country, and the integrity of the American dream—that here is a country which offers equal and full citizenship to all who live in it. The Southerner has as much of a stake in that as anyone else.

This, then, has been, and is, the role of the Southern moderate—to prevent the image of due process of law and that of the inevitability bound up in the Supreme Court's decision from being blurred. The waves have rolled over him. They will again. The clamor of the angry and defiant men now and then have drowned him out. It will again.

If he is no longer in the center of the picture in the Deep South he is still in it, if at the edge. Sometimes he gets cropped off by the picture editors.

And, in the end, of course, the moderates, the reasonable, practical men, the moral men, and those whose convictions are based on religion, will be there to pick up the wreckage left by those who defy the law and the courts and forget their oath to support the Constitution of the United States. The moderates will make it unnecessary to start from scratch.

37

Review
of Winston S. Churchill's
The Great Democracies

There are not quite four hundred pages in Sir Winston Churchill's fourth volume in his history of the English-speaking peoples, *The Great Democracies*. Southerners, in particular, should like it. Of the almost four hundred pages, the War Between the States is given one hundred.

It is to him, of course, the Civil War, which is as it should be. In time, as we mature, we will outgrow the strained technicalities of phrasing. Sir Winston says of that civil war that it was "the noblest and most formidable of all the great mass-conflicts of which till then there was no record." Like all who have read at all deeply of that war, Sir Winston is entranced with the battles and the leaders, military and political.

One of the most fascinating aspects of this whole great series of volumes is that they include so many of Sir Winston's candid personal opinions. He has many criticisms to make of the decisions of Generals Lee and Grant and of Presidents Lincoln and Jefferson Davis, as well as of lesser principals.

Winston S. Churchill, *The Great Democracies*, vol. 4 in *A History of the English-Speaking Peoples* (New York: Dodd, Mead, & Co., 1958). Manuscript provided by Mrs. Ralph McGill from the McGill papers, now at Emory University, Atlanta; written for the *Atlanta Journal* and *Constitution*, and published by permission of Atlanta Newspapers, Inc. Vol. 1 is *Birth of Britain*, vol. 2, *The New World*, and vol. 3, *Age of Revolution*.

But of General Lee he said that he was "one of the noblest of Americans who ever lived, and one of the greatest captains known to the annals of war." It follows naturally that he considers Lee's Army of Northern Virginia to have "made a struggle unsurpassed in history." General Grant seemed to be negative. Churchill speaks of Grant's battles against General Lee as "the negation of generalship."

Sir Winston revered Lincoln. But he thought the president of the Union interfered too much with generals. This will interest British readers and other military men. If there was ever a prime minister who rode herd on his generals it was Sir Winston.

As always, the Churchill prose is wonderful to read. It flows deeply, like a great organ sweep. But it flows. Here is a sample, selected from a chapter closest to the Southern heart, that of the Battle of Gettysburg.

> "General," said Pickett to Longstreet, who stood sombre and mute, "shall I advance?" By an intense effort Longstreet bowed his head in assent. Pickett saluted and set forty-two regiments against the Union centre. We see today, upon this battlefield so piously preserved by North and South, and where many of the guns still stand in their firing stations, the bare, slight slopes up which this grand infantry charge was made. In splendid array, all their battle flags flying, the forlorn assault marched on. But, like the Old Guard on the evening of Waterloo, they faced odds and metal beyond the virtue of mortals.

Of the many who have written of that charge none have done it better, perhaps none have done it so beautifully and eloquently as Sir Winston.

But, he can be brief and tell a whole story in a few words. As, for example, he tells of Meade's delay in following up General Lee and of this delay allowing the Confederate leader to cross the Potomac to safety.

> General Lee carried with him his wounded and his prisoners. He had lost only two guns and the war.

The Great Democracies covers less than a century, from 1815 to the end of the Boer War in 1902. Like the others before it, it is not a history in the usual sense of that word. It is Sir Winston's concept of it, and he gives emphasis here, as in the others, to politics and war. Those subjects interest him most. He has his own sense of history and he thinks, and not immodestly, that great men shape events.

One meets here, of course, much more than the Civil War. After all, it fills but one-fourth of the book. Here are the great figures of English history, and some of those in Europe with which they contended.

Disraeli, Queen Victoria, Gladstone, Palmerstone, Russell, Bismark, Napoleon—they all march majestically through the pages.

For those who like history and great prose this is, of course, a must to add to the other three. [160]

---

[160] See McGill's review of *The Age of Revolution*, in volume 1.

38

Review
of Brainard Cheney's
This is Adam

W hen I was a young reporter I roomed with another member of the staff. He was a Georgian from Fitzgerald and Lumber City, named Brainard Cheney. We burned to be writers, authors of books and of magazine articles.

And, of course, we talked out of our own lives and experiences. Cheney had, as did I, a rural background. His was one of the great lumber area and of plantation-type farming. One of the characters he remembered best was a Negro farm worker, one of those uneducated, but wise men, who had in him the basic essence of man and his best qualities of loyalty, faith, compassion, courage, and the stubborn will to endure.

I watched for this man in Cheney's first two novels, *Lightwood* and *River Rogue*. Both of these had a south Georgia locale and story. Both grew out of the great lumber operations which for years covered the Altamaha with rafts and brought riches, turbulence, folly, cruelty, and ruthlessness in their wake.[161]

Brainard Cheney, *This Is Adam* (New York: McDowell, Obolensky Publishers, 1958). Manuscript provided by Mrs. Ralph McGill from the McGill papers, now at Emory University, Atlanta. Written for *Atlanta Journal* and *Constitution*, and published by permission of Atlanta Newspapers, Inc.

[161]Brainard Cheney, *Lightwood* (Boston: Houghton Mifflin, 1939); *River Rogue* (Boston: Houghton Mifflin, 1942); *Devil's Elbow* (New York: Crown Publishers, 1969).

But now in the third novel, *This is Adam*, comes the character I ·
heard about so often more than thirty years ago. He is called Adam in
this very excellent novel. It is again a Georgia story. Adam had worked
a long time for Colonel Hightower. Then Colonel Hightower died. The
widow had to depend on Adam to be overseer. The time is the turn of
the century when rural areas were isolated. But they were, nonetheless,
pockets of life. They held all the qualities of life, treachery, hypocrisy,
faith, honesty, strength, weakness.

Certain conniving neighbors, putting a pious, all-for-the-best face
on it, set out to get control of the widow's land. She is not experienced.
She is easily deceived. There is only Adam who knows better. And
Adam, of course, is but a Negro field hand. His powers to oppose the
power pattern of his community are, of course, nonexistent. Nor is there
much time. The would-be-stealers of the widow's land must bring off
the deal quickly.

But there is Adam. He must survive if the land is to be held. He
has only his faith, his manhood, and the shrewdness of all those, animal
or man, who of necessity have had to develop what might be called a
technique of survival. Adam, in his old denims and work-scuffed shoes,
must stand before the men and somehow, careful not to offend the power
structure which could instantly destroy him, match wits with them.

It is great drama. Cheney has written a fine book. The characters
are exceptionally well drawn. They live and have being. The writing is
mature and demonstrates that the author is among our better craftsmen
in this field.

It seems to me that in the choice of the title, Cheney has made of
Adam the symbol of man as William Faulkner discussed him in his
magnificent speech accepting the Nobel Prize in literature. Adam is all
men.[162] But all that enables man to endure is his faith, his compassion,
his love. This is Adam. And Adam lives because he has the qualities to
endure.

This is by no means just another Southern book. Nor is it one about
"the problem." It is not a book about the race question, save that the sym-
bolism is an inescapable part of any such problem. Nor is it a book about

---

[162]"Speech at Stockholm on the Occasion of His Receiving the Nobel Prize," in
Faulkner at Nagano, ed. Robert A. Jelliffe (Tokyo: Kenkyusha Lts., 1956) 203-206.

"The South." The locale is south Georgia at the turn of the century, and Cheney knows it well by research and by virtue of having heard the members of his own family and community discuss it. It is a book about life and the part a man played in it. I assuredly recommend it to all who like a good novel with well-drawn characters and a plot which reaches a high peak of drama.

And it is good, too, after all these years to find a character well remembered out of cub-reporter days, at last fittingly pictured in a good book.

39

Speaking
for the South—and to It:
Review of Brooks Hays's
A Southern Moderate Speaks

B rooks Hays, whose lengthy career (1943-1958) as congressman
from the Little Rock district was ended in the last November
election by a write-in purge supported by Gov. Orval Faubus,
has written a brief book quite typical of the man. It is scrupulously honest, the expression of a man to whom his Christian conviction means a
great deal. It is a just book. It does not sit in judgment, and it sees good
in all things. It is the expression of a conciliator, not a fighter or
crusader.

Brooks Hays is a moderate. But, here we are trapped in semantics.
Compared with the more reactionary Deep South congressmen, he is.
But, compared with those moderate Southern senators and House members who refused to sign the Southern manifesto of the spring of 1956,
which document attacked the Supreme Court school decision of 1954 as
an "abuse of Federal power," he is not.

Those who know Mr. Hays will have for him deep respect and appreciation for his integrity, compassion, and his qualities as a man and

---

Brooks Hays, *A Southern Moderate Speaks* (Chapel Hill: University of North Carolina Press, 1959). Review reprinted from the *New York Times*, 15 March 1959, with
permission of Mrs. Ralph McGill and the *New York Times*. Copyright 1959, by The
New York Times Company. An earlier draft of this review is in the McGill papers,
now at Emory University, Atlanta.

friend. The writer holds such an opinion. Because of his honesty, his book which as he says, records conclusions growing out of a lifetime of "observations and reflections," reveals what perhaps is the fatal flaw of the South's one-party politics. The flaw is that at no time before the abuses of civil and voting rights became so intolerable as to produce federal or, as it is called, "outside" action, did any of the Southern moderates in the Congress initiate any reform action of their own.[163]

Brooks Hays's experience could be multiplied many thousands of times. He was, and is, a sensitive man and a dedicated Christian. Even as a boy he saw, and was hurt by, the injustices of "Jim Crow." He records many such sorrows. But, such was the power pattern of the one-party system of his region that no moderation was attempted until federal suits were filed in the white primary and subsequently in the first of the several school cases.

Once these issues were joined, and the emotions loosed, Congressman Hays labored courageously, patiently, and intelligently. But by then it was too late. The battle had begun, and the troops committed. Some of his compromises would have been helpful and productive of progress. But, here again, he could get no help from his Southern colleagues, and this completely nullified his efforts. Those in Congress who had cast their political future on the side of civil rights knew that Congressman Hays was almost a lone voice, and that the compromises, if any, would all be on one side.

About a third of the book concerns itself with "The Little Rock Story."[164] It was Congressman Hays who arranged, with the eager cooperation of then Assistant to the President Sherman Adams, the conference between President Eisenhower and Governor Faubus, at Newport, Rhode Island, 14 September 1957.

Governor Faubus issued a statement after leaving this meeting which generally was interpreted as an agreement to comply with the

---

[163]For more by McGill on Southern moderates see review in this volume of Charles Morgan, Jr., *A Time to Speak*; Hodding Carter, *Southern Legacy*; Frank E. Smith, *A Congressman From Mississippi: An Autobiography*; and articles "The Southern Moderates Are Still There" and "The Case for the Southern Progressive," in volumes 1 and 2.

[164]Officials of Arkansas had been ordered by the Court to allow blacks to enroll in the "white" public schools of Little Rock.

Court decision which he himself described as "the law of the land." It was his later repudiation of his seeming agreement which produced the mob defiance of the Court and made necessary the ordering of troops to Little Rock. (Months later Governor Faubus was to say he had to agree before the president would see him. The reviewer could find no substantiation of this in Congressman Hays's book.)

Mr. Hays, who says he became very fond of the governor during their long vigils, thinks that then United States Attorney General Herbert Brownell erred in not giving Governor Faubus more time to seek "court delays," that is, to wait until the Supreme Court had ruled on the state statutes. The president's reply to this suggestion had been that the matter "fell so completely within the jurisdiction of the courts that little could be done by the Executive in that regard." Mr. Hays believes that, since the Court had issued an order, Attorney General Brownell was determined on a "judicial showdown."

Of most value in this feature of the book is the clearing up of why United States marshals were not sent. There originally was no thought of troops, other than possible federalization of the State Guard and their use to keep order and allow the Court order to be carried out.

School Superintendent Virgil Blossom did ask for marshals. The local district attorney at the behest of Congressman Hays (after a call to Sherman Adams) asked for the marshals. The Justice Department felt it could not send them. A short while before the Senate had deleted Title III from the civil rights bill. This title was the one which proposed to give the Justice Department authority to participate in suits for enforcement of Negroes' rights. The attorney general therefore concluded properly that the Congress had declared that he should exercise no authority in such cases. Mr. Hays believes him to have been only technically correct, though he thinks the moral commitment of the government should have overridden the technicality.

One indisputable fact is made perfectly clear. The president of the United States, once the situation had so deteriorated, had no choice but to sustain the Court or to surrender to anarchy.

There are two other clarifications. Congressman Hays believes that in the beginning there would likely have been no disorder had not Governor Faubus proclaimed publicly his conviction that there would be. He also believes that a speech in Little Rock by Gov. Marvin Griffin of Georgia a few days before the scheduled opening of the school, pledging that he would never permit Georgia schools to accept the Court order, caused Governor Faubus to "think twice" about what he should do. Until that time it generally was believed Governor Faubus would support the school board.

A Southern Moderate Speaks closes with a forthright plea to the South and the nation for faith in the success of our mission to defend democracy in our land and throughout the free world. To do this, Mr. Hays thinks, there must be a substantial contribution from the Christian community.

"The re-evaluation of our faith," he writes, "the re-defining of goals, and the new resolutions, which we as a free people must form to acquire the strength for resisting those who put their confidence in materialism and power are things which must occupy us in the next few years, else we will lose the world conflict and all the human rights we so deeply cherish."

40

As the South Begins to Put Its Burden Down, an Interim Report: Review of William Peters's *Southern Temper*

A t the end of the last page of William Peters's fine book on the problem of desegregation in the South one feels as if one has just read, in excellent reportorial style, an exhaustive diagnostic report on a patient, including the psychiatric findings. There is, of course, a prognosis.

It is a report at times repellent as one encounters the ugly malignant tumors and deep-seated infections affecting the patient. But the patient is not going to die. Diagnostician Peters reveals that there is gradually increasing resistance to the several sources of infection. Indeed, the patient is himself developing new antibodies and will in time be well, even healthy.

Of making many analytical books on the South there is of course no end. Nor should there be. The only regret is that so few of these receive

Review of William Peters, *The Southern Temper* (New York: Doubleday Publishers, 1959). Reprinted from the *New York Times Book Review*, 3 May 1959, by permission of Mrs. Ralph McGill and the *New York Times*. Copyright 1959, by the New York Times Company. An earlier draft of this review is in the McGill papers, now at Emory University, Atlanta.

the patiently thorough research into events, emotions, historical facts, statistics, and persons which Mr. Peters has provided.

It is, in addition, the best-organized piece of writing, or study, yet done on the progress of desegregation. The subject is a large one. Mr. Peters gave it a treatment as perceptive and exhaustive as the late W. J. Cash did the whole South in *The Mind of the South*, published in 1941.[165] Mr. Peters's book is so honest and objective that no effective attack can be made on it. There are certain to be smears and denials. But the integrity of the work will survive intact.

Mr. Peters is from the North. This is one reason, I believe, his book was so soundly written. The Southerner, bred and born in his own particular briar patch, is too often emotionally involved. He knows there are millions of wonderful, decent people in the South whose moral principles, whether of Jewish, Christian, or secular philosophy, have not been shaken. But he has been so busy with the clamor of the fanatics that he could not see with the wide-screen lens which was Mr. Peters's best asset. *The Southern Temper* is such excellent continuity of statistics, events, incidents, and personalities as to be a fascinating story, not a study. It is not, in any sense, a rehash of things written before. Some of the same facts and events necessarily are there, but they are so cogently integrated in the superb organization as to be newly effective.

Morality and law slowly are gaining adherents. Mr. Peters accurately sees the surge of bombings and burnings, the irrationally vicious McCarthy-like smears of all those who support processes of law as Communists, pinks, and leftists, as a confession of impending defeat.[166]

He makes other points in a new and fresh manner. The Negro is winning his rights of equal citizenship because he may now depend on the laws and the Constitution of his country, and not on the paternalistic cloak of a white friend or benefactor. There is a brief, yet adequate his-

---

[165]Wilbur Joseph Cash, *Mind of the South* (New York: A. A. Knopf, 1941).

[166]See Lewis M. Killian, *White Southerners* (New York: Random House, 1970); Raymond W. Mack, ed., *Changing South* (Chicago: Aldine Publishing Company, 1970); John C. McKinney and Edgar T. Thompson, eds., *South in Continuity and Change* (Durham: Duke University Press, 1965); and Thomas H. Naylor and James Clotfelter, *Strategies for Change in the South* (Chapel Hill: University of North Carolina Press, 1975).

tory of the National Association for the Advancement of Colored People. This organization has made local errors. But it advocates only the implementation of law and constitutional interpretations which its most abusive, hysterical critics cannot contend.

Mr. Peters also does a service in stating that both words and ideas have stood in the way of a clear understanding. The Supreme Court, as he makes clear, ordered not integration but an end to compulsory segregation. What is required is the removal of all legal barriers which prevent Negro children from attending any school they could attend if they were white. The proper word is desegregation. And what happens, says Mr. Peters with truth, when schools are desegregated is typically that a few Negro children apply for transfer. Most Southerners willing to think know that if all the schools suddenly were desegregated, fewer than two or three percent of the Negro children would change schools. Integration means a deliberate order of mixing and this the Court has not done.

The author lays several old myths by the heels. One is the favorite that prejudice may not be successfully legislated out of existence. The president of the United States has used this argument. Here again, Mr. Peters argues with clarity and force that the legislation is not aimed at prejudice but discrimination. There was, for example, a great prejudice against women being allowed to vote. Long years of agitation and work were necessary to remove the discrimination. Legislation at last succeeded. The end of this discrimination saw the decline of the prejudice. The comparison may be somewhat oversimplified, but the facts of it are inescapable.[167]

His statistics on discrimination in employment, including that of the government, is a disturbing revelation. Discrimination has helped produce poverty, slums, and ignorance. These factors, Mr. Peters says, are destructive of morals, health, faith, and ambition. It is not then fair to say, "Look at what an unhealthy, bad fellow this is. He must like to live that way."

Mr. Peters sees a gradual growth of the trend of the Southerners in the middle moving away from the segregationist extremists toward a

---

[167]See John Hope Franklin and Isidore Starr, eds., *The Negro in Twentieth-Century America: A Reader on the Struggle for Civil Rights* (New York: Vintage Books, 1967).

new status quo offering some permanency. He is right not to predict the timetable. It cannot be, he says, more than "several years" away. And once the burden is put down he believes the South may become more sincere in application of civil rights than the North.

Harry Golden, sage and philosopher of North Carolina, whose book *Only in America* has long been on the bestseller lists, has written an excellent foreword to this perceptive and valuable book.[168]

---

[168]Harry Golden, *Only in America* (Cleveland: World Publishing Co., 1958).

41

The Crisis of the City

Uncle Remus was telling a story to the Little Boy.
". . . and then," said Uncle Remus, "B'rer Rabbit climbed a tree."
"But, Uncle Remus," protested the Little Boy, "rabbits don't climb trees."
"This time, chile," said Uncle Remus, "B'rer Rabbit was jus' 'bliged to climb a tree."
This story, as much as any other, has relevance to describe the dilemma of the Deep South states, and more particularly, their cities.

They are about at the point where they are 'bliged to begin integration of their schools on at least the screened basis of a pupil-placement law. The alternative is to close their school system. This the rural and White Citizens' Council type extremist politicians are willing to do. But a slow tide of resistance is rising in the cities, and there is an underground of doubt in the rural areas.[169]

Published by permission of Mrs. Ralph McGill and *Saturday Review* (23 May 1959): 15, 45. Copyright 1959, The Saturday Review, Inc.

[169]Neil R. McMillen, *The Citizens' Council* (Urbana: University of Illinois Press, 1971); John Bartlow Martin, *The Deep South Says "Never"* (New York: Ballantine Books, 1957); Francis M. Wilhoit, *The Politics of Massive Resistance* (New York: George Braziller, 1973); and Numan V. Bartley, *The Rise of Massive Resistance: Race and Politics in the South During the 1950's* (Baton Rouge: Louisiana State University Press, 1969).

Atlanta's crisis is perhaps the best illustration of a city in a political straitjacket. Atlanta introduced Negro policemen on the force some fifteen years ago. The extremists said blood would flow in the streets. None did. Today there are Negro officers. Three years ago Atlanta desegregated her seven municipal golf courses despite a demagogic campaign by then Governor Marvin Griffin that the courses be closed or sold. There was not a single incident, nor has there been one. In early 1959, Atlanta's system of buses and electric trolleys was desegregated. After a week there was one incident—two teenagers had a verbal row. A stern warning by the juvenile court took care of that. Atlanta's city government, her newspapers, and most of the people have proceeded with all deliberate speed to try and make these things work within the framework of law. It is the only Deep South city where there is, and has been, a pro and con public debate, particularly on the subject of schools. Atlanta was much too sensible to argue an old tradition as applying to public golf courses, police forces, or trolleys. But Atlanta is helpless to attempt to solve her school problem.

Georgia's cities are even more in bondage than other Southern cities. Georgia has the county unit system, and there is no real opposition party. Democratic nomination means election. Under the unit system the rural counties rule. An Atlanta vote is worth, usually, about one-seventieth of that in a small county. It is possible in Georgia to get the most votes and still lose. A city can't demand, and get, local school-board authority.[170]

About all Atlanta can do is to rattle her political chains. But she vigorously is doing that. Indeed, there are sounds of clinking of metal in other cities of the state.

All cities in America, including New York, the most majestic of them all, suffer from the blight of rural legislative dominance in state legislatures. This blight is really a state of mind. It shuts its eyes to the population losses in the rural areas. It knows, but refuses to face the fact, that the proliferating urban areas provide most of the state revenue, jobs, and markets. This climate of pettiness is the more stubbornly and emo-

---

[170]For further evidence of McGill's personal involvement in constructive social change, see his speeches on race relations in *Ralph McGill: Editor and Publisher*, ed. Calvin McLeod Logue, 2 vols. (Durham: Moore Publishing Company, 1969), and the editor's introduction to this volume.

tionally cultivated in the old cotton states than elsewhere for obvious reasons.

The South, more especially the Deep South, is still conservative, in the traditional rural manner, in its legislative majorities. They represent the region with the largest percentage of Negro population. This area possesses most of the old-plantation-type economy. It is releasing persons from the land at a more accelerated rate. A majority of the rural counties are losing population and the per capita income shrinks. Significantly, and inevitably, the Deep South states of Alabama, Mississippi, South Carolina and Georgia have a long, uninterrupted history of reckless agitation of race for political ends.[171]

These are the basic factors explaining why these four states, as of this writing, almost hysterically refuse their cities, or the counties with few Negroes, the right to plan any attempt at obeying the Supreme Court decision. In these states, and only these four, has there been a complete denial of any sort of official approach to the problem other than total, massive resistance.

The political power pattern, supported presently by a substantial majority of the people, knows that if let alone most of the cities and some of the counties with sparse Negro population would choose to keep their schools open with a token beginning of integration. Such a decision would not necessarily be a basis of agreeing with the Court. Nor would there be in it any great measure of moral acceptance of the principles. It would be largely a matter of reality. All necessary gerrymandering would be done to make the token as small as possible. But since it would be relatively easy and not too involved, they would be willing to go ahead and have a try. They are not so permitted by the most fantastic and, almost surely unconstitutional, state laws.

State legislators and their constituents, like juvenile delinquents, are explained by the same psychology. In general, they reflect the environment, pressures, and experiences of their more malleable years.

---

[171]See Jay R. Mandle, *Roots of Black Poverty: The Southern Plantation Economy After the Civil War* (Durham: Duke University Press, 1978); Paul E. Mertz, *New Deal Policy and Southern Rural Poverty* (Baton Rouge: Louisiana State University Press, 1978); Harriet Laura Herring, *Passing of the Mill Village: Revolution in a Southern Institution* (Chapel Hill: University of North Carolina Press, 1949).

Basically, there is no real ancestral difference between the Tennessean, the North Carolinian, the Kentuckian, all of whom are well into plans of slow integration of their schools, and the people of South Carolina, Georgia, Alabama, and Mississippi. Their ancestors mostly came out of the melting pot of the colonial port of Philadelphia. They moved into the many-folded ranges of the Appalachians. They found the same passes and pushed on to find good land.

But the four states involved grew up with more slavery, more plantation economy, more sense of master and slave, more psychological need of the doctrine of superiority, and a greater feeling of guilt for having kept a human being in slavery. Therefore, while they are the same sort of people in colonial origins, they react differently. They will continue to do so. The resistance in the Deep South will be enduring and lacking in any rationality. This is not surprising nor is it in any degree unexpected.[172]

How does one peer into the future?

There are two major factors at work. The first, and perhaps the most powerful, is that of economics. Closed schools do not go well with new industries. This is especially true when almost every new plant of size includes research men, technicians, engineers, and management. These people will not go where they cannot be sure of schools for their children.

Little Rock's merchants have been hurt. But the real revelation of how things are occurred in early March of this year. The Little Rock Chamber of Commerce, which twice before had refused to poll itself, voted seventy-six percent to reopen the high schools on an integrated basis.

About a year and a half passed before Little Rock's business began to reflect the results of Governor Faubus's actions. It is not only the mills of the gods that grind slowly. The states planning to close their schools can now point to new plants that have made favorable site decisions this year. This is routine. From the time a large corporation's board votes to

---

[172]See Raymond W. Mack, ed., *Changing South* (Chicago: Aldine Publishing Co., 1970); John C. McKinney and Edgar T. Thompson, eds., *South in Continuity and Change* (Durham: Duke University Press, 1965); and Thomas H. Naylor and James Clotfelter, *Strategies for Change in the South* (Chapel Hill: University of North Carolina Press, 1975).

go ahead with a new plant until it is placed, an average period of about a year and a half transpires. If, however, the states do indeed carry out the folly of abolishing public education they will reap an increasingly poor economic harvest.

The prospective economic losses in a region hungry for more industry are just beginning to be seen and comprehended. Sowing a crop of massive resistance means that the good seeds fall upon stones or are crushed out by the thorns of prejudice.

North Carolina, among the first to understand this complex problem, announced plans to construct a great state research plant in the center of the triangle between her three major institutions, Duke University, North Carolina State, and the University of North Carolina. Industry was informed that the schools and colleges of the state would not merely be open, but would provide research aid.

Looking ahead, one may prophesy that while there are at least four states so completely held in political bondage as to destroy their public schools, this leadership will, in time, itself be overthrown by the well-known law that for every action there is an equal reaction.

The second factor is the leadership of cities. They are beginning to plan to fight with every possible legal device. In Atlanta, for example, a spontaneous, local organization was formed called HOPE, Inc. (Help Our Public Education) Their plans are to educate the people to what loss of education will mean. This, plus economics, won't delay the Deep South extremists, who are almost compulsively committed to destroying education, but it will shorten the period of tragedy.

Restoration of education will not be easy. Teachers will have gone elsewhere. A great many quickly constituted "private" schools will be demanding special privileges. Indeed, they already are.

There does not seem to be much hope of avoiding closing the schools. To speak even of closing schools means a previous process of closing the mind has been completed. The states cannot be compelled to maintain a public system. And most of the politicians care more about their own political face than the children.

To be sure, the state laws passed to maintain segregation in the four Deep South states are almost certainly unconstitutional. They eventually will be knocked down like so many dominoes. Even then, if unreasoning fanaticism insists on destruction of public education, it can do as did Samson of old.

But more and more cities are rattling their chains. And if the schools are destroyed and darkness falls, it will be that which comes just before the dawn. Out of it will come a new political leadership and a costly restoration of public education.

42

If the Southern Negro
Got the Vote

On the night of April 25, a fast-working, disciplined mob brutally dragged Mack Charles Parker, Negro, awaiting trial on a charge of rape, from a cell in the unguarded jail at Poplarville, in Pearl River County, Mississippi. On May 4, his body, bearing two gunshot wounds, was found in an eddy of the nearby Pearl River.

None knows what was in the collective mind of the mob, beyond a determination to kill Parker. Yet, despite the surface incongruity of the suggestion, it is likely that the systematic denial of voting rights to Negroes was one of the motivating factors in the hate-heated heads of the murderers.

April 25 was a Saturday. Parker's trial was set for Monday. It would be a jury trial with an all-white jury. For in Pearl River County only qualified voters may serve on juries, and in that county there was not even one Negro on the voting lists. But the Supreme Court has held that contrived exclusion of Negroes from jury duty denies a fair trial to a Negro defendant and is unconstitutional. It was common knowledge in Poplarville that Parker's defense planned to challenge the whole proceeding on this ground.

Reprinted by permission of Mrs. Ralph McGill and the *New York Times*, 21 June 1959. Copyright 1959, by The New York Times Company.

For days there had been sullen talk in the town square to the effect that, in these circumstances, it would never be possible to obtain a valid conviction. Without question, this feeling combined with the more familiar ingredients of prejudice to doom Mack Parker to death on that night when the air was soft with spring and the young people of Poplarville were dancing happily not far from the shabby jail.

The mob, in a manner of all mobs, thus achieved something it did not intend. It focused national attention anew on the almost unbelievable restriction of the right of Negroes to participate in the choice of public officials in the Southern states, particularly those of the old cotton South.

This denial of the ballot does not occur only in isolated places like Poplarville. Nor is its meaning confined simply to inability to vote for candidates for office. The ballot is the basic civil right. Once obtained, it would be the best remedy for all civil grievances.

Any attempt to provide a picture of the status of the Negro voter in the South runs into many difficulties. Accurate registration figures are not easily obtained. Voting lists are not always kept up to date. In a surprising number of counties in most of the Southern states the lists have not been thoroughly checked in years. Names of persons long dead, and those of voters who have left the county or state often are not removed. It is not uncommon to find counties which report white registration totals exceeding the white population of voting age.

Further, Negroes have been enfranchised in the South for only thirteen to fifteen years. Until the mid-forties, when the United States Supreme Court ruled the white primary unconstitutional, the Negro voter was a Deep South rarity.

The white primary—restricting the vote in Democratic primaries to white citizens—was a deliberate device of state Democratic committees to deny the Negro the right to participate in the choice of those who would govern. Since there was no opposition in the one-party South, the elections customarily found the Democratic primary nominees unopposed. The Supreme Court ruled that such a system disfranchised the Negro and was unconstitutional. (The poll tax, a second restrictive device, today is retained by only five states—Alabama, Arkansas, Mississippi, Texas, and Virginia. It has lost some of its deterrent effect with the movement of people from the land to the urban areas and into higher income brackets. [173]

When the white primary was removed there was angry resentment and a hurried putting together of heads to contrive a substitute the courts could not invalidate. While the legal minds worked out their plans for new restrictive legislation, requiring some form of literacy tests of which the registrars would be the sole judges, others resorted to the ready technique of intimidation. In some counties, following the Court ruling, motorcades of masked men drove silently along the roads and through the Negro sections of the county seats. A few crosses were burned before the homes of those Negroes who were regarded as likely to encourage interest in voting. "Uncle Toms," pliant Negroes, were used to carry warnings to the others.

The first so-called literacy law supplanting the white primary was adopted in Alabama in 1944. It required a registrant to "read, write, understand and explain any article" in the Constitution of the United States. In 1949, a federal district court ruled this out as hopelessly vague and also noted that the registrars, not being constitutional lawyers, would not themselves know whether the replies were correct.

In a 1951 law the "understand and explain" clause was therefore omitted. But a severe test was established in its place. In addition to the usual qualifications of age, residence, and lack of a criminal record, the Alabama law provides:

> The following persons . . . shall be qualified to register . . . those who can read and write any Article of the Constitution of the United States in the English language which may be submitted to them by the Board of Registrars, provided, however, that no person shall be entitled to register as electors except those who are of good character and who embrace the duties and obligations of citizenship under the Constitution of the United States and under the Constitution of the State of Alabama, and, provided, further, that . . . each applicant shall be furnished . . . a written questionnaire. . . . Such questionnaire shall be answered in writing by the applicant, in the presence of the Board without assistance. . . .

This, with variations providing registrars with opportunities for wide discrimination, is almost a Southwide pattern. In all states the re-

---

[173]See Jack Bass and Walter DeVries, *Transformation of Southern Politics: Social Change and Political Consequence Since 1945* (New York: New American Library, 1976).

gistrars have powers of discretion, actual or assumed. In rural areas white registrants are "passed" quickly while most or all Negroes are rejected.

In one Alabama county no standard form is used. The registrars may ask on what date the Tenth Amendment was adopted or on what date Oklahoma became a state. Veteran Negro college teachers have been refused registration for failing literacy tests. In still other counties the sheriff has been known to sit in a chair close by where the questioning was going on, compounding the uneasiness most rural Negroes feel in the courthouse, which to them has too often been a symbol of injustice rather than justice. Various other stratagems and forms of intimidation are used—frequent, unannounced changes of hours for registration, highly technical purges of Negro voters, gunshots in the night in the vicinity of those who are known to have talked of registering, a few persons actually killed.

As a result, Negro registration in eleven Southern states—Alabama, Arkansas, Florida, Georgia, Louisiana, Mississippi, North Carolina, South Carolina, Tennessee, Texas, and Virginia—had reached a total of but 1,321,731 in 1958. This is about 25 percent of the 4,980,000 Negroes of voting age. Mississippi has the lowest rate of any state— 30,000 to 35,000 out of a Negro voting-age population of about 500,000. The Southern Regional Council, a highly respected interracial research organization, has found that 80 to 85 percent of Negro voting is in the cities and larger towns of the South.

It should be added that white voter participation in the South is also below the national average. It is held down by the one-party system, low educational and income levels, the dominance of "the courthouse crowd" in most rural counties, the poll tax, and the difficulties of registration— the same factors that discourage Negro voting. Booker T. Washington, the illustrious Negro leader, once said that to hold the Negro in the economic ditch, the white man would have to get down there with him. This prophecy has been painfully accurate and applies, too, in the fields of politics and education.

The familiar bugaboo raised by those who oppose Negro suffrage and who create elaborately contrived legislation to restrict and discourage registration is the cry of "bloc vote," expressing fear of Negro domination through the ballot. The specter of Negro political rule is one constantly cultivated and exaggerated by those determined to maintain the status quo. Extremist demagogues make the most of it.[174]

"You let the civil-rights do-gooders have their way and you'll have a nigger mayor, nigger police, a nigger sheriff, a nigger superintendent of schools and nigger tax collectors," wrote one of the more violent editors in a White Citizens' Council pamphlet given general distribution.[175]

Actually, in the less than twenty years that the Negro may be said to have been partially enfranchised, his voting pattern has proved to be just like everyone else's. If Negroes feel that their interests are directly involved they vote in a bloc—as do farmers, union members, businessmen, or as doctors do on any issue which seems to them to involve socialized medicine. But when racial questions are not at issue, Negro voters tend to split their votes just as consistently as does the rest of the population.[176]

For example, Dr. Rufus Clement, able Negro president of Atlanta University, twice has been elected to the city's school board. Each time he carried the white wards as well as those heavily Negro. In the last election a successful, respected Negro businessman was a candidate for another municipal position. His vote in the Negro wards was far less than that of Dr. Clement, strongly indicating that there is no bloc voting unless the Negro voters' special interests are at stake.

Naturally, once the Negro acquired the right to vote, he would use it to obtain his full civil rights. He would, in addition, become a pres-

---

[174]Cal M. Logue and Howard Dorgan, eds., *Oratory of Southern Demagogues* (Baton Rouge: Louisiana State University Press, 1981).

[175]See William J. Simmons, *The Mid-West Hears the South's Story* (Greenwood MS: The Citizens' Councils, 1958); Thomas P. Brady, *A Review of Black Monday* (Winona MS: Association of Citizens' Councils of Mississippi, 1954); James O. Eastland, *We've Reached Era of Judicial Tyranny* (Greenwood MS: Association of Citizens' Councils of Mississippi, 1955); Neil R. McMillen, *The Citizens' Council* (Urbana: University of Illinois Press, 1971).

[176]See Chandler Davidson, *Biracial Politics: Conflict and Coalition in the Metropolitan South* (Baton Rouge: Louisiana State University Press, 1972); Numan V. Bartley and Hugh D. Graham, *Southern Elections: County and Precinct Data, 1950-1972* (Baton Rouge: Louisiana State University Press, 1978); Steven F. Lawson, *Black Ballots: Voting Rights in the South, 1944-1969* (New York: Columbia University Press, 1976).

sure group in his community, seeking community services in exactly the way white voters have been doing all these years.[177]

In Southern state elections the Negro voter would be a force behind expansion of schools and industry. He would provide, too, the possibility of creating a two-party system where today there is one. It is precisely this which adds to the fears of those who do not want him to vote and which causes them to try to picture the Negro voter as a dangerous factor.[178]

The fear of bloc voting arises in its most caloric form in the few Southern counties where the Negro population is a majority of perhaps 60 to 70 percent. At least a part of it contains an element of guilt—as revealed in the assumption that if Negroes were allowed to vote they would all have reason to vote as a strong antiwhite bloc. But for many white residents the fear also takes tangible form in the visible presence of more Negroes than whites. It understandably is difficult for those so situated to apply reason to the question—and few have tried.

But there would never be a time when all the Negroes would vote. A high percentage of any Negro community—higher than in white communities—is under voting age. Many of the adults in these rural counties are illiterate, though not entirely by their own choice. They could not meet a legitimate test.

Moreover, the Southern Negro population is steadily declining, nowhere more rapidly than in the old plantation, cotton counties where Negro population majorities now exist. It is quite possible that the 1960 census will show that half of the nation's Negro population is outside the Southern states.

Because of the emigration of the Southern Negro, as well as that of the whites, the Bureau of the Census already has said that if the trend continues—and it is continuing—several Southern states will lose some representation in Congress in the reapportionment which will follow the 1960 census. This emigration is speeding up the decline of Southern po-

---

[177]See Brian Rungeling et al., *Employment, Income, and Welfare in'the Rural South* (New York: Praeger, 1977).

[178]See Numan V. Bartley and Hugh D. Graham, *Southern Politics and the Second Reconstruction* (Baltimore: Johns Hopkins University Press, 1975).

litical power in Congress, a process that has already become evident during the past three or four years.

Three basic suggestions for meeting the problems raised by denial of Negro voting rights are indicated by present conditions and unmistakable trends. They are:

(1) Not even the most sincere believer in states' rights, alone with his conscience, can doubt the need for a bolstering of civil rights legislation to at least the moderate, common-sense level requested by President Eisenhower and Attorney General William Rogers. True, law alone is not enough. But history teaches that once prejudice and discrimination lack the sanction of law, both decline.

(2) The Federal Civil Rights Commission, established to look into denial of voting and other rights, may not need to be made permanent. But through the turbulent years immediately ahead, the nation will badly need such a board.

(3) The continuing concentration of Negroes in cities offers an opportunity and an urgent need for a boldly imaginative cooperative civic job of political education by service clubs and other recognized agencies devoted to civic improvement. It should be obvious—as unhappily it is to but a few—that it is necessary and possible to provide for the Negroes (and for that matter, the whites) who leave the mechanized farms honest instruction in the duties and responsibilities of citizenship. Most of those who come to town have little political consciousness. The average field hand or small Negro farmer, with little or no education, knowing that if he does not "keep his place" he may encounter violence, is not aware of the meaning of voting.

But the present pattern of Southern life does not allow for real interracial cooperation in public-service schools for potential voters. Political "education" is left to those who are trampling out the vintage where the grapes of wrath are stored. There is rarely any mention that a moral question as well as one of political health, is involved for the white and Negro leadership of the cities.

So far the more progressive Negro churches have carried the burden of both inspiration and instruction. Some have achieved excellent results. But they would be the first to say they have barely scratched the surface. They must have help from a community which sees the Negro voter as an asset if he has honest leadership and example.

Negro society is as stratified as that of the white population. Its members are by no means a closely knit set bearing aloft the slogan, "All for one, one for all." The Negro knows that some of his own race have exploited him as ruthlessly and have deceived him as cruelly as have white men of like character. He knows, too, that some of his own people have provided some of the most venal examples of Southern politics. Yet one of the best features of the Negro minority now seeking voting rights has been that its leadership has not sought to set it apart and ask for special privileges. It attempts to be more American, not less; to be complete citizens, not semicitizens.[179]

---

[179]For McGill's later view of voting by blacks, see "The State of the South" and "Case for the Southern Progressive," in volume 2.

43

A Changing South
As I See It
1959

C all it the South or the Southeast, as you will. To one bred, born
and reared in it, to one who has lived in it all one's life, save
for the goings-away and the comings-back, it seems somehow
always to have been in motion.

The South traditionally has insisted on a separateness, as if somehow
it were determined to be an unchanging microcosm of an old civilization. Yet, no region in America has been so convulsively, ruthlessly, and
indeed, so often changed.[180]

As a boy, I heard grandmothers tell of the days when the invading
armies came, and of smoke from burning barns and homes staining the
sky. I listened wide-eyed and with quickening pulsebeat while grand-
fathers and great-uncles told of riding with Nathan Bedford Forrest's
"Critter Company," of wild cavalry charges and of the fierce affection
for their leader. I took from them some of their own distaste for General

---

Reprinted by permission of Mrs. Ralph McGill and *Think* magazine, July 1959.
Copyright 1959, by International Business Machines Corporation.

[180]See Charles S. Sydnor, *Development of Southern Sectionalism: 1819-1848* (Baton
Rouge: Louisiana State University Press, 1948); Avery O. Craven, *Growth of Southern
Nationalism: 1848-1861* (Baton Rouge: Louisiana State University Press, 1953); and
Carl N. Degler, *Place Over Time: The Continuity of Southern Distinctiveness* (Baton
Rouge: Louisiana State University Press, 1971).

Braxton Bragg and President Davis. I heard bitter stories, too, of another South, that of the years of reconstruction and the harsh years which followed, made austere and spiritually corrosive by a poverty of almost everything, material, spiritual, educational.

I wondered then what "the old South" and that postwar South must really have been—as my own son questions me, sometimes with laughter, about the South I knew as a boy.

Southerners, I believe, entertain more of a mystique about their region than do those of any other geographic divison. Almost everyone has his own South in his mind and nurtures that image of it.[181]

The physical South itself remains the more constant, though bulldozers and workers of buildings move mountains more easily than faith and tear down structures old and new for urban redevelopment. The ribbons of freeways and highways also are helping remake the terrain.

The South curves south and west from Virginia to Mississippi and Arkansas. The many-folded Appalachians reach into it from New England, to become a vast, disorderly wilderness of smoky peaks, ranges, ridges, and plateaus in the Carolinas and East Tennessee. The last haze-covered buttresses thrust deep into South Carolina and Georgia. There are mountain rivers and valleys with the Indian names on them. Further South are prairies, the wire-grass coastal plains, the pine forests, the Atlantic coast. More distant are the bayous, the tidal rivers, swamps, and the rich deltas.

The mountain ranges and the passes bear names put on them by DeSoto's weary, gold-cursed men, and by the hunters, traders, and settlers who followed after those who were the first to find ways through the tortured folds of the Appalachians.

This section of the nation's geography is a region of myths, legends, and facts. Its song is a medley of fiddle tunes and laughter, the tinkle of a silver spoon stirring a julep in a crystal glass, of gospel hymns and the mournful power of a Negro spiritual crying out of a secret place in the heart of a plowman in a distant field or a woman at the Monday washpot.

---

[181]See T. Harry Williams, *Romance and Realism in Southern Politics* (Athens: University of Georgia Press, 1961); Paul M. Gaston, *New South Creed: A Study in Southern Mythmaking* (New York: Vintage Books, 1970); and C. Dwight Dorough, *Bible Belt Mystique* (Philadelphia: Westminster Press, 1974).

The record is not yet completed. Already the new sounds are there—of many new machines, of generators and the noises of construction.

It is land of many and diverse images. Some are magnificent and true as others are romantically and preposterously contrived. Some are weakness, some are strength.

It is an area which for too many years had almost a compulsion for agriculture. Now it comes with a precipitate rush into the industrial revolution, hot-eyed for industry and payrolls. Yet, for all this eagerness to grasp the hand of the future, there is a reluctance to let go the hand of the past.

Something of the geography is in the people of every region. From the beginning there were many Souths. There were the great river and coastal plantations, where rice, tobacco and Sea Island cotton brought wealth, luxury, slavery, and created a culture which obtained its wines, its linens, and literature from Europe. It put the name of English holdings on its manor houses and developed the sort of civilization which can flourish only in the soil of leisure. These put their stamp on the South. The image, the stereotype is theirs, even though, in 1860, there were but 383,632 slaveholders in a white population of more than 8,000,000. In 1820 one of every four Southerners was a Virginian.[182]

But there was the South of cabins and clearings in the mountains and along the curve of the Piedmont, with its many streams to turn the wheels of gristmills. The smoke went up from mud-and-stick chimneys in the pine forests and on the wire-grass plains. Slaves were rare with these people. Their tie with the Union was forged with the long rifles at King's Mountain. Most of them stayed with the old flag when the test came.

The tapestry of this epoch—this first South—is a rich and brilliant one. It celebrates, in its threads, great men and small, wise men and fools, brave men and ignoble. Its political and emotional leadership was

---

[182]See Kenneth M. Stampp, *The Peculiar Institution: Slavery in the Ante-Bellum South* (New York: Vintage Books, 1956); John W. Blassingame, *The Slave Community: Plantation Life in the Antebellum South*, rev. and enl. ed. (New York: Oxford University Press, 1979); Eugene D. Genovese, *Roll, Jordon Roll: The World the Slaves Made* (New York: Vintage Books, 1972); and Robert William Fogel and Stanley I. Engerman, *Time on the Cross: The Economics of American Negro Slavery* (Boston: Little, Brown and Co., 1974).

determined to maintain and extend a slave-cotton economy. The clamor of the abolitionist and slaveowner bitter-enders merged inevitably into the sound of guns, which were to echo almost continually for four long, demanding years of sorrow, blood and ruin.

There followed another epoch—another South.

It began, one might say, with the insane folly of a pistol shot in a theater box. It was the tragic era of Reconstruction. This was a relatively brief period, as years go, though packed into it was so much of excess that this period, not the war, spawned most of the prejudices, the racial fears and antagonisms, which even yet poison the nation's political wells.

Reconstruction ended in 1877, after the 1876 presidential election was almost certainly taken from Samuel J. Tilden, Democrat, and given to Rutherford B. Hayes, Republican. The South had become a dependency, had given economic suzerainty to the business interests of the East as a price for an end to military occupation and government.[183]

There emerged yet another "new South." It was one of harsh, unrelenting toil and meager return. Poverty and discontent were the legacy of political exploitation. In 1880, the estimated true valuation of property in the United States was $47,642,000,000. The South's share was $5,776,000,000. The per capita wealth was $376 in the South as against an average of $1,086 outside.

But economic exploitation rapidly replaced political. Speculators came to build and sell—empires of timber, mineral lands, railways, and mines.

The prophets began to speak exultantly of the "new South" and poets and orators spoke of the beauty of smokestacks on the horizon. A campaign for public education was begun.

But on the land there were bitterness and want. The Populist revolution grew to explosive power in the late 1880s and into the 1890s. The leaders of both the Republican and Democratic parties were shaken and

---

[183]See C. Vann Woodard, *Reunion and Reaction: The Compromise of 1877 and the End of Reconstruction* (Boston: Little, Brown Publishers, 1966); William C. Harris, *Presidential Reconstruction in Mississippi* (Baton Rouge: Louisiana State University Press, 1967); James Wilford Garner, *Reconstruction in Mississippi* (Baton Rouge: Louisiana State University Press, 1968); and Alan Conway, *Reconstruction of Georgia* (Minneapolis: University of Minnesota Press, 1966).

afraid. By the time Grover Cleveland was elected president of the United States in 1884, the first Democrat since Buchanan, the Populists were on the march. But the old problems of agriculture, of abused soil, credit, and debt, which had so stirred them, were to remain unsettled.

The First World War boomed cotton. So did the immediate postwar years. But by 1922 the disaster of the boll weevil was complete. Men did not know it then, but another South, or epoch, was ending. The war had caused men and women to migrate northward to the new booming industrial centers, particularly Detroit. The ruin of the cotton economy sent thousands more in their steps. The Great Depression came swiftly on. By 1938 a presidential commission would report to the White House that the South was the nation's "Number One economic problem."

What I remember best of those days is of how that report challenged the South. There had been a ferment of discussion all through the worst of the depression years. The collapse of the cotton economy was tragically on display in every town in the dejected persons displaced by it.[184]

The commission report touched off a great debate because it could not be ignored. The state legislatures reverberated with resentment and affirmation. The universities took it up. Communities formed study and forum groups. Out of them came a reversal of the committee's conclusion. If we were the number one economic problem we were quite inescapably the number one opportunity.

It was as if the region had not known how much it had been tied to agriculture. And, truthfully, it had not.

A study by the department of economics at the University of Georgia revealed that in 1930 the South's percentage share of the nation's total industry was about exactly that of 1860. This was a shock.

The impetus of the new legislation to provide credit and aid to agriculture and for construction of roads and public buildings was accelerated by the greater demands of Europe as the Second World War came on. Capital poured into the South as training camps, shipyards, service industries, metal fabricating plants, and demand for timber grew. When the war was ended the South, for the first time in its long history,

---

[184]See Richard H. King, *A Southern Renaissance: The Cultural Awakening of the American South, 1930-1955* (New York: Oxford University Press, 1980), and V. O. Key, Jr., *Southern Politics in State and Nation* (New York: Vintage Books, 1949).

had a store of capital. It had, too, more managerial skills and a great pool of skilled labor. From 1939 to 1950 the South's labor force increased by fifty percent.[185] As 1957 ended, the U.S. Chamber of Commerce reported from its southeastern office that the region had surpassed the average rate of advancement for the nation as a whole. The same source noted that from 1954 to 1957 the twelve southeastern states had a per capita income gain of sixteen percent, second highest in the nation. In employment, the South is fifth in percentage increase.

It is no mere figure of speech to say that the South, in general, is exploding economically. It has the water, the labor, the climate, many of the raw materials for the new industrial growth—wood pulp, resins, cellulose fibers.

There are other changes. By the late 1930s it could be seen, in the postmortem on the Southern epoch which had ended with the depression, that the permanent subordinate position for the Negro, which was a part of that economic system, also was finished. The 1954 school decision did not come without warning. There had been a number of decrees at the graduate school level. Slowly, and not without agony, the adjustment began. Those who were willing to look with open eyes could see that the states which could manage to improve their public schools and university-level education and employment would profit most from the swift pace of industrialization.[186]

That South, possessing its share of wonderful people of both races, all somehow in love with the region, and holding fast to the best human qualities, will in good time move into the mainstream of American life.

---

[185]See Paul E. Mertz, *New Deal Policy and Southern Rural Poverty* (Baton Rouge: Louisiana State University Press, 1978); Frank Burt Freidel, *F.D.R. and the South* (Baton Rouge: Louisiana State University Press, 1965); and Charles Pearce Roland, *Improbable Era: The South Since World War II* (Lexington: University Press of Kentucky, 1975).

[186]See Robert Haws, *Age of Segregation: Race Relations in the South, 1890-1945* (Jackson: University Press of Mississippi, 1978); Numan V. Bartley and Hugh D. Graham, *Southern Politics and the Second Reconstruction* (Baltimore: Johns Hopkins University Press, 1975); Donald R. Matthews, *Negroes and the New Southern Politics* (New York: Harcourt, Brace and World, 1966); Lewis M. Killian, *White Southerners* (New York: Random House, 1970); Raymond W. Mack, ed., *Changing South* (Chicago: Aldine Publishing Co., 1970).

Once rid of the old burdens, it will then be more able than ever before in its history to make the next "new South" match the dreams of its most uninhibited prophets.

44

The Agony
of the Southern Minister

I
n the 131-year-old city of Columbus Georgia, a town on the bank of the Chattahoochee River with a population of eighty-five thousand whites and forty thousand Negroes, Rev. Robert Blakely McNeill, forty-four, endured with faith and patience the slow progress of convalescence following a coronary suffered 10 June.

His severe physical shock came just three days after a spiritual one. A judicial commission of the Southeast Georgia Presbytery had dismissed him from the pastorate of the First Presbyterian Church, its chairman reading the brief, almost curt, notice from the pulpit Mr. McNeill had filled for six and a half years.

Seven long months before, the same commission, after a request for a hearing by seven of the congregation, had said that the racial issue was the central one behind the opposition to the pastor. According to Rob McNeill's friends, this "Spanish-Inquisition-like hostility" was fostered by a hard core of "about fifty church members."

Actually, Rob McNeill, Alabama-born, Southern-reared and educated had never once used his pulpit to urge integration. Even his most bitter enemies admit as much. But in an article published in *Look* magazine in May 1957, he had advocated a moderate course of creative con-

Reprinted by permission of Mrs. Ralph McGill and the *New York Times*, 27 September 1959. Copyright 1959, by The New York Times Company.

tact between the races as a necessary approach to racial harmony and Christian duty.[187] He emphasized that he rejected sexual and contrived social mixing. But he also made it plain he had meant that Negroes should, and must, be accepted in the administration of community affairs.

From that day on, there were those in his congregation who, for these mild statements, remorselessly set out to drive him from the church. By June they were appealing to the Presbytery. Statements like these were heard, "No nigger will ever darken the door of the church," and, "If a nigger comes, I go."

It was even reported that some of the more relentless opponents among the 1,200 professed Christians in the congregation were heard to say, on learning of the coronary that brought Mr. McNeill close to death, that the Lord finally had "taken care of him." Others, seemingly dismayed at the possibility that the illness might create sympathy, said, "It's a fake attack."

However, Rob McNeill was not alone. Members of his congregation manned a reception table outside his hospital room in two-hour shifts from early morning until late at night to greet and register visitors and to protect him from intruders. There were special prayers in hundreds of homes, and his wife and three children, who suffered their share of vile language and death threats by phone, were never without friends.

McNeill's supporters agreed then that he must go to another pastorate, though they longed to confront his opposition in a further church hearing. He was, at the time of his heart attack, considering a call to a large Charleston, West Virginia, church but was unwilling to surrender to the malignant forces against him. But now he has accepted.

A leader among those who opposed him is quoted as saying, "Now we must find a preacher with the right kind of religion."

This story of Robert McNeill, Christian minister in the Deep South, who sought to have his own life reflect the two great command-

---

[187]Robert Blakely McNeill, "A Georgia Minister Offers a Solution for the South," *Look* 21 (28 May 1957). McGill wrote the introduction to McNeill's *God Wills Us Free: The Ordeal of a Southern Minister* (New York: Hill and Wang, 1965), in volume 2.

ments of love as specifically designated by his Master, is—save for the
heart attack and the drama of his unexpected public firing—not an unusual one in the South.[188] In varying degrees it is shared by all Southern
ministers and priests who have the courage to take even the most moderate of positions on racial integration. Pressure from some of the con-
gregational leaders, ostracism and obstruction, repeated telephone calls
in the dead of night, ugly, whispered filth, threats of violence and death
inspired by minds stewing with God alone knows what evil—these are
all part of a pattern familiar to the ministers of Southern churches who
try to take the attitude of tolerance required by Christianity, the ethics
of Western civilization, the Constitution and courts of the United States,
and their own national church organization.[189]

Despite the virulence of the attacks upon them, these moderate ministers do not, in general, take the position that each church should have
a thoroughly mixed congregation. That is not likely to come about in the
South any more than it has or will soon in the North; social and economic patterns of community life preclude it, quite aside from the integration controversy.[190]

The stand these ministers do take is twofold: First, Christians and
Christian churches should, as a matter of principle, be in the forefront
of the forces working for racial tolerance and obedience to the law, particularly in the matter of public school integration. Second, as a token of
this principle, white congregations should cease to reject the very
thought of a Negro crossing the threshold; although Negroes need not
be admitted to full membership, any who wish to worship should be
welcomed.[191]

---

[188]In Mark 12:30-31, Jesus said, "And thou shalt love the Lord thy God with all
thy heart, and with all thy soul, and with all thy mind, and with all thy strength.
. . . And the second is this: thou shalt love thy neighbor as thy self."

[189]For McGill's advice to ministers concerning race relations see his speech to
ministers, Emory University, Atlanta, 21 January 1959 in *Ralph McGill: Editor and
Publisher*, ed. Calvin M. Logue, 2 vols. (Durham: Moore Publishing Co., 1969)
1:163-79.

[190]To see how McGill's views and advice concerning race relations evolved from
the 1940s to 1969 see the editor's introduction to this volume.

[191]See Ralph McGill, "Let's Lead Where We Lag," *Episcopalian* (March 1962),
reprinted in volume 2.

The basic position of the moderates was set forth in November 1957, by 80 Atlanta ministers who issued what came to be known as a manifesto calling for communication between the races, maintenance of public schools, and obedience to law and the courts. A year later 311 ministers and a rabbi representing sixteen denominations in the Atlanta area issued a stronger statement along the same lines, the principles of which the Catholic bishop publicly endorsed. In many other Southern states, ministers and church organizations have published similar assertions of principles.

The views of these Southern moderates are, in every case, fully in keeping with the official policies of national church bodies. No such organization—Protestant, Roman Catholic, Greek Orthodox, or Jewish—today supports segregation in principle or practice.

The General Assembly of the Presbyterian Church, after the U.S. Supreme Court's school decision in 1954, took a forthright, official position in support of it. In subsequent years it reaffirmed it and firmly put down all attempts to repeal that resolution. The National Conference of the Methodist Church has made a similar affirmation.

The Southern Baptist Convention—representing by far the largest Southern denomination—met in St. Louis in June 1954, and adopted a five-point resolution recognizing that "this Supreme Court decision is in harmony with the Constitutional guarantee of equal freedom to all citizens, and with the Christian principles of equal justice and love for all men." In its 1959 convention in Louisville, Kentucky, the convention beat down attempts to repeal this resolution and also heard retiring president Brooks Hays—the former Congressman from Little Rock who was defeated for reelection because of his moderate racial position—read a report denying scriptural basis for the separation of the races.[192]

Bishops of the Episcopal and Roman Catholic Churches have, without exception, ordered that every person is welcome in the House of God. When a Roman Catholic layman's organization in New Orleans angrily and publicly defied a local Church order against segregation and appealed directly to the Pope, the Vatican took a "serious and most unsympathetic view" of the appeal. A high Vatican source said "the Church

---

[192]See McGill's review of Brooks Hays, *A Southern Moderate Speaks* (Chapel Hill: University of North Carolina Press, 1959), reprinted in volume 1.

is unalterably opposed to all forms of discrimination—in New Orleans as much as in South Africa."

Such policy statements by national and regional church organizations are, of course, gratifying. They provide a necessary yardstick. Nor is it fair to say they are without influence at the church or parish level. But church congregations—particularly the dominant Protestant ones of the South—either have or assume considerable local authority.[193]

Most of them harbor an element—perhaps only a minority, but a potent one—who will never agree that a Negro should be admitted to a white church. These all-out segregationists unhesitatingly put the separation of the races ahead of Christian teaching, law, or moral principle.

With an example before them of public officials' defiance of the courts on school integration, they find it easier to bomb churches and schools, to defy Christian teaching and church policies, and to make life miserable, if not impossible, for any minister who seeks to follow his conscience, secular law, and church policy. Publications by extremist states' rights groups and White Citizens' Councils repeatedly urge that "weak-kneed preachers" be "whipped into line" by the withholding of contributions. They sneer at the clergy of all faiths, saying, "Money talks and they all listen."

Lay attacks on ministers rarely are so open as that which attracted national attention in Columbus, Georgia. For the most part, they take the form of relentless, petty harassments and slow destruction of the pastor's program. Some of the "big givers" reduce their pledges and let their dislike become known. Some move to another church where the "religion" is the "right kind." Or the meeting of the church board will produce budget wrangles and decisions which, while not so stated, have the effect of negating the pastor's program.

When, for example, the congregation of an Atlanta church, sensing the intention of some hostile members to reduce their giving, bestirred itself to extra effort and sacrifice and turned in the full amount of the budget anyhow, the board suddenly found a need for an expensive addition to the physical equipment of the church. By this and other de-

---

[193]See McGill's "The Church in a Social Revolution," *Church and Race* 2 (December 1964): 3-4, reprinted in volume 2.

vices, the board so depleted the budget that the pastor's program was wrecked.

One of the largest Methodist churches in Georgia had a strongly worded resolution offered at an April meeting of the stewards which called for the instant dismissal of any church officials (including the pastor) or Sunday school teachers using the facilities of the church to practice or advocate integration. It was defeated—but the chairman of the board said the vote did not mean the church would permit Negroes to attend.

Thus ministers are squeezed between the dictates of conscience and church policy, on the one hand, and the prejudices of those who "run" the church on the other. Save for the so-called Bible floggers, the Ku Klux chaplain breed, and those who are sure that God himself is chief among segregationists, this is a time of agony of spirit for the ministers of sensitive heart and mind. "We are in a long period of Gethsemane," said one recently. "And once again Judas is with us."

Every minister with any shred of awareness sees that, just as the racial issue is the greatest political issue before the world today, so it is for Christianity. If the first great commandment of Jesus, and the second which is "like unto it," have no validity in the minds of church members, then the churches are finished, or eventually will be.

"The thing that gets me," said one minister who has taken a moderate stand, "is the silence I encounter. I go and expose myself to members of my congregation who I know to be in opposition, so that we may talk. They won't. The silence is worst.

"Then, too, it is uncomfortable to see successful business and professional men, who have been old friends and strong financial props, suddenly become cold and aloof because one voices the opinion that a colored person is a child of God and has a right to worship in any of God's houses. You want to kneel and pray with these men or to put your arms around them and say, 'Please, what is it in your hearts that makes you so stubborn and afraid?' But today too many men are wrapped in the armor of unreasonable fears and anger."

Many ministers sorrowfully note another effect of the church's position on desegregation. It is that many people today love their church, but not Christ and the faith He taught.

"It had never occurred to me," said one, as he talked of it, with genuine grief in his voice, "that for so many people the church was the building, the meeting with old friends, the association in the women's organizations, and that Christ meant little, if anything. But it is true. There is a great gulf between what some mean when they say they love the church and what another means for whom Christ has validity. It saddens me to learn how many persons do not want Christ to intrude on them, indeed will not permit it, if he makes them uncomfortable."

A sense of shame and self-accusation is especially noticeable among younger ministers, encountering for the first time the harshness of some older men whom they had regarded as great Christian lay leaders. They have stories to tell which, while sometimes wryly humorous, are always said with disillusionment.

Many a minister today is holding on in a Southern church, developing a technique of survival, merely because he does not want to desert those in the congregation who depend on him and need him. Still others remain, believing that time and God are working together in their behalf.

There are some grounds for this optimism. Slowly but surely, if not always clearly, one may see at work among lay groups the influence of Christian ministers courageous enough, and with status enough to counter some of the fanaticism. More and more individuals, and a slow procession of churches, are making the decision that houses of worship should be open to all seeking God. It will be slow, in some areas tortuously so, but it will come. It will come most slowly of all in those Deep South states where there is sure to be the closing of public schools over the same issue. But there are a few churches even there which welcome Negroes to mass and to worship.

Although no Southern church is integrated in the true sense of the word, almost every Southern city has one or two churches to which Negroes come with some regularity. So far the doors are open mainly in Catholic churches, although beginnings toward desegregation are evident in some others. This development is limited entirely to the cities; solid opposition to integration persists in rural areas.

As some things cannot be measured in dollars and cents, just so the impact of all that has happened, and is in progress, in this field of race, religion, and church, cannot be put down in statistics or any sort of box score. It is something which involves the heart, mind, and adrenal glands.

An example of what could be called an awakening, or impact, is the experience of a Methodist Church congregation in Georgia whose minister has recently accepted a call to a large church in the Southwest. The board of deacons had harassed him for more than a year without ever making the harassment overt. It had depleted his budget unnecessarily. It had dismissed his assistant and otherwise frustrated his program.

The pastor believed most of the members were on his side, but he did not feel he could appeal to them over the heads of his board. The board was, as usual, made up largely of the major financial contributors.

Some few of these had come to him privately to protest and argue that his policy of being willing to admit Negroes to worship was wrecking the church and to urge him to renounce it. Some treated him with contemptuous condescension, saying he was just trying to attain publicity at the expense of the church. One, who said he wanted to talk to him "like a father," appealed to him not to ruin his career by being so radical.

Still another board member, a man of considerable wealth, asked him to his office. "I like you," he said, "but you have outlived your usefulness. I will give you five thousand dollars if you will resign quietly and go elsewhere. It will be a matter between us. No one will know."

The minister managed to restrain his anger, refused and quietly walked out.

The pastor stayed on for about a year. Then, to prevent a tragic, open break, he resigned. He himself did not know what the impact of the affair had been on his congregation. But soon afterward an excited, happy member came to him and said, "We had a meeting to discuss your replacement. And you know, we found that we have just about fifty-three die-hard segregationists in our congregation of more than two thousand. We are going to engage a man with convictions like yours."

Other congregations are slowly learning more about themselves. Without question, the controversy over desegregation is causing soul-searching; the result in the months and years ahead may be to break the race barriers in most churches.

Those ministers who have come to grips with this problem see the church as fulfilling its greatest role in the years ahead—that of binding up the spiritual wounds, and of moving mankind another inch or so forward toward a brotherhood of man, under God, so that this nation, or any nation so dedicated, can and shall have a new birth of freedom. The pastor of one large Southern church has said:

> We are all integrated . . . every one of our churches is integrated. The faces in the pews may all be white. But the Negro is there. He is present in the anger and guilt of some of the congregation. He is present in the consciences of many. He is present in the fears of the ushers who wait each Sunday to see if he will come. He waits in the wings, invisible, but present just the same.
>
> God is at work. Some of the churches may become private clubs and establish rigid rules against the presence of nonmembers. They will never be happy. They will never know peace. We are all integrated and there is nothing we can do about it save ask God's grace to make us see it.[194]

---

[194]See McGill's "Interview on Race and the Church"; also Charles Reagan Wilson, *Baptized in Blood: Religion of the Lost Cause, 1865-1920* (Athens: University of Georgia Press, 1980); and Samuel S. Hill, *Religion and the Solid South* (Nashville: Abingdon Press, 1972).

45

She Sifted the Ashes
and Built a City

I t was 1842. And spring. A stake was driven in the ground in Land Lot 77, in what was then DeKalb County, Georgia.

Wilson Lumpkin, a former governor of Georgia, then disbursing officer of the proposed W. & A. Railroad, went with surveyors and State Engineer Charles F. M. Garnett to the site. It was, Lumpkin recalled eleven years later in a letter to his daughter Martha, "a perfect state of nature . . . a wild, unmolested forest. . . ."

This stake in the ground was Atlanta, Georgia. In the autumn of 1959 it is the center of a metropolitan population of one million persons.

Let us be ballad makers. Or let us imitate the ancient Greek and Roman makers of myths and say that Atlanta was born of steam. Her mother was water. Her father was flame. She was born of the wedding of the two.

She was a child of the young industrial revolution, of furnaces and fabrication of metals. Among her forebears are those who invented the steam engine and the railroad locomotive. From them have descended the gasoline, diesel, and jet engines.

Atlanta was born with energy in her body. In her genes were transportation, movement, drive, the hissing steam, the singing of rails, the

Reprinted from *Atlanta Journal and Constitution*, Autumn 1959, by permission of Mrs. Ralph McGill and Atlanta Newspapers, Inc.

movement of great truck lines along highways, and of swift aircraft in the skies.

Even now men are building, within sight of her ever-enlarging skyline, the great freighters of the air, the huge, jet-prop Hercules, into which will go twice as much freight as can be packed into a railway boxcar. Crews can take it across the Atlantic, or bring back a load, without stop. Already this never-static city is on the way to becoming the air-freight center of the Southeast, and one of the great transportation cities of the nation.

There has always been a song in the city's heart—a rhythm, a symphony, a waltz, a minuet, a spiritual, a hymn. There is in it the sound of clicking rails, of hammers, of saws, the smooth rasp of the bricklayer's trowel, the sound of electric hammers on rivets in steel beams, the sibilant whisper of hurrying heavy rubber tires on highways, the whistling sound of great aircraft wings.

She began as a stake marking the place where a railroad terminus would later be. She was raw and crude and tough when she began. But she was honest enough to call the first two political factions the Rowdies and Non-Rowdies.

She was born among wild magnolias. But she was iron. She was Deep South, yet she never at anytime in her history was a typical Southern town. The magnolias crept into her speech. The Deep South gave her a touch of softness. But from the very beginning she never knew the languor and the sleepy tranquillity of the legendary Old South. She was never lazy, never afraid.

But when the surveyors drove the stake in land lot 77 they were looking toward the future. Atlanta is like that. She is, in a sense, a city without a past. For her, as a poet has said, the past is a bucket of ashes. Atlanta was a young, lusty, sprawling go-ahead town when William Tecumseh Sherman burned it. There were sorrow and loss, anger, and recrimination. But not for long. The sound of hammers and saws, of bricks being laid, of merchants selling goods, of transport and the movement of merchandise drowned out all else.

Bill Arp, a writer for the *Constitution*, had set the tone. When the War Between the States was ended he did not choose to look at the ruin of it and wring his hands in despair. "I killed as many of them as they did of me," he wrote, "and so I went home and made a crop."

Atlanta did not rise out of the fire-blackened ruins by any stroke of luck. She worked. In the fall of 1865 when, one might say, the ashes had not long been cooled, a reporter for Boston and Chicago newspapers wrote back a story saying:

> From all this ruin and devastation a new city is springing up with marvelous rapidity. The narrow and irregular and numerous streets are alive from morning till night with drays and carts and hand-barrows and wagons—with hauling teams and shouting men—with loads of lumber and loads of brick and loads of sand—with piles of furniture and hundreds of packing boxes—with mortar and hod-carriers—with carpenters and masons—with rubbish removers and house builders—with a never-ending throng of pushing and crowding and scrambling and eager and enterprising men. . . . The four railroads here groan with traffic . . . the very genius of the West, holding in one hand all its energies and in the other all its extravagancies, is there; not sitting in the supreme ease of settled pause, but standing in the nervous tension of expected movement. . . .

That was, mind you, the autumn of 1865.

She was a city in the South—but she was western in vision and energy. That was Atlanta—that is Atlanta—never in the ease of settled pause, but always in movement.

It was just a few years later that Gen. William T. Sherman came for a visit. Critics said she should not receive him. And there were some few in the city who were bitter. But Sherman was a part of the past. And Atlanta wanted him to see what they had done. So, the town put on its bib and tucker and made him welcome.

Of course, they had some fun. As the train rolled in a wag said, "Ring the fire bells. The town will be gone in forty minutes." And when it was learned the general would be offered the freedom of the city, yet another wit commented, "He was too damned free with it when he was here before."

Atlanta received the surprised compliments of the general as her just due. She heard him say that the reasons he had to destroy the city were the same reasons which would make her become a great city. He likened, he said, what was left of the Confederacy when he reached Atlanta, to a hand. Atlanta was the palm of it. If he destroyed Atlanta he destroyed all the fingers, too—the rail lines and the towns and cities to which they went. He was a good prophet—was "Crump" Sherman.

In 1870 an English visitor marveled at what he called "a sense of power" in the city. But power, restlessness and vision and the will to work were not all.

Those busy men who were building Atlanta would also go home, wash up, put on a clean shirt and go to hear the Italian opera singers. They did this in 1866. They built an opera house and packed it to see the master tragedian of them all, Edwin Booth, a man weighted with his own tragedy brought on by his extremist brother, John Wilkes Booth.

The bookstore was doing a good business with volumes from England and from the publishing houses in Boston, Philadelphia, and New York.

A valid American aristocracy was building, too. It was not the old aristocracy, possible only in the leisure of a slave economy, which held on in some cities about it like the legendary fly caught in amber. It was a true aristocracy, not imported from the courts of France and Britain, but one which grew as it had to grow, out of the American soil and the developing culture of the new South. It was, and is, an aristocracy, always willing to take off its coat and do its share of work.

A generation ago Atlanta brought the Metropolitan Opera to Atlanta and has kept it coming ever since. It developed as a center of concerts and music and to this day attracts people from all the bordering states to its fall and winter programs.

It was, and is, a city of balance and common sense. One of the reasons this was, and is, possible is the makeup of its people.

They came with the years. Somehow, for all its Deep South location, Atlanta was, and has remained, a city which welcomed all talent and energy. Some of those most damned as carpetbaggers in the heated Reconstruction period stayed on to become leaders and builders of the city, honored for their contributions. Atlanta has never been a walled-in city with the gates closed.

The city early became more cosmopolitan than any other in the Southeast and Southwest. It has remained so. It is a city with some of the elements of energy and alertness of New York and Chicago in its makeup. It is a fortunate city in that the great variety of people who came to it brought with them educated minds from the universities and colleges of the nation, great and small.

Every fall, when the football fervor fills the land, the alumni associations have dinners and remind us that most of the great state and privately endowed universities and the better small ones are essential ingredients of the makeup of Atlanta. The winter meetings of the major educational institutions for women reveal how many of their graduates are a part of the mind, mood, will, and spirit of Atlanta.

It is not, and has not been since it began to rebuild from the ashes, a provincial city, living in some moonlight-drenched, magnolia-scented dream of the past. Atlanta honors the past, but it does not look backward nor cling to that past. It is a proud and intelligent city. And it moves confidently toward the future.

As the advertising agencies and businessmen of the nation have learned, Atlanta is, even as Sherman said, the great market and distributing center for the Southeast and much of the Southwest as well. Let us consider, for example, the letter X.

George Leckie, scholar and brilliant teacher who revised the *Georgia Guide*, wrote of the meaning of this X, now discovered by those who make goods and process foods for sale and distribution.[195]

"Let a line," he wrote, "be drawn on a map from Boston through New York to New Orleans; and another from Chicago to Miami. These will form an immense X that intersects itself at a point slightly northeast of Atlanta." Roughly, the northeast leg of the X's New Orleans-Boston axis will lie just east of the great Appalachian chain, extending southwest from the St. Lawrence Valley in Canada's Quebec province to the coastal plains in Alabama. The passes, or outlets, for highways and railroads in the Appalachian chain funnel into and out of Atlanta. This is also true of the Chicago-Miami axis of the X, with the "pass" at Chattanooga. Likewise, a line from Minneapolis-St. Paul to Miami and another from Kansas City, will create another great X which bisects very close to Atlanta.

So, we see the great highways for trucks and rail lines, and the network of airlines as well, all centering on Atlanta. This makes it now, and for the future, the great distribution center for Georgia and all its neighboring states and those beyond.

---

[195]McGill wrote a foreword for George C. Leckie, *Georgia: A Guide to Its Towns and Countryside* (Atlanta: Tupper & Love, 1940).

And, the thinkers and planners of Atlanta's future should not fail to see the meaning of the two *X*s. This the more so now that the St. Lawrence waterways, at one end of the *X*s, are opened.

Atlanta's spirit is varied and alert because the city is not an enlargement of any one Southern product such, for example, as cotton. Nor is it tied to any plantation system, in tradition or thought. It is a center for communication, finance, transportation, distribution. It is a center, too, of managerial skills.

It has no antebellum homes for annual "pilgrimages" into the past. It possesses, instead, because good architects early came from the North and were made welcome, a very high position, as scholar Leckie pointed out, with regard to good architectural taste among American cities. "This," wrote Leckie, "should be taken as symbolic of its energy and managerial skill. The white columns it has are not monuments over the grave of a dream."

So, the years came and the people came—

The Young Men's Library Association was established in 1867 with a committee composed of new citizens and old. The *Atlanta Constitution* was founded and first published in 1868. The first board of education was elected in 1870, with the legendary ashes still warm. That same year the DeGive opera house was built to supply demand. Today there are our symphony, civic operas, ballet companies, theater groups, and art museum.

Henry Grady was a major source of the early dynamics. As editor of the *Constitution* he was regarded in his time as a liberal and a progressive. Many criticized him. He broke utterly with the "Old South" in spirit and vision. He had deep and abiding love for his state and region. He was emotional about the courage and sacrifices of the people of the Confederacy and its soldiers.[196]

But his first love was his country. And he knew that the future of the South was in being a part of the nation. He argued this over and over again—pleading for a new South which would be in the mainstream of national affairs. He saw the need for industry, for jobs, for skies stained with industrial smokestacks, for skylines dotted with the towers of fac-

---

[196]See Joel Chandler Harris, ed., *Henry W. Grady, Including His Writings and Speeches* (New York: Cassell Publishing Co., 1890).

tories and office buildings. He set out to love the nation into peace—and to make the South a part of it.

He, with the aid of friends in the North and erstwhile carpetbaggers in the South, led a local committee to bring to Atlanta the International Cotton Exposition in 1881. In 1885 came the more ambitious Cotton States and International Exposition with Booker T. Washington, Negro educator, as one of the principal speakers—a step in racial goodwill which was daring for its time—and greatly criticized by the extremists and reactionaries of that time.[197]

It should here be noted there was not then in Atlanta any vested interests with old, obsolete plants and machinery. Since there was no such interest to keep out other industries to protect their own—a fate suffered by many Southern cities—this dynamic of Atlanta was early established.

The churches, vigorous, courageous and sane, are an essential part of the Atlanta spirit. The city has been remarkably free of religious demogogues and has given short shrift to the few who have appeared.

The years came—the people came. Errors were made. Fires now and then burned some of the city. There were, of course, always some who were afraid and who wanted to stay put. They are around today. There were always some who had made their fortunes in the city and put little, if anything back. But, by and large, the city has taken its leadership from those who looked and planned ahead.

Joel Chandler Harris used to go home to West End for lunch, putting down an Uncle Remus story or an editorial to be finished on return. He liked driving the horse car which ran past his house while the driver ate lunch. He saw the first automobiles.

The factories came—the great automobile companies, the manufacturers of farm equipment, furniture, glass, the makers of parts, and of many, varied items. The transportation facilities burgeoned. The communications systems of telephone, telegraph, radio and television, joined in the growing.[198]

---

[197]Booker T. Washington, "Atlanta Exposition Speech," in *American Speeches*, ed. Wayland Maxfield Parrish and Marie Hochmuth (New York: Longmans, Green and Co., 1954) 461-65.

[198]See Kenneth Coleman, ed., *A History of Georgia* (Athens: University of Georgia Press, 1977).

The serpentine Chattahoochee River, especially pleasing to poets in its mountain reaches, is slowly but steadily developing and already one can see Atlanta as a seaport for the great industrial barges of the inland waterways tied into the St. Lawrence waterways which reach out into the seven seas of the world. That, too, is a part of the dream—a feature of the two big Xs and their meaning.

The spirit of Atlanta—it began with a dream and a surveyor's stake in the wilderness, and the dream has never become tarnished or its flame unattended.[199]

---

[199]See McGill's "Why I Live in Atlanta," "The Housing Challenge," and "Georgia Tech: Lighthouse to the Postwar South," in volumes 1 and 2.

46

Saving the Schools

One of the tragedies of the Deep South position has been that almost all the political and much of the lay leadership has, for almost five years, perpetuated the myth that state legislatures, state courts, and governors of states had the power to override the constitutional interpretations by the United States Supreme Court.

For some weeks now, it has been possible to detect a slight sobering in public attitude as the reality of the Supreme Court's decision becomes more and more evident. The action of the Supreme Court of Virginia was probably as effective in bringing home this reality as were the several decisions of federal courts.

Unhappily, for the public schools, the children, and the industrial future in four Southern states—namely, Mississippi, Alabama, South Carolina, and Georgia—the political leadership has not left itself room in which to manuever. The outlook in these states is for a worsening of the situation and the closing of at least some of the schools. Nonetheless, even in those states there is a realization that defiance or massive resistance will not save the schools.

In the months ahead Florida's proposal of a parents-opinion plan almost surely will gain favor. It permits parents to withdraw a child from

Reprinted by permission of Mrs. Ralph McGill and the *Christian Science Monitor,* 1959.

an integrated school and receive a sum equal to that child's share of state and county educational funds.

This proposal by Florida would retain the public school system but would give withdrawal assistance to those parents who did not wish their child to attend them. It is the only positive proposal yet made which seems to have the status of constitutionality.

All of these factors do help the moderate. Indeed, the moderate is beginning to emerge as the person who, from the beginning, has proposed the proper course.[200]

---

[200]For vital speeches delivered by McGill in support of the South's public schools see *Ralph McGill: Editor and Publisher*, ed. Calvin McLeod Logue, 2 vols.(Durham: Moore Publishing Co., 1969); and articles in this volume and volume 2.

47

Foreword
to Mildred E. English's
College in the Country

arely is it given to see a relatively large community change from one of apathy and lack of outlook to one of vitality, vision, and participation in all the issues of our day. I first saw Carrollton, Georgia about thirty years ago. It was a trading town in an agricultural center of small farmers. Its industrial development consisted of two small cotton mills. The intense depression and its corrosive effects weighed heavily upon the town and the county of which it is the seat.

Into this community came a teacher and doer, Irvine S. Ingram, as president of West Georgia College. He and his tireless faculty along with town leaders like Richard O. Flinn, Jr., a young Presbyterian minister of great faith and energy, were the original magnets which attracted to them a group more interested in giving than receiving.

Out of these beginnings have come the several and exciting programs of adult education now called College in the Country. But years before this flowering, Carrollton, Georgia and West Georgia College had become a center of learning and of service. The entire country began to look at itself and to study how to do something about the obvious

Foreword to Mildred E. English, *College in the Country: A Program of Education for Adults* (Athens: University of Georgia Press, 1959). Reprinted by permission of Mrs. Ralph McGill and the University of Georgia Press.

tion, has been a very real assistance in helping to expand the idea and to make it known over the United States wherever adult education is attempted. Without the fund, the program would not have been possible and the debt to the fund is great. But the fund itself would be the first to wish known the already established success, energy, and imaginative concepts of the local people which had first attracted it. This fact is why the fund became interested.

For a good many years Dr. Ingram's chief lieutenant has been the very able J. Carson Pritchard, who has contributed greatly in vision and philosophy, as well as in work.

But all who have been involved in the College in the Country join in the knowledge that they have been blessed with a very notable man, in the full meaning of the phrase, in Dr. Irvin S. Ingram. This very worthwhile book is a tribute to many men and women who have given much. But all these join in the knowledge that they have been followers of a truly great teacher and leader.[201]

---

[201]See McGill's "West Georgia College Honors Day Speech," in *Ralph McGill: Editor and Publisher*, ed. Calvin McLeod Logue, 2 vols. (Durham: Moore Publishing Company, 1969) 2:135-39.

48

Memories
of Bellamy and FDR

I remember in the New York theater, when the final curtain had gone down on "Sunrise at Campobello," I walked out trying to hide the fact I had been weeping. And then I saw, all about me, that others were also wet of eye. Indeed, some few women were sobbing as they held to the arms of their escorts.

It has been my pleasure to see some great moments in the theater, going back to John Drew, Otis Skinner, David Warfield, Cyril Maud, and others of the old days. But not one was more thrilling than that last scene in Campobello when Ralph Bellamy, as Franklin D. Roosevelt, struggling along on crutches for the first time after polio, clutches the podium at Madison Square Garden and pulls himself erect to the roar of the convention waiting for him to nominate Al Smith. This is the play which Atlanta will see this week at the Tower Theater.

For Ralph Bellamy it is necessary to summon forth that overworked adjective *great*. He is a great actor in the full meaning of the word. He had the hard, demanding schooling in stock companies.

My first job as a reporter was in Nashville, Tennessee. I did everything they'd allow. I wrote politics, covered police, reviewed books and

Reprinted from the *Atlanta Constitution*, 25 January 1960, by permission of Mrs. Ralph McGill and Atlanta Newspapers, Inc.

plays. I had also a yen to be an actor and carried spears in touring Shakespearean plays which played at the old auditorium.[202]

That was in the time before the movies had taken over all the local
theaters. There was a "road" and the provinces got to see the great of the
stage of that time.

It was the time of the summer stock shows. Almost every city of size
had a company. And one summer the Bellamy Players came to
Nashville.

There was Bellamy Sr., but the star of each comedy or drama was
the young son—Ralph Bellamy. I remember him suffering in "Seven
Keys to Baldpate."

This was before the days of air conditioning. The time of the play is
winter and the set showed snow at the windows. Bellamy sweated
through his coat but, of course, only cub reporters playing at being critics noted things like that. I remember all his parts that summer—melodrama and the light plays calculated to ease the tedium of summer.

Anyhow, the town took the Bellamy Players at heart. It was a good
summer. And when it was done and the company was gone, leaving
Nashville a much duller place, a lot of us knew that the name of Ralph
Bellamy would be in the news for years to come. It has been, too, and
always in the best of ways. He had leading roles in more than eighty
movies.

The role of FDR in "Sunrise at Campobello" is his sixth stage part
of prominence. He played, for example, the lead in the Pulitzer Prize
play, "State of the Union," which ran for two years on Broadway. Television has featured him on "Studio One," "Theater Guild," and other
dramatic productions.[203]

There are not many actors in our time who have been schooled in
their craft as has Bellamy, and it is a fine and warming thing to have
him on the road with a play which picks one up and makes one live with

---

[202]For information on McGill's early interest in theater, see *Ralph McGill: Editor
and Publisher,* ed. Calvin McLeod Logue, 2 vols. (Durham: Moore Publishing Company, 1969) 1:25-44.

[203]For more by McGill on artists, see "The Caring People," in *Southern Encounters: Southerners of Note in Ralph McGill's South,* ed. Calvin M. Logue (Macon: Mercer University Press, 1983).

the high moments of Franklin Roosevelt's life from the time polio struck him down until he took those first agonizing, yet glorious, steps, all alone, to the podium with the great swelling roar of the Democratic convention in his ears. There had been rumors he would never walk again, that he was through. But there he was, only thirty-four months after being stricken.

There is a fine cast with Bellamy—there would be. Its members will pardon me if I write of him, because of the old tie of stock-company days in Nashville, and the magnificent integrity of person and artist which has marked his career.

The play opens on that summer season at the Roosevelt home in New Brunswick, Canada. They are young—Eleanor and Franklin Roosevelt and the children.

There comes the afternoon when the young Roosevelt comes in from sailing and swimming, and complains of weariness and a pain as he goes up the stairs to the bed.[204] There follows, such is the mastery of Dore Schary's writing, some of the most poignant scenes, some of the most tender, delightful, and moving scenes the theater has seen.

There is an insight into the closeness of the family; the tensions caused by the stern old mother who wanted to give all the orders, and the crippled man—fighting. And one sees, too, the strength and help of the young wife.

It was a part of my experience to see Franklin D. Roosevelt with some frequency, both at Washington and in Warm Springs. I went to the play in New York sure that Ralph Bellamy would do a masterful job, but feeling that since no one really could look like FDR it might be somewhat unreal for one who knew him. I couldn't have been more wrong. Ralph Bellamy doesn't try to look like him. He simply uses his great artistry to become Franklin Roosevelt. He studied the voice for days and days. He watched movies for mannerisms. He talked with the children, with Mrs. Roosevelt, and friends.

The play was but minutes old when I had forgotten it was Bellamy on the stage. He missed none of the small details—a great actor doesn't.

---

[204]For more by McGill on Roosevelt, see review of *F.D.R.: His Personal Letters*, in volume 1.

There was the matter of the paralyzed legs. Few persons realized
how completely paralyzed those legs were. Bellamy's legs became paralyzed for the play. Many weary, painful hours were required to learn
how to *be* paralyzed in both legs.

There is laughter, tears, and inspiration in this play. In New York
even hardened Republicans were stirred to cheers and tears—and said
so in print.

It is not a political play—it is a magnificent bit of theater about a
vivid, world-known character. To see this play is to see one of the great
actors of our time—in a truly magnificent play about three years in the
life of a man whose whole life was a drama. To see "Sunrise at Campobello" is to give yourself a memory which will be warm and vivid all
the days of your life.

Notes for United Negro College Fund Meeting

M r. John D. Rockefeller, who is chairman of the United Negro College Fund, accurately has described the contribution of the member colleges and universities as increasingly important in scholarship, teaching, and science. Future demands, with an ever upward climb in enrollment and applications, require that these institutions have support.

I think it not amiss to recall the origins of these colleges because they so vividly highlight the progress made and justify the belief of those who founded them that a need was present which could not be ignored. Most of them had very humble beginnings. The University of Atlanta, for example, began in a freight car. Fisk University was started in an abandoned Civil War hospital. Tuskegee began operations in two old farm buildings.

Their accomplishment in the past sixty years is a magnificent tribute to the determined faculties and students and those who have assisted them. In the year 1900, for example, there were enrolled in all of the Negro colleges in the country only 2,624 students. It is now well over

Notes for a speech for the United Negro College Fund meeting, 25 April 1960, Boston. Manuscript provided by Mrs. Ralph McGill, from the Ralph McGill papers, now at Emory University, Atlanta.

100,000, of which about 20,000 are enrolled in white institutions in the East and West.

A survey of Lincoln University's students made a few years ago revealed that of almost 5,000 graduates, 1,100 became ministers, 800 doctors, 550 teachers, and 225 lawyers. Ten colleges and twenty-five high schools have been founded by Lincoln's graduates. This example, which can be multiplied by others, is evidence enough of why these colleges are important now and also why their role in the future will become more important, especially in the South.

For thirty-one years I have been, I believe, a reasonably close observer of the great center of education which is located in Atlanta. Through all these years the fine institutions in it have served as a bridge of communication between the two races. I like to think that Atlanta has done, within the existing pattern, a rather outstanding job in this field. These things could not have been done had it not been for the long years of contact with the Negro educational institutions. I hear today, for example, that relations between the races have deteriorated badly. This is a generality and like all generalities it is filled with error. In one aspect it is true that race relations have worsened. But in another, they have improved. There is a better foundation. They are based now on constitutional interpretations and law and they are therefore the sounder and have a basis on which genuine, enduring progress can be had.

As for what is happening and may happen in the South one can, with reason, be either optimistic or drown in frustration and despair. Some of us experience both of these emotions on alternate days. Certainly it is a fascinating subject.

I believe that the South, which is moving in a great tide of transition from agriculture to industry and research, one day will develop the political potency and maturity to match its economic progress.

It is a dangerous oversimplification to assume that the Supreme Court's school decision, the new but always legitimate aspirations and rising status of the Negro, are the sole cause of the South's many paradoxes, her angers and her traditional malaise.

We cannot overlook the effect of a revolution not quite comprehended by the rest of the nation. In a few short years the South has experienced an industrial revolution which was spread over several generations in the rest of the nation. In the first ten years after the Second World War the South added four thousand new manufacturing plants. A third of this growth was accounted for by only thirty-seven of the larger urban areas. Smaller cities also showed similar gains. By 1955 the average per capita income of Southerners had climbed to 257 percent of the 1929 level as against 141 for the rest of the country. But, this surging advance still left us well below the national per capita income level.[205]

During the forties your cities grew at at a rate of 15.4 percent, those of the South at 39 percent. In those years more than four million native Southerners, more than half of them Negroes, moved out of the region entirely. A smaller, yet quite sizeable group, of Northerners and Westerners moved in with the new industry.[206]

I ask you to observe how abruptly this has occurred. A region long rural, and for generations a study in lacks and needs, swiftly was changed. The cities were crowded with newcomers, most of them poorly educated, unskilled, and unaccustomed to city ways. This is true of our cities, as of others. Fear and insecurity and anxiety are in all of them. Racial antagonism flourishes in the fears and frustrations in any economic and social revolution. The tendency is to cling all the tighter to the status quo—to the familiar. We do ourselves and the future an injustice if we fail to see this fact as an essential ingredient of racial discord. The backdrop is transition. But, even in the South, this is not generally understood. When to this climate of unease and insecurity is added open defiance of the processes of law by state and public leaders, all other elements of lawlessness are encouraged to go and do likewise. Anti-Semiticism, for example, flourishes.

Governor LeRoy Collins, of Florida, a friend whom I cherish and honor, noted this in a recent speech. He said:

> The greatest danger in the South is that our people will fail to understand the change taking place all around them. They must not forget that the first

---

[205]See Brian Rungeling et al., *Employment, Income, and Welfare in the Rural South* (New York: Praeger, 1977); Vivian W. Henderson, *Economic Status of Negroes: In the Nation and in the South* (Atlanta: Southern Regional Council, 1963).

[206]See Charles Pearce Roland, *Improbable Era: The South Since World War II* (Lexington: University Press of Kentucky, 1975); V. O. Key, Jr., *Southern Politics in State and Nation* (New York: Vintage Books, 1949); Donald R. Matthews, *Negroes and the New Southern Politics* (New York: Harcourt, Brace & World, 1966).

law of nature is change and that the second is the survival of those who put themselves in accord with this change. This is what Southern leadership must recognize if it expects to be listened to on the national scene.

A tremendous lesson is to be learned from the tragic example of Edmund Ruffin, the Virginian who happened to be the one who fired the first shot upon Fort Sumter. By no means was this his greatest achievement. Ruffin had a remarkable foresight and understanding of what the South could be if it would practice sound soil conservation, then a scoffed-at innovation.

The Civil War kept him from ever seeing his vision and hopes materialize. He was consumed with his hostility to the Union and his devotion to the cause of the Confederacy. When he got the news that the South had lost the war, Ruffin, asking that his body be wrapped in a Confederate blanket and buried, took his own life in abject despair. Had he been able to devote his energies to saving the South's soil, a mission for which he was so conspicuously qualified, our region doubtless would have been spared many long years of suffering.

If the South should wrap itself in a Confederate blanket and consume itself in racial furor, it would surely miss its greatest opportunity for channeling into a wonderful future the products of change now taking place. And the South must face up to the further fact that it would also bury itself politically for decades to come.[207]

There are signs, even in the Deep South states, that change and the need of intelligence to meet it are now beginning to be understood. Elsewhere there is more substantial progress to report.[208]

I cannot say that anything has happened in this process which was not expected, save for Governor Faubus's folly and shame in Arkansas. We did have the bad luck, because of a failure to prepare public opinion, to have the Court decision fall into the hands of lawyers and politicians for resolution, instead of the educators. Here was a tragic example of heads in sand. The Court's ruling was not unexpected. It had been long and publicly in the making in the form of previous decisions. But, nowhere had there been any planning for it. We speak with the value of hindsight, but I like to think of what might have happened had the National Educational Association, a national committee from the colleges

---

[207]See McGill's "LeRoy Collins: Florida's Nominee for Governor Started out in a Grocery Store," in *Southern Encounters: Southerners of Note in Ralph McGill's South*, ed. Calvin M. Logue (Macon: Mercer University Press, 1983).

[208]See John C. McKinney and Edgar T. Thompson, eds., *South In Continuity and Change* (Durham: Duke University Press, 1965); Raymond W. Mack, ed., *Changing South* (Chicago: Aldine Publishing Co., 1970).

and universities, and a president's committee, been at work for at least a year conditioning public opinion for the change.[209]

Even so, if we wish to be optimistic let us look. Kentucky has just about completed its process of integrating its schools. West Virginia has completed her process. We must remember, in this context, that both Missouri and Oklahoma long ago did the same. In vast Texas more than one hundred small communities have peaceably, and without publicity, effected the change. Delaware, Maryland, and the District of Columbia are others in this list. North Carolina, Tennessee, and Arkansas have towns and cities where beginnings have been made. Virginia, which originally gave massive resistance strength by throwing her great prestige and history behind it, had the character to reverse her position and attempts now a plan of free choice.

There are but five states with complete segregation. If one wishes to be pessimistic one can note that as of last September only six percent of the Negro students were in integrated schools. But, it must also be kept in mind that legal resistance has been possible and that even now, in the states with complete resistance, there is but one court case pending. This is in Atlanta.

Political leadership in these states has deceived the people from the start with assurances that the Court decision could not be made applicable, that the public schools were in no danger. They now desperately need a new vocabulary, and it may be they will adopt that of Virginia's. Georgia has had the experience of a legislature-created study commission which held public meetings in each of the ten congressional districts. To the surprise of the state, and the commission, five of the ten produced more witnesses for keeping schools open at any cost than for closing them. Not only this, but the hearings provided the districts with opportunity for a dialogue, which before had been impossible.

It is certain there will be, in the months ahead, some schools closed.[210] It is conceivable this could include state universities. In the

---

[209]See McGill's "Speech to National Education Association," *Ralph McGill: Editor and Publisher,* ed. Calvin McLeod Logue, 2 vols. (Durham: Moore Publishing Company, 1969) 1:245-56.

[210]For McGill's speeches concerning open public schools in the South see *Ralph McGill: Editor and Publisher,* vols. 1 and 2.

states where this is likely to happen, Negro members of the state system would be closed. Here we can see what a tremendous burden the private Negro colleges which are members of this fund will need to shoulder. Their role in the years of readjustment will be vital.

The sit-in demonstrations were a shock to the South. Yet, for all the immediate reaction against them, the net will be healthy. Indeed, this already is true. The moral issue at last had an inning. Heretofore, all the emphasis has been on law and courts, and few ever mentioned a moral issue was involved. That a Negro customer could buy toothpaste, buttons, clothing, toys, books, etcetera, in the ten-cent stores but couldn't purchase a soft drink or a sandwich, was so preposterous a situation that only the most extreme could defend it. Nor should it be overlooked that white students joined in support, especially in Tallahassee, Florida. It was the moral issue which brought them out. Most church organizations and many individual ministers also joined in endorsement of the objectives.[211]

Here we had starkly dramatized the need for what Mr. Walter Lippmann has called a public philosophy. Most of the stores coping with sit-ins have Eastern headquarters and direction. One of the great failures of our time is that American business leadership does not have a public philosophy for the great issues before the nation.[212]

The sit-ins are not directed against local laws, but against customs and traditions which cannot be justified. When some stores solve it by removing the stools at lunch counters and say it is all right for Negroes to stand up and have a Coke but it is against custom to sit down, that custom has become too preposterous to have any acceptance.

---

[211]See John Hope Franklin and Isidore Starr, eds., *The Negro in Twentieth-Century America: A Reader on the Struggle for Civil Rights* (New York: Vintage Books, 1967).

[212]For McGill's personal philosophy of public involvement see the editor's introduction.